Sport Tourism Destinations: Issues, Opportunities and Analysis

Sport Tourism Destinations: Issues, Opportunities and Analysis

A.R. Chauhan

RANDOM PUBLICATIONS
NEW DELHI (INDIA)

Sport Tourism Destinations: Issues, Opportunities and Analysis

ISBN 978-93-5111-330-0

Published in 2014 in India by

RANDOM PUBLICATIONS

4376-A/4B, Gali Murari Lal, Ansari Road
New Delhi-110 002
Phone : +91-11-43580356, +91-11-23289044
e-mail: randomexports@gmail.com, sales@randompublications.com,
info@randompublications.com

Type Setting by : Keystoneprintads, Delhi-110051
Printed at : Printed at Thomson Press (India) Ltd

Preface

Tourism is travel for recreational, leisure, or business purposes. The World Tourism Organization defines tourists as people "traveling to and staying in places outside their usual environment for not more than one consecutive year for leisure, business and other purposes".

Sports tourism, or more correctly, Sport Tourism refers to travel which involves either observing or participating in a sporting event staying apart from their usual environment. Sport tourism is a fast growing sector of the global travel industry and equates to $600 billion a year. There are several classifications on sport tourism. Gammon and Robinsom suggested that the sports tourism are defined as Hard Sports Tourism and Soft Sports Tourismwhile Gibson suggested that there are three types of sports tourism included Sports Event Tourism, Celebrity and Nostalgia Sport Tourism and Active Sport Tourism.

The book endeavors to introduce readers to the field of sport tourism while analyzing the fundamental components of sport tourism offers key definitions examines the relationship between sport tourism and other established form of tourism sectors and puts forward various typologies to help the reader understand the nature and scope of sport tourism.

I thank all members of my team who have helped in the preparation of the book. My special thanks go to "Random Publications" who have published the book.

—A.R. Chauhan

Contents

1

Tourism: An Introduction

Tourism is travel for recreational, leisure or business purposes. The World Tourism Organization defines tourists as people who "travel to and stay in places outside their usual environment for more than twenty-four hours and not more than one consecutive year for leisure, business and other purposes not related to the exercise of an activity remunerated from within the place visited." Tourism has become a popular global leisure activity. In 2008, there were over 922 million international tourist arrivals, with a growth of 1.9% as compared to 2007. International tourism receipts grew to US$944 billion (euro 642 billion) in 2008, corresponding to an increase in real terms of 1.8%. As a result of the late-2000s recession, international travel demand suffered a strong slowdown beginning in June 2008, with growth in international tourism arrivals worldwide falling to 2% during the boreal summer months.

This negative trend intensified during 2009, exacerbated in some countries due to the outbreak of the H1N1 influenza virus, resulting in a worldwide decline of 4% in 2009 to 880 million international tourists arrivals, and an estimated 6% decline in international tourism receipts. Tourism is vital for many countries, such as Egypt, Greece, Lebanon, Spain, Malaysia and Thailand, and many island nations, such as The Bahamas, Fiji, Maldives, Philippines and the Seychelles, due to the large intake of money for businesses with their goods and services and the opportunity for employment in the service industries associated with tourism. These service industries include transportation services, such as airlines, cruise ships and taxicabs, hospitality services, such as accommodations, including hotels and resorts, and entertainment venues, such as amusement parks, casinos, shopping malls, music venues and theatres.

ETYMOLOGY OF TOURISM

Theobald (1994) suggested that "etymologically, the word tour is derived from the Latin, 'tornare' and the Greek, 'tornos', meaning 'a lathe or circle; the movement around a central point or axis'. This meaning changed in modern English to represent 'one's turn'. The suffix–ism is defined as 'an action or process; typical behaviour or quality', while the suffix,–its denotes 'one that performs a given action'. When the word tour and the suffixes are combined, they suggest the action of movement around a circle. One can argue that a circle represents a starting point, which ultimately returns back to its beginning.

Therefore, like a circle, a tour represents a journey in that it is a round-trip, *i.e.*, the act of leaving and then returning to the original starting point, and therefore, one who takes such a journey can be called a tourist." In 1941, Hunziker and Krapf defined tourism as people who travel "the sum of the phenomena and relationships arising from the travel and stay of non-residents, insofar as they do not lead to permanent residence and are not connected with any earning activity."

In 1976, the Tourism Society of England's definition was: "Tourism is the temporary, short-term movement of people to destination outside the places where they normally live and work and their activities during the stay at each destination. It includes movements for all purposes." In 1981, the International Association of Scientific Experts in Tourism defined tourism in terms of particular activities selected by choice and undertaken outside the home.

In 1994, the United Nations classified three forms of tourism in its Recommendations on Tourism Statistics:

- Domestic tourism, involving residents of the given country travelling only within this country.
- Inbound tourism, involving non-residents travelling in the given country.
- Outbound tourism, involving residents travelling in another country.

HISTORY OF TOURISM

Wealthy people have always travelled to distant parts of the world, to see great buildings, works of art, learn new languages, experience new cultures and to taste different cuisines. Long ago, at the time of the Roman Republic, places such as Baiae were popular coastal resorts for the rich. The word tourism was used by 1811 and tourist by 1840. In 1936, the League of Nations defined foreign tourist as "someone travelling abroad for at least twenty-four hours". Its successor, the United Nations, amended this definition in 1945, by including a maximum stay of six months.

Leisure travel

Leisure travel was associated with the Industrial Revolution in the United Kingdom–the first European country to promote leisure time to the increasing industrial population. Initially, this applied to the owners of the machinery of production, the economic oligarchy, the factory owners and the traders.

These comprised the new middle class. Cox and Kings was the first official travel company to be formed in 1758. The British origin of this new industry is reflected in many place names. In Nice, France, one of the first and best-established holiday resorts on the French Riviera, the long esplanade along the seafront is known to this day as the Promenade des Anglais; in many other historic resorts in continental Europe, old, well-established palace hotels have names like the Hotel Bristol, the Hotel Carlton or the Hotel Majestic–reflecting the dominance of English customers. Many leisure-oriented tourists travel to the tropics, both in the summer and winter. Places of such nature often visited are: Bali in Indonesia, Brazil, Cuba, the Dominican Republic, Malaysia, Mexico the various Polynesian tropical islands, Queensland in Australia, Thailand, Saint-Tropez and Cannes in France, Florida, Hawaii and Puerto Rico in the United States, Barbados, Sint Maarten, Saint Kitts and Nevis, The Bahamas, Anguilla, Antigua, Aruba, Turks and Caicos Islands and Bermuda.

Winter tourism

Although it is acknowledged that the Swiss were not the inventors of skiing it is well documented that St. Moritz, Graubünden, became the cradle of the developing winter tourism: Since that year of 1865 in St. Moritz, many daring hotel managers choose to risk opening their hotels in winter but it was only in the seventies of the 20th century when winter tourism took over the lead from summer tourism in many of the Swiss ski resorts. Even in Winter, portions of up to one third of all guests (depending on the location) consist of non-skiers.

Major ski resorts are located mostly in the various European countries (*e.g* Andorra, Austria, Bulgaria, Czech Republic, France, Germany, Iceland, Italy, Norway, Poland, Serbia, Sweden, Slovenia, Spain, Switzerland), Canada, the United States (*e.g*. Colorado, California, Utah, New York, New Jersey, Michigan, Montana, Vermont, New England) New Zealand, Japan, South Korea, Chile, Argentina, Kenya and Tanzania.

Mass tourism

Mass tourism could only have developed with the improvements in technology, allowing the transport of large numbers of people in a short space of time to places of leisure interest, so that greater numbers of people could begin to enjoy the benefits of leisure time. In the United States, the first seaside resorts in the European style were at Atlantic City, New Jersey and Long Island, New York.

In Continental Europe, early resorts included: Ostend, popularised by the people of Brussels; Boulogne-sur-Mer (Pas-de-Calais) and Deauville (Calvados) for the Parisians; and Heiligendamm, founded in 1793, as the first seaside resort on the Baltic Sea.

Adjectival Tourism

Adjectival tourism refers to the numerous niche or specialty travel forms of tourism that have emerged over the years, each with its own adjective.

Many of these have come into common use by the tourism industry and academics. Others are emerging concepts that may or may not gain popular usage.

Examples of the more common niche tourism markets include:

- Agritourism
- Culinary tourism
- Cultural tourism
- Ecotourism
- Extreme tourism
- Geotourism
- Heritage tourism
- LGBT tourism
- Medical tourism
- Nautical tourism
- Pop-culture tourism
- Religious tourism
- Slum tourism
- Space tourism
- War tourism
- Wildlife tourism

DEVELOPMENTS OF TOURISM IN 21ST CENTURY

There has been an upmarket trend in the tourism over the last few decades, especially in Europe, where international travel for short breaks is common. Tourists have high levels of disposable income, considerable leisure time, are well educated, and have sophisticated tastes. There is now a demand for a better quality products, which has resulted in a fragmenting of the mass market for beach vacations; people want more specialised versions, quieter resorts, family-oriented holidays or niche market-targeted destination hotels.

The developments in technology and transport infrastructure, such as jumbo jets, low-cost airlines and more accessible airports have made many types of tourism more affordable. WHO estimates that up to 500,000 people are on planes at any time.

There have also been changes in lifestyle, such as retiree-age people who sustain year round tourism. This is facilitated by internet sales of tourism products. Some sites have now started to offer dynamic packaging, in which an inclusive price is quoted for a tailor-made package requested by the customer upon impulse. There have been a few setbacks in tourism, such as the September 11 attacks and terrorist threats to tourist destinations, such as in Bali and several European cities. Also, on December 26, 2004, a tsunami, caused by the 2004 Indian Ocean earthquake, hit the Asian countries on the Indian Ocean, including the Maldives. Thousands of lives were lost and many tourists died. This, together with the vast clean-up operation in place, has stopped or severely hampered tourism to the area.

The terms tourism and travel are sometimes used interchangeably. In this context, travel has a similar definition to tourism, but implies a more purposeful journey. The terms tourism and tourist are sometimes used pejoratively, to imply a shallow interest in the cultures or locations visited by tourists.

Sustainable tourism

"Sustainable tourism is envisaged as leading to management of all resources in such a way that economic, social and aesthetic needs can be fulfilled while maintaining cultural integrity, essential ecological processes, biological diversity and life support systems." (World Tourism Organization) Sustainable development implies "meeting the needs of the present without compromising the ability of future generations to meet their own needs" (World Commission on Environment and Development, 1987) Sustainable tourism can be seen as having regard to ecological and socio-cultural carrying capacities and includes involving the community of the destination in tourism development planning.

It also involves integrating tourism to match current economic and growth policies so as to mitigate some of the negative economic and social impacts of 'mass tourism'. Murphy (1985) advocates the use of an 'ecological approach', to consider both 'plants' and 'people' when implementing the sustainable tourism development process.

This is in contrast to the 'boosterism' and 'economic' approaches to tourism planning, neither of which consider the detrimental ecological or sociological impacts of tourism development to a destination. However, Butler (2006) questions the exposition of the term 'sustainable' in the context of tourism, citing its ambiguity and stating that "the emerging sustainable development philosophy of the 1990s can be viewed as an extension of the broader realization that a preoccupation with economic growth without regard to it social and environmental consequences is self-defeating in the long term." Thus 'sustainable tourism development' is seldom considered as an autonomous function of economic regeneration as separate from general economic growth.

Ecotourism

Ecotourism, also known as ecological tourism, is responsible travel to fragile, pristine, and usually protected areas that strives to be low impact and (often) small scale. It helps educate the traveler; provides funds for conservation; directly benefits the economic development and political empowerment of local communities; and fosters respect for different cultures and for human rights.

Pro-poor tourism

The pro poor tourism has to help the very poorest in developing countries has been receiving increasing attention by those involved in development and the issue has been addressed either through small scale projects in local communities and by Ministries of Tourism attempting to attract huge numbers of tourists. Research by the Overseas Development Institute suggests that neither is the best way to encourage tourists' money to reach the poorest as only 25% or less (far less in some cases) ever reaches the poor; successful examples of money reaching the poor include mountain climbing in Tanzania or cultural tourism in Luang Prabang, Laos.

Recession tourism

Recession tourism is a travel trend, which evolved by way of the world economic crisis. Identified by American entrepreneur Matt Landau (2007), recession tourism is defined by low-cost, high-value experiences taking place of once-popular generic retreats. Various recession tourism hotspots have seen business boom during the recession thanks to comparatively low costs of living and a slow world job market suggesting travellers are elongating trips where their money travels further.

Medical tourism

When there is a significant price difference between countries for a given medical procedure, particularly in Southeast Asia, India, Eastern Europe and where there are different regulatory regimes, in relation to particular medical procedures (*e.g.* dentistry), travelling to take advantage of the price or regulatory differences is often referred to as "medical tourism".

Educational tourism

Educational tourism developed, because of the growing popularity of teaching and learning of knowledge and the enhancing of technical competency outside of the classroom environment. In educational tourism, the main focus of the tour or leisure activity includes visiting another country to learn about the culture, such as in Student Exchange Programmes and Study Tours, or to work and apply skills learned inside the classroom in a different environment, such as in the International Practicum Training Programme.

Creative tourism

Creative tourism has existed as a form of cultural tourism, since the early beginnings of tourism itself. Its European roots date back to the time of the Grand Tour, which saw the sons of aristocratic families travelling for the purpose of mostly interactive, educational experiences. More recently, creative tourism has been given its own name by Crispin Raymond and Greg Richards, who as members of the Association for Tourism and Leisure Education (ATLAS), have directed a number of projects for the European Commission, including cultural and crafts tourism, known as sustainable tourism. They have defined "creative tourism" as tourism related to the active participation of travellers in the culture of the host community, through interactive workshops and informal learning experiences. Meanwhile, the concept of creative tourism has been picked up by high-profile organizations such as UNESCO, who through the Creative Cities Network, have endorsed creative tourism as an engaged, authentic experience that promotes an active understanding of the specific cultural features of a place. More recently, creative tourism has gained popularity as a form of cultural tourism, drawing on active participation by travellers in the culture of the host communities they visit. Several countries offer examples of this type of tourism development, including the United Kingdom, the Bahamas, Jamaica, Spain, Italy and New Zealand.

Dark tourism

One emerging area of special interest has been identified by Lennon and Foley (2000) as "dark" tourism. This type of tourism involves visits to "dark" sites, such as battlegrounds, scenes of horrific crimes or acts of genocide, for example: concentration camps. Dark tourism remains a small niche market, driven by varied motivations, such as mourning, remembrance, education, macabre curiosity or even entertainment. Its early origins are rooted in fairgrounds and medieval fairs.

Doom tourism

Also known as "Tourism of Doom," or "Last Chance Tourism" this emerging trend involves travelling to places that are environmentally or otherwise threatened (the ice caps of Mount Kilimanjaro, the melting glaciers of Patagonia, The coral of the Great Barrier Reef) before it is too late. Identified by travel trade magazine TravelAge West editor-in-chief Kenneth Shapiro in 2007 and later explored in The New York Times, this type of tourism is believed to be on the rise. Some see the trend as related to sustainable tourism or ecotourism due to the fact that a number of these tourist destinations are considered threatened by environmental factors such as global warming, over population or climate change. Others worry that travel to many of these threatened locations increases an individual's carbon footprint and only hastens problems threatened locations are already facing.

GROWTH IN TOURISM INDUSTRY

The World Tourism Organization (UNWTO) forecasts that international tourism will continue growing at the average annual rate of 4%. With the advent of e-commerce, tourism products have become one of the most traded items on the internet. Tourism products and services have been made available through intermediaries, although tourism providers (hotels, airlines, etc.) can sell their services directly. This has put pressure on intermediaries from both on-line and traditional shops. It has been suggested there is a strong correlation between tourism expenditure per capita and the degree to which countries play in the global context. Not only as a result of the important economic contribution of the tourism industry, but also as an indicator of the degree of confidence with which global citizens leverage the resources of the globe for the benefit of their local economies.

This is why any projections of growth in tourism may serve as an indication of the relative influence that each country will exercise in the future. Space tourism is expected to "take off" in the first quarter of the 21st century, although compared with traditional destinations the number of tourists in orbit will remain low until technologies such as a space elevator make space travel cheap. Technological improvement is likely to make possible air-ship hotels, based either on solar-powered airplanes or large dirigibles. Underwater hotels, such as Hydropolis, expected to open in Dubai in 2009, will be built. On the ocean, tourists will be welcomed by ever larger cruise ships and perhaps floating cities.

Sports tourism

Since the late 1970s, sports tourism has become increasingly popular. Events such as rugby, Olympics, Commonwealth games, Asian Games and football World Cups have enabled specialist travel companies to gain official ticket allocation and then sell them in packages that include flights, hotels and excursions.

Latest trends

As a result of the late-2000s recession, international arrivals suffered a strong slowdown beginning in June 2008. Growth from 2007 to 2008 was only 3.7% during the first eight months of 2008. The Asian and Pacific markets were affected and Europe stagnated during the boreal summer months, while the Americas performed better, reducing their expansion rate but keeping a 6% growth from January to August 2008. Only the Middle East continued its rapid growth during the same period, reaching a 17% growth as compared to the same period in 2007.

This slowdown on international tourism demand was also reflected in the air transport industry, with a negative growth in September 2008 and a 3.3% growth in passenger traffic through September. The hotel industry also reports a slowdown, as room occupancy continues to decline. As the global economic situation deteriorated dramatically during September and October as a result of the global financial crisis, growth of international tourism is expected to slow even further for the remaining of 2008, and this slowdown in demand growth is forecasted to continue into 2009 as recession has already hit most of the top spender countries, with long-haul travel expected to be the most affected by the economic crisis.

This negative trend intensified as international tourist arrivals fell by 8% during the first four months of 2009, and the decline was exacerbated in some regions due to the outbreak of the influenza AH1N1 virus.

TOURISM IN THE FACE OF 21ST CENTURY'S CHALLENGES

It is difficult to pin-point in a short publication all the problems which will determine the direction of tourism's development in the twenty-first century. This difficulty results from dynamic transformations which are in our modern civilization. Twenty years ago in his book entitled „The Third Wave", A. Toffler wrote that humanity will stand in the face of new challenges, and it appears that these processes are in the future. According to the author the title „The Third Wave", like the previous two indicate, „...will squeeze out previous cultures and civilizations bringing it's morals into effect, which was inconceivable for people who had been born earlier".

The speed of our everyday life was considerably slower, as the first wave, the agricultural revolution, needed one thousand years to run its course. The Industrial revolution, or the second wave, needed only three hundred years from the beginning to the end. However, these prior transformations are incomparable to the speed and progress of our modern civilization.

This third wave has been dubbed the technological revolution and is now in process. Some of the more visible processes in our modern life include; the quick development of the technology, the revolution in genetics, the conquest of outer space, the rapid development of cities, and the changes in our jobs and lifestyles. With this information we can state that A. Toffler was correct in saying „The third wave will burst into history within a few decades time.

Thus we will feel the effects of the third wave in our lifetime". Toffler's vision of radical changes in economics accompanied by worldviews of new "liberal opportunities" will create the disintegration of the industrial society. Traditional industries will be replaced with new industries based on modern technology, causing transformation between the relationships of our home and work place, working time and free time, and prosperity versus poverty. The meaning of the natural environment will become more important as the world will be seeking new values resulting in changes of cultures and ideologies. Lifestyles and family functions will change, taking on new meaning with concepts such as science, careers, and unemployment. However, the question remains, what impact will these new changes have on tourism? Will tourism use these opportunities, or will it be an enclave in which we can rest from civilization.

Tourism is a dynamic discipline and is affected by these processes previously discussed. The analysis of trends in the modern tourist market show there are many changes suggesting that tourism in the future will differ from present day affairs. The complexity of tourism will bring about many difficulties throughout its development. J. Krippendorf stated, „ it is possible that tourism, an antidote for the industrial world, has become an industry and predacious devourer of the environment". The more difficult challenge of the twenty-first century will be the protection of the environment. Fortunately the tourism industry has begun using modern technology in the fields of computer science, communications, and the building of transportation to preserve the environment. The development of tourism is also known to be an asset to social economics, however, there tends to be strong speculations to the overall benefits in this aspect.

The Conditions and Prognosis in the Development of Tourism at the Beginning of the 21st Century

Consider the further of tourism and the challenges it will face at the beginning of the twenty-first century. The prognosis is very optimistic as suggested in publicised rapport. The rapport talks about quick development and states that during the next twenty years tourism will be one of the fasts growing departments in the world's economy. However, tourism is far from the end of its development, as for now it consists of a small percentage of the world's citizens.

The main hazards in development are problems with the political situation in the world, especially conflicts within the Balkans, the instability of the Arab world, and the disorganisation between authorities and conflict in the former territory of the Soviet Empire. Slightly less hazardous factors deal with economics such as recession and the increase of gas prices. Nevertheless the outlook on tourist development remains optimistic. The quantitative development of tourism is accompanied by multi-aspects including qualitative and structural transformations.

The recent geopolitical changes made in different regions of the world has had a great influence on the scale and structure of tourism. The downfall of communism and democratisation of societies in former socialist countries are events which have an impact on modern tourism, and other parts of the world have witnessed similar processes within their societies. The development of international tourism will take on new dynamic and important changes in spatial structures. Generally speaking an increase in share of the tourist structure shows no connection with an increase in share of the profit structure.

There is no guarantee of an even distribution in the benefits of tourism. A good example is Africa, which last years shares in total scale of tourist arrivals increased while the total scale of shares in receipts from tourism rapidly decreased. Some interesting changes in the quality of the tourist market are connected with the supply and demand. These aspects of needs, motivations, and demands lead to new directions in tourist firms.

A quick tempo of bringing modern technologies into tourism may herald a real revolution in the organisation of the tourist system. These examples show that tourism, like all repeats of civilization, odder-go changes and the question remains; what tasks will tourism face in the beginning of the new century? There are many factors which will shape the future of the tourist market and it should be noted that some are out of the control of the market. In an attempt to answer some of these questions there must be an analysis of the trends involved with tourism. The diagram presents two basic groups of factors which will decide about tourism in the twenty-first century.

The first group are exterior factors called "megatrends". The second group are interior factors connected with the tourist market. Because of the limited frames in this publication the developing megatrends are on table one, while the factors from the second group are in the complex tables. For more convenient analysis they are split into two groups, one concerned with the demand and one the supply.

Megatrend Influences on the Tourist Market

The end of the twentieth century was a time of great transformation in all fields of life. There were many fast paced changes throughout social conditions, the economy, and technology, which brought about many transitions within tourism. The constant tendencies to observe and gain knowledge about the markets basic condition are needed to succeed with each activity and the trends within tourism can change quickly. The ability to forecast and stimulate these developmental processes is the key to making the correct decisions for the future.

The fluxuation and competition within the tourist market not only requires constant observation and the ability to anticipate change, but also being able to react to the new trend before it becomes the norm. This shows the importance of knowledge in the action of these megatrends, which can be classified into six basic groups; demographics, politics, social and cultural, economics, technology, and ecology. In each of these groups there are positive factors, which will either stimulate or deter the development of tourism, each with variability in strength and effect.

These constituents will decide about the dynamics and expansion of tourism with the difficulty being verification. These megatrends, especially demographics, social, cultural, ecology, and technology hold such a strong influence on the maturation of tourism that such events as a political crisis or economic recession (in some regions) would be unable to hinder such progress.

The Main Trends in Tourist Demands

There are many interesting publications about change within the field of tourist demands and many studies, which analyse the direction of these changes in development, have been publicised recently.

The majorities are unanimous regarding the expansion and direction on the transformations of demands, so much so that there is even an accepted concept known as "Hard and Soft Tourism". It is based on the observational changes within the sphere of former and actual clients in travel agencies and set the standard characteristics of two opposite kinds of tourism: the traditional tourist and the modern tourist. There is a vision of which tourism will dominate the future, characterised by a more active tourist and less interest in passive tourism.

The prediction is that traditional tourism, refereed to as 3 X S (sun sea and sand) will be squeezed out by tourism based on a new formula involving 3 X E (entertainment, excitement, and education). During recent years there has become intensified interest in travelling to historical cities, the so-called "green tourist" with additional concern for a tendency in business tourism. Nevertheless it could be halted through the development of telecommunications and shorter but more frequent trips consisting of sightseeing and holiday could become more popular.

The useful system of "bridges" between a national holiday leading to the extension of weekends has brought about a prognosis for a renaissance in national tourism. V.T.C. Middleton claimed that for tourists, who quite often may be 'experienced,' a trend in national tourism may become more attractive now then ever, including the sixties. The smaller interest in international tourism is in the neighbouring countries, or places where many Europeans have had vacation. In 1990 European travel represented about seven per cent of all international travel, although this number was up to about ten per cent in 1996, and Europeans are not the only ones concerned with these numbers.

A poll conducted recently by the Travel Trade Gazette concerning international tourism showed these tendencies in change also pointed to the tourist industry representatives. One director of a travel agency was quoted saying 'a person who was in Spain ten years ago at present is probably in Penang". The quick increase in numbers of individual trips along with package tours is the prediction of the future. Today Individuality has a strong influence on cars, clothes and other daily needs as well, and the gaining interest of individual travel is one of the most important tendencies in today's tourist demands.

The Main Trends in Tourist Supply

The advancements and inclinations characterised previously have caused fundamental changes in present and future actions of travel agencies. During the last thirty years the developed markets have been dominated primarily by the supply, however, in the future we can expect to see increased importance in the demand factors as well. Agencies, which are not well informed about the market, could feel the effects and begin losing clients.

Today a tourist offer has a different meaning then it did several years ago, when the identical packaged product was selling to a maximum number of clients. This is when the main task of an agency was to secure transportation and hotels for the tourists in an identified town near similar beaches and the local supply had to answer the whimsical requirements of the tourist. Today's tourists expect something different and the prognosis for the twenty-first century is different then it has been in past centuries.

The totality of tourists activities will be one of the most characteristic features in the early dawn of the twenty-first century, and covering borders in economical activity and the concentration of capital are visible in all spheres of the international economy.

These inclinations at the tourist market level are quite visible where huge companies are creating the new direction in trend bringing the end of the small travel agencies drawing to a close. The tourist market has been captured by the huge American and Western European companies with Asian, Japanese, and Chinese companies expected to join them in the near future.

Obviously there are some smaller travel agencies which will be needed to look after some special services, but for the most part this will be the change of the movement in the international tourist structure. The expected changes in Russia and China could bring the largest investments into these two countries. It seems that the tourists supply will have a more violent nature than the demand and the odds are that the supply, at the same time, will be the main point of stimulation and transformation.

THE TOURISM INDUSTRY

For people who think this is the industry for them, strongly suggest that they really think about their personality and be sure they can thrive (and survive) in the atmosphere. It truly is different from anything else. It is critical that they work for a hotel while they are still in school, preferably in a few different hotels, and departments, so they can get a feel for it and know where they would be the happiest and most successful. The growth in the services sector of the worldwide economy has been phenomenal in the last 25 years. In the United States, services currently account for more than 75 per cent of the gross domestic product (GDP), which is a popular measure of an economy's productivity.

Similarly, on an international scale, services continue to account for an ever-increasing percentage of economic activity. Most new jobs are created in the service sector, and the growth in the hospitality and tourism industry is a major contributor. Until the mid-1980s, the emphasis within the marketing community was on products. Now services have surpassed products and have taken on a more important role in marketing.

Services, such as those offered by providers in the hospitality and tourism industry, have developed marketing strategies and practices that are unique. It has been established that the strategies, tactics, and practices that have been used successfully for product marketers do not always work successfully for those who market services. With the distinct differences between products and services in mind, the field of services marketing has evolved.

Services Defined

Unlike products, which are tangible, services are usually intangible. A service is not a physical good; rather, it is the performance of an act or a deed. This performance often requires consumers to be present during the production or delivery of the service. Service industries, including hospitality and tourism, are actually selling consumers an experience. Services have been defined to "include all economic activities whose output is not a physical product or construction, is generally consumed at the time it is produced, and provides added value in forms (such as convenience, amusement, timeliness, comfort or health) that are essentially intangible concerns of its first purchaser."

Service employees such as front desk agents, housekeepers, hostesses, wait staff, car rental agents, flight attendants, and travel agents are responsible for creating positive experiences for customers. These frontline employees are critical to the success of service firms and play boundary-spanning roles because of their direct contact with customers.

These roles are important because customers' perceptions of service firms are formed as a result of their dealings with the boundary-spanning employees. Several reasons underlie the remarkable growth in services. Two leading services marketing experts, Christopher Lovelock and Lauren Wright, cite numerous reasons for this growth:

- *Changing patterns of government regulation:* The reduction in government regulation has spurred the growth of services. In recent years, there has been a very noticeable shift towards the government taking a much less active role in the regulation of business activities. The most noteworthy of these shifts have been in the airline, trucking, telecommunication, and electrical generation and distribution industries. All of these industries have seen significant changes, as the barriers to entry have been removed and regulations governing such marketing elements as price have also been relaxed or entirely removed.
- *Relaxation of professional association restrictions on marketing:* A new element of competition has been introduced into professions such as law and medicine as more of the practitioners in these areas advertise their services. Bans or restrictions on promotion have been largely removed. Within the hospitality and tourism industry, standards have also changed. We have seen an increase in advertising focusing on direct comparisons, or attacks, on competitors' products and services. This type of advertising strategy creates, or sustains, the perception of superiority in the mind of the consumer in favour of the brand being advertised.
- *Privatization of some public and nonprofit services:* The term privatization was first used in Great Britain when the government adopted the policy of returning national industries from government to private ownership. This transformation has resulted in a greater emphasis on cost containment and a clearer focus on

customers' needs. Later, in Central and Eastern Europe, following the fall of communism, we witnessed a continuing transformation from planned or government-run economies to market-driven economies fueled by private companies. Many of these countries' governments have released the control of airlines and travel agencies to private firms.

- *Technological innovation:* Technology continues to alter the way firms do business and interact with consumers. In all types of businesses, consumers take a more active role in the service delivery process. For example, airlines, in an effort to reduce labor costs and increase speed of service to customers, have aggressively promoted self-check-in, both at the ticket counter and through their Web sites prior to arrival at the airport. Customers print boarding passes, receipts, and other documents without intervention by an airline employee. Express checkout for hotel guests has been in place for many years, but hotel chains continue to experiment with ways to enhance the service, thereby reducing labour costs and/or increasing the customers' perceived value.

  In other settings, touch-screen computers collect feedback from guests, in much the same manner that comment cards have been used previously. The ease with which a company can maintain and access a database has permitted the development of sophisticated reservation systems and has led to more sophisticated frequent traveller programmes. The use of more sophisticated reservations and property management systems has allowed hospitality and tourism firms to improve the level of service provided to guests. Guest history data serve as another example of how a hospitality organization can use technology to gain a competitive advantage. If a hotel guest requests a specific type of pillow, staff can record this preference within the individual's guest history file. When this guest checks into another hotel operated by the chain, the items that were previously requested can be waiting, without the guest even having to request them.
- *Growth in service chains and franchise networks:* Much of the growth in service firms, including the hospitality industry, has been the direct result of franchising efforts by some of the major companies. Franchising represents a contractual arrangement whereby one firm (the franchisor) licenses a number of other firms (the franchisees) to use the franchisor's name and business practices. Notable lodging organizations such as Choice Hotels International and Marriott International, as well as food service firms such as McDonald's, Burger King, Taco Bell, and Wendy's, have all used franchising as a major vehicle for growth. The continued growth of the hospitality industry by means of franchising has put additional stress on

independent owners and operators. In fact, each year the percentage of hospitality and tourism operations that are independently operated decreases.

- *Internationalization and globalization:* Increasing shareholder value often remains directly associated with increasing company sales and profits, and globalization is one means of achieving this. As more and more of the prime locations are developed domestically, companies look internationally for expansion opportunities. This has been particularly true for fast-food franchisors: a significant proportion of their expansion during the last few years has occurred outside of their traditional domestic markets.
- *Pressures to improve productivity:* In many industries within the service economy, competition stays very intense. This factor, when combined with the pressure from investors for higher returns on capital, has resulted in pressure to increase productivity and reduce costs. In many cases, managers seek to reduce labour costs by running leaner operations or using technology to replace humans for some tasks An example of this was when Delta Airlines encouraged passengers to check in via the Internet, thereby reducing the number of passengers who wanted to check in at the airport. They offered an incentive of 1,000 extra frequent-flyer miles to any passenger who used this service. While increasing productivity and profits remains a highly desirable goal, it must not be done at the expense of long term customer satisfaction. Without long-term satisfaction, future profitability may exist in jeopardy.
- *The service quality movement:* With the advent of consumerism, the public's perception is that service quality has declined. In response, successful firms are using the customer's perception of quality to set performance standards, rather than relying solely on operationally defined standards for service quality. They often conduct extensive research to determine the key elements that impact the customer's perception of service quality. When Ritz-Carlton won the Malcolm Baldrige National Quality Award, this was tangible evidence that paying careful attention to customers' service expectations can have a dramatic impact on the firm.
- *Expansion of leasing and rental businesses:* The expansion of businesses that lease equipment and personnel to firms has been a contributing factor in the growth of the service sector. More and more firms are looking to outsource some elements of their operation, and they often start with elements that are not part of the firm's core product or business. For example, most hotels that host meetings and conventions have outsourced the servicing of the audiovisual needs of groups to a company that specializes in that type of business. The company in turn leases the audiovisual equipment to groups

that are holding meetings in the hotel. The company is able to provide more up-to-date and specialized equipment to groups than the hotel might if it provided the service itself. The hotel does not have to maintain an inventory of equipment, and therefore capital costs are reduced.

- *Manufacturers as service providers:* Some of the firms that traditionally manufactured and distributed tangible products have found it profitable to provide services as well. For example, most automobile manufacturers have consumer credit agencies to facilitate the leasing and purchasing of automobiles. In the hospitality industry, PepsiCo decided to enter the restaurant industry and distribute its products through acquisitions such as Taco Bell and KFC, but the company later reconsidered this strategy and sold these brands to Yum! Brands, Inc. In the computer industry, firms such as IBM and Hewlett-Packard provide services in addition to hardware and software. In most cases, the profit margins on services are higher than on products, contributing significantly to the bottom line of the firm.
- *Pressures on public and nonprofit organizations to find new income sources:* All organizations are under pressure to increase sales, which often becomes difficult within the traditional products that a firm sells. There are many reasons for this, but increasing competition and mature industries are often contributing factors. In an effort to find new sources of income, firms often seek new services that will generate new net sales, without cannibalizing sales of existing products. For example, a limousine company might expand its city tour business in addition to the other services offered.
- *Hiring and promotion of innovative managers:* In the past, managers in the service industries often spent their entire careers within a single industry, or perhaps even with the same firm. This situation no longer reintroduction to services marketing mains the same, especially at the corporate level of management. Firms often hire individuals from other industries to provide a fresh perspective and fresh ideas. The results can become dramatic. One such individual is Steven Bollenback, president and CEO of Hilton Hotels. Prior to his very positive impact on Hilton Hotels, he had engineered innovative financing at both Marriott International and Trump Hotels and Resorts.

The Nature of Services

Along with the growth in services, an appreciation for the ways in which services are different from products has developed. The traditional ways of marketing tangible products are not equally effective in services marketing. In many industries, marketing involves tangible manufactured products, such as automobiles, washing machines, and clothing, whereas service industries focus on intangible products such as travel and foodservice.

However, before we can explore how services get successfully marketed, we need to examine the ways services differ from products. Lovelock and Wright have identified nine key differences.

No ownership by customers: A customer does not take ownership when purchasing a service. There is no transfer of assets.

- *Service products as intangible performers:* The value of owning a high performance car or the latest computer lies in the physical characteristics of the product and to some extent the brand image it conveys. The value of purchasing services lies in the nature of the performance. For example, if you decide to celebrate a birthday or anniversary by dining at an expensive restaurant, the value lies in the way in which the service actors perform. When servers come to the table and present all the entrees simultaneously, the choreographed presentation appears in the same manner as a choreographed play or performance.
- *Greater involvement of customers in the production process:* Because consumers tend to be present when receiving service within a hospitality operation, they remain involved in the service production. In many instances, they are directly involved through the element of self-service. Examples of this can be seen in fast-food restaurants as well as in hotels that provide automated check-in and checkout by means of either a machine or a video connection through the television. Airlines have greatly expanded self-service within their operations as a means of reducing labour costs. In any case, the customer's level of satisfaction depends on the nature of the interaction with the service provider, the nature of the physical facilities in which the service gets provided, and the nature of the interaction with other guests present in the facility at the time the service is provided.
- *People as part of the product*: People or firms that purchase services come in contact with other consumers as well as the service employees. For example, a hotel guest waits in line at the front desk or the concierge desk with other guests. In addition, the guests share facilities such as the pool, the restaurant, and the fitness centre. Therefore, service firms must also manage consumer interactions to the best of their abilities to ensure customer satisfaction. For example, a hotel's sales office would not want to book group business with a non drinking religious group at the same time as a reunion of military veterans. The two groups are significantly different in behaviour, and the expectation is that they would not mix well within the facilities at the same time. Similarly, restaurants separate smokers and

nonsmokers, and they should try to separate other patrons that show some potential for conflict.

- *Greater variability in operational inputs and outputs:* In a manufacturing setting, the operational production can be controlled very carefully. For example, staff carefully manage inventory and precisely calculate production times. Services, however, are delivered in real time, with many variables not being fully under the control of managers. For example, if a guest has been promised an early check-in but all of the guests from the preceding night are late in checking out, it becomes more difficult for the hotel to honour the arriving guest's request. A service setting remains a more difficult site in which to control quality and offer a consistent service experience. Service firms try to minimize the amount of variability between service encounters, but much of the final product stays situational. There are many uncontrollable aspects of the delivery process, such as weather, the number of consumers present, the attitudes of the consumers, and the attitudes of the employees. Therefore, it becomes impossible to consistently control the quality for services in the same manner as the quality of manufactured products.
- *Harder for consumers to evaluate:* Consumers can receive considerable information regarding the purchase of products; however, they often do not obtain it for services. Prior to buying a product, a consumer can research the product attributes and performance and use this information when making a purchase decision, especially an important one.
- *No inventories for services:* Due to the intangible nature of services, they cannot be inventoried for future use. Therefore, a lost sale can never be recaptured. When a seat remains empty on a flight, a hotel room stays vacant, or a table stays unoccupied in a restaurant, the potential revenue for these services at that point in time becomes lost forever. In other words, services are perishable, much like produce in a supermarket or items in a bakery. It remains critical for hospitality and tourism firms to manage supply and demand in an attempt to minimize unused capacity. For example, restaurants offer early-bird specials and airlines offer deeply discounted fares in an attempt to shift demand from peak periods to non peak periods, thereby increasing revenue and profits.
- *Importance of time:* Hospitality services are generally produced and consumed simultaneously, unlike tangible products, which are manufactured, inventoried, and then sold at a later date. Customers must be present to receive the service. There are real limits to the amount of time that customers are willing to wait to receive service. Service firms study the phenomenon of service queues, or the maximum amount of time a customer will wait for a service before

it has a significant (negative) impact on his or her perception of service quality. Airline companies offer curbside check-in for the most time-conscious passengers, and restaurants have devised practices such as providing guests with pagers and expanding the bar area in order to reduce the negative effect that results from waiting for service.

- *Different distribution channels:* The distribution channel for services is usually more direct than the traditional channel (*i.e.*, manufacturer-wholesaler retailer-consumer) used by many product firms. The simultaneous production and consumption normally associated with service delivery limits the use of intermediaries. The service firm usually comprises both the manufacturer and the retailer, with no need for a wholesaler to inventory its products. Consumers are present to consume the meals prepared in a restaurant, to take advantage of the amenities in a hotel, and to travel between cities by plane.

Search, Experience, and Credence Qualities

Consumer behaviour is covered in greater depth, but a brief introduction to the subject as it relates to services becomes useful at this point. When consumers make purchase decisions, they move through a series of steps that explain the thought process leading up to and following the purchase of a product or service. Prior to making a purchase decision, consumers look for information about the product or service. Search qualities are attributes that the consumer can investigate prior to making a purchase.

When purchasing hospitality and tourism services, consumers rely heavily on word of mouth and on promotional elements such as advertising and publicity. Since services are intangible, search qualities can be difficult to evaluate. However, advances in technology and the increase in consumer advocacy groups have resulted in more information being available to consumers prior to purchase. The second set of qualities consumers use to evaluate services are experience qualities.

These refer to the attributes that can be evaluated only after the purchase and consumption of a service. The intangible nature of services forces consumers to rely heavily on experience qualities in the final evaluation of services. Therefore, a high risk remains associated with the purchase of services. For example, consumers who want to purchase an automobile will test-drive the car and review and consult the consumer performance data that are available on that model. Conversely, consumers who rent cars cannot evaluate their purchases until after they have committed their payment. Few consumers will take the time or make the effort to test-drive potential rental cars prior to making a decision at the time of rental. Similarly, consumers are taking a risk when they choose a restaurant because they cannot sample meals before they are purchased.

Finally, credence qualities are those attributes that are difficult to evaluate even after the service is consumed. Even though you arrive safely at your destination after a flight, you cannot evaluate the pilot's work in any real depth. In many cases, you know a service was not performed correctly only when an obvious mistake exists. For example, bacteria often appear on food served in restaurants, but the public becomes aware of it only when major ramifications such as food poisoning or deaths get publicized.

Purchase decisions related to services are more difficult to make because of the lack of search qualities and the difficulty in evaluating credence qualities. Consumers tend to rely on their own past experiences and those of others when making purchase decisions. Therefore, service firms must obtain as much feedback from consumers as possible. If consumers do not return, the firm may not know why, and the consumers will probably tell others about their experience. Service firms should know if consumers are not satisfied so that appropriate actions can be taken to improve the quality of service and increase repeat business.

Service Quality

Firms use two basic strategies to compete: become a low-cost provider of a particular service and focus on price competition, or focus on quality and try to differentiate your service from those offered by your competitors. Firms that can project high-quality images can charge higher prices. Service quality is a perception resulting from attitudes formed by customers' long-term, overall evaluations of performance.4 Maintaining high quality service in the hospitality and tourism industry remains difficult because of the variability in service delivery mentioned earlier in this chapter. Service quality is affected by all of the individuals who have contact with customers. If one employee provides below-standard service or fails to satisfy the customer, a negative experience could result. Therefore, it is important to understand the entire process of service delivery that leads to consumer perceptions of quality.

The Service Quality Process

The service quality process is the product of the expectations and perceptions of a firm's management, its employees, and the customers it serves. Whenever there are differences in expectations or perceptions between the people involved in the delivery and the consumption of services, a potential for a gap in service quality exists. Firms should diagnose any service quality gaps because there is a direct relationship between service quality and customer satisfaction. Simply stated, when customers are satisfied, they are much more likely to purchase from the service provider again. Over time, if they remain satisfied, they become loyal customers.

The service gap is the final gap that exists when there is a difference between customers' expectations of a service and their perceptions of the actual service once it is consumed. When this difference occurs, it is the result of one or more gaps that occur earlier in the service quality process. The first potential gap is referred to as the knowledge gap, which occurs when management's perception of what consumers expect is different from the consumers' actual expectations. This gap may lead to other gaps in the service quality service quality process, and it is usually the result of a failure in the firm's research programme or organizational structure. Firms need to obtain feedback from customers and employees that can be used to design services that will appeal to customers.

If the current service offering is not satisfying customers, then the firm should know from its customer surveys or because its employees are willing, and able, to provide valuable information that they obtain from customers, either voluntarily or involuntarily. The second potential gap is referred to as the standards gap, which refers to the discrepancy that can occur between management's perception of what customers expect and how the service delivery process is designed to meet those expectations. Management establishes the specifications to provide the desired service at the desired level of quality.

Therefore, even if management remains accurate in its perception of customer expectations, a gap could still exist in service because the delivery process does not accomplish the goals of the firm. For example, management may have correctly determined the amount of time that customers are willing to wait to check in to a hotel, but they may not schedule enough front desk clerks to meet the customers' expectations. This could result from a lack of commitment on the part of management or the result of management trying to reduce the firm's operating costs. One of the techniques used by management is to develop a service blueprint— a flow chart that details the delivery process, including the points of contact with customers. This will help to uncover any shortcomings in the delivery process that may lead to a gap in service quality. Management should document each step in the process to identify areas for improvement.

The third potential gap is referred to as the delivery gap, which occurs when there is a difference between the service delivery specifications and the actual service delivery. Management may have correctly assessed customer expectations and developed specifications that will meet these expectations, but employees may not deliver the service properly. For example, a restaurant may specify that wait staff should approach customers within two minutes of seating.

However, the wait staff may stand around discussing their plans for later in the evening and ignoring the specifications. Firms must find ways to create an atmosphere for employees that ensures their willingness to perform the job tasks as desired by management. Employee selection and training are critical in this process, as are the rewards and recognition provided for good performance. The fourth potential gap is referred to as the communications gap, which occurs when there is a difference between the service delivered and the service quality promised through the firm's external communications with customers. Many firms have a tendency to promise more than they can deliver in an attempt to persuade customers.

For instance, advertisements for hospitality and tourism firms lead customers to believe that in the event of a problem or mishap the firms will do whatever they can to satisfy customers. Making promises to consumers that cannot be delivered is a big mistake that service providers often make. It results in service performance levels that are below consumer expectations, leading to dissatisfaction. Each individual consumer makes purchase decisions and has established, based on past experiences, a set of expectations for the performance of a product or service.

Anyone who travels on a regular basis can provide stories related to experiences with airlines, hotels, and restaurants. Ironically, firms that advertise 100 per cent satisfaction guarantees are banking on the fact that most customers will not complain or force the issue. In other cases, firms simply neglect to inform customers about procedures or policies that would affect their expectations.

For example, a good waitress will make sure that customers know that a dish is spicy or that a certain entree will take longer to properly prepare, so that customers can make informed decisions and are less likely to become dissatisfied, because the actual performance will more closely match consumer expectations.

If any of the first four gaps occur, then the service gap will occur because the actual service will not meet the customer's expectations. Comment cards and basic surveys will often uncover a service gap, but they may lack the detail needed to evaluate the other potential gaps. Therefore, firms should have a mechanism in place to obtain feedback from customers and employees that can be used to examine the entire service quality process. If services do not meet customers' expectations of quality, then the customers become dissatisfied and will likely not return. Also, they will convey these negative experiences to their friends and colleagues.

Managing Service Quality

To provide high-quality service, all members of the staff, from the highest to the lowest level on the organizational chart, must view the guest as the highest priority. Delivering high-quality service is based on an attitude of serving customers. For example, the mission statement of The Greenbrier, a well-known resort, states, "We are ladies and gentlemen serving ladies and gentlemen." Developing an attitude that places the customer as the highest priority for the business remains critical. Without satisfied customers and repeat patron-age, the business will not succeed in the long term.

To develop a service quality orientation, customers should be perceived in the following way:

- Each customer is the most important person in any business.

- Customers are not dependent on us, but we are dependent on them.
- Customers do not interrupt our work. They are the purpose for it.
- Customers do us a favour when they call. We are not doing them favours by providing them services.
- Customers are part of our business, not outsiders.
- Customers are human beings like us, with the same feelings and emotions.
- Customers bring us their wants, and it is our job to fulfill them.
- Customers deserve the most courteous and attentive service we can provide.
- Customers are the lifeblood of every business.

Firms that use a customer orientation become more successful at providing products and services that meet customers' needs and expectations. In contrast, firms that assume they know what is best for the customer are more likely to fail. This is further illustrated by those firms that successfully engage in relationship and internal marketing.

RELATIONSHIP MARKETING

All progressive companies devote marketing resources to attract and retain new customers. Relationship marketing is based on the proposition that it is less expensive to keep the customers you already have than to acquire new customers. It is shortsighted to think that merely attracting new customers will keep the business headed in a successful direction. Rather, an equal amount of attention and resources should be devoted to keeping the customer base that already exists. In times of slow market growth and increasing competition, it will be less expensive to maintain an existing customer base than to seek new customers.

Relationship marketing involves attracting, developing, and retaining customer relationships. This long-term view towards the customer must be seen as being equal in importance to attracting new customers. Many firms make the mistake of focusing on new customers at the expense of existing customers, and the level of service quality diminishes. For example, hotel sales managers are expected to develop new accounts with corporate and association groups.

Sometimes they spend so much time trying to get these new accounts that they neglect some of their existing accounts. This lack of attention may cost the hotel the group's future business because they took the customer for granted. Service firms should build relationships and maintain them.

A relationship marketing approach is highly desirable upon meeting the following conditions:

- A customer has an ongoing or periodic desire for the service.
- The service customer controls the selection of the service organization.
- Alternative service providers make it easy for customers to switch.

All three of these conditions are present in the hospitality and tourism industry. Many firms offer special prices and additional services to highly desirable customers in an attempt to build long-term relationships. These practices are most commonly used with business accounts and frequent users. For example, hotels provide contract rates for corporations that supply a high volume of annual business.

Airlines receive one of the lowest rates possible in hotels near airports because they have flight crews who need guest rooms on a daily basis. Also, airlines build relationships with frequent flyers by providing them with additional services such as preboarding, free upgrades, and airport clubs where they can rest or conduct business away from crowded lounges at departure gates.

INTERNAL MARKETING

In addition to focusing efforts on consumers, firms can achieve higher levels of service quality by marketing to their employees. Internal marketing encompasses all activities used by a firm in an effort to improve the marketing effectiveness of its employees. Efforts should be made to communicate with all employees, especially those in boundary spanning roles who come in contact with customers. The ability to deliver consistent, high-quality service depends on the organization's ability to recruit, train, retain, and motivate dedicated service personnel.

First, service firms need to select and hire employees who are willing and able to provide high-quality service. There are many people in the job market, and firms need to create attractive positions that appeal to highly motivated individuals.

A range of potential service exists that an employee can provide from the minimum necessary to retain the position and not be penalized to the maximum possible service. This variability in the level of possible service is referred to as discretionary effort.

For example, if an airline passenger leaves a carry-on item on a flight, the airline's personnel have some discretion as to the level of service they will provide. They can take their time and forward the item to the traveller's next destination, or they can try to deliver it to the traveller before he or she boards the next plane or leaves the airport. Second, service firms should provide employees with adequate training so they possess the skills that are required in performing their job tasks.

In addition, the firm should communicate with employees so they are aware of changes within the organization as well as upcoming events. If service personnel are well trained and they understand what management expects, the environment is right for success. Firms can use both internal communi-cations, such as newsletters and e-mail, and external communications, such as advertising and public relations, to convey their expectations to employees.

An advertisement can be used to create and manage consumer perceptions and expectations, but at the same time, the ad can be used to educate employees as well. One of the major airlines aired a commercial on television that showed an athletic employee running through the airport to catch a traveller who left his briefcase at the check-in counter.

This commercial served two purposes:

- It let customers know that the airline provided high-quality service, and
- It gave employees an idea of the firm's service expectations.

Finally, firms need to provide employees with rewards and recognition when they perform at a high level of discretionary effort. This motivates service providers to continue performing at high levels and to remain loyal to the firm. Retaining good employees is important in providing high-quality service, and it reduces the costs associated with turnover. It takes a great deal of time and effort to hire and train good employees. Firms can use extrinsic rewards such as salary increases and bonuses or intrinsic rewards such as recognition and job satisfaction to motivate employees. Many firms recognize "employees of the month" by honouring them with plaques displayed where customers can see them or allowing them to use special parking spaces close to the building.

CUSTOMER SATISFACTION

Most firms understand the importance of customer satisfaction and will provide basic training to their employees. The more sophisticated firms actually have instruments that they use to measure customer satisfaction and establish benchmarks for future comparisons. Benchmarking is a process whereby a firm establishes a level of performance by comparing current performance against past performance, or by comparing current performance against the performance of other companies or an entire industry.

Data are used to create benchmarks, which then become the standard against which current and customer satisfaction future performance is evaluated. Unfortunately, many firms still only pay lip service to customer satisfaction and the complaints received from customers. The following information was collected through the efforts of the Technical Assistance Research Programme in the 1980s, but it remains accurate today:

- The average business does not hear from 96 per cent of its unhappy customers.
- For every complaint received, 26 other customers have the same problem.
- The average person with a problem tells 9 or 10 people, and 13 per cent will tell more than 20.
- Customers who have their complaints resolved to their satisfaction tell an average of 5 people about the experience.

- Complainers are more likely to do business with you again than non complainers who have a problem: 54–70 per cent if resolved, and 95 per cent if resolved quickly. These statistics support the contention that a dissatisfied customer tells people about a bad experience more often than a satisfied customer tells people about a good experience. However, firms should take note that it is beneficial to have customers voice their complaints so that they can be resolved and increase the likelihood that the customers will return.

Improving Customer Service and Customer Satisfaction

Improving customer service should be a top priority of all managers working in the hospitality and tourism industry. Customer satisfaction occurs when a firm's service, as perceived by customers, meets or exceeds expectations.

Firms that can consistently meet or exceed customer expectations will develop good reputations and often good quality images. When we travel, we encounter service providers in hotels and restaurants who provide exceptional service. This type and consistency of service does not happen by accident; it begins with a commitment by management to make it that way. Conversely, when the opposite occurs, the finger should be pointed at management as well.

- *Define your standards of quality service with measurable indicators:* Before you can evaluate the level of service provided by employees within your organization, you must establish the standards by which they will be judged. These standards, or benchmarks, should be observable and measurable. For example, it might be reasonable to expect front desk agents to answer the telephone within four rings or room service to deliver meals within 30 minutes of when the order was received. Once these standards are developed, they must be communicated to all personnel. It remains crucial that standards be clearly defined before any plans are developed to improve the level of service. Martin suggests two major dimensions to define quality service: the procedural dimension and the convivial dimension. The procedural dimension includes incremental flow of service, timeliness, accommodating consumer needs, anticipating consumer needs before they occur or are requested by the consumer, communicating in a clear and concise manner, customer satisfaction. obtaining consumer feedback, and coordinating through proper supervision. The convivial dimension includes displaying a positive attitude and body language, using the guest's name as a means of delivering personal attention, attending to the guest on a personal basis, providing guidance to guests who are indecisive, and solving problems that arise.
- *Assess your current situation*: As in any continuous improvement

programme, before you move forward, you must determine your current position. This can be done by objectively assessing the level of service currently provided within the organization; this involves conducting an audit of the services provided by service personnel within the organization. As a result of the audit, the strengths and weaknesses of the firm can be determined; this will provide a means of building on the aspects of service that are positive and improving the areas that are deficient. Audits can be conducted using mystery shoppers, or corporations may use staff members to audit the performance of units within the company.

- *Develop effective service improvement strategies:* This must be accomplished through well-planned and thorough training of service providers. Attention must be paid to identifying objectives for the training and providing specific instructions and clear descriptions of the expected outcome (s) of the training.
- *Initiate your solutions carefully:* As with any plan, implementation is the most critical stage. You should proceed with caution, taking steps incrementally rather than all at once. You should build on small successes, rather than trying to accomplish too much too soon.
- *Provide feedback, recognition, and rewards:* Positive feedback must be provided if the change in behaviour continues. A reward structure must be provided that will maintain the level of interest and enthusiasm among the service providers throughout their careers. This represents a major challenge for management, but one that is well worth the effort. Finally, management must continually evaluate the performance of its employees and make the appropriate changes. Over time, customers' expectations of service firms change, and competitive firms may increase the level of service that is considered the standard in an industry. Therefore, firms must constantly reassess their strategies and redefine their service standards. Service performance and customer satisfaction should be measured and evaluated using benchmarks established during previous periods. Also, direct comparisons with the performance of firms considered industry leaders are an excellent way to establish goals for future improvement.

Service Failures, Customer Complaints, and Recovery Strategies

Service failures occur at critical incidents, or "moments of truth," in the service encounter, when customers interact with a firm's employees. It is important to provide service personnel with the authority and the recovery tools necessary to correct service failures as they occur. This section will discuss the types of service failures, common consumer complaints, and recovery strategies that can be used to repair the service failures.

SERVICE FAILURES

The timeliness and form of response by service providers to service failures will have a direct impact on customer satisfaction and quality perceptions.

Service failures are assigned to one of three major categories:

- Responses to service delivery system failures,
- Responses to customer needs and requests, and
- Unprompted and unsolicited employee actions.

The first category, system failures, refers to failures in the core service offering of the firm. These failures are the result of normally available services being unavailable, unreasonably slow service, or some other core service failure that will differ by industry. For example, a hotel's pool may have a leak and be closed, a customer may have to wait a long time for the shuttle to an airport car rental agency, or an airline might mishandle a passenger's luggage.

The second category, customer needs failures, are based on employee responses to customer needs or special requests. These failures come in the form of special needs, customer preferences, customer errors, and disruptive others (*i.e.*, disputes between customers). For example, a hotel guest may want to have a pet in the room, a customer may want to be switched to an aisle seat on an airplane, a customer at an event may lose his ticket, or a customer in a restaurant may be smoking in a nonsmoking section.

The third category, unsolicited employee actions, refers to the actions, both good and bad, of employees that are not expected by customers.

These actions can be related to the level of attention an employee gives to customers, to unusual actions that can be performed by employees, to an action's reinforcement of a customer's cultural norms, or to an employee's actions under adverse conditions. For example, a hostess in a restaurant could anticipate the needs of a family with a small child, a hotel front desk clerk could give a free upgrade to a guest who waited in line too long, a flight attendant could ignore passengers with children, or a cruise ship employee could help to evacuate passengers during a crisis. customer satisfaction

Customer Complaint Behaviour

As mentioned earlier in this chapter, certain undesired outcomes are associated with dissatisfied customers. Two of the most common are to engage in negative word of mouth and to change service providers. A third, less common reaction is to engage in some form of retaliation. This retaliation can range from a negative word-of-mouth campaign to causing physical damage or launching a major protest. The way a firm approaches and handles complaints will determine its long-term performance. Some firms show a dislike for customers who complain, while other firms create an atmosphere that encourages customers to voice their concerns.

For example, Bertucci's Brick Oven Pizzerias, headquartered in Massachusetts, offers customers a tollfree number that they can call to register a complaint. One of the primary reasons for doing this is to provide dissatisfied customers with an outlet to have their concerns heard and to take immediate steps to resolve the complaint. By doing so, the firm hopes to reduce negative word of mouth and to retain customers. Most customers complain in an attempt to reverse an undesirable state.

Other more complicated reasons for complaining are to release pressure, to regain some form of control over a situation, or to get the sympathy of others. Whatever the reason, the outcome is that customers are not completely satisfied, and it is in the firm's best interest to know when this occurs. There are many other dissatisfied customers who do not complain because they don't know what to do or they don't think it will do any good.

Recovery Strategies

When customers complain, firms are presented with the opportunity to recover from service failures. Recovery strategies, and actions occur when a firm's reaction to a service failure results in customer satisfaction and goodwill. In fact, customers who are involved in successful service recoveries often demonstrate higher levels of satisfaction than customers who do not report service failures or complain.

The following list describes popular service recovery strategies:

- *Cost/benefit analysis:* Service firms should compare the costs of losing customers and obtaining new customers with the benefits of keeping existing customers. Most firms place a high value on retaining customers. However, some guests take advantage of satisfaction guarantees and complain on every occasion. Many hotel chains, such as Doubletree, maintain a database on complaints and will flag chronic complainers.
- *Actively encourage complaints:* It is better to know when customers are not satisfied so that action can be taken to rectify the situation. It is important to note that while unhappy customers may not complain to service firms, they will often complain to their family and friends. Hospitality and tourism firms use comment cards and toll-free numbers to encourage customers to provide feedback. Also, service personnel are trained to ask customers whether everything was satisfactory.
- *Anticipate the need for recovery:* Service firms should "blueprint" the service delivery process and determine the moments of truth, or critical incidents, where customers interact with employees. The process can be designed to avoid failures, but recovery plans should be established for use in the event that a failure occurs.

- *Respond quickly:* The timelier the response in the event of a service failure, the more likely that recovery efforts will be successful. Once a customer leaves a service establishment, the likelihood of a successful recovery falls dramatically. Based on this principle, firms such as Marriott International provide service hotlines at each hotel to help resolve problems quickly. Managers and associates know that the speed with which they respond is often as critical as what the final resolution becomes.
- *Train employees:* Employees should be informed of the critical incidents and provided with potential strategies for recovery. For example, some hotel training programmes use videotaped scenarios of service failures to show employees potential problems and the appropriate solutions.
- *Empower the front line:* In many cases, a successful recovery will hinge on a frontline employee's ability to take timely action and make a decision. Firms should empower employees to handle service failures at the time they occur, within certain limits.

For example, Ritz-Carlton allows its employees to spend up to $1,000 to take care of dissatisfied customers. One of the classic examples of a service failure involved Northwest Airlines during a major winter storm at the Detroit airport. Unfortunately, due to the heavy snow, many outbound flights were canceled, and no gates were available for unloading passengers from the inbound flights. This traffic jam left many passengers stranded as the airplanes sat on the taxiways for as long as eight hours. Northwest's inability to provide the passengers with information or a solution resulted in hundreds of unhappy passengers and a class action lawsuit. Having delayed flights and a shortage of gates is not a new phenomenon at airports in climates such as Detroit's, and Northwest Airlines should have had a viable service recovery programme in place that could have lessened the severity of the problem.

Techniques to Assess Customer Satisfaction

One of the critical components of a firm's commitment to customer satisfaction is feedback that provides an assessment of the firm's performance. Then benchmarks can be established and future progress can be evaluated. Also, these measures can be used to reward service personnel in a way that stays consistent with a firm's customer satisfaction goals. The following section describes the most common techniques used by firms to assess customer satisfaction.

SPOKEN COMMENTS AND COMPLAINTS

Listening to consumer comments and complaints remains the most straightforward way to evaluate customer satisfaction. Service firms should set up formal systems that encourage customer and employee feedback regarding service experiences. Management should not overlook the value of the information obtained by boundary-spanning personnel through their normal contact with customers. One of the most recent approaches is providing toll-free numbers so that customers can call to voice complaints.

Surveys and Comment Cards

Many hospitality and tourism firms leave comment cards in guest rooms, on tables in restaurants, and at other points of contact so that they can obtain feedback. One of the problems associated with this method is the lack of representation.

The response rate is small, and it tends to be biased towards those who are most upset and chronic complainers. Larger operations will conduct surveys through the corporate offices by either telephone or mail. Surveys will normally be more representative than comment cards and provide more detailed information. These types of surveys also provide for a more representative sample of customers.

Number of Repeat Customers

Service firms can gauge customer satisfaction by keeping track of repeat business. Higher levels of satisfaction would be associated with higher percentages of repeat customers. This models an unobtrusive method of assessing customer satisfaction, but it does not provide much detail.

Trends in Sales and Market Share

Another way to evaluate customer satisfaction without direct contact with customers is to examine the firm's internal sales records. Comparisons can be made on a month-to-month basis and with the same period of the previous year. Higher levels of satisfaction would be associated with increases in sales. However, firms should be careful with this method because there are many possible explanations for increases in sales.

For example, the firm may have launched a new advertising campaign, a competitor may be renovating or going out of business, or the firm may have decreased its prices. In addition to examining sales records, firms should also look at market share. This measure considers sales in relation to the competition, which is a more accurate assessment of improved market performance. However, there could also be other explanations for changes in market share besides customer satisfaction.

Shopping Reports

Another approach used by hospitality and tourism firms involves having someone consume a service just like any other customer. The "secret shopper" can be an employee of the firm, an outside person chosen by the firm, or an employee of an outside firm that specializes in this service assessment activity. These shoppers are normally equipped with detailed evaluation forms based on company guidelines that can be used to record the desired information. It is often recommended that someone outside the firm be used in an attempt to maintain some level of objectivity. It is important to have a particular operation evaluated by more than one shopper on several occasions throughout the desired period. Doing so will result in a more representative sample of service experiences.

SERVICE TRENDS AFFECTING THE HOSPITALITY AND TOURISM INDUSTRY

Identifying trends within any business is one of the keys to success. Being in a position to identify what is occurring and what is likely to occur in the future remains very important. As discussed earlier, when studying trends in a broad sense, one should examine five major areas: the competitive environment, the economic environment, the political and legal environment, the social environment, and the technological environment.

Several issues and trends are critical to understanding hospitality and tourism marketing. They help put into proper perspective what occurs within the competitive marketplace. Three trends that are having an impact on the hospitality industry and will continue to do so are shrinking customer loyalty, increasing customer sophistication, and increasing emphasis on the needs of individual customers.

Shrinking Customer Loyalty

Advertising and promotion for the hospitality and tourism industry's product-service mix have traditionally focused on the product, the services service trends affecting the hospitality and tourism industry provided, and the physical plant or atmosphere in which the customer enjoys the product-service mix.

Today, many hospitality and tourism firms focus their promotions on price; that is, heavy price competition exists along with a good deal of discounting. Unfortunately, price discounting exists as a short-term strategy that seldom builds brand loyalty. Consumers often shop around for the best deal and are loyal only to organizations that give them a consistently superior one.

Recognizing this, companies have sought ways to increase brand loyalty, especially among heavy users of the product service mix. The best examples of this approach are the frequent flyer programmes promoted by the airlines and the frequent traveller programmes promoted by the lodging companies. These loyalty programmes are commonplace in the lodging industry; all of the major chains use loyalty programmes to encourage and reward frequent guests.

The strategy behind loyalty programmes is to hook the customer with points which can be redeemed for products or services. The more frequently the customer stays at a hotel operated by the company, the more points are earned.

The basic concepts common to all of these programmes are:

- Identify individuals who frequently purchase your product-service mix.
- Recognize the contribution those individuals make to the success of your company.
- Reward those individuals with awards and incentives that will increase their loyalty to your company and its brands.

Tie-ins with other companies providing travel-related services are also frequently used. For example, airlines, hotels, and car rental companies frequently offer bonus points within their programmes if the traveller uses the services offered by one of the companies participating in the tie-in. Both the airlines and the hotel companies are constantly making minor alterations to their programmes.

Increasing Consumer Sophistication

The budget segment of the lodging industry has undergone significant growth in the last several years. This growth has been fueled by the consumer demand for affordable accommodations that provide good value. In fact, consumers focus more on value and less on quality or price alone. Consumers have become more sophisticated and understand the concept of value at any price level. Hotels have responded that offer good quality service at an affordable price. Each of these brands features nicely appointed guest rooms, limited or no public meeting space, limited or no food service provided on the hotel site, and a complimentary continental breakfast for guests. These limited-service brands incur lower development and operating expenses and thereby can provide guests with a lower price and good value, something that all consumers are seeking.

Hotels in the upscale segment are also trying to increase the consumer's perception of value. They continually provide a broad assortment of amenities, such as health clubs on the property, business centres, rooms that provide more work space for business travellers, and personalized concierge service. These properties are striving to become "one-stop" destinations, providing a complete product-service mix that includes many food and beverage outlets, in-house office services, a wide variety of meeting room configurations, and other services, such as recreation, that will appeal to potential guests.

Within the fast-food service segment, companies often "bundle" their products in an attempt to increase sales and provide a better value for their customers. For example, they combine a sandwich, a large order of french fries, and a large soft drink at a price lower than what the items would cost if purchased separately. Similarly, tour operators and travel agents attempt to provide customers with more value by "bundling" the various components of travel (*e.g.*, airline ticket, hotel room, car rental, and tickets for tourist at service trends affecting the hospitality and tourism industry tractions) at a price lower than the sum of the individual components. This approach is known as product bundling.

Increased Emphasis on the Needs of Individual Customers

The markets within both hospitality and tourism segments have been segmented for a long time. In the past 5 to 15 years, this trend has become even more pronounced. Mass marketing has become a thing of the past as more firms extend their product lines to meet the specific needs of smaller segments of travellers and diners. This phenomenon has become most apparent in the lodging industry.

During the last decade, most of the major lodging chains developed several new brands or types of lodging properties to appeal to market segments that they were not currently serving. In addition, many hotel chains have merged with or acquired other hotel chains that focus on different market segments. Improvements in technology have given firms the ability to maintain large databases that detail consumer purchasing behaviour and preferences.

This information can be used to direct marketing efforts towards individual customers or market segments. Instead of relying on the mass media for promotions, a marketer can target past customers through direct mail and e-mail with special promotions and incentives that have a higher probability of being successful. There is more customization of products and promotions and less wasted coverage with media campaigns.

It began by defining services and explaining the characteristics that separate tangible products and services. Services are intangible and cannot be inventoried. This requires changes in the distribution process, and it makes it difficult to maintain consistent quality. It also requires more involvement on the part of customers, who actually become part of the product. The intangible nature of services results in more of an emphasis on experience qualities that are evaluated after a product becomes consumed, and less on search qualities that can be evaluated prior to purchase.

The concept of service quality remains important because consumers form perceptions of a firm based on its ability to provide a consistent level of service. This chapter introduced the service quality process and the potential gaps that could occur throughout the process. These gaps in service will decrease the level of service quality and lead to a decrease in customer satisfaction. Firms learn to manage service operations and improve quality through employee selection and training.

Once a firm focuses on the needs of consumers, it can build customer loyalty through relationship marketing. The overall performance of the firm can be improved through internal marketing efforts that attempt to communicate with employees and provide them with an environment for success. Customer satisfaction exists as the ultimate goal for a firm because it leads to brand loyalty and repeat purchases. Firms must meet or exceed customer expectations on a consistent basis in order to satisfy them. This chapter discussed ways to improve customer service and increase customer satisfaction.

There are critical incidents, or moments of truth, when customers interact with employees and service failures can occur. Firms should encourage customers to voice their complaints so that the firms can anticipate and avoid possible failures. Also, firms can prepare service recovery strategies and train their employees to use them.

A firm's progress concerning customer satisfaction can be assessed using the techniques provided in this chapter, and benchmarks can be set for future comparisons. Finally, the chapter discussed some of the current trends in the hospitality and tourism industry that affect service operations. First, there is shrinking customer loyalty. Customers have many alternatives for fulfilling their needs, and it is easy to compare these alternatives using all of the information that is available.

The stronger the competition, the more incentives customers are given to switch service providers. Second, consumers are becoming more sophisticated. Consumers have access to a proliferation of information about products and services. This information allows them to focus on overall value, rather than price or quality alone. Also, consumer advocacy organizations provide helpful tips for getting bargains and avoiding firms with poor reputations. Finally, there is an increased emphasis on the individual needs of customers.

Improved technology has made database marketing possible, allowing more precise targeting of markets and less wasted coverage with promotions. Firms are able to service more market segments by introducing new brands or forming relationships with other firms (*e.g.*, strategic alliances, mergers, and acquisitions).

Case Study

Service Quality at the Excelsior Hotel

Kristen Adams had recently transferred to the Excelsior Hotel to improve the level of customer service. She had been with the company for five years and had been quite successful in improving the level of customer satisfaction at the two previous hotels to which she had been assigned. Kristen knew that the Excelsior was going to be a real challenge. The mix of business was 60 per cent individual transient guests and 40 per cent group business. Of this group business, about one-third was motor coach tour groups.

On her first day on the job, she witnessed quite a sight. There was a line of about 20 guests waiting to check in when two motor coaches arrived and more than 80 additional guests and guides walked into the lobby to check in. Needless to say, the two front desk agents had a look of terror in their eyes as they worked diligently to process the registrations for those waiting to check in.

Some 40 minutes later, everyone had been checked in, but the general manager said to Kristen, "I'm glad that you are here; we need to work out a better system. Let's meet for lunch tomorrow to discuss your initial ideas."

Kristen had just picked up a pen to start brainstorming ideas to present to the general manager when a guest approached her desk. "Hello, my name is Bill Foster, and I stayed at your hotel last night with my family. We really did not have a good experience, and I want to tell you about it. I want to make sure that this does not happen again, to me or anyone else." Mr. Foster then proceeded to tell Kristen his account of the events. "I was traveling with my wife and our son, who is four years old. Our connecting flight was delayed, so we did not arrive at our final destination until 10 p.m. The Excelsior had an advertised check-in facility at the airport, and I assumed that I would be able to secure my room while waiting for the luggage.

When I approached the employee at the hotel's airport facility, I was told that check-in service was not available at that time of the day.

I found this to be surprising, since this was the very type of situation in which an airport facility would be beneficial. "Next, my family took a shuttle van from the airport to the hotel, where we were given directions to the front desk. Two front desk clerks were on duty when the passengers from the airport shuttle arrived a little before 11 p.m.

However, one of the front desk clerks was apparently going off duty at 11, and she proceeded to close her drawer at that exact moment.

This left a line of approximately 10 or 12 guests to be checked in by one clerk. Needless case study to say, it took some time to process all of the guests, and we had to wait 20 or 30 minutes for our turn.

We were assigned to a room, but at this point we had a few bags and my son was fast asleep and had to be carried. When I asked for assistance with our luggage, I was told that no one was available at that time of night. The hotel was large, having over 1,000 rooms, and the rooms were spread out among several adjacent buildings.

Our room was two buildings away from the lobby area. My wife and I struggled to carry the luggage and our son to the room. We arrived there about 11:30 and attempted to enter the room. The key unlocked the door, but the door would not open. After a couple of attempts, we heard a woman's voice in the room. Obviously, the room had been double-booked and the woman woken from her sleep. I used the house phone to call the front desk and explain the predicament.

The front desk manager offered a quick apology and said that she would send someone with a key to a nearby room. About ten minutes later, a housekeeper happened to be going through the hallway, and she let my family into the room that I had been given over the phone.

However, the housekeeper had no idea what was going on and took my word. After we had been in the room for ten minutes, the phone rang and I spoke with the front desk manager. She acted as though she had sent the housekeeper to open the room, but she still needed to send someone with the room keys. She apologized one last time and told me to call the front desk if I had any other problems."

TOURISM INFRASTRUCTURE

This chapter seeks to introduce some of the important concepts and concerns associated with expanding the economic benefits of tourism through investment in infrastructure. It is adapted from previous work by the author and colleagues, and was presented in part in a World Tourism Organization publication.

There is growing recognition that innovative approaches must be adopted in order to maintain the economic health of many countries, communities and regions. While conditions vary from region to region, tourism has been seen as an important form of economic development. It has also been promoted as a somewhat benign agent of economic and social change, a promulgator of peace through interaction and dialogue, and a service-based industry capable of creating employment and income.

The perception that tourism has only positive economic benefits has lessened in recent years, due to the growing awareness and knowledge of the more intangible and indirect economic costs of tourism. While it can be argued that tourism does offer an important alternative form of economic activity, it must be seen as only one component of a larger series of development initiatives within any economic system. That is not to say that tourism in selected circumstances cannot be the major source of income and jobs in a community or region, but rather that the impact and role of tourism will vary from region to region.

Experience has shown that tourism may take many forms and meet a number of tourist motivations. Experience has also shown that destinations can rise and fall in popularity, driven by various factors in the destination's internal and external environment.

A destination that is entirely dependent on tourism is much more vulnerable to these shifts than an economy that is well diversified and has tourism as just one of its industries.

ECONOMIC EFFECTS OF TOURISM

The ability of a tourism destination to attract tourism revenues and investment in infrastructure is influenced by a complex number of characteristics, such as:

- Political constraints and incentives;
- The resources and conveniences offered;
- Market characteristics;
- Political stability;
- The ability of the destination to market and promote itself effectively.

The primary and secondary effects of tourism expenditures are discussed later in this chapter. In its simplest form, the economic impact of tourism can be measured as the difference in economic well-being between the income levels that would have existed without tourism activity and the income levels after tourism activity. There are a number of potential tangible and less tangible economic benefits and costs; these are summarized below.

The potential economic benefits of tourism development include:

- Increased resources for the protection and conservation of natural and cultural heritage resources;
- Increased income and improved standard of living from tourist expenditures;
- Increased induced income from tourism expenditures;
- New employment opportunities;
- Increased community visibility leading to other economic development opportunities;
- New induced employment opportunities;
- Increased tax base;
- Improved infrastructure and facilities;
- Development of local handicrafts.

The potential costs include:

- Seasonal employment;
- Low status/paying jobs;
- Inflation;
- Increased costs;
- Pollution;
- Increased traffic/congestion;
- Negative impacts on cultural and natural heritage resources;
- Increased crime;
- Increased taxes;
- Leakage of revenues and external domination;
- Over-dependence on tourism as a prime economic activity.

There are other costs that may have an indirect or long-term impact on the economic contributions of tourism. For example, land values may change as high-priced projects replace traditional and less profitable land uses. If agricultural landowners choose to sell or develop their land for tourism purposes, the tourism economy may have to rely on some food imports to feed the tourists and locals. The loss of traditional land values can also have an impact on the local heritage and sense of place. Moreover, conflict may arise between those landowners who do not wish to see the loss of the historic character of their community and area, and pro-tourism proponents.

Residents and speculators who suffer or benefit from rising land prices might join in the fray. Such conflict could escalate as tourism pressures increase, and the resulting scars on the community might take a long time to heal. This short example helps to illustrate that understanding and measuring economic impacts is more complex than simply measuring direct impacts. It is also important to view economic impacts from a long-term perspective. Environmental degradation and pollution will result in short-term environmental costs and associated economic costs incurred in repairing the damage caused by the pollution. There could also be considerable long-term economic costs to the local, regional, and national economies if the destination is no longer desirable due to the effects of degradation and pollution.

MEASURING ECONOMIC IMPACTS OF TOURISM

A major objective of any tourism planning and development process should be to minimize negative impacts and ensure that the benefits are realised in an equitable manner. While there are significant problems on the road to achieving this objective, there is growing recognition that sustainable tourism approaches will help in reaching this goal. There are a number of methods for measuring the economic impacts of tourism activity, some of which are discussed below.

Measuring the economic impact and employment creation activities of tourism should be carried out in an integrated fashion, taking into account direct and indirect job creation as well as the economic well being of the community.

While employment creation is seen as an important objective, concern for the overall local economy must also be a major consideration. As has been discussed, this implies that jobs and economic benefits may be realised from a number of sources other than tourism. It may also imply that jobs are created as the result of private sector entrepreneurial activity as well as community initiative.

SUPPLY-DEMAND AND PRICE ELASTICITIES

The economic contribution of tourism activity to a community or region is influenced by a diverse number of factors within and outside the destination. Given that diversity, it is difficult to calculate impacts due to the wide range of effects associated with tourism economic activities, the diverse number of participants involved in those activities, and the complex interrelationships between various sectors. Tourism economic activity is often explained using the concept of supply and demand. A number of variables influence the demand and supply of a tourism product or service. For example, if the price of a hotel room increases, demand may decrease, as visitors seek other locations or accommodation sources, and the supply of available hotel rooms therefore increases.

The supply-demand relationship of tourism goods and services can be influenced by factors such as the price elasticity of demand for tourism. When demand is price elastic, a lower price could generate a higher demand and hence higher revenues.

Similarly, if demand is price inelastic, a lower price could result in lower overall revenues. Knowing the price elasticity of demand can aid tourism service providers in designing their product mix. However, a number of factors affect price elasticity, making it difficult to calculate.

DIRECT AND INDIRECT EFFECTS OF TOURISM EARNINGS

The economic benefits of travel and tourism can be derived directly or indirectly. The primary effect is direct benefits that result from direct tourist expenditures for goods and services in the destination. These are realised through business receipts, income, employment and government receipts from the sectors that directly receive the tourism expenditure. Indirect benefits are generated by the circulation of tourism expenditures in the destination country through domestic inter-business transactions. For example, indirect benefits can be generated from the investment and spending by the businesses that benefit directly from tourism expenditures. The direct business receipts, when re-funneled as investments or used to purchase other goods and services from domestic suppliers, stimulate income and employment in other sectors. In addition, tourism spending within the destination area can create induced benefits.

As income levels rise due to the direct and indirect effects of change in the level of tourism expenditure, some of the additional personal income is spent within the destination. This results in induced benefits, such as local income and jobs in the local goods and service sector. Hence, the spending by tourists at the destination can create direct benefits in tourism-related services and sectors such as accommodation, hospitality, attractions, events and transportation. This spending can also create a significant amount of indirect and induced benefits in other sectors such as agriculture, construction and manufacturing. Indirect and induced benefits are also referred to as the secondary effect.

MULTIPLIER MODEL OF TOURISM REVENUE TURNOVER

Multipliers measure the effect of expenditures introduced into an economy. Tourism multipliers are used to determine changes in output, income, employment, business and government receipts, and balance of payments due to a change in the level of tourism expenditures in an area. For example, if tourism expenditures increase by 15 per cent due to attendance at a special event in the destination, some of this added revenue may be used by the event to purchase food and other goods from the local economy, as well as on payment of wages, salaries, government taxes etc.

The suppliers to the event may then spend the money received from the event on other goods, services, taxes etc., thus generating yet another round of expenditures. Employees from the events and local suppliers to the events may use the additional personal income, derived from the direct and indirect effects of the increase in tourism expenditures, to consume local goods and services. Some of the added revenues from the increase in tourism expenditures may, however, undergo leakage. For example, revenues may leak out of the local economy in the form of payment for imports or monies saved. Import payments can take several forms, such as repatriation of profits to foreign corporations and salaries to non-local managers, as well as payment for imported goods and promotion and advertising by companies based outside the destination.

Tourism-related commodities and services could be purchased from within the destination, thereby reducing leakages through the creation of economic interrelationships among the goods and service providers in the destination. The net effect of the successive rounds of spending of added tourism expenditure is the multiplier effect.

In essence, tourism multipliers attempt to describe the relationship between direct tourism expenditure in the economy and the secondary effect of that expenditure upon the economy.

Some of the factors that affect the multiplier are the size of the local economy, the propensity of tourists and residents to buy imported goods or services, as well as the propensity of residents to save rather than spend. In mathematical terms.

Some common multipliers are:

- The income multiplier, which measures the extra domestic income generated by an extra unit of tourism expenditure;
- The employment multiplier, which measures the increased number of primary and secondary jobs created by an extra unit of tourism expenditure;
- The government multiplier, which measures the extra government revenue created by an extra unit of tourism expenditure.

Multipliers can be calculated for a country, region or community. However, the information provided by tourism multipliers has to be very carefully evaluated. Factors such as the size of the destination can significantly affect the multiplier. A smaller economy may have a much smaller multiplier than a larger one since more goods and services might be imported to meet the tourists' needs, resulting in a greater leakage of revenues out of the destination. Hence, multipliers may vary greatly among communities within a country or region.

Furthermore, since tourism multipliers can be calculated in a number of different ways, care must be taken when comparing the multipliers of different countries. Multipliers should be examined together with other measurements and indicators in order to determine the positive and negative economic impacts of tourism on the community.

INPUT-OUTPUT ANALYSIS

Studies of the economic impacts of tourism generally include inputoutput analysis. This kind of analysis helps to demonstrate how economic sectors are related, the number of linkages and the effect of these linkages. This form of analysis is, therefore, a means of analyzing inter-industry relationships in the flow of goods and services in an area's economy, through the chain of producers, suppliers and intermediaries to the final buyer.

Input-output analysis commences with the development of a table that illustrates, in matrix form, how transactions flow through the economy over a given time period. The rows of the matrix show the sales of the total output by each sector to every other sector. The columns demonstrate the inputs required by every sector from the other sectors. When assessing tourism accommodation, the rows in the table would demonstrate the output, *i.e.*, the revenues generated by each industry from the sale of products or services, including accommodation, meals, tour guides and related services such as laundry, medical services etc.

The columns would allow us to see the inputs that go into the output of the accommodation sector, including food, utilities, paper products, advertising and promotion services, wage and salary levels etc. Using a combination of matrix manipulations, multipliers can be calculated to provide an assessment of the effects of different sectors on each other. While input-output tables are helpful in understanding the linkages of the sectors in the economy, it must be remembered that the information obtained provides a snapshot of inter-industry economic actions at only one point in time.

TOURISM SATELLITE ACCOUNTS

Satellite accounts provide comprehensive information on a field of economic activity, and are generally tied to the economic accounts of a nation or region. The Tourism Satellite Account is a relatively new phenomenon. For example, the British Columbia Ministry of Development, Trade and Tourism has developed a Tourism Satellite Account as a separate input-output model designed to display tourism's contributions to the province related to the overall input-output model of the province.

A Tourism Satellite Account has also been developed by Statistics Canada in order to assess the significance of tourism to Canada. The account uses concise definitions of tourism and attempts to provide a clear and real measure of tourism-related economic activity. Both direct and indirect tourism activities are accounted for in areas such as, but not limited to, demand, supply, employment, taxes etc. Such a tool is crucial in determining the complex spending patterns of visitors as well as the goods and services that cater to their needs.

Some of the advantages of the Tourism Satellite Accounts can be summarized as follows:

- They help governments and businesses determine the value of tourism to the economy, and thereby develop strategies for ensuring competitive advantage;
- They identify the amount of benefit enjoyed by various sectors, and

the employment, income, taxes and other benefits that flow from those sectors;

- They provide a comprehensive picture of the size and scale of tourism in a country, and can help to gather support for ensuring adherence to the principles of sustainable tourism development.

COST-BENEFIT EVALUATION

By applying a number of economic tools and methods, destinations are able to obtain a large array of economic information on tourism; this information can then be used to make decisions. In assessing this information, analysts, planners, and managers have to determine not just whether jobs and wealth are created, but also how the benefits are distributed, what costs result from the development process, and whether the benefits of tourism outweigh the economic, social and cultural costs.

It is clear that economic analysis needs to be integrated with other data in order to provide a reasonable indication of whether tourism is a good strategy for the destination. Cost-benefit analysis is an important activity to perform, but is also difficult to carry out, since a number of the costs are very difficult to quantify. How does one measure the "sense of place" or "spiritual happiness" of a population?

How does one quantify the loss value of habitat fragmentation to ecological integrity? While strides are being taken to develop full-cost, environmentally-based accounting, some measures may need to remain qualitative rather than quantitative.

Full-scale cost-benefit analysis, while recommended, can therefore be time consuming, expensive and difficult to conduct. Another challenge of cost-benefit analysis lies in identifying who benefits from, and who pays the costs of, tourism. Smaller cost-benefit analyses can be conducted on specific issues to provide information related to tourism.

OBSTACLES TO CREATING ECONOMIC DEVELOPMENT FROM TOURISM

There are a number of obstacles to creating economic development through tourism. These obstacles are discussed below.

Market Obstacles

The potential for a region or municipality to attract tourists on a long-term basis is a key factor. Tourism activities, to a very large degree, are dictated by what is considered "popular" at a given point in time.

In addition, the ability and interest of tourists to travel and how far they are willing to travel is dependent on a variety of factors, such as income levels, cost of fuel, job security, physical condition and mobility, and travel motivations. The ability of a destination to conduct a reliable market survey, identify a positioning strategy and promote itself is essential. However, this requires skill and knowledge that is often lacking in many areas. In addition, cooperation in the marketing effort is important but difficult to achieve in many urban and rural settings.

Community Obstacles

Negative perceptions of tourism are often found at the local level. Tourism activities are not generally viewed as "viable" or "appropriate" business ventures. Generally, tourism is viewed as a short-term activity until more appealing and profitable employment can be found, since many tourism positions pay low wages and are seen as low-status occupations. These perceptions act as a deterrent to local people participating in tourism-related employment.

Lack of Infrastructure

As is discussed later in this study there are a number of infrastructure elements that are crucial to the success of tourism at all levels of a country or region. As tourism tastes change and become more sophisticated, and as the competitive environment further develops, countries and destinations will require adequate infrastructure to meet market demands as well as environmental regulations.

Environmental Obstacles

The emphasis in most tourism activities tends to be on attracting larger numbers of tourists to a region or site, posing problems for environmentally sensitive areas. It is clear that some environments may have to generate high-yielding tourist activities to generate sufficient income while protecting social and natural environments. This is difficult to accomplish in the highly competitive tourism market.

Lack of Integration

There is limited integration and cooperation between many tourism businesses given that, for the most part, the local tourism industry tends to be fragmented or lacking in tourism expertise.

Institutional Obstacles

There is very little coordinated governmental support and promotion for tourism development and initiatives. In addition, governmental activities are often poorly structured to help plan and manage tourism. In other instances, political and other ideologies make tourism planning and management difficult to implement.

Employment and Training Obstacles

There is a serious lack of training and education opportunities in tourism planning and management. The training that is available is often very narrow in focus, and does not address the broader context of tourism and the range of potential opportunities.

The scarcity of employment equity and opportunities for women is a serious obstacle in ensuring an equitable distribution of the benefits of tourism activity. In addition, access to education and training is limited for a number of disadvantaged groups. It is clear from this discussion that there are a number of factors and obstacles that need to be considered in the expansion of tourism. It is essential that an integrated approach be taken. The role of infrastructure in that particular process will be explored in the remaining portion of this study.

DEVELOPMENT OF TOURISM INFRASTRUCTURE

PUBLIC-RELATED TOURISM INFRASTRUCTURE

The operation of tourism facilities, services and amenities are often dependent on a number of travel infrastructure networks. These networks may include transportation, water supply, energy/power, waste disposal and telecommuni-cations. There is some ambivalence towards the view that all the infrastructure networks must be in place before tourism activity can take place.

The reason is that in some developing countries, resort developments appear to function adequately and to the satisfaction of their clients without full infrastructure systems being in place. In the case of some forms of tourism development, the lack of a complete network of modern highways may be advantageous in that the absence of the network acts as a deterrent to the penetration of mass tourism to environmentally sensitive areas.

For some isolated tourism development, such as independent and sometimes remote integrated resorts, all the basic operating infrastructure systems are incorporated in the overall design, while in regard to infrastructure the resort may be self-sufficient without needing any connection to any more general urban or regional systems.

The problem with the independent resort unit may be that it solves satisfactorily all its infrastructure needs within its own territory, but by doing so, may "export" some of the water supply and waste disposal problems to other areas.

The most usual case in tourism development is for infrastructure development to precede the completion of the tourism facilities. This may mean that the installation of the infrastructure becomes a public sector responsibility, with some escalation of the cost for development as a contribution to the overall costs of tourism development.

A rationale for the infrastructure services being a public sector responsibility includes consideration of the following factors:

- The network of services is most likely available to both tourists and residents of the area;

- Achievement of consistency in standards is desirable;
- The construction of an integrated system may facilitate non-tourism development within the region;
- The network will facilitate development that contributes to the economic welfare of the resort or region;
- The network will need to be maintained by public agencies to ensure that prescribed standards are met.

Transportation

Easy access to tourism destinations in terms of international transport and facilities for easy movement within the destinations are generally considered to be prerequisites for the development of tourism. In addition, these two elements are best considered as complementary and a part of a comprehensive communications system.

One of the forces that may impede the cohesiveness and comprehensiveness of a communications strategy is the fragmentation of responsibility for the various modes of transportation and the different route systems and networks. For planning and management purposes, transportation infrastructure in the Asia-Pacific region can be seen as comprising:

- International air services and international airports;
- Domestic air services;
- Land transport systems and routes;
- Water transport.

International Air Services

One of the controlling factors of the nature and magnitude of the international visitor market is the availability of international air access. The significant determinants of international visitor numbers using international air services include flight schedules and frequency, seat capacity of aircraft on the routes, proportion of seat capacity dedicated to intermediate points, flight routes and linkages, journey times, fares, flight origins and choice of airline.

Some of these determinants are themselves affected by such factors as the operating characteristics of the international terminal, including:

- Operational time-frame;
- Operational category;
- Operational characteristics including the navigation system, runway, apron and handling capacity, passenger terminal capacity, cargo handling capacity, fuel storage and car parking;
- Facilitation processes;
- Special facilities.

A satisfactory performance level of all these factors will only partially determine the success of tourism activity.

Domestic Air Services

Some countries have a poorly developed and serviced internal or domestic air network, whereas others have a reasonable network of airports. It is clear that if the full economic benefits of tourism are to be realised, then a viable network of airports is necessary to accommodate growth and distribute tourism activity. The private sector must be encouraged to set up safe and reliable services to outer regions.

Land Transport Systems and Routes

It is necessary to develop an efficient land transport system to complement a land-use strategy, in order that:

- Major circulation systems can be identified, planned and provided with an adequate budget;
- Major centres and points of tourism can be linked;
- Road systems can be placed into appropriate hierarchical categories;
- Routes can be used to open up new areas and properly service emerging tourism resorts, while also providing access to natural tourism attractions and circuits for tours

It is not necessary to achieve a comprehensive road network to service tourism; in fact, some routes may be left undeveloped to restrict and limit visitor access. In a comprehensive land transport system, assessments need to be made of the availability to tourists of adequate private vehicles, buses, taxis, private rental vehicles, and any indigenous "means of transport". These are matters best left to private enterprise and market forces, with licensing controls by the government.

Water Transport

From the point of view of tourism development, water-based transport is an important item. It can be used to provide access to areas with no road connections, restrict development at other destinations and, in some instances, provide a unique and indigenous tourism experience.

In the development of the water transport component of the transport strategy, due recognition should be given to the different types of vessels and their distinct purposes, which include:

- Inter-transport;
- Circuit transport and access vessels to transport tourists from the "mainland" to offshore resorts;
- Day-trip, sightseeing and excursion boats;
- Short-duration cruise transport;
- Specialized boats for diving, snorkelling, offshore marine pursuits, sport fishing, lagoon cruising and underwater viewing.

The nature of water-based transport is such that a specialized government agency should be responsible for licensing operators.

Water Supply Systems

One of the most important requirements for the development of tourism facilities is an adequate and continuous supply of safe water for drinking purposes as well as domestic and recreational use. In some developing countries, the responsibility for the supply and treatment of water lies with the tourism development project; in other cases it is a responsibility that is accepted by the government in the interests of both the visiting and residential communities. For some countries, there is an uneven quality and quantity of water in the major townships, smaller townships and rural areas. The upgrading of the various aspects of the water systems then becomes a responsibility of the tourism developer, and there may be a benefit to the adjoining local community.

Water needs are diverse and are increasing. Supply requirements for tourism developments include water for:

- Domestic purposes;
- Hotels and restaurants;
- Laundries;
- Swimming pools and other recreational uses;
- Street cleaning;
- Irrigation;
- Fire-fighting.

There are basic quantitative measurements that, while useful, do not take into account the special demands generated by particular factors.

These factors can include such aspects as:

- Climatic conditions;
- The tendency towards extravagance in water use by holidaymakers;
- Increased levels of water use in food and drink preparation in remote locations;
- The tendency for corporate and government agencies to be more lavish in their use of water in the maintenance of sites in areas that experience high levels of tourist visitation.

Assessment of the capacity of systems is sometimes frustrated by acts of vandalism, leakage and breakdown of inefficient systems leading to reduction in water pressure, and failures. Storage systems are needed to ensure adequate supply and constant pressure, in order to provide a reserve against interruptions of flow and for emergency and fire-fighting requirements.

The location and siting of reservoirs are critical and must be incorporated into the integrated infrastructure plan. Distribution systems will be determined by the factors of source and storage.

In developed areas with major townships, the water distribution system may be a public responsibility, so that a reticulated system linking many of the developed sectors of the urban areas is in place or is being constructed.

For other situations, a direct flow system from storage to usage points such as resorts or hotels may be the only feasible option. In some countries, especially those with visitors, or dispersed townships or communities, it may be necessary for each major resort and tourism facility to make provision for its own water supply, treatment, storage and distribution. For some resorts, desalination plants may offer the only realistic source of usable water.

Energy and Power

Power demand reflects the expectations of international visitors who want the standard of services to which they are accustomed. Important considerations are the adequacy of supply to meet peak-load requirements, certainty of service, and compatible power supply types. If each major resort and hotel is not required to be responsible for its own power supply, then the public system needs to be designed so as to meet the demands of tourism development created by such requirements as:

- Air-conditioning;
- Swimming pools, spas and other water circulation systems;
- Cooking and food preparation, dishwashing, laundry, dry-cleaning, lighting, entertainment including videos, television, radio, night clubs and discos, and basic hotel servicing, cleaning, and elevators;
- Residents' needs.

The generating capacity of many countries may often be at a crucial threshold, because available supply creates its own increasing demand. In some countries and regions, it may be necessary for each of the major tourism developments to incorporate their own generating facilities to cover the circumstances of local power generating or supply failure. In many cases, the existing power systems are operating close to maximum load conditions, so that major power users such as hotels and integrated resorts need emergency generating capacity.

There needs to be a requirement that all new major developments should proceed only after consultation with any national or regional electricity or power generating authority, to ensure that demands for supply are within the capacity of the existing system, or that suitable alternative plans can be prepared. Power distribution systems take one of two forms: underground systems or above ground systems.

There are significant aesthetic, operational, maintenance and cost differentials between the systems, which need to feature in the preparation of any integrated power distribution plan. In sensitive environmental areas and prestigious tourism districts, it may be that the adoption of underground distribution systems is determined according to aesthetic, rather than cost and operational factors. There must be stringent safety codes related to power generation and power distribution.

Waste Disposal Systems

The disposal of various types of waste is a matter of critical concern, given that the adequacy of the methods chosen for the disposal of liquid waste and solid waste will play a significant role in the protection of the health of tourists and the resident community. The adequacy of the method will influence the condition of the environment in general, and of reefs, lagoons, beaches, streams, lakes and groundwater in particular.

Tourism destinations retain attractiveness if, among other things, the environment is clean, pleasant and pollution-free. If the methods of waste disposal prove to be inadequate, then the environment will deteriorate as the result of pollution; the outcome could well be a reduction in tourist visitation levels, with resultant reduced economic benefits. In addition, environmental degradation will be unacceptable to local communities.

The principal objectives of all waste disposal systems should be the complete elimination of health risks and environmental damage.

This issue should be considered at two levels:

- The policy level, where the principal consideration is to achieve the highest level of effective waste disposal and the lowest level of environmental degradation;
- The technical level, where the choice and design of the most effective system should be in the hands of planners, architects and engineers, working within the framework of environmental impact assessment procedures.

Post and Telecommunication Services

The accessibility of post and telecommunication services is crucial, especially in view of the size of the Asian and Pacific region. The ease and reliability of communications is especially critical for the business traveller. The infrastructure system of post and telecommunication services includes postal services, telephones, telexes, facsimile and other electronic machines, and radio and television relay.

In addition to the public networks for such services, some large resorts may operate internal systems of their own. Infrastructure plans for this group of services need to identify transmission route exchanges and relay stations, antenna systems and relays. This is an area of infrastructure that is susceptible to rapid technological changes, with progress into the realm of advanced technology requiring new skills in management and operation.

Pollution Control Mechanisms

It is becoming recognized that the need to achieve and maintain a clean environment is imperative. In general, the degree of environmental cleanliness, the extent to which the environment is pollution-free, and the degree to which the aesthetic environment is pleasant will influence the tourism attractiveness of a destination. If adequate facilities and infrastructure are not provided to cope with solid and liquid waste products, and if there are inadequate mechanisms of control, then it is likely that the pre-visit expectations of the international visitors will not be met. Consequently, the tourist potential and expected economic benefits will be reduced.

Thus, not only will environmental pollution have reduced economic benefit for tourism but the quality of the environment will also have declined for all users, including the local communities.

To be effective, pollution control mechanisms need the support of a structure that includes:

- Appropriate legislation, supported by laws, ordinances and regulations;
- An agency, or group of agencies, charged with the statutory authority to provide leadership in order to monitor practices and enforce the regulations;
- A set of performance standards;
- An organized system of surveillance, probably public-sector managed;
- A set of penalties for violations and poor performance.

FACILITIES AND SERVICES INFRASTRUCTURE

In addition to the provision of public infrastructure the success of any tourism destination is dependent to a large degree on the nature of the facilities and services infrastructure that are available to the tourist.

It is convenient to examine these aspects in three groups:

- Primary tourist facilities and services;
- Secondary tourist facilities and services;
- Tertiary tourist facilities and services.

The underlying attitude of the national governments to the concept and process of planning are essential to determining the success of tourism development. For some Asia-Pacific countries, the planning philosophy may be market driven, so that the existence of the various facilities and services, their quality and quantity, and their geographical distribution and association is the outcome of the interplay of market forces. In contrast, some countries with a philosophical commitment to government guidance or control over tourism development may prefer to pursue policies and practices fitting any development to a carefully prepared land use and economic strategy.

The commentary in this chapter is generally relevant to both approaches, although its application is more likely in the controlled approach to tourism planning. For tourism resort areas, planned on an integrated basis, it is possible to rationalize the provision of facilities and services so that they are complementary in standard, range, distribution and scale.

In general, the basic characteristics of tourism facilities and services include:

- Diversity in range, scope, scale, quality and quantity;
- Enclaves or precincts, with some tendency towards linear arrangements along principal linkages and routes;

- Common features of architecture, advertising or site preferences;
- Dominance of "magnet" facilities, either in the form of a major enterprise, a distinctive district or precinct of similar enterprises, or in the form of a major retail store.

There is a tendency for facilities and services to concentrate according to type, quality, standard, status and historic legacy. In addition, depending upon local attitudes and visitor expectations, the distribution of facilities and amenities may be determined by outlets for indigenous crafts, arts and performances.

Another aspect that reflects local circumstances is the degree to which the conventional facilities and services are augmented by the loose arrangements of open-air markets. These markets may be held at a defined time of day or perhaps on a particular day in the week in public market places. The range of tourism planning opportunities and possibilities will be dictated as much by the peculiarity of local circumstances as by the claimed efficiency of these guidelines.

Accommodation and Restaurants

In terms of investment, especially private investment, tourist accommodation represents the most expensive facility in tourist resorts. In the early stages of integrated plan preparation it is essential to undertake detailed survey of existing tourist accommodation, and a projection of trends and requirements. In addition, at this early stage of planning, assessments should be made of preferred geographical positioning and arrangement and preferred architectural styles. There is evidence that the character and composition of tourist accommodation has undergone considerable change in the past few decades.

New types of accommodation, such as self-catering units, budget hotel accommodation and camping sites, have evolved to meet market demands for increased levels of independence, self-sufficiency, informality, economy and convenience. Such changes have been influenced by the emergence of the new types of traveller and the tourist who invests in a holiday home or unit in a preferred tourism destination. As the spectrum of travellers has undergone transformation, there have also been changes in the requirements for traditional hotel accommodation. Noticeable changes have occurred in recent years in the preferences of international tourists in relation to restaurant facilities. The previous inclination to use the restaurant facilities of the tourist hotel, because it formed an integral component of the hotel or resort enclave, is being replaced progressively by a trend towards eating in restaurants of different types.

It is claimed, for example, that the provision of good restaurants and other food outlets is a crucial determinant of visitor satisfaction at a tourist destination. The changing demand is adding local and indigenous cuisine to the range of international cuisine.

This demand is being met with the development of restaurants independent of the hotels and integrated resorts. Such restaurants are often based on Asian cuisine, local indigenous cuisine, and use of local products, especially seafood, vegetables and fruit.

Shopping

Shopping is another complementary experience that contributes to the overall attractiveness of a tourism destination. As such, it should be considered as an element in the integrated tourism plan. In an increasing number of tourism plans, special consideration is being given to improving the attractiveness of shopping by providing more attention to the detailed design of shopping areas and shopping precincts, together with the hours when shops are open.

In terms of the range of merchandise, most commonly the attention of tourism planning is given to outlets that retail imported quality goods, indigenous handicrafts, duty-free merchandise and leisure wear. There are two principal tourism planning issues: the location and distribution of shopping facilities; and the range of goods available, especially the potential contribution by locally made goods.

Travel and Tour Services

Travel and tour services are essential elements in a national integrated tourism plan. These service providers are the intermediaries between tourism destinations and the potential visitors.

Their functions include greeting services, airport transfers, sightseeing tour operations, servicing individual travellers, servicing tour groups, providing ticketing and accommodation reservation services, and providing links with off-shore tour agencies.

In addition, these travel and tour service providers link the tourist with local tourism services and facility operators. A tangible element of the travel and tour services is attention to detail, especially in supervising the standard of accommodation booked on behalf of clients and the standard of the vehicles used. Another element of the travel and tour service that may be a cause of concern is the standard of tour guiding. Some countries are progressing rapidly to a style of training and licensing to ensure that quality service is provided.

In addition to tour guiding, many of the activities of the travel and tour services are suited to the operations of indigenous entrepreneurs. There are increasing examples, especially in the development of ecotourism operations, of indigenous entrepreneurs seizing opportunities to capitalize on advantageous natural and cultural circumstances.

Recreation and Entertainment

It is axiomatic that recreation and entertainment facilities should be deliberately arranged so as to generate interest, to invite participation, facilitate the linkage of complementary tourism land uses and activities, and create an image of vitality and excitement. It may be necessary to ensure that recreation and entertainment venues are buffered from adjoining uses that they might otherwise disturb.

The range of recreation and entertainment facilities will depend not only on the visitor profile and the resultant demand, but also on the scale and location of the resort area.

The range may include:

- Cinemas;
- Multipurpose halls for concerts, theatres, social meetings and local entertainment;
- Open-air theatres;
- Libraries and reading rooms;
- Museums and galleries with exhibits of indigenous crafts, art, folklore and history;
- Night clubs and dance halls;
- Casinos;
- Playgrounds and parks;
- Sports halls;
- Swimming pools;
- Golf courses.

Health Care, and Emergency and Safety Systems

This group of services and facilities provide the community support base for the more high-profile services of accommodation, restaurants, shopping, entertainment and recreation.

The principal services and facilities in this group are:

- Health care;
- Emergency and safety.

In addition to the general provision of the physical structures and the service personnel, it is becoming incumbent on the major resorts, major hotels and large commercial enterprises to ensure that proper hygiene and sanitary standards are maintained on the premises and in the immediate environs.

INFRASTRUCTURE FINANCING POSSIBILITIES

With the maintenance and, in some cases, increasing levels of interest in tourism opportunities available in the Asian and Pacific region, the potential for investment is significant. This potential is often facilitated and encouraged by deliberate policies of governments in the region. In addition to general opportunities for investment and development, the range of opportunities comprises two types. First, there are infrastructure needs and opportunities in already established tourism destinations or in new, less-developed destinations.

Second, opportunities exist to invest in:

- Accommodation;
- Ancillary services;
- Support services;
- Tourism enterprises.

Public infrastructure investment needs remain significant if destinations are to remain competitive and, at the same time, the destination environment is to be safeguarded. The range of infrastructure investment is significant, from larger projects such as airports to smaller-scale concerns such as sewage and water supply at the local level. Despite the present and potential tourism activity in Asia-Pacific countries, the available hotel and tourism facilities in many areas are limited. In addition to the small critical mass, potential investors may be discouraged by the difficulty of dealing with some government agencies, inadequate infrastructure, the difficulties of tackling the complex land tenure system, and insufficient investment incentives.

These difficulties are being addressed and, in many cases, overcome in most countries in the Asia-Pacific region; this is particularly so because it is realised by the governments that if they do not, the economic benefits of their countries may be at risk. Most conspicuously, many governments have introduced investment promotion incentives, investment legislation, and trade and business directories.

The region, as a whole, presents the potential investor with a number of differences:

- The differences in government systems between the Asia-Pacific countries, each with its own approach to investment and development;
- The differences in tourism development needs;
- The differences in the range of information available on investment support, incentives promotion and application procedures.

This part presents a generalization of known practices and opportunities for the development of financing mechanisms that may provide an informed or satisfactory basis for the support and promotion of tourism activity. To finance the full range of tourism infrastructure needs, several strategies and sources may be tapped. Among these sources are domestic private investment, foreign private investment sources, and foreign aid. These matters will be considered in this part. In addition, where appropriate, reference will be made to development incentives, relevant legislative structures, government decisionmaking processes, fiscal incentives and financial incentives. A brief part that examines investment requirements will precede these considerations.

Investment Requirements

Most Asia-Pacific countries have reached the stage of development where it has become necessary to prepare formal development plans within established objectives, and to facilitate and mobilize resources to achieve the required level of economic development. For many Asia-Pacific countries, development strategies emphasize the need to encourage foreign direct investment.

This emphasis is based on the large capital requirements for many large-scale, technically complex infrastructure and up-market forms of development in tourism. For many of the smaller economies, there is an insufficient domestic investment base to underwrite large projects. As a result, many countries have introduced various forms of assistance directed at encouraging foreign investment encapsulated in special legislation or administrative guidelines and regulations.

It is necessary to clarify the purposes of the investment and the type of projects for which offshore investment is required. The scope for significant tourism expansion in the immediate future exists in most of the Asian and Pacific region.

However, achieving this expansion will require considerable funds in order to overcome what are often major constraints, such as:

- Air transportation;
- Basic infrastructure services;
- Suitable accommodation facilities;
- Recreational facilities (including secondary tourism);
- Promotion and marketing;
- Support services and industries.

In the preparation of a tourism strategy, due recognition should be given to the cost implications and, by inference, the investment requirements. The accuracy of the cost structures and the investment requirements will always be subject to fluctuations in the costs of construction, materials, services and supporting activities, and professional services, all of which will be influenced by exchange rates, the costs of raising finance and general inflationary pressures.

Investment in tourism "hardware" will include:

- Water supply, sewage, telecommunications, roads, power generation;
- New and/or refurbished tourism accommodation (hotels, integrated resorts, guesthouses, and camping sites);
- Specialized ethnic or regional restaurants as the expectations of tourists expand;
- Transport facilities (airports, ports, harbours, road systems and car parks);
- Transport vehicles (motor vehicles, ferries, other maritime vessels, aircraft, helicopters and bicycles);
- Visitor attractions, natural attractions, cultural attractions and recreational facilities.

In addition to this "hardware", considerable investment will be required in such "software" items as:

- Tourism administration in governments;

- Ancillary administration in governments (customs, immigration and quarantine);
- Marketing and promotion;
- Information exchange;
- Travel and tour agencies;
- Education and training facilities and services;
- Affiliations and memberships in regional and international organizations.

Investment Sources

The basic sources of investment available to Asia-Pacific countries include:

- Domestic private capital;
- Foreign private capital;
- Foreign aid (bilateral and multilateral assistance);
- Government finance.

Foreign investment has played a crucial role in developing many of the leading economic sectors in many of the Asia-Pacific countries.

The reasons include:

- The scarcity of local capital funds;
- The scarcity of local technical and professional expertise;
- The lack of preparedness to take risks by private investors;
- The legacy of colonial funding;
- The willingness of multilateral agencies to focus particular assistance on the needs of the Asian and Pacific region;
- The emergence of capital sources (private or public) in developed neighbouring countries that believe they have a responsibility to assist with the development of the region.

Foreign Aid

For most Asia-Pacific countries, foreign aid continues to play a vital role in meeting government budgetary and development needs as well as the provision of foreign exchange. Official development assistance is bilateral (including targeted aid from one donor nation to a recipient nation) or multilateral (including targeted aid to a recipient nation or group of nations from international or multinational agencies). In the case of both sources, dependency on foreign aid may limit the freedom of action of those nations that are recipients.

These limitations may:

- Impose structures on the local economy;
- Limit flexibility in those structures (because of accountability);
- Result in large public sector agencies for maintaining and managing the aid;

- Cause inefficiencies in the private sector;
- Cause strains in the local economy (because it looks stronger than it really is);
- Reduce self-reliance;
- Bring inflationary pressures;
- Inflate consumer demand (especially for tourism and hospitality);
- Expose recipients to pressures from donors.

However, for many countries there are few if any options to the acceptance of foreign aid, no matter what the perceived negatives and disadvantages are. Sources of foreign aid may not be stable, especially as donor sources review their commitments, priorities, interests and availability of funds. Bilateral sources, in particular, may be subject to fluctuations occasioned by changes in political priorities of the donor nation. Foreign aid to the region comes from multilateral aid (mainly from international organizations), bilateral aid (on a government-to-government basis) and special aid arrangements.

The principal bilateral aid arrangements are conducted on the government-to-government level, and result in aid transfer as budgetary assistance. These arrangements are conducted between members of particular geopolitical groupings. Special aid arrangements may be negotiated on a government-togovernment or government-to-agency basis for particular prestige projects, schemes of environmental rehabilitation or schemes of regional cooperation. Asia-Pacific governments need to pursue aggressive strategies to gain access to funding or technical assistance.

In addition to national and international aid agencies, the national or reserve banks of many countries around the Pacific Rim are supportive of foreign aid programmes, particularly with regard to lending bank-to-bank support. It is important for national tourism offices to raise the profile of their claims for aid assistance within the total package being negotiated by the senior economic advisors.

Unless the negotiation team is convinced of the need for aid support for tourism projects and development (including institutional support), it is unlikely that tourism matters will achieve priority that is high enough to gain funding. If the national government is seen to be less than enthusiastic, the donor source may delete tourism from the list of worthy projects. If it is difficult to gain high priority for tourism in general government searches for foreign aid, tourism agencies may resort to advocating support from more project-focused donor agencies, including conspicuous infrastructure components that may be attractive to such agencies.

They may also target specialist donor agencies (such as the World Tourism Organization or the United Nations Development Programme (UNDP) to solicit support for plan preparation exercises.

Donor agencies will scrutinize the projects, programme cost structure, time scale and recommended staffing arrangements. It may be that to secure national preferences, Asia-Pacific governments will need to concede to operational preferences of the donor agencies.

Foreign Private Investment

It has been established that the presence of any of the following factors will frustrate potential private foreign investment:

- Inadequate government support;
- Insufficient investment incentives;
- A lack of supporting infrastructure;
- Difficulties in tackling complex land tenure systems;
- A multiplicity of agencies, many with overlapping functions;
- Excessive time required to obtain decisions;
- A lack of adequate local expertise;
- Inadequate training schemes.

These are matters over which national governments have some control and influence. In order for privately funded tourism investment to be encouraged and facilitated, it is necessary for Asia-Pacific countries to introduce a range of financial and other incentives, appropriate legislation and appropriate decision-making systems.

It is evident that, in many cases, the national policy on tourism (if there is one) is often unclear or poorly articulated, and information on the tourism sector is usually inadequate for potential investors. These factors continue to create a poor image. Therefore, to attract foreign investment, Asia-Pacific governments have to improve the image of their competence. There is evidence that most governments in the region have recognized the need to attract foreign investment to provide economic growth in their countries, and they are responding to that need by introducing investment promotion measures and investment legislation, together with business and investment guides and directories.

In order for governments to encourage and facilitate foreign investment in tourism projects in their countries, it has become necessary to introduce an appropriate legislative framework and develop a set of decisionmaking procedures.

These decision-making processes must be capable, within a reasonable timeframe, of achieving an outcome in the best interests of the potential investor, the national government and the local community.

Alternatives to a legislative framework include:

- Specific legislation that focuses on tourism development in general, or on particular facets of tourism development (such as hotels), with the opportunity for the general provisions to be carried over into other aspects of tourism development;
- Specific legislation that establishes an agency with responsibility for overseeing tourism planning and development, such as a tourism development authority or tourism bureau;

- General legislation that facilitates, monitors, controls and regulates foreign investment for any development purpose.

Each of these alternatives has its advantages and disadvantages. Some national governments exercise control through general powers supervising the economy. Although there may be some merit in operating without legislation that can be used specifically to manage tourism development, the existence of a specific legislative framework is indicative to the investment community that tourism is being taken seriously. An additional procedural matter is the establishment of conspicuous decision-making mechanisms.

Such mechanisms should include clear articulation of the ministry responsible for supervising tourism planning and development, specification of monitoring processes, nomination of promotion responsibilities, and specification of the sequence of decision-making. This process should culminate in the nomination and identification of the point in the decision chain at which decisions can be expected.

The most important specifications are:

- Governmental agencies to be included;
- The sequence of steps;
- The first point of access into the decision process;
- The participants in each of the steps;
- The responsibilities of those participants (in general and at each step)
- The expected outcomes of each step;
- The likely points of negotiation and partners in those negotiations;
- The final outcome (certificate of approval, letter of eligibility, and a development license or a similar document).

It will be necessary for national governments to determine the configuration of the decision-making structure that is most suited both to its governmental structure as well as the nature and level of development of tourism in that country. Not all Asia-Pacific countries will need (or could operate) a complex decision-making system.

In order for the system to work efficiently, it may be necessary to create special agencies or committees with responsibility for:

- Carefully screening the off-shore interests incorporated in tourism projects, especially the sources of finance;
- Scrutinizing tourism projects and investment applications of particular types;
- Scrutinizing the documentation at crucial phases in the decision sequence;
- Facilitating coordination between different government departments and other agencies;
- Ensuring the efficient passage of any proposal or application.

Such committees may be ad hoc entities, formed as and when necessary. Alternatively, they may be permanent, standing committees with a regular calendar of meetings.

Types of Incentives

The mobilization of the tourism development strategy is dependent upon a partnership of public sector investment (especially in infrastructure) and private sector investment (especially in projects and enterprises). At every stage of implementation, there is a need for governments to stimulate private investment by creating a favourable context for investment in general with specific tourism-related fiscal, financial and other incentives. This need is sometimes met by a series of general investment incentives under some form of enterprise stimulation legislation or by being incorporated in revenue and taxation legislation or in the form of particular tourism project legislation.

In the Asian and Pacific region, there is considerable variation in the legislative framework for stimulating private investment in tourism development. Clearly, there is no one model that will fit easily into the different governmental systems and structures or into the various levels of maturity achieved by Asia-Pacific countries.

Several broad categories of incentives may be used:

- Financial incentives, through which a government provides grants or loans from its own resources or through a government financial institution;
- Quasi-financial incentives, through which a government provides loan guarantees, subsidies or exchange rate guarantees, or a differential grant that covers the gap between official and commercial lending rates;
- Fiscal incentives, through which a government provides tax holidays and deductions, customs duty exemptions, concessions or capital expenditure allowances;
- Other incentives of considerable diversity, including training facilities, profit repatriation and work permits.

Before embarking upon any strategy of incentives in any of the categories, governments should develop a preferred expectation on such matters as:

- Whether the government should interfere in market forces;
- Whether the government should assume particular development and investment responsibilities in infrastructure development and incentives, provision of training facilities and programmes, supporting transport services, and the construction and operation of facilities such as hotels and attractions;
- Whether the government should become involved directly in a commercial enterprise or partnership, and if so to what level and type of risk;
- Whether the government should use its various structures and systems to guide tourism development into particular strategies with a particular emphasis (such as strategies and development in ecotourism);

- Whether the government should relieve the private sector of some of the essential services, for example, by operating the national airline, in order to reduce dependency on off-shore commercial decisions;
- Whether the government should facilitate development, especially by providing assistance in land negotiations with indigenous owners.

These various matters are important pre-conditions for the creation of an appropriate tourism investment strategy.

Other important considerations include:

- The determination of the overall nature and scope of tourism activity that will fit comfortably with national economic, socio-cultural and environmental strategies;
- The prescription of levels of resident-foreign ownership and involvement;
- The determination of levels of importation (goods, services and skills) before the balance of payments becomes distorted, as well as prescriptions that will control the leakage of benefits.

In addition, governments must decide which types and by how far the range of incentives are to be direct, with active government involvement in finance, or indirect, with a government pursuing a multiplicity of roles in terms of support, facilitation, encouragement and assistance. The following subsections briefly refer to the scope of the various types of incentives that may be considered. It is not claimed that each type will be suited to the circumstances of every government, or that each type needs to be included in the range of incentives offered by any particular government. As with all aspects of policy and planning, the precise government response will be determined by local circumstances.

Financial and Quasi-financial Incentives

The need for financial or quasi-financial incentives will depend on the general availability of financial services to the private sector and on the government's attitude towards its responsibility for complementing private investment with public investment.

This responsibility can include construction and maintenance of infrastructure services (water supply, waste disposal and road construction), as well as grants and loans for the construction and operation of tourist facilities such as accommodation, resort complexes, and entertainment and recreation venues.

Government involvement through direct incentives may be possible for major development projects through the provision of direct loans to private developers and negotiations with international agencies for funding. In the case of finance for small-scale indigenous projects, the government may provide direct finance (grants or loans) or support the project by assisting with professional services.

If a government is to become involved in direct financial incentives, it will need to determine such matters as the scale of loans, grant limitations, predetermination of project viability, periods of repayment, conditions on the use of the finance provided, and conditions on such matters as training for local residents. In addition, that government will need to develop a policy on the use of loans from foreign sources.

Fiscal Incentives

These incentives are less direct than grants and loans. Their indirect nature does not make any specific financial demands on, or commitments from, governments. In most cases, the implication for the national budget is that these are a source of revenue.

Each government must decide whether the incentives are sufficient inducements for tourism development; however, there are no precise criteria for making such decisions. The intention of the fiscal incentives is to make investment in tourism projects more attractive, less risk-prone, more capable of returning a profit and more sustainable. The range of fiscal incentives is extensive.

Fiscal incentives may include:

- Allowances (*e.g.*, for underpinning investment, supporting projects, depreciation or modernization and refurbishment);
- Concessions (*e.g.*, for losses due to payment of tax, to offset construction costs of new vessels, on import duties, for providing training to employees, and on port and excise taxes);
- Tax assistance (*i.e.*, exemptions from company tax, reduced tax levels during pioneer status, tax holidays, moratoriums, tax credit for interest on foreign loans, tax exemption on re-invested profit, tax deductions for providing training, income tax exemption for foreign employees, and tax deductions for support of national marketing programmes).

In some cases, the investment incentives may be tied to requirements and assistance that are related to:

- Concession periods;
- Limitations of scope;
- Assurances that the supported project will incorporate employment of local labour, use of local produce, provision of training opportunities to upgrade the skill levels of local labour and provisions to assist the general promotion of the tourism area.

Despite the scope of fiscal incentives, which can be the outcome of shrewd financial planning and strategy formulation by governments, such incentives may not be sufficient to attract the level of tourism development that is considered desirable and appropriate. Therefore, governments may need to generate a range of companion incentives.

Companion Incentives

Several acute problems exist in various Asia-Pacific countries that need to be addressed if private investment is to be attracted. These issues include the problem of obtaining land for the development of hotels and resort facilities in suitable and attractive locations, the peculiarities of land ownership and land leasing, the level of availability of government savings and private savings, and the availability of local entrepreneurial and managerial skills and experience.

Because the availability of fiscal and financial incentives may not be sufficient to attract the level of private investment considered necessary, governments may need to consider a range of companion or complementary incentives, including:

- Seed money as loan equity;
- Assistance with land negotiations, especially with indigenous land owners;
- Providing training facilities (*i.e.*, courses, schools, colleges and teaching staff);
- Guarantees of promotion through the Visitor's Bureau;
- Ease of repatriation of profits;
- The provision of work permits for key workers and staff;
- Write-off costs of critical appliances and plants (air conditioners and solar heaters).

A major incentive, in certain circumstances, may be the declaration of the nation as a "tax haven", with the removal of restrictions on corporate tax, income tax, estate duties, capital gains tax and sales tax. It must be realised that the strategy of incentives is to provide a competitive edge for one resort destination/nation over another. In the highly competitive environment of tourism, that edge of advantage may not be of long duration.

In any case, incentives alone will not ensure the creation and maintenance of a satisfactory level of tourism activity. Any tourism destination will need a combination of economic, environmental and socio-cultural advantages to begin to make a mark in the region and then to progress positively through the life cycle of tourism destination areas.

Having reached a stage of maturity, the destination area will need to build additional attractive features, including investment incentives, if it is not to lose its edge to competition in the region. This competitive advantage will cause the strategy of incentive creation to be dynamic, designed to meet the peculiar circumstances of each Asia-Pacific nation.

Incentive Protocols

In a few cases, formal legislative or regulatory provisions exist that govern incentives for foreign and/or local investment, for the economy in general or for tourism in particular. Governments generally consider most investment proposals to be beneficial to national development. Some governments have statutes that confer discretionary powers to grant incentives, including tax exemptions and customs duty concessions. However, there are few cases of an extensive, integrated system.

In most cases, application for investment projects has to be made to relevant ministers, and those applications are passed through a network of committees and advisors; they may be judged, not against a set of published criteria, but on a case-by-case basis. This means that the granting of approval for the project and the granting of incentives will depend on the merit of the proposal. Some governments have established a specific bureau or committee to appraise, evaluate and recommend action for major proposals. The relevant minister may make the final decision for small-scale projects, while the Cabinet may decide on large-scale projects involving high levels of capital investment. It is likely that the administration of investment incentives on a case-by case basis will not be conducive to effective decision-making (because of problems of consistency, confidence or equity), the implementation of the tourism strategy (because of the distortions decisions may impose) or efficient, delay-free decision processes.

The investment incentive process must be conspicuous, transparent, regular (following a time scale), clear and defined, supported by legal enactment and composed of a package of incentives (fiscal, financial and companion incentives). In addition, as events have demonstrated in the region, political and economic stability is an over-riding requirement for the creation of a favourable investment climate.

The purposes of the incentive package are to relieve the national budget of undue burdens, provide initial development momentum, support programme acceleration of that momentum, and provide flexibility so that projects can be encouraged and facilitated. Such a package should not be considered immutable or permanent. Each aspect of investment incentives should be subject to regular review, with a frequency at least as regular as the national economic strategy.

Domestic Investment

With the exception of the more economically developed countries in the Asian and Pacific region, the lack of an adequate local capital base for major projects is a major constraint to tourism development. It is generally accepted that tourism development in the Asian and Pacific region will be dependent largely on foreign investment.

However, there are opportunities for the involvement of local communities and indigenous entrepreneurs through joint ventures, land for equity exchanges, employment, and training schemes to achieve the necessary entrepreneurial, managerial and operational skills. There is a strong case to be made that Asia-Pacific countries should develop strategies that, in the long term, may lead to reduced dependence on foreign sources of investment finance. Such a case may be predicated on the expectation that a heavy dependence on foreign sources may contribute to undermining national and individual initiative.

The vulnerability to external forces could be reduced by a number of internal strategies, such as:

- Revision of subsistence strategies, so that even without large injections of capital, surplus production in rural areas can be accessed by tourism resorts ("subsistence affluence");
- Involvement of indigenous communities in low technology and low environmental impact projects, especially to meet the preference of some tourists for authentic experiences;
- Creation by government of a tourism development fund (to be operated within the framework of the national development bank).

The creation of a national tourism development fund specifically to assist local entrepreneurs could be considered an imperative strategy, given the generally low level of reserves of domestic private capital. This would become the responsibility of the government, operated through the national development bank, and targeted at domestic entrepreneurs seeking funding for small-scale enterprises for which commercial banks are reluctant to lend.

INSTITUTIONAL FRAMEWORK FOR INFRASTRUCTURE DEVELOPMENT

There is considerable evidence of the need for an effective institutional framework if tourism development is to be coordinated, efficiently supervised, monitored and integrated into the overall scope of national economic, environmental and social planning. It is important that the institutional framework encompasses organizations from both the public and private sectors.

A coordinated framework is necessary because of the fragmented nature of the tourism industry. The public sector, the private sector, non-profit organizations and the community play important roles in tourism planning and infrastructure development. The principal perspective of the public sector is to manage development in order to achieve community goals within the public interest. For the private sector, the principal function is to provide facilities and services to tourists while maximizing returns on the investment. The World Tourism Organization has described the distinctiveness of the roles of the public and private sectors by the principle that governments should not seek to do what the private sector is able and willing to do.

However, in many cases of large-scale development, the private sector and the government may work in a partnership. Other partnerships may develop where governments assist indigenous landowners with the commencement of an enterprise to be managed eventually by indigenous communities. One of the principal purposes of tourism planning is to bring into harmonious balance the different interests of the various stakeholders.

This balance may be achieved through the establishment of an appropriate multi-faceted institutional framework. In some tourism development plans, an effective institutional framework is considered to be one of the principal determinants of successful tourism development.

SUGGESTED MEASURES FOR CREATING A FAVOURABLE ATMOSPHERE FOR INVESTMENT IN TOURISM INFRASTRUCTURE

A variety of strategies and measures can be implemented to ensure a favourable atmosphere for investment in tourism infrastructure. In this chapter, the range of measures is presented for consideration by member economies as well as regional organizations and agencies.

NATIONAL LEVEL

Create a Clear Picture of the Role of Tourism in Solving Social, Economic and Environmental Problems

There is an urgent need for countries to emphasize, both to their own population as well as to the external community, the important role that tourism can play in solving a range of social, economic and environmental problems. This will require detailed studies of existing problems and the role that sustainable tourism development can play in achieving societal objectives such as the alleviation of poverty and the improvement of the quality of life of women.

It is only with this kind of information that government departments as well as aid agencies will understand that tourism is an essential development tool. Even more importantly, emphasis should be placed on the fact that if economic and social issues are to be dealt with, investment decisions in overall infrastructure development must support tourism initiatives.

Creation of Tourism Investment Information Centres

Within an increasingly competitive global market there is an urgent need to provide investors with relevant information on infrastructure possibilities. Countries could therefore consider the establishment of tourism investment information centres to assist national as well as foreign investors. The centres would provide a one-stop service for tourism investment by providing information on investment opportunities and regulations in the tourism industry.

Encourage Cooperation and Integrated Tourism Development Planning

Given the fragmented nature of the public sector as well as private sector aspects of the industry, there is an urgent need for cooperation among all relevant stakeholders.

Specific steps could include:

- The encouragement of other governmental agencies in addition to tourism departments to become involved in tourism investment;
- Increased cooperation between various organizations including the international community, the private sector and relevant government agencies, in order that tourism infrastructure investment is seen as a legitimate development tool for country economies;
- The development of investment programmes and policies in consensus with all the stakeholders. This cooperation will ensure that various government departments as well as the private sector will be more likely to work with one another;
- Involvement of the town and country planning agencies in integrating area development plans with tourism development.

Creation of a Positive Investment Climate

Evidence now suggests that investors are looking for stable and transparent economies in which to invest. In order to achieve this condition, the following strategies could be considered:

- The creation of official procedures that will encourage investment in all aspects of infrastructure and remove the need for corruption as a means of getting things done;
- The development of a comprehensive and transparent legal system and framework as well as legislation that will allow effective implementation and support of infrastructure investment;
- Improvement of the investment environment on a continuous basis, *e.g.*, by alleviating administrative regulations and providing efficient support for information distribution;
- Making incentives more flexible, through consultation or negotiation if necessary, with individual foreign investors rather than by the uniform criterion that may not recognize specific needs and local conditions;
- Increasing lease periods on land and reviewing land rents on a regular basis in an open and transparent manner;
- The provision of strong protection for foreign investment, backed by the force of law;
- Making revolving lines of credit available to the private sector for tourism projects that support strategic societal objectives.

Creation of Special Tourism Investment Zones

Consideration should be given to establishing special zones where investment incentives and clearly understood procedures are in place for tourism development. Within the zones there could be support for infrastructure development, especially in key environmental and public sector areas such as water supply, electricity and telephone. Within those areas there must also be special interest bank loans for infrastructure investment.

Support Human Resource Development

Attracting investment requires that governments as well as private sector stakeholders are aware of the investment procedures and conditions of the global market. In addition, investors must be assured that there is a reliable source of trained personnel in all aspects of tourism activity. Governments and the private sector should therefore consider the establishment of tourism institutes in order to supply the required work force. It is important to stress that training and capacity-building must address actual demands.

Create Opportunities for Strategic Product Development

Given the definition of infrastructure adopted in this study, it is vital that all aspects of the tourism environment be considered. This requires strategic investment in infrastructure that will support local as well as national development.

Specific strategies can include:

- Increased accessibility for existing and potential tourist markets by investing in various forms of transportation facilities and modes;
- Investment in cultural as well as natural heritage sites and attractions, given the importance of these aspects of a destination in meeting overall tourism needs;
- Development of places of pilgrimage by providing the requisite infrastructure facilities;
- Development of the attraction of tourism destinations based on several themes including: islands and beaches, highland resorts, eco-tourism, historical places, cultural attractions and technical parks.

Adopt Innovative Means of Delivering Quality Infrastructure Development

Countries should assess the adoption of build-operate-transfer arrangements to attract foreign investment in tourism infrastructure development. This will require that careful study be undertaken of the costs and benefits of such arrangements, and that public officials are well trained in the development of contracts and arrangements that will benefit all stakeholders. In addition, very careful analysis should be made of the feasibility of such arrangements before any contractual commitments are made.

Other Measures

Other measures that could be implemented in order to create favourable conditions for investing in tourism infrastructure include:

- Increasing local autonomy. Special consideration should be given to ensuring that the autonomy of local government is further enhanced thereby providing local authorities with the incentive to develop policies and approaches to attract and support foreign investment in infrastructure;

- Investing portions of the results of taxation in tourism infrastructure development. Mechanisms should be put into place to tax those benefiting from the tourism economy. One way to ensure that tourism strategies are supported is to direct portions of the tax receipts directly back into investment in tourism infrastructure. This will convince taxpayers that their money are being used in an open and productive manner;
- Development and use of appropriate applications of new technologies for promoting tourism products. Development of the information technology aspects of tourism is essential if the full benefits of tourism infrastructure investment are to be realised;
- Stopping income leakages at the local level. One of the major issues in trying to encourage local investors to contribute to the infrastructure development relates to the significant leakages that often occur from tourism activity. Stopping such leakages also has the added advantage of ensuring that the economic and social needs of local people are enhanced through tourism development. Specific actions can include:

– Involving local communities at all levels in all aspects of the policy-making, planning, and management decisionmaking process;

– Training and the provision of financial as well as technical assistance that will support the creation of locally owned and operated small and medium-sized enterprises. This will help to maintain tourism incomes within the community;

– Encouraging tourism development that makes use of local agricultural products and materials. This may require some investment, but the long-term benefits are that the local community will have the capacity to benefit directly from tourism development;

– Creating taxes that stay within the local community to help to support infrastructure development;

– Ensuring that capacity-building initiatives are designed to develop trained local workers to assume both managerial as well as lower-level positions within the tourism industry. Local governments may wish to give preference to tourism developments that employ local labour and help to build capacity of local people.

Monitoring the Effectiveness of Investment in Tourism Infrastructure

It is essential that governments at all levels effectively monitor the benefits as well as the costs of investment in tourism infrastructure. This information is vital not only to guiding national as well as local level public sector investments, it is also an essential area of information for encouraging investment by the private sector at the national or and international levels.

REGIONAL LEVEL

A great deal can be done at the regional level to ensure that there are sufficient resources to expand opportunities for investment in tourism infrastructure at all levels. Some of this effort can occur through cooperation between countries, and some initiatives can be taken by organizations such as ESCAP to achieve these objectives.

Specific strategies could include:

- A review of current initiatives and existing strategies to assess their effectiveness in encouraging tourism investment;
- The Asian Development Bank (ADB) and the World Bank could ensure that their existing policies view investment in tourism infrastructure as an essential dimension of their social and environmental programmes;
- Multilateral agencies and institutions should assist governments in recognizing the economic and social contribution of tourism, and they should include tourism in mainstream programmes for job creation, export promotion and investment stimulation;
- ESCAP could take initiatives to establish an information technology network through which the member countries could provide and use information related to investment in tourism infrastructure;
- ESCAP could provide consultative services on investment in the member countries.

CONCLUSIONS

The search for sustainable tourism does not entail "throwing the baby out with the bath water". Direct and indirect forms of government intervention might be necessary to ensure the protection of natural resources and the equitable distribution of economic benefits from tourism development. At the same time, incentives have to be provided to the private sector to encourage financial investment in development activity that adheres to the principles of sustainable tourism.

Encouraging cooperation and collaboration among the diverse actors, as well as public-private sector partnerships, should assist in reducing potential and actual conflicts of interests and values. In addition, these actions should facilitate the more efficient use of resources and capabilities to achieve the destination's economic objectives.

If countries, regions and communities are to be in a position to take advantage of tourism as a form of economic development, a number of changes will be required and specific programmes will need to be put in place to encourage investment in infrastructure.

Such changes and programmes include:

- Better tourism planning and management practices;
- Coordination of activities at all levels of government operations;
- Improved cooperation between businesses and communities, as well as between the public and private sectors;
- Improved impact assessment and monitoring practices;
- The design and delivery of a wide range of tourism-related educational and training opportunities;
- The provision of marketing and promotional assistance;
- More equitable access to employment, promotion, education and training for marginalized population groups;
- The establishment of tourism support and resource centres.

One important strategy will be to eliminate obstacles to the creation of economic development in the tourism sector.

These actions can include:

- Ensuring tourism strategies and plans must be linked with a broader set of initiatives and community or economic development plans;
- Providing for more coordination, both at the policy and action levels among the various agencies involved and between the different levels of government;
- Fostering cooperation among businesses and tourism operators, which is essential given that one business or operation can be directly affected by the success or quality of another. Models of tourism partnerships must be explored in the areas of planning, management, marketing, and funding for tourism ventures;
- Encouraging financial institutions to play a role by working with local communities and entrepreneurs to help provide investment funds;
- Educating all stakeholders in the fact that cooperation among neighbouring regions and communities is most important;
- Education and training programmes that are necessary in order to ensure that local residents are in a position to obtain the necessary skills and knowledge for participating effectively in the tourism process;
- National, regional and local tourism-related policies, which are required for providing direction for sustainable tourism development. Maintaining local government control over decision-making and keeping tourism within the capacity of local resources are two strategies for managing the core-periphery problem. Hence, government policies may have to be set on foreign investment in tourism (addressing forms, types, profit distribution, etc.), training

and educating of local residents within the destination areas, and on the use of natural and common goods. Stimulating domestic tourism and encouraging local participation in tourism development can also help to address core-periphery problems;

- Financial incentives and assistance, which are required in aiding tourism service providers to cope with the problems that are created by the seasonal nature of most tourism activity. For example, financial assistance may allow diversification into off-season and shoulder season activities by attracting specific user segments during these periods through marketing and promotion assistance.

2

Types of Tourism

RELIGIOUS TOURISM

Religious tourism, also commonly referred to as faith tourism, is a form of tourism whereby people of faith travel individually or in groups for pilgrimage, missionary, or leisure purposes.

The International Conference on Religious Tourism estimates the worldwide faith tourism industry at $18 billion. North American religious tourists comprise an estimated $10 billion of this industry.

TOURISM SEGMENTS

Religious tourism comprises many facets of the travel industry including:

- Christian and faith-based camps
- Crusades, conventions, and rallies
- Faith-based cruising
- Leisure vacations
- Missionary travel
- Monastery visits and guest-stays
- Pilgrimages
- Religious tourist attractions
- Retreats

STATISTICS

Although no definitive study has been completed on worldwide religious tourism, some segments of the industry have been measured,

- The Religious Conference Management Association, in 2006 more than 14.7 million people attended religious meetings, an increase of more than 10 million from 1994 with 4.4 million attendees.
- The U.S. Office of Travel and Tourism Industries, Americans traveling overseas for "religious or pilgrimage" purposes has increased from 491,000 travellers in 2002 to 633,000 travellers in 2005.
- The World Tourism Organization, an estimated 300 to 330 million pilgrim's visit the world's key religious sites every year.

- One-quarter of travellers said they were currently interested in taking a spiritual vacation. More than one in ten travellers said they were more interested now compared to five years ago in taking a spiritual vacation. The appeal of a spiritual vacation spans the ages, with approximately one-third of each age group expressing current interest in taking such a vacation.
- Religious attractions including Sight and Sound Theatre attracts 800,000 visitors a year while the Holy Land Experience and Focus on the Family Welcome Centre each receives about 250,000 guests annually. Religious tourism, also commonly referred to as faith tourism, is a form of tourism whereby people of faith travel individually or in groups for pilgrimage, missionary, or leisure purposes. The International Conference on Religious Tourism estimates the worldwide faith tourism industry at $18 billion.
- The 50,000 churches in the United States with religious travel programmes
- The Christian Camp and Conference Association states that more than eight million people are involved in CCCA member camps and conferences, including more than 120,000 churches.
- The United Methodist Church experienced an increase of 455% in mission volunteers from 1992 with almost 20,000 volunteers compared to 110,000 volunteers in 2006.

COUNTRIES, TOURIST BOARDS AND RELIGIOUS TOURISM

- *Bahamas*: One of the few countries with a Director of Religious Tourism and staff dedicated to attracting faith-based visitors
- *Cypress*: Launching new marketing efforts to increase religious tourism of its current 100,000 faith-based visitors annually
- *India*: Largest portion of visitors are religious pilgrims
- *Israel*: Tourism ministry looks to boost tourism from North America
- *Italy*: Religious tourism in Italy alone generates over $4.5 billion each year.
- *Jordan*: Promoting niche markets such as religious tourism is a large part of Jordan's overall tourism strategy
- *Scotland*: Projected to triple from religious tourism dollars of GBP 80-100 to GBP 300 million by 2014
- *Switzerland*: Seeking to highlight its religious sites and attract more visitors

PILGRIMAGE

In religion and spirituality, a pilgrimage is a long journey or search of great moral significance. Sometimes, it is a journey to a sacred place or shrine of importance to a person's beliefs and faith. Members of every major religion participate in pilgrimages. A person who makes such a journey is called a pilgrim. Buddhism offers four sites of pilgrimage: the Buddha's birthplace at Kapilavastu, the site where he attained Enlightenment Bodh Gaya, where he first preached at Benares, and where he achieved Parinirvana at Kusinagara.

Israel acts as a focal point for the pilgrimages of many religions, such as Judaism, Christianity, Islam and the Bahá'í Faith. In the kingdoms of Israel and Judah, the visitation of certain ancient cult-centres was repressed in the 7th century BC, when the worship was restricted to Jahweh at the temple in Jerusalem. In Syria, the shrine of Astarte at the headwater spring of the river Adonis survived until it was destroyed by order of Emperor Constantine in the 4th century AD. In mainland Greece, a stream of individuals made their way to Delphi or the oracle of Zeus at Dodona, and once every four years, at the period of the Olympic games, the temple of Zeus at Olympia formed the goal of swarms of pilgrims from every part of the Hellenic world.

When Alexander the Great reached Egypt, he put his whole vast enterprise on hold, while he made his way with a small band deep into the Libyan desert, to consult the oracle of Ammun. During the imperium of his Ptolemaic heirs, the shrine of Isis at Philae received many votive inscriptions from Greeks on behalf of their kindred far away at home. Although a pilgrimage is normally viewed in the context of religion, the personality cults cultivated by communist leaders ironically gave birth to pilgrimages of their own.

Prior to the demise of the USSR in 1991, a visit to Lenin's Mausoleum in Red Square, Moscow can be said to have had all the characteristics exhibiting a pilgrimage—for Communists. This type of pilgrimage to a personality cult is still evident today on people who pay visits of homage to Mao Tse Tung, Kim Il Sung, and Ho Chi Minh.

BELONGINGS ON TRADE

Pilgrims contributed an important element to long-distance trade before the modern era, and brought prosperity to successful pilgrimage sites, an economic phenomenon unequalled until the tourist trade of the 20th century. Encouraging pilgrims was a motivation for assembling relics and for writing hagiographies of local saints, filled with inspiring accounts of miracle cures. Lourdes and other modern pilgrimage sites keep this spirit alive.

NEW PILGRIMAGE

Pilgrimages are still made throughout the world: modern-day pilgrimages include the Way of St. James, the Hajj, and the pilgrimage to Mount Kailash. In modern usage, the terms pilgrim and pilgrimage can also have a somewhat devalued meaning as they are often applied in a secular context. For example, fans of Elvis Presley may choose to visit his home, Graceland, in Memphis, Tennessee. Similarly one may refer to a cultural centre such as Venice as a "tourists' Mecca".

PILGRIMAGE CENTRES IN DIFFERENT TIMES AND CULTURES

Antiquity

Many ancient religions had holy sites, temples and groves, where pilgrimages were made.

- Baalbek Lebanon.
- Delphi, Greece. Oracle.
- Dodona, Epirus, Greece. Oracle.
- Ephesus Temple of Diana.
- Karnak, Egypt.
- Kurukshetra, India
- Thebes, Egypt.

Bahai Faith

Bahai Faith grimage currently consists of visiting the holy places in Haifa, Akka, and Bahji in Northwest Israel. Bahais do not have access to other places designated as sites for pilgrimage. Bahaullah decreed pilgrimage in His Motherbook to two places: the House of Bahaullah in Baghdad, Iraq, and the House of the Bab in Shiraz, Iran. In two separate Tablets, known as Suriy-i-Hajj, He prescribed specific rites for each of these pilgrimages. It is obligatory to make the pilgrimage, "if one can afford it and is able to do so, and if no obstacle stands in one's way".

Bahais are free to choose between the two Houses, as either has been deemed sufficient. And although women are not bound to perform pilgrimage, they are certainly not prohibited to do so.

Buddhism

Gautama Buddha spoke of the four sites most worthy of pilgrimage for his followers to visit:

- *Bodh Gaya*: Place of Enlightenment
- *Kusinara*: Where he attained mahaparinirvana.
- *Lumbini*: Birth place
- *Sarnath*: Where he delivered his first teaching

Other pilgrimage places in India and Nepal connected to the life of Gautama Buddha are: Savatthi, Pataliputta, Nalanda, Gaya, Vesali, Sankasia, Kapilavastu, Kosambi, Rajagaha, Varanasi.

Other famous places for buddhist pilgrimage in various countries include:

- *Cambodia*: Angkor Wat, Silver Pagoda.
- *China*: Yung-kang, Lung-men caves.
- *India*: Sanchi, Ellora, Ajanta.
- *Indonesia*: Borobudur.
- *Japan*: Kyoto, Nara.
- *Laos*: Luang Prabang.
- *Myanmar*: Bagan, Sagaing Hill.

- *Nepal*: Bodhnath, Swayambhunath.
- *Sri Lanka*: Polonnaruwa, Temple of the Tooth, Anuradhapura.
- *Thailand*: Sukhothai, Ayutthaya, Wat Phra Kaew, Wat Doi Suthep.
- *Tibet*: Lhasa, Mount Kailash, Lake Nam-tso.

Communism

- *China*: Peking, Mausoleum of Mao Tse Tung in Tiananmen Square.
- *Germany*: Trier, Birthplace of Karl Marx in Trier
- *USSR*: Moscow, Mausoleum of Lenin in Red Square.

Christianity

Pilgrimages were first made to sites connected with the birth, life, crucifixion and resurrection of Jesus. Surviving descriptions of Christian pilgrimages to the Holy Land date from the 4th century, when pilgrimage was encouraged by church fathers like Saint Jerome. Pilgrimages also began to be made to Rome and other sites associated with the Apostles, Saints and Christian martyrs, as well as to places where there have been apparitions of the Virgin Mary. The crusades to the holy land are also considered to be mass armed pilgrimages. The second largest single pilgrimage in the history of Christendom was to the Funeral of Pope John Paul II after his death on April 2, 2005.

An estimated four million people travelled to Vatican City, in addition to the almost three million people already living in Rome, to see the body of Pope John Paul II lie in state. World Youth Day is a major Catholic Pilgrimage, specifically for people aged 16-35. It is held internationally every 2-3 years. In 2005, young Catholics visited Cologne, Germany. In 1995, the largest gathering of all time was to World Youth Day in Manila, Philippines, where four million people from all over the world attended.

The major Christian pilgrimages are to:

- *Constantinople*: Former capital of the Byzantine Empire and the see of one of the five ancient Patriarchates and spiritual see of the Eastern Orthodox Church. Hagia Sophia, former cathedral and burial place of many Ecumenical Patriarchs.
- *Jerusalem*: Site of the crucifixion and resurrection of Jesus.
- *Lourdes, France*: Apparition of the Virgin Mary. The second most visited Christian pilgrimage site after Rome.
- *Rome on roads such as the Via Francigena*: Site of the deaths of Saint Peter, Saint Paul and other early martyrs. Location of sacred relics of various saints, relics of the Passion, important churches and headquarters of the Catholic Church.
- *Santiago de Compostela in Spain on the Way of St James*: This famous medieval pilgrimage to the shrine of Saint James is still popular today.

Other important Christian pilgrimage sites include:

- Assisi, Italy, St. Francis of Assisi and St Clare, relics
- Avila, Spain, St Theresa of Avila, relics
- Bethlehem, in Israel, Birthplace of Jesus and King David.
- Canterbury Cathedral associated with Saint Thomas Becket.
- Cap-de-la-Madeleine, Quebec, Canada in honour of Our Lady of the Cape.
- Carey, Ohio to the Basilica and National Shrine of Our Lady of Consolation. Catholic pilgrims from the Middle East journey here to mark the Feast of the Assumption.
- Cathedral of Chartres, France.
- *Cologne, Germany*: Relics of the Three Magi.
- Conques, France
- *Croagh Patrick, Ireland*: Saint Patrick.
- *Czestochowa, Poland*: Black Madonna of Czêstochowa is housed pernamently in theJasna Góra Monastery
- *Fatima, Portugal*: Apparition of the Virgin Mary.
- Glastonbury, England. St Joseph of Arimathea.
- Goa, India. St. Francis Xavier
- Guadalupe, Spain
- Hill of Crosses, Lithuania
- House of the Virgin Mary, Turkey. Pope John-Paul II declared the Shrine of Virgin Mary as a pilgrimage place for Christians.
- *Issoudun, France*: Notre-Dame du Sacré-Coeur
- Kapel in 't Zand, Limburg
- Kevelaer, Germany
- Knock, Ireland
- Lakefield, Ontario, Canada
- Licheñ Stary, Sanctuary of Our Lady of Licheñ
- *Lisieux, France*: Saint Therese of Lisieux, burial place.
- *Lourdes, France*: Apparition of the Virgin Mary. Place of healing.
- *Mariazell, Austria*: Marian Shrine to Austria and Hungary
- *Meaugorje, Bosnia-Herzegovina*: Apparitions of the Virgin Mary at the present.
- *Miercurea Ciuc, Transylvania, Romania*: Whit Sunday gathering of Catholics.
- *Montserrat, Catalonia, Spain*: The Virgin of Montserrat is housed pernamently in the monastery of Santa María de Montserrat.
- *Mount Athos, Greece*: Orthodox monastic centre.
- *Mount Nebo, Jordan*: Traditional site of the death of Moses.
- Mount Sinai, Egypt, holy mountain to the ancient Hebrews, traditional site has been commemorated since time of Constantine
- Nazareth, Israel, hometown of Jesus

- Nidaros, Trondheim, Norway. Shrine of St. Olav. 4th most visited pilgrimage site in Middle Ages.
- Padua, Italy, St Anthony, relics
- Paris
- PemaiEion Kalvarija, Samogitia, Lithuania.
- Rosslyn Chapel, Scotland
- *Sacri Monti, Italy*: The Sacred Mountains of Piedmont and Lombardy.
- San Giovanni Rotondo, Italy, St Pio from Pietrelcina
- Sea of Galilee, Israel, site of Jesus' early ministry.
- Shrine of Our Lady of Guadalupe, Mexico City. Apparition of the Virgin Mary.
- St. Andrews, Scotland, it is said that Saint Andrew was given, by God, directions to the location of St Andrews
- St. Patrick's Purgatory, Donegal, Ireland
- St. Thomas Mount, India. Place where St. Thomas was martyred.
- Taize Community, France, modern monastery that actively encourages pilgrimages to it
- *Trondheim, Norway*: Nidaros Cathedral, shrine of St. Olav.
- *Turin, Italy*: Holy Shroud.
- Vailankanni, India. 16th-century Mary apparition site.
- Vierzehnheiligen, Germany.
- *Walsingham, England*: Virgin Mary apparition site.
- *Wittenberg, Germany*: Church of Martin Luther and centre of the Protestant Reformation.

Hinduism

Hindus are required to undertake pilgrimages during their lifetime.

Most Hindus who can afford to go on such journeys travel to numerous sites including those below:

- Allahabad
- Arunachala
- Ayodhya
- Benares
- Chidambaram
- Dakshineshwar
- Dharmasthala
- Dwarka
- Gaya
- Guruvayoor
- Hampi
- Haridwar
- Kalahasti
- Kanchipuram
- Kanyakumari
- Kateel
- Kollur
- Kumbakonam
- Kukke Subramanya
- Kunrakudy
- Madurai
- Mahabalipuram
- Marudamalai
- Mathura
- Mandher Devi temple
- Mayapur

in Mandhradevi

- Mount Kailash
- Nashik
- Nathdwara
- Palani
- Pazhamudircholai
- Puri
- Pushkar
- Puttaparthi
- Rameswaram
- Rishikesh
- Sabarimala
- Shirdi
- Sikkal
- Sivagiri, Kerala
- Somnath
- Sringeri
- Srirangam
- Swamimalai
- Swamithope
- Talapady
- Tanjavur
- Thiruchendur
- Thiruparamkunram
- Thiruthani
- Tirupati
- Ujjain
- Udupi
- Malai Mandir
- Vaishno Devi
- Vayalur
- Viralimalai
- Virpur
- Vrindavan
- Badrinath
- Gangotri
- Kedarnath
- Yamunotri

The last four sites in the list together comprise the Chardham, or four holy pilgrimage destinations. It is believed that travelling to these places leads to moksha, the release from samsara. Vrindavan is most important place of pilgrimage for every Vaishnava, especially for the followers of Gaudiya Vaishnavism who regard Krishna as the original Personality of Godhead. Here one can attain love of God.

Islam

The pilgrimage to Mecca–the Hajj–is one of the Five Pillars of Islam. It should be attempted at least once in the lifetime of all able-bodied Muslims who can afford to do so. It is the most important of all Muslim Pilgrimages. Many Muslims also undergo ziyarat, which is a pilgrimage to sites associated with the prophet Muhammad, his companions, or other venerated figures in Islamic history, such as Shi'a imams or Sufi saints. Sites of pilgrimage include mosques, graves, battlefields, mountains, and caves.

Local Pilgrimage traditions-those undertaken as ziarah visits to local graves, are also found throughout Muslim countries. In some countries, the grave sites of heroes have very strong ziyarah traditions as visiting the graves at auspicious times is a display of national and community identity. Some traditions within Islam have negative attitudes towards grave visiting. The third religiously sanctioned pilgrimage for Muslims is to the Al Quds mount in Jerusalem which hosts Al-Aqsa Mosque and the Dome of the Rock.

Judaism

Within Judaism, the Temple in Jerusalem was the centre of the Jewish religion, until its destruction in 70 AD, and all who were able were under obligation to visit and offer sacrifices known as the korbanot, particularly during the Jewish holidays in Jerusalem. Following the destruction of the Second Temple and the onset of the diaspora, the centrality of pilgrimage to Jerusalem in Judaism was discontinued. In its place came prayers and rituals hoping for a return to Zion and the accompanying restoration of regular pilgrimages. Until recent centuries, pilgrimage has been a fairly difficult and arduous adventure. But now, Jews from many countries make periodic pilgrimages to the holy sites of their religion. The western retaining wall of the original temple, known as the Wailing Wall, or Western Wall remains in the Old City of Jerusalem and this has been the most sacred site for religious Jews. Pilgrimage to this area was off-limits from 1948 to 1967, when East Jerusalem was controlled by Jordan. Some Reform and Conservative Jews who no longer consider themselves exiles, still enjoy visiting Israel even if it is not an official "pilgrimage."

ADVENTURE TOURISM

Adventure tourism is a type of niche tourism involving exploration or travel to remote areas, where the traveller should expect the unexpected. Adventure tourism is rapidly growing in popularity as tourists seek unusual holidays, different from the typical beach vacation. Adventure Tourism can take many forms with the increase in numbers of people with disabilities around the World and recent veterans from Wars have opened the doors to Adventure Travel for the Disabled. Albeit this may not be in exotic areas some tourism areas that have been developing include Australia, USA and Canada.

Whistler and Vancouver British Columbia, Canada have been taking the lead with the 2010 Paralympics coming up fast. Adapting to the needs of the Disabled to attract a $ 13 billion dollar a year industry in North America alone. The global Adventure Travel Trade Association, "adventure travel" may be any tourist activity including two of the following three components: a physical activity, a cultural exchange or interaction. Mountaineering expeditions, trekking, bungee jumping, rafting and rock climbing are frequently cited as an examples of adventure tourism.

MOUNTAINEERING

Mountaineering is the sport, hobby or profession of walking, hiking, trekking and climbing up mountains. It is also sometimes known as alpinism, particularly in Europe. While it began as an all-out attempt to reach the highest point of unclimbed mountains, it has branched into specializations addressing different aspects of mountains and may now be said to consist of three aspects:

rock-craft, snow-craft and skiing, depending on whether the route chosen is over rock, snow or ice. All require great athletic and technical ability, and experience is also a very important part of the matter.

Snow

While certain compacted snow conditions allow mountaineers to progress on foot, typically some form of mechanical device is required to travel efficiently over snow and ice. Crampons 10-12 point spikes which are attached to a mountaineers boots, are used on hard snow and ice to provide additional traction and allow very steep ascents and descents. There a many different varieties, ranging from lightweight aluminum models intended for walking on glaciers to aggressive steel models intended for vertical and overhanging ice and rock.

Snowshoes can be used to walk through deep snow approaching the mountain or on lesser slopes up the mountain. Skis can be used almost everywhere snowshoes can and also in steeper, more alpine landscapes although it takes more practice to develop sufficiently strong skiing skills for difficult terrain. The practice of combining the techniques of alpine skiing and mountaineering to ascend and descend a mountain is a form of the sport by itself, called Ski Mountaineering. Ascending and descending a snow slope involves many different techniques of the feet and an ice axe which have been developed over the last hundred years, originating in Europe. The progression of footwork from the lowest angle slopes to the steepest terrain is first to splay the feet to a rising traverse, to kick stepping, to front pointing the crampons.

The progression of the ice axe technique from the lowest angle slopes to the steepest terrain is to use the ice axe first as a walking stick, then a stake, then to use the front pick as a dagger below the shoulders or above, and finally to swing the pick into the slope over the head. This also involves different designs of ice axe depending on the terrain to be covered, and even whether a mountaineer uses one or two ice axes.

Glaciers

When traveling over glaciers, crevasses pose a grave danger. These giant cracks in the ice are not always visible as snow can be blown and freeze over the top to make a snowbridge. At times snowbridges can be as thin as a few inches. Climbers use a system of ropes to protect themselves from such hazards. Basic gear for glacier travel includes crampons and ice axes. Teams of two to five climbers tie into a rope equally spaced. If a climber begins to fall the other members of the team perform a self-arrest to stop the fall. The other members of the team enact a crevasse rescue to pull the fallen climber from the crevasse.

Ice

Multiple methods are used to safely travel over ice. If the terrain is steep but not vertical, then protection in the form of pickets or ice screws can be driven into the snow or ice and attached to the rope by the lead climber. Each climber on the team must clip past the anchor, and the last climber picks up the picket. This allows for safety should the entire team be taken off their feet. This technique is known as Simul-climbing. If the terrain becomes vertical then standard ice climbing techniques are used.

Shelter

Climbers use a few different forms of shelter depending on the situation and conditions. Shelter is a very important aspect of safety for the climber as the weather in the mountains is very unpredictable. Tall mountains require many days of camping on the mountain.

Hut

The European alpine regions, in particular, have a network of mountain huts. Such huts exist at many different heights, including in the high mountains themselves–in extremely remote areas bivouac shelters may have been provided. The mountain huts are of varying size and quality but each is typically centred on a communal dining room and have dormitories equipped with mattresses, blankets or duvets, and pillows–guests are expected to bring and to use their own sleeping bag liner.

The facilities are usually rudimentary but, given their locations, huts offer vital shelter, make routes more widely accessible and offer good value. In Europe, all huts are staffed during the summer and some are staffed in the spring. Elsewhere, huts may also be open in the fall. Huts also may have a part that is always open, but unmanned, a so-called winter hut. When open and manned, the huts are generally run by full-time employees, but some are staffed on a voluntary basis by members of Alpine clubs. The manager of the hut, termed a guardian or warden in Europe, will usually also sell refreshments and meals–both to those visiting only for the day and to those staying overnight.

The offering is surprisingly wide–given that most supplies, often including fresh water, must be flown in by helicopter–and may include glucose-based snacks on which climbers and walkers wish to stock up, cakes and pastries made at the hut, a variety of hot and cold drinks, and high carbohydrate dinners in the evenings. Not all huts do offer a catered service, though, and visitors may need to provide for themselves. Some huts offer facilities for both, enabling visitors wishing to keep costs down to bring their own food and cooking equipment and to cater using the facilities provided. Booking for overnight stays at huts is deemed obligatory, and in many cases is essential as some popular huts–even with over 100 bed spaces-may well be full during good weather and at weekends. Once made, the cancellation of a reservation should be advised to the hut as a matter of courtesy–and, indeed, potentially of safety, as many huts keep a record of where climbers and walkers state they planned to walk to next. Most huts are contactable by telephone and most take credit cards as a means of payment for the service they provide.

Bivy

A bivy or bivouac is simply getting a sleeping bag and Bivouac sack and laying down to sleep. Many times small half sheltered areas like cracks in rocks or simply a trench dug in the snow are used to provide a basic means of shelter as well.

This technique is performed by most people only in cases of emergency, however in good weather this can be pleasant. Some climbers steadfastly committed to Alpine Style climbing plan on bivying in order to save the weight of a tent when snow conditions are not suitable for a snow cave.

Tent

Tents are the most common form of shelter used on the mountain. A four season tent is recommended for any camp above timberline in the mountains. Some climbers do not use tents at high altitudes unless the snow conditions do not allow for snow caving, although digging a snow cave is a time consuming and work intensive endeavor.

Sometimes walls of snow or rock can be built instead to shelter the tent from high winds and storms. One of the downsides to tenting is that high storm winds and snow loads can be unnerving and cause the tent to collapse, however modern mountaineering tents are usually tested for wind speeds up to 125 mph. Even so, constant flapping of the tent fabric can hinder sleep and raise doubts about the security of the shelter in windy conditions.

Snow Cave

Snow caves are another way for some climbers to shelter high on the mountain. Unlike tents snow caves are silent and actually warmer. A correctly made snow cave will hover around freezing, which relative to outside temperatures can be very warm.

They require carrying a snow shovel, which some may consider to be extra equipment, to build easily. They can be dug from a deep snowdrift, out of a slope, or anywhere there is at least four feet of snow. Another shelter that works well is a quinzee, which is excavated from a pile of snow that has been work hardened or sintered. Igloos are used by some climbers, but are deceptively difficult to build and require specific snow conditions.

Hazards

The craft of climbing has been developed to avoid three main types of danger: the danger of things falling on the climber, the danger of the climber falling and inclement weather. The things that may fall include rocks, ice, snow, other climbers or their gear; the mountaineer may fall from rocks, ice or snow, or into a crevasse. In all, there are eight chief dangers: falling rocks, falling ice, snow-avalanches, falls, the climber falling, falls from ice slopes, falls down snow slopes, falls into crevasses and dangers from weather. To select and follow a route using one's skills and experience to mitigate these dangers is to exercise the climber's craft.

Falling Rocks

Every rock mountain is slowly disintegrating due to erosion, the process being especially rapid above the snow-line. Rock faces are constantly swept by falling stones, which are generally possible to dodge. Falling rocks tend to form furrows in a mountain face, and these furrows have to be ascended with caution, their sides often being safe when the middle is stoneswept. Rocks fall more frequently on some days than on others, just as to the recent weather. Ice formed during the night may temporarily bind rocks to the face but warmth of the day or direct sun exposure may easily dislodge these rocks. Local experience is a valuable help on determining typical rockfall on such routes. The direction of the dip of rock strata often determines the degree of danger on a particular face; the character of the rock must also be considered. Where stones fall frequently debris will be found whilst on snow slopes falling stones cut furrows visible from a great distance. In planning an ascent of a new peak mountaineers must look for such traces. When falling stones get mixed in considerable quantity with slushy snow or water a mud avalanche is formed. It is vital to avoid camping in their possible line of fall.

Falling Ice

The places where ice may fall can always be determined beforehand. It falls in the broken parts of glaciers and from overhanging cornices formed on the crests of narrow ridges. Large icicles are often formed on steep rock faces, and these fall frequently in fine weather following cold and stormy days. They have to be avoided like falling stones. Seracs are slow in formation, and slow in arriving at a condition of unstable equilibrium.

They generally fall in or just after the hottest part of the day, and their debris seldom goes far. A skillful and experienced ice-man will usually devise a safe route through a most intricate ice-fall, but such places should be avoided in the afternoon of a hot day. Hanging glaciers often discharge themselves over steep rock-faces, the snout breaking off at intervals. Their track should be avoided.

Falls from Rocks

The skill of a rock climber is shown by one's choice of handhold and foothold, and his adhesion to those one has chosen. Much depends on a correct estimate of the firmness of the rock where weight is to be thrown upon it. Many loose rocks are quite firm enough to bear a person's weight, but experience is needed to know which can be trusted, and skill is required in transferring the weight to them without jerking. On rotten rocks the rope must be handled with special care, lest it should start loose stones on to the heads of those below. Similar care must be given to handholds and footholds, for the same reason.

When a horizontal traverse has to be made across very difficult rocks, a dangerous situation may arise unless at both ends of the traverse there be firm positions. Mutual assistance on hard rocks takes all manner of forms: two, or even three, people climbing on one another's shoulders, or using an ice axe propped up by others for a foothold. The great principle is that of co-operation, all the members of the party climbing with reference to the others, and not as independent units; each when moving must know what the climber in front and the one behind are doing. After bad weather steep rocks are often found covered with a veneer of ice, which may even render them inaccessible. Crampons are useful on such occasions.

Avalanches

The avalanche is the most underestimated danger in the mountains. People generally think that they will be able to recognize the hazards and survive being caught. The truth is a somewhat different story. Every year, 120-150 people die in small avalanches in the Alps alone. The vast majority are reasonably experienced male skiers aged 20-35 but also include ski instructors and guides. There is always a lot of pressure to risk a snow crossing.

Turning back takes a lot of extra time and effort, supreme leadership, and most importantly there seldom is an avalanche to prove the right decision was made. Making the decision to turn around is especially hard if others are crossing the slope, but any next person could become the trigger.

The Slab Avalanche

This type of avalanche occurs when a plate of snow breaks loose and starts sliding down; these are the largest and most dangerous.

- Hard slab avalanche-formed by hard-packed snow in a cohesive slab. The slab will not break up easily as it slides down the hill, resulting in large blocks tumbling down the mountain.
- Soft slab avalanche-formed again by a cohesive layer of snow bonded together, the slab tends to break up more easily.

The Loose Snow Avalanche

This type of avalanche is triggered by a small amount of moving snow that accumulates into a big slide. Also known as a "wet slide or point release" avalanche. This type of avalanche is deceptively dangerous as it can still knock a climber or skier off their feet and bury them, or sweep them over a cliff into a terrain trap.

Dangerous slides are most likely to occur on the same slopes preferred by many skiers: long and wide open, few trees or large rocks, 30 to 45 degrees of angle, large load of fresh snow, soon after a big storm, on a slope 'lee to the storm'. Solar radiation can trigger slides as well. These will typically be a point release or wet slough type of avalanche. The added weight of the wet slide can trigger a slab avalanche. Ninety per cent of reported victims are caught in avalanches triggered by themselves or others in their group.

When going off-piste or traveling in alpine terrain, parties have a moral responsibility to always carry:

- Avalanche beacon
- Probe
- Shovel

Paradoxically, expert skiers who have avalanche training make up a large percentage of avalanche fatalities; perhaps because they are the ones more likely to ski in areas prone to avalanches, and certainly because most people do not practice enough with their equipment to be truly fast and efficient rescuers. Even with proper rescue equipment and training, there is a one-in-five chance of dying if caught in a significant avalanche, and only a 50/50 chance of being found alive if buried more than a few minutes. The best solution is to learn how to avoid risky conditions.

Ice Slopes

For travel on slopes consisting of ice or hard snow, crampons are a standard part of a mountaineer's equipment. While step-cutting can sometimes be used on snow slopes of moderate angle, this can be a slow and tiring process, which does not provide the higher security of crampons. However, in soft snow or powder, crampons are easily hampered by balling of snow which reduce their effectiveness. In either case, an ice axe not only assists with balance but provides the climber with the possibility of self-arrest in case of a slip or fall. On a true ice slope however, an ice axe is rarely able to effect a self-arrest.

As an additional safety precaution on steep ice slopes, the climbing rope is attached to ice screws buried into the ice. True ice slopes are rare in Europe, though common in mountains located in the tropics, where newly-fallen snow quickly thaws on the surface and becomes sodden below, so that the next night's frost turns the whole mass into a sheet of semi-solid ice.

Snow Slopes

Snow slopes are very common, and usually easy to ascend. At the foot of a snow or ice slope is generally a big crevasse, called a bergschrund, where the final slope of the mountain rises from a snow-field or glacier. Such bergschrunds are generally too wide to be stepped across, and must be crossed by a snow bridge, which needs careful testing and a painstaking use of the rope.

A steep snow slope in bad condition may be dangerous, as the whole body of snow may start as an avalanche. Such slopes are less dangerous if ascended directly than obliquely, for an oblique or horizontal track cuts them across and facilitates movement of the mass.

New snow lying on ice is especially dangerous. Experience is needed for deciding on the advisability of advancing over snow in doubtful condition. Snow on rocks is usually rotten unless it is thick; snow on snow is likely to be sound. A day or two of fine weather will usually bring new snow into sound condition.

Snow cannot lie at a very steep angle, though it often deceives the eye as to its slope. Snow slopes seldom exceed 40°. Ice slopes may be much steeper. Snow slopes in early morning are usually hard and safe, but the same in the afternoon are quite soft and possibly dangerous; hence the advantage of an early start.

Crevasses

Crevasses are the slits or deep chasms formed in the substance of a glacier as it passes over an uneven bed. They may be open or hidden. In the lower part of a glacier the crevasses are open. Above the snow-line they are frequently hidden by arched-over accumulations of winter snow. The detection of hidden crevasses requires care and experience. After a fresh fall of snow they can only be detected by sounding with the pole of the ice axe, or by looking to right and left where the open extension of a partially hidden crevasse may be obvious.

The safeguard against accident is the rope, and no one should ever cross a snow-covered glacier unless roped to one, or even better to two companions. Anyone venturing onto crevasses should be trained in crevasse rescue.

Weather

The primary dangers caused by bad weather centre around the changes it causes in snow and rock conditions, making movement suddenly much more arduous and hazardous than under normal circumstances.

Whiteouts make it difficult to retrace a route while rain may prevent taking the easiest line only determined as such under dry conditions. In a storm the mountaineer who uses a compass for guidance has a great advantage over a merely empirical observer.

In large snow-fields it is, of course, easier to go wrong than on rocks, but intelligence and experience are the best guides in safely navigating objective hazards. Summer thunderstorms may produce intense lightning.

If a climber happens to be standing on or near the summit, they risk being struck. There are many cases where people have been struck by lightning while climbing mountains. In most mountainous regions, local storms develop by late morning and early afternoon. Many climbers will get an "alpine start"; that is before or by first light so as to be on the way down when storms are intensifying in activity and lightning and other weather hazards are a distinct threat to safety.

Altitude

Rapid ascent can lead to altitude sickness. The best treatment is to descend immediately. The climber's motto at high altitude is "climb high, sleep low", referring to the regimen of climbing higher to acclimatize but returning to lower elevation to sleep. In the South American Andes, the chewing of coca leaves has been traditionally used to treat altitude sickness symptoms.

Common symptoms of altitude sickness include severe headache, sleep problems, nausea, lack of appetite, lethargy and body ache. Mountain sickness may progress to High Altitude Cerebral Edema and High Altitude Pulmonary Edema, both of which can be fatal within 24 hours.

In high mountains, atmospheric pressure is lower and this means that less oxygen is available to breathe. This is the underlying cause of altitude sickness. Everyone needs to acclimatize, even exceptional mountaineers that have been to high altitude before. Generally speaking, mountaineers start using bottled oxygen when they climb above 7,000 m. Exceptional mountaineers have climbed 8000-metre peaks without oxygen, almost always with a carefully planned programme of acclimatization. In 2005, researcher and mountaineer John Semple established that above-average ozone concentrations on the Tibetan plateau may pose an additional risk to climbers.

Locations

Mountaineering has become a popular sport throughout the world. In Europe the sport largely originated in the Alps, and is still immensely popular there. Other notable mountain ranges frequented by climbers include the Caucasus, the Pyrenees and the Tatra mountains. In North America climbers frequent the Rockies and Sierra Nevada of California, the Cascades of Washington and the high peaks of Alaska. There has been a long tradition of climbers going on expeditions to the Greater Ranges, a term generally used for the Andes and the high peaks of Asia including the Himalaya, Pamirs and Tien Shan.

In the past this was often on exploratory trips or to make first ascents. With the advent of cheaper long-haul air travel mountaineering holidays in the Greater Ranges are now undertaken much more frequently and ascents of even Everest and Vinson Massif are offered as a "package holiday". Other popular mountaineering areas of more local interest include the Southern Alps of New Zealand, the Japanese Alps the Scottish Highlands and the mountains of Scandinavia.

HISTORY

- Though it is unknown whether his intention was to reach a summit, Ötzi ascended at least 3,000 m in the Alps about 5,300 years ago. His remains were found at that altitude, preserved in a glacier.

- The first recorded mountain ascent in the Common Era is Roman Emperor Hadrian's ascent of Etna to see the sun rise in 121.
- Peter III of Aragon climbed Canigou in the Pyrenees in the last quarter of the 13th century.
- The first ascent of the Popocatépetl was reported in 1289 by members of a local tribe
- Jean Buridan climbed Mont Ventoux around 1316.
- The Italian poet Petrarch wrote that on April 26, 1336 he, together with his brother and two servants, climbed to the top of Mont Ventoux. His account of the trip was composed later as a letter to his friend Dionigi di Borgo San Sepolcro.
- The Rochemelon in the Italian Alps was climbed in 1358.
- In the late 1400s and early 1500s ascents were made of numerous high peaks in the Andes, for religious purposes by the citizens of the Inca Empire and their subjects. They constructed platforms, houses and altars on many summits and carried out sacrifices, including human sacrifices. The highest peak they are known for certain to have climbed is Llullaillaco. They may also have ascended the highest peak in the Andes, Aconcagua as a sacrifice victim has been found at over 5,000 m on this peak.
- In 1492 the ascent of Mont Aiguille was made by order of Charles VIII of France. The Humanists of the 16th century adopted a new attitude towards mountains, but the disturbed state of Europe nipped in the bud the nascent mountaineering of the Zurich school.
- Leonardo da Vinci climbed to a snow-field in the neighbourhood of the Val Sesia and made scientific observations.
- In 1642 Darby Field made the first recorded ascent of Mount Washington, then known as Agiocochook, in New Hampshire.
- Konrad Gesner and Josias Simler of Zurich visited and described mountains, and made regular ascents. The use of ice axe and rope were locally invented at this time. No mountain expeditions of note are recorded in the 17th century.
- Richard Pococke and William Windham's historic visit to Chamonix was made in 1741, and set the trend for visiting glaciers.
- In 1744 the Titus was climbed, the first true ascent of a snow-mountain.
- The first attempt to ascend Mont Blanc was made in 1775 by a party of natives. In 1786 Dr Michel Paccard and Jacques Balmat gained the summit for the first time. Horace-Bénédict de Saussure, the initiator of the first ascent followed next year.
- The Norwegian mountain climber, Jens Esmark was the first person to ascend Snøhetta in 1798, part of the Dovrefjell range in Southern Norway. The same year he lead the first expedition to Bitihorn, a

small mountain in the southernmost outskirts of Jotunheimen, Norway. In 1810 he was the first person to ascend Mount Gaustatoppen in Telemark, Norway.

- The Jungfrau was climbed in 1811, the Finsteraarhorn in 1812, and the Breithorn in 1813. Thereafter, tourists showed a tendency to climb, and the body of Alpine guides began to come into existence as a consequence.
- Citlaltépetl was first climbed in 1848 by F. Maynard and G. Reynolds.
- Systematic mountaineering, as a sport, is usually dated from Sir Alfred Wills's ascent of the Wetterhorn in 1854. The first ascent of Monte Rosa was made in 1855.
- The Alpine Club was founded in London in 1857, and was soon imitated in most European countries. Edward Whymper's ascent of the Matterhorn in 1865 marked the close of the main period of Alpine conquest–the Golden age of alpinism–during which the craft of climbing was invented and 'perfected', the body of professional guides formed and their traditions fixed.
- Passing to other ranges, the exploration of the Pyrenees was concurrent with that of the Alps. The Caucasus followed, mainly owing to the initiative of D. W. Freshfield; it was first visited by exploring climbers in 1868, and most of its great peaks were climbed by 1888.
- The Edelweiss Club Salzburg was founded in Salzburg in 1881, and had 3 members make the First Ascent on 2 Eight-thousanders, Broad Peak and Dhaulagiri.
- Trained climbers turned their attention to the mountains of North America in 1888, when the Rev. W. S. Green made an expedition to the Selkirk Mountains. From that time exploration has gone on apace, and many English and American climbing parties have surveyed most of the highest peaks; Pikes Peak having been climbed by Mr. E. James and party in 1820, and Mt. Saint Elias by the Duke of the Abruzzi and party in 1897. The exploration of the highest Andes was begun in 1879-1880, when Whymper climbed Chimborazo and explored the mountains of Ecuador. The Cordillera between Chile and Argentina was visited by Dr. Gussfeldt in 1883, who ascended Maipo and attempted Aconcagua. That peak was first climbed by the Fitzgerald expedition in 1897.
- The Andes of Bolivia were first explored by Sir William Martin Conway in 1898. Chilean and Argentine expeditions revealed the structure of the southern Cordillera in the years 1885-1898. Conway visited the mountains of Tierra del Fuego.
- New Zealand's Southern Alps were first visited in 1882 by the Rev.

W. S. Green, and shortly afterwards a New Zealand Alpine Club was founded, and by their activities the exploration of the range was pushed forward. In 1895, Major Edward Arthur Fitzgerald, made an important journey in this range. Tom Fyfe and party climbed Aoraki/Mount Cook on Christmas Day 1894, denying Fitzgerald the first ascent. Fitzgerald was en route from Britain with Swiss guide Matthias Zurbriggen to claim the peak. So piqued at being beaten to the top of Mount Cook, he refused to climb it and concentrated on other peaks in the area. Later in the trip Zubriggen soloed Mount Cook up a ridge that now bears his name.

- The first mountains of the arctic region explored were those of Spitzbergen by Sir W. M. Conway's expeditions in 1896 and 1897.
- Of the high African peaks, Kilimanjaro was climbed in 1889 by Dr. Hans Meyer, Mt. Kenya in 1899 by Halford John Mackinder, and a peak of Ruwenzori by H. J. Moore in 1900.
- The Asiatic mountains were initially surveyed on orders of the British Empire. In 1892 Sir William Martin Conway explored the Karakoram Himalaya, and climbed a peak of 23,000 ft. In 1895 Albert F. Mummery died while attempting Nanga Parbat, while in 1899 D. W. Freshfield took an expedition to the snowy regions of Sikkim. In 1899, 1903, 1906 and 1908 Mrs Fannie Bullock Workman made ascents in the Himalayas, including one of the Nun Kun peaks. A number of Gurkha sepoys were trained as expert mountaineers by Major the Hon. C. G. Bruce, and a good deal of exploration was accomplished by them.
- The Rucksack Club was founded in Manchester, England in 1902.
- The American Alpine Club was founded in 1902.
- In 1902, the Eckenstein-Crowley Expedition, lead by mountaineer Oscar Eckenstein and occultist Aleister Crowley, was the first to attempt to scale Chogo Ri. They reached 22,000 feet before turning back due to weather and other mishaps.
- In 1905, Aleister Crowley led the first expedition to Kanchenjunga, the third highest mountain in the world. Four members of that party were killed in an avalanche. Some claims say they reached around 21,300 feet before turning back, however Crowley's autobiography claims they reached about 25,000 feet.
- The 1950s saw the first ascents of all the eight-thousanders but two, starting with Annapurna in 1950 by Maurice Herzog and Louis Lachenal. The world's highest mountain, Mount Everest was first climbed on May 29, 1953 by Sir Edmund Hillary and Tenzing Norgay from the south side in Nepal. Just a few months later, Hermann Buhl made the first ascent of Nanga Parbat, a remarkable solo climb, the only eight-thousander to be solo'd on the first ascent.

K2, the second highest peak in the world was first scaled in 1954. In 1964, the final eight-thousander to be climbed was Shishapangma, the lowest of all the 8,000 metre peaks.

BACKPACKING

Backpacking combines hiking and camping in a single trip. A backpacker hikes into the backcountry to spend one or more nights there, and carries supplies and equipment to satisfy sleeping and eating needs. A backpacker packs all of his or her gear into a backpack. This gear must include food, water, and shelter, or the means to obtain them, but very little else, and often in a more compact and simpler form than one would use for stationary camping.

A backpacking trip must include at least one overnight stay in the wilderness. Many backpacking trips last just a weekend but long-distance expeditions may last weeks or months, sometimes aided by planned food and supply drops. Backpacking camps are more spartan than ordinary camps. In areas that experience a regular traffic of backpackers, a hike-in camp might have a fire ring and a small wooden bulletin board with a map and some warning or information signs. Many hike-in camps are no more than level patches of ground without scrub or underbrush. In very remote areas, established camps do not exist at all, and travellers must choose appropriate camps themselves. In some places, backpackers have access to lodging that are more substantial than a tent.

In the more remote parts of Great Britain, bothies exist to provide simple accommodation for backpackers. Another example is the High Sierra Camps in Yosemite National Park. Mountain huts provide similar accommodation in other countries, so being a member of a mountain hut organization is advantageous to make use of their facilities.

On other trails there are somewhat more established shelters of a sort that offer a place for weary hikers to spend the night without needing to set up a tent. Most backpackers purposely try to avoid impacting on the land through which they travel.

This includes following established trails as much as possible, not removing anything, and not leaving residue in the backcountry. The Leave No Trace movement offers a set of guidelines for low-impact backpacking.

Professional Backpacking

For some people, backpacking is a necessary and integral part of their job. In the military a framed backpack is referred to as a "rucksack" or simply a "ruck". Soldiers who serve in the militaries of most nation-states usually receive at least some rudimentary backpacking training while infantrymen are often trained to a more advanced backpacking skill level. They share many common attributes with amateur backpackers: being self-contained, use of land-navigation skills and actively minimizing their environmental foot-print.

Although there are also a few differences such as the need to carry an assault rifle, other weapons, ammunition and communication equipment as well as at times maintaining "noise and light discipline", which means remaining silent and in darkness to avoid detection. Other professional backpackers may be scientific and academic researchers, professional guides, photographers, park-rangers and "search and rescue" personnel.

Motivation

People are drawn to backpacking primarily for recreation, to explore places that they consider beautiful and fascinating, many of which cannot be accessed in any other way. A backpacker can travel deeper into remote areas, away from people and their effects, than a day-hiker can. However, backpacking presents more advantages besides distance of travel. Many weekend trips cover routes that could be hiked in a single day, but people choose to backpack them anyway, for the experience of staying overnight. These possibilities come with disadvantages.

The weight of a pack, laden with supplies and gear, forces backpackers to travel more slowly than day-hikers would, and it can become a nuisance and a distraction from enjoying the scenery. In addition, camp chores can easily consume several hours every day. Backpackers face many risks, including adverse weather, difficult terrain, treacherous river crossings, and hungry or unpredictable animals.

They are subject to illnesses, which run the gamut from simple dehydration to heat exhaustion, hypothermia, altitude sickness, and physical injury. The remoteness of backpacking locations exacerbates any mishap.

However, these hazards do not deter backpackers who are properly prepared. Some simply accept danger as a risk that they must endure if they want to backpack; for others, the potential dangers actually enhance the allure of the wilderness.

BUNGEE JUMPING

Bungee jumping is the sport that originated from New Zealand and was created by maverick daredevil A J Hackett, and his original jump from a bridge in Greenhithe, Auckland. The sport denotes jumping from a tall structure while connected to a large rubber cord. The tall structure is usually a fixed object, such as a building, bridge, or crane; but it is also possible to jump from a movable object, such as a hot-air-balloon or a helicopter, that has the ability to hover over one spot on the ground; fixed-wing aircraft are clearly unsuitable because they only stay aloft when moving rapidly forward.

The intense thrill comes as much from the free-falls as from the rebounds. When the person jumps, the cord stretches to absorb the energy of the fall, then the jumper flies upwards again as the cord snaps back. The jumper oscillates up and down until all the energy is used up. The word bungee first appeared around 1930 and was the name for rubber eraser. The word bungy, as used by A J Hackett, is said to be "Kiwi slang for Elastic Strap". Cloth-covered rubber cords with hooks on the ends have been available for decades under the generic name bungee cords. In the 1950s David Attenborough and a BBC film crew had brought back footage of the "land divers" of Pentecost Island in Vanuatu, young men who jumped from tall wooden platforms with vines tied to their ankles as a test of courage.

This film inspired Chris Baker of Bristol, England to use elastic rope in a kind of urban vine jumping. The first modern bungee jump was made on 1 April 1979 from the 250ft Clifton Suspension Bridge in Bristol, and was made by four members of the Dangerous Sports Club. The jumpers, led by David Kirke, were arrested shortly after, but continued with jumps in the US from the Golden Gate and Royal Gorge bridges, spreading the concept worldwide.

By 1982 they were jumping from mobile cranes and hot air balloons, and putting on commercial displays. One of the first operators of a commercial bungee jumping concern enabling the general public to experience these leaps of faith was New Zealander, A J Hackett, who made his first jump from Auckland's Greenhithe Bridge in 1986. During the following years Hackett performed a number of jumps from bridges and other structures building public interest in the sport. Hackett remains one of the largest commercial operators, with concerns in several countries.

The worlds first permanent commercial bungee site was the Kawarau Bridge Bungy at Queenstown in the South Island of New Zealand. Despite the inherent danger of jumping from a great height, several million successful jumps have taken place since 1980. This is attributable to bungee operators rigorously conforming to standards and guidelines governing jumps, such as double checking calculations and fittings for every jump. As with any sport, injuries can still occur, but there have been few fatalities. A relatively common mistake in fatality cases is to use too long a cord.

The cord should be substantially shorter than the height of the jumping platform to allow it room to stretch. When the cord reaches its natural length the jumper either starts to slow down or keep accelerating. depending upon the speed of descent. One may not even start to slow until the cord has already stretched somewhat, because the cord's resistance to distortion is zero at the natural length, and increases only gradually after, taking some time to even equal the jumper's weight.

RAFTING

Rafting or whitewater rafting is a recreational activity utilizing a raft to navigate a river or other bodies of water. This is usually done on whitewater or different degrees of rough water, in order to thrill and excite the raft passengers. The development of this activity as a leisure sport has become popular since the mid 1970s. Rafting is one of the earliest means of transportation, used as a means for shipping people, hunting, and transferring food. In 1842, Lieutenant John Fremont of the U.S. Army first journalized his rafting expedition on the Platte River.

Horace H. Day designed the equipment he used in rafting. Day's rafts were constructed from four independent rubber cloth tubes and wrap-around floor. In 1960s, rafting was then recognized and paths like Grand Canyon were routed and whitewater rafting companies were established. In 1970s, rafting marked its major development as a leisure sport when it was then included in the Munich Olympic Games.

In 1980s, as rafting continued to gain its popularity, a lot of rivers were opened for rafting activities. Rivers in South America and Africa were just a few of them. In 1990s, rafting was included in major game events like the Barcelona Games in 1992, Atlanta Games in 1996, and the whitewater events of the Summer Olympic Games hosted by Ocoee River in Tennessee Valley.

In addition, the International Federation of Rafting was instituted in 1997 and in 1999 the first Official International Championship was held. Nowadays, river rafting is still gaining popularity among extreme water sports in order to thrill and excite the raft passengers.

ROCK CLIMBING

Rock climbing, broadly speaking, is the act of ascending steep rock formations. Normally, climbers use gear and safety equipment specifically designed for the purpose. Strength, endurance, and mental control are required to cope with tough, dangerous physical challenges, and knowledge of climbing techniques and the use of essential pieces of gear and equipment are crucial.

Although the practice of rock climbing was an important component of Victorian mountaineering in the Alps, it is generally thought that the sport of rock climbing began in the last quarter of the nineteenth century in various parts of Europe. Rock climbing evolved gradually from an alpine necessity to an athletic sport in its own right.

As rock climbing matured, grading systems were created in order to more accurately compare relative difficulties of climbs. Over the years, both climbing techniques, and the equipment climbers use to advance the sport, have evolved in a steady fashion.

ADVENTURE TOURISM IN INDIA

ANGLING IN INDIA

Today, in India, the sport of angling is combined with conservation. As per the existing Indian protection laws, the fish is allowed to be caught, but must be released within a stipulated time period. The average time taken to land a Mahseer is in ratio to its weight—5 minutes to 5 lbs. With just enough time to record its weight, and preserve your moment of glory with the prize catch of film, before the fish is revived-you have to be really quick or else it could just end up as one of those fishy stories of, "the great one that got away."

CAMEL SAFARI IN INDIA

Thar Desert Camel Safaris of India are now one of Asia's fastest selling adventure holidays. These include camel treks ranging from short rides around Jaisalmer to extensive trips that remind you of Lawrence of Arabia on his epic journey across the Sahara, Marco Polo, on the historic silk route, a medieval trader leading his caravan through the hostile spice route or a royal caravan serai heading for one of the medieval kingdoms of the Thar desert-without many of the hardships of course! They are a great way to see the desert and to enjoy a novel and adventurous holiday.

The Great Indian Desert may not have great expanses of sand dunes and incredible spaces of wilderness as large as those of the Sahara and Namibia, but more than makes up for it with some glorious citadels and extremely colourful and unspoilt villages. Its sand dunes are more easily accessible from airports and railway stations than those of many African countries.

CAMEL SAFARI CIRCUIT IN INDIA

The Camel Safari Circuit in India comprises of Jaisalmer, Jodhpur, and Bikaner, all in Rajasthan. They were the princely kingdoms in the desert belt of India Rajasthan. Each was comparable in size to many modern nations of Europe. All the former capitals prospered from trade with the camel caravans that traveled from West Asia and Europe to Mongolia, and were impressively fortified to protect these riches. The result was a wealth of palaces built for royalty, havelis or courtyard mansions built for merchants and nobility and intricately carved temples for the subjects.

Materials used were normally sandstone, which was easily available and provided a better medium to the silavats who specialized in making stone resemble lace. A camel safari is a great way to see the desert-visiting the villages, seeing wildlife, and riding across the open desert sands. Typical camel safaris organized around Jaisalmer take in the architectural ruins of Lodurva which was the former capital of the Bhatti Rajput desert kingdom before the founding of Jaisalmer, the Anasagar oasis, the sand dunes of Samm and the water source of Moolsagar where village women gather with pitchers at dusk. Night halts on basic safaris are at villages on the way or temporary bivouac camps in the desert scrub where camels are hobbled and let out to browse.

CAMEL SAFARI IN INDIA-TRAVEL KIT

The climate is extreme in the desert-afternoons may seem much hotter than the actual 26-30 degree temperature may suggest. Night temperatures may drop below zero on the dunes. It is essential to stock both woolen and cotton clothing. Shorts and skirts are comfortable wear for camel safaris but remember some of the off beat routes visit villages that have not seen many tourists and locals may look askance at ladies who do not wear ankle length clothing and men in shorts.

Sun hats with large rims or cotton caps that can be dipped in water when it gets too hot around midday, are essential preferably with a balaclava or scarf for covering the neck and forehead.

At Jodhpur you can buy umbrellas that are quite convenient for camel safaris. Sunscreen cream, moisturizers and lip salve area must. A water bottle can be comfortably slung on the camel saddle and it is practical also to carry tangerines as even on a deluxe safari it may not be practical to dismount each time to drink from the carted water supply. Bottled mineral water is available at Jodhpur and Jaisalmer. Find out if the baggage is being transferred by camel cart or vehicle.

In case of the latter, a small handbag can carry the essentials you are likely to need on the way. If prone to sickness, carry suitable medication against the swaying gait of the camel. A torch, penknife an even cutlery will be required. Finally patience is an important piece of baggage on a camel safari as it takes time to get to grips with camel travel and to reach destinations that may be on your travel priorities.

MOUNTAINEERING IN INDIA

Mountaineering as a sport has a history as old as the history of the evolution of human race itself. Mountaineering started when the need was felt for people who could climb difficult heights and terrains to meet people across the border, to trade, or to conquer new territories. In the course of time, man developed new modes of transportation and communication and venturing out on these difficult routes were not needed. Nevertheless, what remained was his nature to take risks and getting pleasure in conquering something totally unknown and unexplored.

This inner urge to take up challenges has led man to do things that are quite daring. In India, mountaineering as a sport came with the Europeans in the 18th century. That was a time when entire Europe was experiencing a new phase.

New regions were being explored, won, and native peoples were being made to become civilized. This zeal of adventurism found its ultimate fruition in the Himalayas-lofty, extremely difficult to conquer, and challenging enough to send a man back to his mother's womb. But, being men, these challenges were accepted and there began a tussle between men's ambitions and nature's reluctance.

New heights were conquered, new routes were discovered, many lives lost, but the mission was accomplished. Today, almost all the major peaks are conquered and even general people have started taking mountaineering as a serious hobby. For starters, India offers a wide spectrum of options for mountaineering as well as other related sports. Peaks and trekking routes are classified and maps are available for the interested travellers. Many institutes provide basic and advanced level courses in mountaineering and other related sports. All the equipment is locally available and other support resources can be found here.

PARAGLIDING IN INDIA

If you like Icarus ever wished to fly, as suggested, make your dream realise. The adventure of paragliding is something you just cannot miss. Soar over the hills, dip whenever you aspire to get a better view of the Earth, glide and sail, feel the freedom of the bird. The adventure of being at the altitude needs an attitude! No noise pollution, no smoke just plain fun. The thrill of have your own wings, the big wide sky with no traffic jams is a safe and easy aero adventure.

Paragliding is fun for the people who constantly would love to reach new heights. Be amongst the stars during the day and count the constellations at night! Live life happily in the lap of Mother Nature. The package offers training for the novice too. Come fly, with us. The paraglider, harness, helmets, radios and ankle boots are equipments required for the adventure. Besides the monsoon season, the sky is your road for the escapade, come on touch the sky.

ELEPHANT SAFARI

How about a safari atop an elephant? Jeeps and other mechanical means of transportation may distract the fellow animals in the jungle. The Elephant is the best possible option available to admire the beauty of nature. The wildlife adventure in India is incomplete if an Elephant safari is not include in the itinerary. Come and explore the wild terrain of the Corbett National Park on the most majestic animal of all. Even horse safaris do well with the tourists in India. The strong and sturdy animal has since long been galloping across the terrific terrain in India.

ROCK CLIMBING IN INDIA

It is not quite easy to define rock climbing, but it is not difficult too. Anyone who claims to be a rock climber has his own version of the game. Rock climbing for some is to challenge their spirits and explore new heights, to give a fillip to their unbounded imaginations; for others, it is a way telling the world that he/she has finally arrived. For many of the professional rock climbers, it is not a sport.

Can you call a mission to moon a sport or pastime? If not, then why should rock climbing be called a sports is the argument. For them, rock climbing is an adventure of the greatest magnitude; it is a fight against self, against the elements, and the ultimate goal is to reach the summit and return back alive.

SCUBA DIVING IN INDIA

One of the greatest adventures in life can be to explore the totally unknown and unexplored world under sea. The joy of floating inside the sea like a fish where every creature is your friend and every new sight is a discovery can be immense. In addition, the sheer thrill of watching the rich flora and fauna of the sea in their natural habitat is unparalleled. The curiosity to know the underwater world of the sea is not a new phenomenon for human civilization. We have so many stories from the epic Ramayana describing the world beneath the sea when Hanuman was crossing the sea to reach Lanka.

The origin of many mythical characters and objects are related to the sea. There is a legend about Samudra Manthan that tells us that the sea was churned around a hill known as Meru with a snake around it. The gods pulled one end of the snake while the other end was pulled by the demons. Many amazing things came out of this exploration-an elephant called Airavata that became the property of Indra, a tree called Kalpavriksa that could grant anything, a cow known as Kamdhenu that gave milk everyday, the Goddess of wealth Lakshmi, the god of Ayurveda Dhanawantari, the Visha and Amrit. Scuba diving and snorkeling as sports came with the Europeans who saw the vast expanse of the Indian coastline. Besides, many Indians who experienced this unique adventure also brought with them a new and exciting option for their fellow countrymen.

Stretching many thousand kilometers, the Indian coastline spans the mighty waters of the Arabian Sea, the Indian Ocean and the Bay of Bengal. Dotted with the finest beaches, cliff promontories, mangroves, backwater, jewel-like island groups and marine life, there are wide diving possibilities. While there are many popular easily accessible sites, many more can be explored which are not at all known.

The sight of the smashing waves creating foaming breakers on the coral reef, which enclose azure lagoons whose crystal clear waters wash the fine grained white sands of the palm dotted low islands, is one of the few marvels of God's creations left untouched by the encroaching hands of industrialization and progress. The underwater city is a unique and diverse collection of colourful and weirdly patterned sea animals. Corals take pride of place in these reef cities.

Rich in variety and colour, the thousands of types of corals range from tall sea fans to small hydroids, from languidly waving sea anemones to glassy jellyfish. Danger there is, but only enough to add to the sense of adventure and thrill. This fun is multiplied many times over as you don the scuba gear. This gear has been especially devised for the deep sea diver and gives an opportunity for thrill and adventure unparalleled and unimagined by ones who think of the sea as nothing but a large saltwater lake.

India is fast becoming the adventure tourism destination of the world; and scuba diving and snorkeling as well as other water sports are going to be an integral part of this. If you have not had adventure in India, you do not know what adventure is all about.

SKIING IN INDIA

The sheer joie de vivre inspired by one's first successful slide down a ski slope defies description. Once limited to a privileged few, the adrenalin-producing pastime of skiing has been brought within the range of the common man now. For the purist, there is unsullied, powdery snow. For the accomplished and ego-conscious, there are punishing runs. For wobbly beginners and confident intermediates, there are easy slopes and understanding instructors who soon inspire dreams of Olympic glory.

With a first run to buoy one under the belt, there follows a succession of blissful days. Each day brings a fresh challenge to conquer and relish when you are at any skiing resort. Mastering the twists and turns and jumps of skiing, completing a longer ski run, and achieving faster speed are all part of this process.

Every winter in the Indian Himalayas the slopes are warmed by the excited cries and laughter of entrants being introduced to the joys of winter sports: the magic of the wind rushing past as you whiz down a slope of skis, or the sheer pleasure of gliding gracefully, artistically cutting figures of eight in the snow. Skiing, like any other high-altitude adventure sports in India, is a contribution of the Europeans. The summers in north India have always been unpleasant, more so for the Europeans who were mostly from the cold countries.

To save themselves from this oppressive heat, they went to the Himalayas, not too far from major centres in north India. Many hill stations were established, the prominent among them being Shimla, Manali, Mussoorie, and Nainital. These places served not only as the home away from home for them but also as the centre where they could participate in recreational activities like skiing and trekking. Some of these places still have the best skiing slopes in the country. Affluent Indians started participating in this sport even before independence.

After independence, with the efforts of adventure sport bodies, local youths were encouraged to participate in this sport. They took to it enthusiastically and later helped in training hordes of tourists coming from other parts of the county and even abroad.

Today, skiing is quite popular in the hill stations of North India and new facilities have added up to make it more popular among the masses.

TREKKING IN INDIA

Off late, trekking in India is becoming popular among the tourists all over the world. This might have been a new phenomenon for the travellers from abroad, for Indians, these mountains signify not only the natural beauty but also a source of spiritual guidance.

Trekking has remained men's passion from the day he took his first step on the earth. He always ventured out of home and his natural surroundings to explore something new, a world that was unknown to him. It is astonishing to learn that the human race migrated from one continent to another when there were no means of communication, no helping hands, and most of them who left their home could never return back.

WHITE WATER RAFTING IN INDIA

If you want to get some kick, some change in life, or just to have some fun, river rafting can satisfy most of your desires. If you have the zeal, then go for the challenge and show others that you can do it. White-water rafting is not for fashionable thrill seekers, but for those who thrive on hair-soaking risks, which keep the adrenalin flowing overtime! The thrill of rushing down fast-flowing mountain streams a froth with huge waves, dashing against dangerous boulders and dizzy rapids, while you cling for dear life dependent on a fragile, inflatable rubber raft or dinghy. Be swept along a rushing river in a rubber raft, tumble over rapids, plunge over waterfalls and feel the icy spray splash on your face, as your raft races along a mountain river in India.

Experience the thrill of white water rafting in India along tumbling snow-fed Himalayan rivers in summer destinations in India. River rafting in India is an exhilarating experience that you can enjoy on your Indian Holiday. One of the best regions for river rafting in India is the stretch upto Rishikesh in Uttaranchal. White water rafting on Alaknanda, Bhagirathi and Ganga rivers is a popular adventure tourism activity in summer in India. For the more adventurous traveller, white water rafting tours in India can also be organized on the Indus River in Ladakh and Brahmaputra River in Arunachal Pradesh White water rafting in India on the Alaknanda River is the most easily accessible white water river rafting stretch from Delhi. We drive from Delhi to Rishikesh and further north to Devprayag, where the Alaknanda River and Bhagirati River combine to form the Ganges, a river considered holy by Hindus in India.

Further North is Rudraprayag, where the Alaknanda and Mandakini Rivers combine. The white water rafting Alaknanda tour, consists of an approximately 130 Km long stretch from Rudraprayag to Shivpuri near Rishikesh in Uttaranchal, India. You will be given training by experienced river rafting instructors and guides. You will travel in groups in rafts, with an instructor at all times. Life jackets and other essential safety equipment are provided. You can stay overnight in luxury tents, pitched on beaches alongside the river, as we halt each night.

You can also enjoy campfires and bonfire nights on river rafting tours in India. As you swoop and tumble over the rapids with exotic names such as 'Roller Coaster;' 'Crossfire' and 'The Wall' you will feel the excitement and heart-racing thrill of white water rafting in India, on adventure tours to India this summer, with Indian Holiday.

MEDICAL TOURISM

Medical tourism can be broadly defined as provision of 'cost effective' private medical care in collaboration with the tourism industry for patients needing surgical and other forms of specialized treatment. This process is being facilitated by the corporate sector involved in medical care as well as the tourism industry-both private and public. Medical tourism refers to traveling to other countries to obtain medical, dental, and surgical treatment.

At the same time they could also tour, and fully experience the attractions of the countries they visit. Exorbitant costs of healthcare in industrialized nations, ease and affordability of international travel, favourable currency exchange rates in the global economy, rapidly improving technology and standards of care in many countries of the world, and most importantly proven safety of healthcare in select foreign nations have all led to the rise of medical tourism. Medical tourism is a term initially coined by travel agencies and the mass media to describe to the rapidly-growing practice of traveling to another country to obtain health care.

Such services typically include elective procedures as well as complex specialized surgeries such as joint replacement cardiac surgery, dental surgery, and cosmetic surgeries. The provider and customer use informal channels of communication-connection-contract, with less regulatory or legal oversight to assure quality and less formal recourse to reimbursement or redress, if needed. Leisure aspects typically associated with travel and tourism may be included on such medical travel trips.

The concept of medical tourism is not a new one. The first recorded instance of medical tourism dates back thousands of years to when Greek pilgrims traveled from all over the Mediterranean to the small territory in the Saronic Gulf called Epidauria. This territory was the sanctuary of the healing god Asklepios. Epidauria became the original travel destination for medical tourism. Spa towns may be considered an early form of medical tourism.

DESCRIPTION

Factors that have led to the recent increase in popularity of medical travel include the high cost of health care or wait times for procedures in industrialized nations, the ease and affordability of international travel, and improvements in technology and standards of care in many countries of the world. Medical tourists can come from anywhere in the world, including Europe, the UK, Middle East, Japan, U.S. and Canada.

This is because of their large populations, comparatively high wealth, the high expense of health care or lack of health care options locally, and increasingly high expectations of their populations with respect to health care. A large draw to medical travel is convenience and speed. Countries that operate public health-care systems are often so taxed that it can take considerable time to get non-urgent medical care. The time spent waiting for a procedure such as a hip replacement can be a year or more in Britain and Canada; however, in Singapore, Hong Kong, Thailand, Cuba, Colombia, Philippines or India, a patient could feasibly have an operation the day after their arrival. In Canada, the number of procedures in 2005 for which people were waiting was 782,936. Additionally, patients are finding that insurance either does not cover orthopedic surgery or imposes unreasonable restrictions on the choice of the facility, surgeon, or prosthetics to be used.

Medical tourism for knee/hip replacements has emerged as one of the more widely accepted procedures because of the lower cost and minimal difficulties associated with the traveling to/from the surgery. Colombia provides a knee replacement for about $5,000 USD, including all associated fees such as FDA approved prosthetics and hospital stay over expenses. However, many clinics quote prices that are not all inclusive and include only the surgeon fees associated with the procedure. Medical tourists may seek essential health care services such as cancer treatment and brain and transplant surgery as well as complementary or 'elective' services such as aesthetic treatments.

A research found in an object by a famous university: "the cost of surgery in Bolivia, Argentina, Cuba, India, Thailand, Colombia, Philippines or South Africa can be one-tenth of what it is in the United States or Western Europe, and sometimes even less. A heart-valve replacement that would cost US$200,000 or more in the U.S., for example, goes for $10,000 in the Philippines and India—and that includes round-trip airfare and a brief vacation package. Similarly, a metal-free dental bridge worth $5,500 in the U.S. costs $500 in India or Bolivia and only $200 in the Philippines, a knee replacement in Thailand with six days of physical therapy costs about one-fifth of what it would in the States, and Lasik eye surgery worth $3,700 in the U.S. is available in many other countries for only $730.

Cosmetic surgery savings are even greater: A full facelift that would cost $20,000 in the U.S. runs about $3,000 in Cuba, $2,700 in the Philippines or $2,500 in South Africa or $ 2,300 in Bolivia."To understand the phenomenon of medical travel, we can compare the average costs of cosmetic surgeries between the industrialized nations and Latin America countries where medical tourism and cosmetic surgery tourism are becoming popular, such as Argentina, Bolivia, Brazil, Costa Rica, Colombia, Philippines, and Mexico.

Popular medical travel worldwide destinations include: Brunei, Cuba, Colombia,Hong Kong, Hungary, India, Israel, Jordan, Lithuania, Malaysia, The Philippines, Singapore, South Africa, Thailand, and recently, UAE and New Zealand. Popular cosmetic surgery travel destinations include: Argentina, Bolivia, Brazil, Colombia, Costa Rica, Cuba, Mexico and Turkey. In Europe Belgium, Poland and Slovakia are also breaking into the business. South Africa is taking the term "medical tourism" very literally by promoting their "medical safaris": Come to see African wildlife and get a facelift in the same trip. However, perceptions of medical tourism are not always positive.

In places like the U.S., where most have insurance and access to quality health care, medical tourism is viewed as risky. In some parts of the world, wider political issues can influence where medical tourists will choose to seek out health care; for example, in late 2006, some patients from the Middle East were choosing to travel to Singapore or Hong Kong for health care rather than to the U.S. because of international tensions. While the tourism component might be a big draw for some Southeast Asia countries that focus on simple procedures, India is positioning itself the primary medical destination for the most complex medical procedures in the world.

India's commitment to this is demonstrated with a growing number of hospitals that are attaining the U.S. Joint Commission International accreditation to help to capture the US medical tourism market, while others looking beyond just the US market to potential clients from the United Kingdom, Europe and Australia may also look towards other international healthcare accreditation schemes for brand advantage. Singapore positions itself as a medical hub for health care services, medicine, biomedical research and pharmaceutical manufacturing converge. Singapore has made international news for many complex surgeries in specialties such as neurology, oncology, and organ transplants procedures.

Currently Singapore boasts the largest number of U.S. Joint Commission accredited hospitals in the region. In South America, countries such as Argentina, Bolivia, Brazil and Colombia lead on plastic surgery medical skills relying on the vast experience their surgeons have in treating the style-obsessed. It is estimated that 1 in 30 Argentineans have had plastic surgery procedures, making this population the most operated in the world after the U.S. and Mexico. In Bolivia and Colombia, plastic surgery has become quite common. The "Sociedad Boliviana de Cirugia Plastica y Reconstructiva", more that 70% of middle and upper class women in the country have had some form of plastic surgery. Colombia also provides advanced care in cardiovascular and transplant surgery.

Companies are beginning to offer global health care options that will enable North American and European patients to access world health care at a fraction of the cost of domestic care. Companies that focus on 'Medical Value Travel' typically provide experienced nurse case managers to assist patients with pre-and post-travel medical issues. They also help provide resources for follow-up care upon the patient's return. While these services will initially be of interest to the self-insured patient, several studies indicate that the rapid growth of Health Savings Accounts in the U.S. will also drive interest to health care in other countries.

INDIA

India is known in particular for heart surgery, hip resurfacing and other areas of advanced medicine. The government and private hospital groups are committed to the goal of making India a world leader in the industry. The industry's main appeal is low-cost treatment. Most estimates claim treatment costs in India start at around a tenth of the price of comparable treatment in America or Britain. Estimates of the value of medical tourism to India go as high as $2 billion a year by 2012.

The Indian government is taking steps to address other infrastructure issues that can serve as a deterrant to the country's growth in medical tourism. The south Indian city of Chennai has been declared India's Health Capital, as it nets in 45% of health tourists from abroad and 30-40% of domestic health tourists.

CULTURAL TOURISM

'Cultural tourism' is the subset of tourism concerned with a country or region's culture, especially its arts. It generally focuses on traditional communities who have diverse customs, unique form of art and distinct social practices, which basically distinguishes it from other types/forms of culture. Cultural tourism includes tourism in urban areas, particularly historic or large cities and their cultural facilities such as museums and theatres. It can also include tourism in rural areas showcasing the traditions of indigenous cultural communities and their values and lifestyle. It is generally agreed that cultural tourists spend substantially more than standard tourists do. This form of tourism is also becoming generally more popular throughout Europe.

DEFINITION

By definition, the term destination refers broadly to any given area where tourism is a relatively important activity, like for instance having an economy significantly influenced by tourism revenues. However, it is complicated by the fact that a single, recognizable destination may include several cities, towns or municipalities, provinces, or other government entities-in island archipelago it may be the entire country.

LIVING CULTURAL AREAS

Due to globalization, technology and the onset of cultural tourism and ecotourism, the number of living cultural areas is continually declining. For an indigenous culture that has stayed largely separated from the surrounding majority, tourism can present both advantages and problems. On the positive side are the unique cultural practices and arts that attract the curiosity of tourists and provide opportunities for tourism and economic development. On the negative side is the issue of how to control tourism so that those same cultural amenities are not destroyed and the people do not feel violated.

Chiloe, Chile

Chiloe is Chiloes largest island, located at the midway point between the capital, Santiago, and the country's extreme south at Tierra del Fuego. Chiloe is the site of the Chiloé Model Forest, member of the same network as the Calakmul and Eastern Ontario Model Forests. Having evolved for centuries isolated from mainland Chile, the "Chilotes" developed a strong, self-reliant culture, rich in folklore, mythology and tradition.

This very identity is what constitutes the island's major attraction for domestic tourists in Chile and increasingly, for international tourists. As in the Calakmul case above, tourism to Chiloé is very strongly based on the island's cultural heritage, predominantly consisting of crafts markets, appreciation of cultural landscapes, museum exhibitions, seafood cuisine and architectural heritage.

However, the average tourist to the island will have little opportunity to see Chilotes involved in their living cultural activities, such as the elaborate preparation of the islands famous "curanto" meal, rich in shellfish, meat and potatoes, the management practices of their farm and forest lands, boat building and more. In order to overcome the cultural and organizational barriers that keep suppliers of living cultural heritage and tour operators apart, the Chiloé diocese of Ancud established a private foundation called "Fundación con Todos". Among other activities, the Foundation has played a key role in helping a number of Chilote households organize themselves into an "agrotourism" network.

The Foundation helped Chilote households make the preparation required to accommodate tourists and complemented this effort with a professional marketing campaign. These works were undertaken with the financial support of other agencies. Again, in cooperation with the EOMF and the Chiloé Model Forest, a cultural and natural heritage tour was organized to Argentina and Chile, including a three-day visit to Chiloé, permitting some of the Chilote households to host a group of cultural heritage tourists for the first time. The visits were very successful and should be the first of more to come, helping establish the credibility of Chiloé's agrotourism network among other tour operators.

Orrissa Tribes

Nestling on the eastern coast of India, Orissa is one of the most exquisite regions dominated by exotic sandy beaches, plenteous wild life, and holy temples famous for their architectural splendor and primitive lifestyle.

The charm of the city is still well-nigh chaste and unrevealed by the visitors, up to its full extent. The other lure of the city lies in its tribal population dotted with more than 62 tribal communities. The tribal communities of Orissa constitute about 23% of its total population. Orissa is inhabited by tribes like Saora or Sabar that had a respectable mentioning in the epic of Mahabharata. Mostly the Orissa tribes are high land habitats with opulent ethnic trait, cultures and customs dominated by varying languages. The culture conscious tribes are able to preserve their social customs and dignified values. The most primitive tribes are Bondas, Gadabas, Koyas, Kondhas and Sauras. The culture of tribal Orissa is affluent with their own folk songs and dances, their tattoos. Tribal culture of Orissa is well depicted in its modern city in form of poems, art and craft or music. The tribes have adapted the Hindu traditions and culture from centuries, which is mixed with their own culture giving a distinct zest to the entire racial. Songs and dances are the essence of the tribal culture of Orissa. The traditions and the ceremonies for wedding, birth and death all are represented by singing songs, rural dances along with feasts. The Tribal Folk Orissan tribes are strong, assiduous and simple hospitable tribes, normally like to be reserved and maintain distance from the people of other communities, as they are too shy. The major occupation of these tribes is agriculture and fishing and hunting.

Men usually wear loin attire and women rap long stretch of cloth around them. Women are adorned with ornaments like bangles, armlets, bracelets, necklaces, rings, hairpins etc usually made of silvers, aluminum, and brass. The practice of tattooing is prevalent among women folk. Girls above 5 years are found with tattoo mark on their faces and hands. Festival Celebration Numbers of deities are worshiped by the tribes for their happy life. Many festivals are also celebrated with much of enthusiasm and excitement. The ceremony rituals are observed through out the year in order to appease their deities and ascendant. The most significant festival of the year are the chaita parab and push parab-this day all able men of the village go on a hunting expedition. The tribes with their cultural dance, song and music all distinguish custom of their artistic life, which demarcate them from the other non tribal groups.

Orissa acquire every thing Orissa is a state, embellished with hilly terrain of the Eastern Ghats, where primitive tribes dwell and a beautiful stretch of the Indo-Aryans coast where modern life persists. A blend of 2 discrete civilization with contrast cultures, beautiful landscapes, beaches, rich wildlife, offers the best of India to its visitors. As the issue of globalization takes place to this modern time, the challenge of preserving the few remaining cultural community around the world is becoming hard. In a tribal based community, reaching economic advancement with minimal negative impacts is an essential objective to any destination planner. Since they are using the culture of the region as the main attraction, sustainable destination development of the area is vital for them to prevent the negative impacts because of tourism.

MANAGEMENT ISSUES

Certainly, the principle of "one size fits all" doesn't apply to destination planning. The needs, expectations, and anticipated benefits from tourism vary greatly from one destination to another. This is clearly exemplified as local communities living in regions with tourism potential develop a vision for what kind of tourism they want to facilitate, depending on issues and concerns they want to be settled or satisfied.

DESTINATION PLANNING RESOURCES

Culture: The Heart of Development Policy

It is important that the destination planner takes into account the diverse definition of culture as the term is subjective.

Satisfying tourists' interests such as landscapes, seascapes, art, nature, traditions, ways of life and other products associated to them-which may be categorized cultural in the broadest sense of the word, is a prime consideration as it marks the initial phase of the development of a cultural destination.

The quality of service and destination, which doesn't solely depend on the cultural heritage but more importantly to the cultural environment, can further be developed by setting controls and policies which shall govern the community and its stakeholders.

It is therefore safe to say that the planner should be on the ball with the varying meaning of culture itself as this fuels the formulation of development policies that shall entail efficient planning and monitored growth.

Local Community, Tourists, the Destination and Sustainable Tourism

While satisfying tourists' interests and demands may be a top priority, it is also imperative to ruminate the subsystems of the destination's. Development pressures should be anticipated and set to their minimum level so as to conserve the area's resources and prevent a saturation of the destination as to not abuse the product and the residents correspondingly. The plan should incorporate the locals to its gain by training and employing them and in the process encourage them to participate to the travel business.

Keep in mind that the plan should make travellers not only aware about the destination but also concern on how to help it sustain its character while broadening their travelling experience.

SOURCES OF DATA

The core of a planner's job is to design an appropriate planning process and facilitate community decision. Ample information which is a crucial requirement is contributed through various technical researches and analyses.

Here are some of the helpful tools commonly used by planners to aid them:

- Key Informant Interviews
- Libraries, Internet, and Survey Research
- Census and Statistical Analysis
- Spatial Analysis with Geographical Information System and Global Positioning System technologies

KEY INSTITUTIONS

Participating structures are primarily led by the government's local authorities and the official tourism board or council, with the involvement of various NGOs, community and indigenous representatives, development organizations, and the academe.

Cultural and Ecotourism in the Mountainous Regions of Central Asia and in the Himalayas

Tourism is coming to the previously isolated but spectacular mountainous regions of Central Asia, the Hindu Kush and the Himalayas. Closed for so many years to visitors from abroad, it now attracts a growing number of foreign tourists by its unique culture and splendid natural beauty. However, while this influx of tourists is bringing economic opportunities and employment to local populations, helping to promote these little-known regions of the world, it has also brought challenges along with it: to ensure that it is well-managed and that its benefits are shared by all.

As a response to this concern, the Norwegian Government, as well as the UNESCO, organized an interdisciplinary project called the Development of Cultural and Eco-tourism in the Mountainous Regions of Central Asia and the Himalayas project.

It aims to establish links and promote cooperation between local communities, national and international NGOs, and tour agencies in order to heighten the role of the local community and involve them fully in the employment opportunities and income-generating activities that tourism can bring.

Project activities include training local tour guides, producing high-quality craft items and promoting home-stays and bed-and-breakfast type accommodation. As of now, the project is drawing on the expertise of international NGOs and tourism professionals in the seven participating countries, making a practical and positive contribution to alleviating poverty by helping local communities to draw the maximum benefit from their region's tourism potential, while protecting the environmental and cultural heritage of the region concerned.

ETHNIC TOURISM

Ethnic tourism is related to the more popularly known nature or eco-tourism. In nature tourism, people visit a region, usually in a third world country, in order to enjoy its natural beauty. Nature tourism can also imply social awareness because it "creates an understanding of cultural and natural history, while safeguarding the integrity of the ecosystem and producing economic benefits that encourage conservation".

Ethnic tourism is the addition of an indigenous or traditional group of people who live in this environment and interact and depend upon it. Visitors enjoy both the natural environment and the singular ethnic experience. Because of the ethnic groups' dependence on the environment, it is difficult to separate ethnic tourism from the landscape in which it occurs. Hence, nature and ethnic tourism are often interrelated and inseparable. From the visitor's point of view, ethnic tourism is "travel motivated by the search for the firsthand, authentic and sometimes intimate contact with people whose ethnic and/or cultural background is different from the tourists". Ethnic tourists are also driven by the desire to see some of the "threatened" cultures which may soon disappear through assimilation into the nation's majority. The visitor's experience usually includes opportunities to see and photograph people in their traditional dress, observe their living conditions, and purchase local handicrafts.

Ethnic and nature tourism can help protect indigenous people and their environments by providing a sustainable alternative to subsistence agriculture and extractive activities such as timber harvesting. The added income and exposure can satisfy national goals of development while contributing to cultural pride and autonomy. Ethnic tourism can also have many negative consequences including commoditization of culture, social tension, and loss of cultural identity. In any case, tourism brings changes as groups gain or lose ownership, access, and use rights, and adjust to a new economic system. The varying controllers of tourism play a major role in the changes and effects wrought by tourism on the resident population.

National parks and similar protected areas are the most recognizable forms of nature and ethnic tourism. These large scale, federally controlled land management systems preserve the land which is often in danger of encroachment and extraction activities. Some national parks are designed to protect the environment and the indigenous group dependent on that environment such as Odzalla National Park in Congo, the Kalahari Reserves in Botswana, Manu Park in Peru, Gates of the Arctic Monument in Alaska, Kluane Park in the Yukon, Kakadu National Park in the Northern Territory in Australia, Varirata National Park in Papua New Guinea, and Honduras Rio Platano Biosphere Reserves. However, federal control of these lands often neglect the needs or input of the parks' residents.

For example, the nomadic Masai who migrate seasonally with their cattle through Amboseli and Serengeti National Parks in Kenya and Tanzania have increasingly come into conflict with park administrators who have placed priority on preserving large tracts of savanna woodlands and wildlife over that of the Masai's traditional sustainable lifestyle. Although most tourists come to see the wildlife, increasing numbers also want to view the Masai. This form of ethnic tourism brings few benefits for the Masai who have hardly any crafts and no control over tourism.

In other parks, like Sagarmatha National Park in Nepal, much of the resident population does benefit from tourism. The Sherpa have supplemented their herding lifestyle with jobs relating to tourism but have little control over tourist access. As the national government promotes Sagarmatha for tourism, the demand for material needs like wood for heat increases. As the environment is degraded due to deforestation, the Sherpa must compete with outsiders for their own resources. Hence, national parks sometimes hurt more than help the local populations who live in and around these protected areas. An alternative to national, people-exclusive projects is a project or approach to tourism that includes the resident population and recognizes the value of traditional techniques that can help manage the environment.

Outside assisted projects vary from obvious governmental or organizational influence and control to projects promoted as "grassroots" or "bottom-up" but which include outside influence in planning and implementation. "Local participation at all stages" is a phrase included in most project documents but not always strictly followed. Outside assistance can provide ideas and needed capital but can also produce many problems. One example is the Toraja of southern Sulawesi in Indonesia who receive federal assistance in planning, promotion, and infrastructure.

Although the Toraja have some control and earn most of the benefits, government interference has designated some areas over others as tourist destinations, so that competition and animosity between formerly cooperative communities has begun. Less obvious outside interference from the national majority has caused social problems among the Ladakhi of Northern India. Most tourism benefits go to the small percentage of hotel owners and to outside tour operators.

To help remedy this situation, the Swedish-backed Ledeg foundation has helped the Ladakhi develop souvenirs and promote native dancing which builds on their traditional background. It remains to be seen if Ledeg's involvement helps distribute benefits more uniformly or just allows another minority to profit over others. Outside involvement is not always apparent.

The Kuna of Panama have developed a rainforest reserve with the administrative and monetary help of multinational organizations including the Inter-American Foundation and the World Wildlife Fund. The Kuna benefit from selling their colourful weavings but have seen a decline in tourist visitation since the implementation of their project because it severed cooperative relations with individuals and groups who formerly helped to advertise, transport, and provide lodging for the visitors. One alternative to outside assistance is no assistance. This allows an approach to tourism to evolve from the existing social order and within the limits of the natural environment and culture. Of course, economic unfairness and social disruption can still occur. Indigenous-developed tourism has some clear advantages.

Tourism on Taquile island on Lake Titicaca is one example of indigenous-controlled tourism. In order to develop a tourist infrastructure, the Quechua-speaking residents of Taquile pooled together their money and energy. They bought a boat motor to speed tourist transport to the island and take turns lodging the guests.

3

Effective Marketing, Planning, Communication and Promotion for Sport Tourism

DEFINITION OF MARKETING

The concept of marketing can be viewed from social and managerial perspectives. At its simplest, marketing can be defined as exchange transactions that take place between the buyer and the seller. Marketing is the management function, which organizes and directs all those business activities involved in assessing and converting customer purchasing power into effective demand. Philip Kotler defines marketing as "a social process by which individuals and groups obtain what they need and want through creating, offering and freely exchanging products and services of value with others".

ASPECTS OF MARKETING CONCEPT

The important aspects of marketing concept are:

- *Creation of demand*: Marketing tries to create demand through various means. The producers first ascertain what the customers want and then produce goods just as to the needs of the customers. There is a systematic effort to sell goods and services just as to the needs of the customers.
- *Customer Orientation*: Marketing involves undertaking a range of business activities directed at the creation of customer satisfying products and services.
- *Integrated Marketing*: The customer orientation alone is not enough on the part of management. To be effective must be backed by an appropriate set up within the country. The responsibility of marketing department is to ensure coordination of the various departments of the company *i.e.*, finance, purchase, research and development.

- *Profitable sales volume through customer satisfaction*: Marketing tries to realise long-term goals of profitability, growth and stability through satisfying customers' wants. All the basic activities of a company are planned to meet the wants of customers and still making reasonable profits. Modern marketing thus begins with the customer and ends with the customer.

MARKETING MIX

Marketing concepts had been originally developed in the context of tangible consumer goods. Marketing mix refers to the ingredients or the tools, which the marketer mixes in order to interact with a particular market. Kotler defines marketing mix as "set of marketing tools that the firm uses to pursue its marketing objectives in the target market". Each of the elements in the marketing mix is important and has an influence on the customer.

4 P'S OF MARKETING MIX

McCarthy has classified the main elements of a marketing programme in terms of 4 Ps-Product, Price, Promotion and Place.

- Product includes design, features, quality, range, size, models, appearance, packaging, and warranties. It also includes pre-sales and post-sale services like training for use, repairs, maintenance or replacements.
- Price includes concessions on basic price, discounts, rebates, credits, installation facilities and delivery terms.
- Promotion includes advertising, publicity media choices, messages, and frequency of exposure, campaigns, sales promotion, point-of-purchase, displays and merchandising.
- Place or channels of distribution includes retail outlets, wholesalers, transportation, warehousing, inventory levels, order processing procedures, etc.

Consumers generally form their perceptions of products and services based on prices. Pricing products and services is a complex process. It is based on the uniqueness of product attributes and the perceived value, which the consumer is willing to pay. Pricing strategies are planned just as to consumers' cultural norms and the political, legal and social environment of the place where the tourist product is located.

Example of Price: Indian Airlines has offered Super Saver tickets in January 2006, a multicoupon ticket is being offered with each coupon valid for travel between any two domestic destinations connected by a direct flight. The offer gives two options, one is about four-ticket option priced at ₹20000 in Economy class and the other is ₹28000 in Executive class. This is an example of good Bargain. There is also the option of buying additional ticket at incredibly low prices. Such convenience of booking provides the comforts of flying with wide choice of travel. Distribution systems or channels serve as the intermediary between consumers and suppliers and are an essential part of the travel and hospitality marketing strategy.

Many companies such as hotels or airlines use their central reservation systems to facilitate sales directly to customers. Example of Channels of Distribution: It is estimated that in the year 2004, out of a total 730 million Internet users, only 35.8 per cent use English language websites. Therefore, local language should be part of the distribution strategy and many hospitality companies also provide localized websites with several languages.

Let us understand how a marketer uses the tools of marketing mix by taking the example of a product like 'Tanishq' watches by Titan Industries. The watch is packed in plastic box, has a design, features, quality and company ensures warranty. It has list price but at times the dealer permits discount or rebate. The company distributes the watch through exclusive retail outlets. The company promotes it by using advertising and sales force. All the activities of Titan are the ingredients that have gone into the making of 'Tanishq' for the purpose of creating exchanges with the potential customers.

TARGET MARKET

The term 'market' refers to the collective of existing and prospective customers for the product. People who need to stay outside their usual residence use a hotel. A person may not have such a need but if such a need arises later, he is a prospective customer. The marketing effort is aimed at such prospective customers who would choose to buy the marketer's hotel services. However, all persons who need to stay outside are not prospective customers for the 5-star hotels. They may stay at budget hotels.

Hence, the market for the five star hotels is only part of the total market of total hotel users. Such parts are called segments of the market. The customers of the hotel are those who come to stay as well as users of other facilities. They are different groups and each group constitutes different segments since the needs and expectations of each one of these groups are different. For example, segmentation is possible on the basis of usage of swimming pool. The segments using the pools for training are different from regular guests in terms of age, behaviour, attention required, hours spent in the pool or cleanliness demanded and so on.

MARKET SEGMENTATION

Market segmentation is the process of identifying groups of buyers of the total market with different desires. Most markets are too large for an organization to provide all the products and services needed by all buyers in that market. This leads organizations selecting target markets necessitating market segmentation.

Market segmentation has certain obvious advantages in that the organization is:

- Better placed to spot and compare marketing opportunities,

- Cater to the specific needs of the buyers,
- Develop marketing programmes for specific market segments.

In tourism, market segmentation is very important. The strategy of market segmentation in tourism is to divide the present and the potential market on the basis of some characteristic and then concentrate marketing efforts like pricing, supply and promotion efforts to the target markets.

BASES FOR MARKET SEGMENTATION

Segmentation is usually done on the basis of one or more of the following characteristics:

- *Buying behaviour*: Volumes of purchase, delivery requirements.
- *Demographic*: Family size, religion, gender, income, occupation, language, education.
- *Geographic*: Region, district, density of population, climate, urbanrural.
- *Psychographics*: Value system, lifestyles, and personality types.

Usually the tourist market is segmented in terms of demographic, geographic, psychographic, social and economic criteria. For example the market for a particular area might be the businessmen in the age group of 40-60 years who have an income of over $100,000 per year and who live in southern parts of Germany.

The tourist market may be segmented on the basis of:

- Destinations.
- Economic status and spending tendencies.
- Place or origin of tourists.
- Preferences of staying, like camping, luxury hotels, caravans, etc.
- Preferences of travel, like air, sea, road, or rail.
- Purpose of tour like holidays, pilgrimage, sightseeing, shopping, etc.

Each segment of the market differs in terms of needs and expectations. No one organization can cater to the needs of all segments. Each organization has to decide on the particular segment or segments it would cater to. The segment so identified is called the target segment. Having identified the market, all activities will have to be planned keeping this target market in mind.

The services being offered, the messages in communication, the media used for communication, the pricing policies, the arrangements have to be consistent with the preferences and behaviour patterns of the target market. For example, if the hotel is targeting on the domestic tourists at religious places, then providing foreign food or advertising in business magazines would be the waste of resources. Instead, provide vegetarian thali food and advertise in religious magazines and on channels like Aastha and Sanskar.

TOURISM MARKETING

It is a well known fact that as long as the inherent sense of curiosity and adventure dwells in the hearts of human beings, the desire to travel in order to see new sights and experience new things, to live under different environments will always grows.

The marketing in tourism industry has evolved as part of the process initiated by the desire for travel in people. Without exception, all human beings will always nurture a desire to travel in order to see places.

The question arises that if the desire is ever present in people to travel and experience new things, why then would the tourism industry need marketing efforts at all? The marketing problems in tourism is quite different from marketing problems in other industries, and this justifies making marketing in tourism, a subject for separate and specialized enquiry.

The concepts and principles, the techniques and methods of marketing can be equally applied to tourism. The concept of tourism marketing can be better understood by identifying and considering the differences between markets for physical, tangible goods on the one hand and the market for tourism on the other. Tourism marketing could be defined as the systematic and coordinated efforts exerted by tourist enterprises at international, national and local levels to optimize the satisfaction of tourists, groups and individuals, in view of a sustained tourism growth. Krippendorf, "Marketing in tourism is to be understood as the systematic and coordinated execution of business policy by tourist undertakings, whether private or state owned, at local, regional, national or international levels to achieve the optimal satisfaction of the needs of identifiable consumer groups, and in doing so to achieve an appropriate return."

Tourism is a very complex industry because of its multifaceted activities, which together produce the tourist products otherwise considered as independent industry. Besides, its complexity lies mostly in the fact that tourists are located in different places, have different socio-economic structures, different needs, tastes, attitudes, expectations, and behaviour patterns. The marketing concept helps the tourist organization to establish a consistent and effective communication system with actual and potential tourists in the selected markets. It also helps them to know their customers' wishes, needs, motivations, likes and dislikes.

SPECIAL FEATURES OF TOURISM MARKETING

From ancient times when travel was a prerogative of a select few who travelled in search of adventure to the present day jet travel, there have been many changes. Travel in ancient times was a simple affair. The type of facilities that were required by the people to travel was provided by a handful of suppliers of such services. In the present scenario of travel expansion, markets necessitated the application of marketing techniques. Marketing of tourist products has certain peculiarities.

The difference arises due to peculiar nature of tourist products:

- *A tourist product is assembled by many producers*: The tourist product cannot be provided by a single enterprise. In tourism, airline provides 'seat' to travel, hotels provide 'accommodation', a travel agent 'bookings' while a museum provides 'place of experience'. So, the tourist product is an amalga-mation of many components, which together make a complete product.

- Intermediaries play a dominant role: In tourism, sales intermediaries like tour operators, travel agents, reservation services and hotel brokers play a dominant role. They determine to a large extent which services will be sold and to whom.
- *Production and consumption of tourist services are closely Interrelated*: The travel agent who sells his product cannot store it since there is a close link between production and consumption of tourist services. Production can only take place or can only be completed if the customer is actually present.
- *Tourism demand is highly unstable*: Tourism demand is influenced by seasonal, economic, political and other such factors. For example, political unrest affects inflow of tourist to a particular destination.
- *Tourism is an intangible, non-material product*: Unlike a tangible product, no transfer of ownership of goods is involved in tourism. Instead certain facilities are made available for a specified time and for a specified use like a seat in an aeroplane or room in a hotel.
- *Travel motivations are diverse in nature*: The reasons, expectations, and desires, which influence tourists' choice for certain holiday destinations, types of accommodation and vacation activities are varied. Very often people make exactly the same choice for entirely different reasons.

To a considerable extent, tourism marketing depends on various market factors. Therefore, marketing of tourism as compared to other industries needs a somewhat different approach.

PRODUCT IN TOURISM

The needs of the tourist relate to comfort and pleasure in travel, stay, food arrangements and visiting spots of interest and attraction.

Hence, the tourist expectations are:

- Able to experience the new places–their life-styles, food, culture, heritage, etc. as per one's own choice.
- Be able to visit places of interest, spend adequate time at such places.
- Facility of transportation available.
- Facing no risk to one's person or belongings, etc.
- Getting suitable food to one's tastes and health.
- Not to be hurried or hustled against the preferred place.
- To be looked after and cared for.

The three basic components of a tourist product are:

- Attractions,
- Facilities, and

- Accessibility.

Attractions constitute an important feature of the product. Attractions are those elements in the tourist product, which determine the choice of the particular tourist product, to visit one particular destination rather than another. These are things to see and enjoy like cultural sites, historical buildings, beaches, mountains, national parks, or events like trade fairs, exhibitions, music festivals, etc. Facilities are those elements in the tourist product, which are a necessary aid to the tourist centre. The facilities complement the attractions. These include accommodation, food, communications, guides and so on.

Accessibility is a means by which a tourist can reach the areas where attractions are located. Tourists' attractions are of little importance if their locations are inaccessible by the normal means of transport. It also relates to the formalities in reaching the places like visas, customs, bookings etc.

In Tourism, the products are varied. A travel agent may arrange for itineraries and airline bookings and may also help in getting passport, visas, foreign exchange clearances, embarkation facilities at airport and so on. Similarly attractions are added to a destination. For example, 18 rooms of Buckingham Palace have been opened to visitors, which are a major tourist attraction to visitors. Apart from the Throne Room, Drawing Room and the Picture Gallery, the Souvenir shop selling white china mugs with Buckingham Palace written on it or Crystal Balls with details from the State Dining Room is also a part of the attraction. A product in tourism is the place of destination and what one may experience while proceedings to and staying at that destination.

For example,

- Sentose islands of Singapore, is packaged as a place where there are no shops, no skyscrapers, no offices-a place of quiet and tranquility, to relax and be with nature, so different from Singapore. Travelling by cable car to the island is also a part of the package.
- Places in Rajasthan like Jaisalmer are being offered as tourism products to experience the life-style of Maharajas, living in real palaces with kingly comforts, travelling on ' Palace on Wheels', the luxuriously fitted railway train, going hunting on elephant back and so on. The product is not merely the city of Jaisalmer and what it may offer as historical and cultural importance. The product is the total experience of travel and other attractions, all related to the royalty of Jaisalmer.

The tourism product may be developed with emphasis on art, architecture, culture, religion, history, sports, leisure, temples, life-styles, etc.

- Himalayas are a product not only for sports and adventure tourism, but also for nature lovers and spirituality.
- Varanasi is a product based on religion, the Ganges capturing the essence of Oldest Hindu heritage.

- The accommodation provided, is as much a part of the safari in the African forests as the prospect of seeing wild-life. Many prefer and pay more to live in the open country 'with nature' instead of in five-star comfort.

CHARACTERISTICS OF TOURISM PRODUCTS

A product is something that a producer makes and offers to consumers to provide satisfaction of needs. Like all products, tourism also needs marketing and it is different from marketing of manufactured goods since tourism product has different characteristics.

INTANGIBLE

Manufactured goods are tangible in the sense that they have physical dimensions and attributes and can be seen, felt, or tasted. The tourism product is an intangible product. Take for example, an aviation industry. One can see the airplane, the facilities provided within, etc. But none of these would determine the nature and quality of services imparted by the airline. One cannot see, feel, smell, touch or measure a service performed. It can only be experienced from the effects produced during the journey.

INSEPARABILITY

A physical product is produced in the factory, bought in the shop and consumed in the customer's premises at his convenience. But when the customer buys a service like travelling in an airline, the production and consumption of the services takes place at the same time. The experience of the tourist product exists when it is produced as well as consumed. The service in the airline is the promptness of delivery of baggage or courtesy of the airhostess or safety of travel.

PERISHABILITY

A manufacturer of a physical product can anticipate the demand in advance and store the goods in warehouse and deliver them to the customers at the time of need. But the supply of the tourism product cannot be stored because tourism products are highly perishable. A seat in the plane or a room in the hotel not used today is a total waste. If an advertisement placed in the media channel is not seen or read, it is a waste. If the supply is not used, it perishes. So, the seats in an aircraft, the rooms in the hotels, the space in the ship, the services of a tourist guide, the time of the travel agency, etc. all perish if not utilized when available. What is not sold cannot be carried forward like stocks to be sold the next day or at any other time.

OWNERSHIP

No ownership passes from seller to buyer in a service. The buyer only acquires the right to certain benefits of what the seller offers. One may have the right to use a hotel room or a railway berth for a period of time, but the ownership of the room or berth remains with the hotel or the railways.

MARKETING MIX IN TOURISM MARKETING

Tourist marketing mix is largely a complex group of factors to achieve the 'end products', which helps the marketing manager to understand the demand in relation to supply and marketing investments. A balanced mix is necessary to reach this targeted result.

The tourist marketing mix can include the following elements:

- *The Product*:
  - Image, reputation, positioning
  - Size and facilities offered
  - Staff members and their attitudes
  - The characteristics of the product
- *The Price*:
  - Corporate
  - Discounted
  - Normal
  - Promotional
  - Seasonal
  - Wholesaler rates
- *The Promotion*:
  - Advertising
  - Direct mail
  - Public relations
  - Sales promotion
- *The Distribution*:
  - Airlines
  - Channels of distribution
  - Clubs/Associations
  - Intermediaries
  - Reservation systems

'Marketing mix' has both short-term as well as long-term aspects. Long-term plans are based on study of natural, economic, social and technological aspects of the markets and customers. The short-term aspects relate to price reduction, aggressive promotion, or introduction of a new product in the market.

TOURISM MARKETING STRATEGY

One of the basic considerations for successful marketing strategy is the need for research. It provides the information base for effective marketing. It relates to providing answers to various questions pertaining to the marketing activities. Market research can be defined as the "systematic collection of information relating to supply and demand for the product in such a way that the information may be used to make decisions about its policies and objectives". In order to formulate any marketing strategy, it is essential for a tourist organization and others engaged in marketing of tourist products to know the answer of following questions:

- Who are the persons engaged in tourism and where do they live?
- Who are the potential customers and where do they come from?
- What are their likes and dislikes?
- What are their travel preferences and interests?
- What do they buy and where do they stay?
- What mode of transport do they use?
- What are their entertainment preferences?
- What are the trends in competition?
- What type of marketing programmes would be needed?

Market research provides answers to all the above questions. To make the overall marketing efforts effective and successful, as in the case of manufactured products, the tourist organization has to be totally aware of the trends in travel habits, vacation habits and complete knowledge about potential customers. It is very important to have detailed information on all aspects of a market. Results of such research will work as a guideline for designing and launching a successful marketing programme. A lot of data can be collected through publications, commercial analysis, trade information, press cuttings, previous studies etc.

Other ways to obtain data are:

- Tourism Departments,
- Discussion with tourists,
- Observation of customers at premises,
- Observations and discussions with visitors in exhibitions and trade shows,
- Attitudes, image perceptions and awareness studies,
- Advertisement and other media response studies,
- Studies of usage pattern.

UNDERSTANDING TOURISM PLANNING

Tourism is one of many activities in a community or region that requires planning and coordination. Here we provide a simple structure and basic guidelines for comprehensive tourism planning at a community or regional level. Planning is the process of identifying objectives and defining and evaluating methods of achieving them. By comprehensive planning we mean planning which considers all of the tourism resources, organizations, markets, and programmes within a region. Comprehensive planning also considers economic, environmental, social, and institutional aspects of tourism development.

TWO SIDES OF TOURISM PLANNING

Tourism planning has evolved from two related but distinct sets of planning philosophies and methods. On the one hand, tourism is one of many activities in an area that must be considered as part of physical, environmental, social, and economic planning. Therefore, it is common to find tourism addressed, at least partially, in a regional land use, transportation, recreation, economic development, or comprehensive plan.

The degree to which tourism is addressed in such plans depends upon the relative importance of tourism to the community or region and how sensitive the planning authority is to tourism activities. Tourism may also be viewed as a business in which a community or region chooses to engage. Individual tourism businesses conduct a variety of planning activities including feasibility, marketing, product development, promotion, forecasting, and strategic planning.

If tourism is a significant component of an area's economy or development plans, regional or community-wide marketing plans are needed to coordinate the development and marketing activities of different tourism interests in the community. A comprehensive approach integrates a strategic marketing plan with more traditional public planning activities.

This ensures a balance between serving the needs and wants of the tourists versus the needs and wants of local residents. A formal tourism plan provides a vehicle for the various interests within a community to coordinate their activities and work towards common goals. It also is a means of coordinating tourism with other community activities.

STEPS IN THE PLANNING PROCESS

Like any planning, tourism planning is goal-oriented, striving to achieve certain objectives by matching available resources and programmes with the needs and wants of people. Comprehensive planning requires a systematic approach, usually involving a series of steps.

The process is best viewed as an iterative and on-going one, with each step subject to modification and refinement at any stage of the planning process.

There are six steps in the planning process:

- Define goals and objectives.
- Identify the tourism system.
    - Resources
    - Organizations
    - Markets
    - Generate alternatives.
- Evaluate alternatives.
- Select and implement.
- Monitor and evaluate.

STEP ONE

Obtaining clear statements of goals and objectives is difficult, but important. Ideally, tourism development goals should flow from more general community goals and objectives. It is important to understand how a tourism plan serves these broader purposes. Is the community seeking a broader tax base, increased employment opportunities, expanded recreation facilities, better educational programmes, a higher quality of life? How can tourism contribute to these objectives? If tourism is identified as a means of serving broader community goals, it makes sense to develop plans with more specific tourism development objectives.

These are generally defined through a continuing process in which various groups and organizations in a community work together towards common goals. A local planning authority, chamber of commerce, visitors bureau, or similar group should assume a leadership role to develop an initial plan and obtain broad involvement of tourism interests in the community. Public support for the planning process and plan is also important. Having a good understanding of tourism and the tourism system in your community is the first step towards defining goals and objectives for tourism development.

The types of goals that are appropriate and the precision with which you are able to define them will depend upon how long your community has been involved in tourism and tourism planning. In the early stages of tourism development, goals may involve establishing organizational structures and collecting information to better identify the tourism system in the community. Later, more precise objectives can be formulated and more specific development and marketing strategies evaluated.

STEP TWO

Identifying Your Tourism System When planning for any type of activity, it is important to first define its scope and characteristics. Be clear about exactly what your plan encompasses. A good initial question is, "What do you mean by tourism?" Tourism is defined in many ways. Generally, tourism involves people traveling outside of their community for pleasure. Definitions differ on the specifics of how far people must travel, whether or not they must stay overnight, for how long, and what exactly is included under traveling for "pleasure".

Do you want your tourism plan to include day visitors, conventioneers, business travellers, people visiting friends and relatives, people passing through, or seasonal residents? Which community resources and organizations serve tourists or could serve tourists? Generally, tourists share community resources with local residents and businesses.

Many organizations serve both tourists and locals. This complicates tourism planning and argues for a clear idea of what your tourism plan entails.

You can begin to clarify the tourism system by breaking it down into three subsystems:

- Tourism resources,
- Tourism organizations, and
- Tourism markets.

An initial task in developing a tourism plan is to identify, inventory, and classify the objects within each of these subsystems.

Tourism Resources are any:

- Natural,
- Cultural,
- Human, or
- Capital resources that either are used or can be used to attract or serve tourists.

A tourism resource inventory identifies and classifies the resources available that provide opportunities for tourism development. Conduct an objective and realistic assessment of the quality and quantity of resources you have to work with. Some data suggested classification to help obtain a broad and organized picture of your tourism resources. Tourism Organizations combine resources in various proportions to provide products and services for the tourist.

A partial list and classification of organizations that manage or coordinate tourism-related activities. It is important to recognize the diverse array of public and private organizations involved with tourism. The most difficult part of tourism planning is to get these groups to work towards common goals. You should develop a list of these organizations within your own community and obtain their input and cooperation in your tourism planning efforts.

Setting up appropriate communication systems and institutional arrangements is a key part of community tourism planning.

TOURISM RESOURCES

- *Natural Resources*:
  - Climate-seasons
  - Fauna-fish and wildlife
  - Flora-forests, flowers, shrubs, wild edibles
  - Geological resources-topography, soils, sand dunes, beaches, caves, rocks and minerals, fossils
  - Scenery-combinations of all of the above
  - Water resources-lakes, streams, waterfalls
- *Cultural Resources*:
  - Anthropological resources
  - Cuisine
  - Ethnic cultures
  - Historic buildings, sites

  - Industry, government, religion, etc.
  - Local celebrities
  - Monuments, shrines
- *Human Resources*:
  - Craftsman and artisans
  - Hospitality skills
  - Local populations
  - Management skills
  - Other labour skills from chefs to lawyers to researchers
  - Performing artists-music, drama, art, storytellers, etc.
  - Seasonal labour force
- *Capital*:
  - Availability of capital, financing
  - Infrastructure-transportation roads, airports, railroads, harbors and marinas, trails and walkways
  - Infrastructure: utilities water, power, waste treatment, communications.

Tourism Management Organizations and Services

Off-Site

Coordination, planning, technical assistance, research, regulation:

- Educational organizations and consultants, *e.g.*, Travel and Tourism Research Association; U.S. Travel Data Centre; Travel Reference Centre, Univ. of Colorado, Boulder; Travel, Tourism, and Recreation Resource Centre, Michigan State University.
- Federal and state departments of commerce, transportation, and natural resources
- Federal, state, regional, and local tourism associations
- Travel information and reservation services

On-Site

Development, promotion and management, of tourism resources:

- Federal agencies, NB. departments of commerce, transportation, and land management agencies.
- Local government organizations, *e.g.*, visitor information, chamber of commerce, convention and visitor's bureaus, parks.
- State agencies, NB. departments of commerce, transportation, and land/facility management agencies

Businesses:

- *Accommodations*: Hotels, motels, Lodges, resorts, bed and breakfast cabins and cottages, Condominiums, second homes, Campgrounds
- *Food and Beverage*: Restaurants, Grocery, Bars, nightclubs, Fast food, Catering services

- *Information*: Travel agencies, Information and reservation services, Automobile clubs
- Transportation: Air, rail, bus; Local transportation: taxi, limo, Auto, bicycle, boat rental; Local tour services

Recreation Facilities and Services

Winter sports: Ski, skating, snowmobile areas; Golf courses, miniature golf; Swimming pools, water slides, beaches; tennis, handball, racquetball courts, bowling alleys; Athletic clubs, health spas; Marinas, boat rentals and charters; hunting and fishing guides; Horseback enterprises; Sporting goods sales and rentals:

- *Entertainment*: Nightclubs, amusement parks, spectator sport facilities; Gambling facilities: casinos, horse racing, bingo; video arcades; art galleries and studios, craft shops, studios, demonstrations; performing arts: theater, dance, music, film; historic and prehistoric sites; museums: art, history, science, technology; arboreta, zoos, nature centres,
- *Support services*: Auto repair, gasoline service stations; boat and recreation vehicle dealers and service; retail shops: sporting goods, specialties, souvenirs, clothing; health services: hospitals, clinics, pharmacies; laundry and dry cleaning; beauty and barber shops; babysitting services; pet care; communications: newspaper, telephone; banking and financial services

Tourism Markets

Tourists makeup the third, and perhaps most important subsystem. Successful tourism programmes require a strong market orientation. The needs and wants of the tourists you choose to attract and serve must be the focus of much of your marketing and development activity. Therefore, it is important to clearly understand which tourism market segments you wish to attract and serve. Tourists fall into a very diverse set of categories with quite distinct needs and wants. You should identify the different types of tourists, or market segments that you presently serve or would like to serve. This may involve one or more tourism market surveys.

A visitor survey identifies the size and nature of the existing market and asks the following questions:

- How did they find out about your community?
- How satisfied are they with your offerings?
- What are the primary market segments you presently attract?
- What attracted them to the community?
- What local businesses and facilities do they use?
- Where do they come from?

A market survey (usually a telephone survey) also can be conducted among households in regions from which you wish to attract tourists. This type of study helps identify potential markets, and means of attracting tourists to your area.

Tourism Market Segments

In a general tourism plan, some clear target tourism market segments should be identified. You might begin by defining the market area from which you will draw most of your visitors.

The size of your market area depends upon the uniqueness and quality of your "product", transportation systems, tastes and preferences of surrounding populations, and your competition. Identifying the market area will help target information and promotion and define transportation routes and modes, competition, and characteristics of your market.

Next, divide your travel market into the following trip length categories:

- Day trips from 50 to 200 miles away,
- Day trips from a 50 mile radius,
- Extended overnight vacation trips.
- Overnight trips of 1 or 2 nights (most likely weekends), and
- Pass-through travellers,

After you have an idea of your market area and kinds of trips you will be serving, begin defining more specific market segments like vehicle campers, downhill skiers, sightseers, family vacationers, single weekenders, and the like. These segments can be more clearly tied to particular resources, businesses, and facilities in your community. What kinds of products and services are likely to attract each of these groups? Tourist needs as well as their impact on the local community are quite different for day tourists versus overnight tourists.

Areas catering primarily to weekend traffic will experience large fluctuations in use. In deciding the relative importance of these different segments, communities need to assess both their ability to provide required services (do you have enough rooms?), as well as the demand for different types of trips relative to the supply and your competition.

THE ENVIRONMENT

A tourism plan is significantly affected by many factors in the broader environment. Indeed, one of the complexities of tourism planning is the number of variables that are outside of the control of an individual tourism business or community. These include such things as tourism offerings and prices at competing destinations, federal and state policy and legislation, currency exchange rates, the state of the economy, and weather. These factors are discussed more fully in Extension bulletin E-1959 as part of the market environment analysis. Local populations also must be considered in tourism planning. As they compete with tourists for resources, they can be significantly affected by tourism activity, and they are an important source of support in getting tourism plans implemented.

A survey of local residents can be conducted to assess community attitudes towards tourism development, identify impacts of tourism on the community, and obtain local input into tourism plans. Public hearings, workshops, and advisory boards are other ways to obtain public involvement in tourism planning. Local support and cooperation is important to the success of tourism programmes and should not be overlooked.

STEP THREE

Generating alternative development and marketing options to meet your goals requires some creative thinking and brainstorming. The errors made at this stage are usually thinking too narrowly or screening out alternatives prematurely. It is wise to solicit a wide range of options from a diverse group of people.

If tourism expertise is lacking in your community, seek help and advice outside the community. Tourism planning involves a wide range of interrelated development and marketing decisions.

The following development questions will get you started:

- How much importance should be assigned to tourism within a community or region?
- What are the relative roles of public and private sectors?
- Which general community goals is tourism development designed to serve?
- Which organization(s) will provide the leadership and coordination necessary for community tourism planning?

Tourism marketing decision questions include:

- *Place*: Where should tourism facilities be located?
- *Price*: What prices should be charged for which products and services. Who should capture the revenue?
- *Product*: What kinds of tourism products and services should be provided? Who should provide what?
- *Promotion*: What kinds of promotion should be used, by whom, in which media, how much, when? What community tourism theme or image should be established?
- *Segments*: Which market segments should be pursued; geographic markets, trip types, activity or demographic subgroups?

STEP FOUR

Tourism development and marketing options are evaluated by assessing the degree to which each option will be able to meet the stated goals and objectives. There are usually two parts to a systematic evaluation of tourism development and marketing alternatives:

- Feasibility analysis, and
- Impact assessment.

These two tasks are interrelated, but think of them as trying to answer two basic questions:

- Can it be done?, and
- What are the consequences?

A decision to take a specific action must be based both on feasibility and desirability. Feasibility Analysis: First, screen alternatives and eliminate those that are not feasible due to economic, environmental, political, legal, or other factors. Evaluate the remaining set of alternatives in more paying particular attention to the market potential and financial plan. Make a realistic assessment of your community's ability to attract and serve a market segment or segments. This requires a clear understanding of the tourism market in your area and how this market is changing. Also carefully identify your competition and evaluate your advantages and disadvantages compared to the competition. Plan towards the future because it takes time to implement decisions and for your actions to take effect. Therefore, look at the likely market and competition for several years to come. Review forecasts for the travel market in your area, if available. Careful tracking of tourism trends in your own community can help identify changes in the market that you will have to adapt to.

Impact Assessment

When evaluating alternative development and marketing strategies it is important to understand the impacts, both positive and negative, of proposed actions. A classification of economic, environmental, and social impacts associated with tourism development. The types of impacts and their importance vary across different communities and proposed actions.

Generally, the size, extent, and nature of tourism impacts depend upon:

- Degree of concentration/dispersal of tourist activity in the area
- How well tourism is planned, controlled, and managed.
- Length and nature of tourist contacts with the community
- Similarities or differences between local populations and tourists
- Stability/sensitivity of local economy, environment, and social structure
- Volume of tourist activity relative to local activity

Look at both the benefits and costs of any proposed actions. While tourism development can increase income, revenues, and employment, it also involves costs.

Evaluate benefits and costs of tourism development from the perspectives of local government, businesses, and residents.

IMPACTS OF TOURISM

- *Economic Impacts*:
  - Economic base and structure
  - Employment

- Fiscal impact-taxes, infrastructure costs
- Prices
- Sales, revenue, and income

- *Environmental Impacts*:
  - Air
  - Flora and fauna
  - Infrastructure
  - Lands
  - Waters
- *Social Impacts*:
  - Community spirit and cohesion
  - Congestion and crowding
  - Education
  - Occupations
  - Population structure and distribution
  - Quality of life
  - Safety and security
  - Values and attitudes

Impacts on Local Government

Local government provides most of the infrastructure and many of the services essential to tourism development, including highways, public parks, law enforcement, water and sewer, garbage collection and disposal. Evaluate tourism decisions with a clear understanding of the capacity of the local infrastructure and services relative to anticipated needs, and take into account both the needs of local populations and tourists.

A fiscal impact analysis evaluates the impact of tourism on the community's tax base and local government costs. It entails predicting the additional infrastructure and service requirements of tourism development, estimating their costs, deciding who will pay for/provide them, and how. Will tourism generate increased local government revenue through fees and charges, local sales or use taxes, increased property values or property tax rates, or larger local shares of federal and state tax revenues?

Impacts on Business and Industry

Businesses that are directly serving tourists benefit from sales to tourists. Through secondary impacts, tourism activity also benefits a wide range of businesses in a community. For example, a local textile industry may sell to a linen supply firm that serves hotels and motels catering primarily to tourists. A local forest products industry sells to a lumberyard where local woodcarvers or furniture makers buy their supplies.

They in turn sell to tourists through various retail outlets. All of these businesses benefit from tourism. If most products and services for tourists are bought outside of the local area, much of the tourist spending "leaks" out of the local economy. The more a community is "self-sufficient" in serving tourists, the larger the local impact.

Impacts on Residents

Local residents may experience a broad range of both positive and negative impacts from tourism development. Tourism development may provide increased employment and income for the community. Although tourism jobs are primarily in the service sectors and are often seasonal, part time, and low-paying, these characteristics, are neither universal nor always undesirable. Residents may value opportunities for part time and seasonal work. In particular, employment opportunities and work experiences for students or retirees may be desired. Residents may also benefit from local services that otherwise would not be available.

Tourism development may mean a wider variety of retailers and restaurants, or a better community library. It may also mean more traffic, higher prices, and increases in property values and local taxes. The general quality of the environment and life in the community may go up or down due to tourism development. This depends on the nature of tourism development, the preferences and desires of local residents, and how well tourism is planned and managed.

STEPS FIVE AND SIX

As suggested, not attempt a complete discussion of decision making, plan implementation, and monitoring, but these are critical steps in the success of a tourism plan. A set of specific actions should be prescribed with clearly defined responsibilities and timetables.

Monitor progress in implementing the plan and evaluate the success of the plan in meeting its goals and objectives on a regular basis. Plans generally need to be adjusted over time due to changing goals, changing market conditions, and unanticipated impacts. It is a good idea to build monitoring and evaluation systems into your planning efforts.

CONCLUDING REMARKS

Successful tourism planning and development means serving both tourists and local residents. The bulletins in this series stress the importance of a market orientation for attracting and serving tourists. This market orientation must be balanced with a clear view of how tourism serves the broader community interest and an understanding of the positive and negative impacts of tourism development.

Remember, tourism should serve the community first and the tourist second. Tourism development must be compatible with other activities in the area and be supported by the local population. Therefore, the tourism plan should be closely coordinated with other local and regional planning efforts, if not an integral part of them.

NATIONAL AND REGIONAL TOURISM PLANNING

The importance of effective tourism planning in ensuring economic benefit and sustainability is now widely recognized. Here we introduce concepts of national and regional tourism planning and look at the basic approaches, techniques and principles applied at this level. It is now recognized that tourism must be developed and managed in a controlled, integrated and sustainable manner, based on sound planning. With this approach, tourism can generate substantial economic benefits to an area, without creating any serious environmental or social problems. Tourism's resources will be conserved for continuous use in the future.

There are numerous examples in the world where tourism has not been well planned and managed. These uncontrolled developments may have brought some short-term economic benefits. Over the longer term, however, they have resulted in environmental and social problems and poor quality tourist destinations. This has been detrimental to the area's residents, and tourist markets have been lost to better planned destinations elsewhere. Many of these places are now undergoing redevelopment. It is obviously better to plan for controlled development initially, and prevent problems from arising in the first place.

Tourism planning is carried out at all levels of development-international, national, regional and for specific areas and sites. National and regional planning lays the foundation for tourism development of a country and its regions. It establishes the policies, physical and institutional structures and standards for development to proceed in a logical manner. It also provides the basis for the continuous and effective management of tourism which is so essential for the long-term success of tourism. This publication is divided into two parts. The first part briefly explains planning concepts and describes planning and marketing methodologies. Emphasis is placed on the integrated approach, balancing economic, environmental and socio-cultural factors, and achieving sustainable development. Importance is also given to techniques that need to be used in implementing plans. Without adopting and applying these techniques, tourism plans cannot be realised.

The second part presents case studies of tourism policies and plans which have actually been prepared and, for the most part, are being implemented. The case studies have been selected to represent the several different elements of plans that must be considered in integrated development. Most of the case studies are ones that have been prepared by the WTO for several countries and regions during the past decade.

One of the important functions of the WTO is its technical cooperation activities. The organization has assisted many countries throughout the world in preparing planning, marketing, economic and other types of tourism studies, advising on all aspects of tourism development, and training local tourism-related personnel.

Both Parts I and II of this publication reflect the WTO's basic approach to planning for the integrated and sustainable development of tourism in its global technical cooperation activities. The WTO hopes that this publication will provide tourism officials, planners and others involved in tourism with an understanding of national and regional tourism planning. Their application of sound planning practice can then provide the basis for their countries to achieve successful tourism development.

THE IMPORTANCE OF PLANNING TOURISM

Planning tourism at all levels is essential for achieving successful tourism development and management. The experience of many tourism areas in the world has demonstrated that, on a long-term basis, the planned approach to developing tourism can bring benefits without significant problems, and maintain satisfied tourist markets. Places that have allowed tourism to develop without the benefit of planning are often suffering from environmental and social problems.

These are detrimental to residents and unpleasant for many tourists, resulting in marketing difficulties and decreasing economic benefits. These uncontrolled tourism areas cannot effectively compete with planned tourist destinations elsewhere. They usually can be redeveloped, based on a planned approach, but that requires much time and financial investment. Tourism is a rather complicated activity that overlaps several different sectors of the society and economy. Without planning, it may create unexpected and unwanted impacts.

Tourism is also still a relatively new type of activity in many countries. Some governments and often the private sector have little or no experience in how to develop tourism properly.

For countries that do not yet have much tourism, planning can provide the necessary guidance for its development. For those places that already have some tourism, planning is often needed to revitalize this sector and maintain its future viability. First, tourism should be planned at the national and regional levels. At these levels, planning is concerned with tourism development policies, structure plans, facility standards, institutional factors and all the other elements necessary to develop and manage tourism. Then, within the framework of national and regional planning, more detailed plans for tourist attractions, resorts, urban, rural and other forms of tourism development can be prepared. There are several important specific benefits of undertaking national and regional tourism planning.

These advantages include:

- Developing tourism so that its natural and cultural resources are indefinitely maintained and conserved for future, as well as present, use.
- Establishing the guidelines and standards for preparing detailed plans of specific tourism development areas that are consistent with,

and reinforce, one another, and for the appropriate design of tourist facilities.

- Establishing the overall tourism development objectives and policies- what is tourism aiming to accomplish and how can these aims be achieved.
- Integrating tourism into the overall development policies and patterns of the country or region, and establishing dose linkages between tourism and other economic sectors.
- Laying the foundation for effective implementation of the tourism development policy and plan and continuous management of the tourism sector, by providing the necessary organizational and other institutional framework.
- Making possible the coordinated development of all the many elements of the tourism sector. This includes inter-relating the tourist attractions, activities, facilities and services and the various and increasingly fragmented tourist markets.
- Offering a baseline for the continuous monitoring of the progress of tourism development and keeping it on track.
- Optimizing and balancing the economic, environmental and social benefits of tourism, with equitable distribution of these benefits to the society, while minimizing possible problems of tourism.
- Providing a physical structure which guides the location, types and extent of tourism development of attractions, facilities, services and infrastructure.
- Providing a rational basis for decision-making by both the public and private sectors on tourism development.
- Providing the framework for effective coordination of the public and private sector efforts and investment in developing tourism.

The planned approach to developing tourism at the national and regional levels is now widely adopted as a principle, although implementation of the policies and plans is still weak in some places. Many countries and regions of countries have had tourism plans prepared. Other places do not yet have plans, but should consider undertaking planning in the near future.

In some countries, plans had previously been prepared but these are now outdated. They need to be revised based on present day circumstances and likely future trends. Founded on accumulated experience, the approaches and techniques of tourism planning are now reasonably well understood. There is considerable assurance that, if implemented, planning will bring substantial benefits to an area.

APPROACHES TO TOURISM PLANNING

It is important to understand the basic approaches to planning and managing tourism development.

PLANNING TOURISM AS AN INTEGRATED SYSTEM

An underlying concept in planning tourism is that tourism should be viewed as an inter-related system of demand and supply factors. The demand factors are international and domestic tourist markets and local 'residents who use the tourist attractions, facilities and services. The supply factors comprise tourist attractions and activities, accommodation and other tourist facilities and services. Attractions include natural, cultural and special types of features-such as theme parks, zoos, botanic gardens and aquariums-and the activities related to these attractions. Accommodation includes hotels, motels, guest houses and other types of places where tourists stay overnight.

The category of other tourist facilities and services includes tour and travel operations, restaurants, shopping, banking and money exchange, and medical and postal facilities and services. These supply factors are called the tourism product.

Other elements also relate to supply factors. In order to make the facilities and services usable, infrastructure is required. Tourism infrastructure particularly includes transportation (air, road, rail, water, etc.), water supply, electric power, sewage and solid waste disposal, and telecommuni-cations.

- *Demand Factors*:
  - Domestic tourist markets
  - International tourist markets
  - Residents' use of tourist attractions, facilities and services
- *Supply Factors*:
  - Attractions and activities Ïper cent Accommodation
  - Institutional elements
  - Other infrastructure
  - Other tourist facilities and services Ïper cent Transportation

Provision of adequate infrastructure is also important to protect the environment. It helps maintain a high level of environmental quality that is so necessary for successful tourism and desirable for residents. The effective development, operation and management of tourism requires certain institutional elements.

These elements include:

- Availability of financial capital to develop tourist attractions, facilities, services and infrastructure, and mechanisms to attract capital investment.
- Education and training programmes, and training institutions to prepare persons to work effectively in tourism.
- Marketing strategies and promotion programmes to inform tourists about the country or region, and induce them to visit it, and tourist information facilities and services in the destination areas.
- Organizational structures, especially government tourism offices and private sector tourism associations such as hotel associations.

- Tourism-related legislation and regulations, such as standards and licensing requirements for hotels and tour and travel agencies.
- Travel facilitation of immigration (including visa arrangements), customs and other facilities and services at the entry and exit points of tourists.

The institutional elements also include consideration of how to enhance and distribute the economic benefits of tourism, environmental protection measures, reducing adverse social impacts, and conservation of the cultural heritage of people living in the tourism areas. As an inter-related system, it is important that tourism planning aim for integrated development of all these parts of the system, both the demand and supply factors and the physical and institutional elements.

The system will function much more effectively and bring the desired benefits if it is planned in an integrated manner, with coordinated development of all the components of the system. Sometimes, this integrated system approach is also called the comprehensive approach to tourism planning because all the elements of tourism are considered in the planning and development process.

Just as important as planning for integration within the tourism system is planning for integration of tourism into the overall development policies, plans and patterns of a country or region. Planning for this overall integration will, for example, resolve any potential conflicts over use of certain resources or locations for various types of development. It also provides for the multi-use of expensive infrastructure to serve general community needs as well as tourism. Emphasis is given to formulating and adopting tourism development policies and plans for an area in order to guide decision-making on development actions.

The planning of tourism, however, should also be recognized as a continuous and flexible process. Within the framework of the policy and plan recommendations, there must be flexibility to allow for adapting to changing circumstances. Planning that is too rigid may not allow development to be responsive to changes. There may be advancements in transportation technology, evolution of new forms of tourism and changes in market trends.

Even though allowed to be flexible, the basic objectives of the plan should not be abrogated although the specific development patterns may be changed. Sustainable development must still be maintained. Planning for tourism development should make recommendations that are imaginative and innovative, but they must also be feasible to implement. The various techniques of implementation should be considered throughout the planning process.

This approach ensures that the recommendations can be accomplished, and provides the basis for specifying the implementation techniques that should be applied. Implementation techniques can also be imaginative and not only rely on established approaches. It is common practice for a tourism plan to include specification of implementation techniques, and sometimes a separate manual on how to achieve the plan recommendations.

PLANNING FOR SUSTAINABLE DEVELOPMENT

The underlying approach now applied to tourism planning, as well as to other types of development, is that of achieving sustainable development. The sustainable development approach implies that the natural, cultural and other resources of tourism are conserved for continuous use in the future, while still bringing benefits to the present society The concept of sustainable development has received much emphasis internationally since the early 1980s, although tourism plans prepared even before that period often were concerned with conservation of tourism resources. The sustainable development approach to planning tourism is acutely important because most tourism development depends on attractions and activities related to the natural environment, historic heritage and cultural patterns of areas. If these resources are degraded or destroyed, then the tourism areas cannot attract tourists and tourism will not be successful. More generally, most tourists seek destinations that have a high level of environmental quality-they like to visit places that are attractive, clean and neither polluted nor congested.

It is also essential that residents of the tourism area should not have to suffer from a deteriorated environment and social problems. One of the important benefits of tourism is that, if it is properly developed based on the concept of sustainability, tourism can greatly help justify and pay for conservation of an area's natural and cultural resources. Thus, tourism can be an important means of achieving conservation in areas that otherwise have limited capability to accomplish environmental protection and conservation objectives. A basic technique in achieving sustainable development is the environmental planning approach.

Environmental planning requires that all elements of the environment be carefully surveyed, analysed and considered in determining the most appropriate type and location of development. This approach would not allow, for example, intensive development in flood plain and steep hillside areas. An important aspect of sustainable development is emphasizing community-based tourism. This approach to tourism focuses on community involvement in the planning and development process, and developing the types of tourism which generate benefits to local communities. It applies techniques to ensure that most of the benefits of tourism development accrue to local residents and not to outsiders.

Maximizing benefits to local residents typically results in tourism being better accepted by them and their actively supporting conservation of local tourism resources. The communitybased tourism approach is applied at the local or more detailed levels of planning, but it can be set forth as a policy approach at the national and regional levels. The benefits accruing to local communities are also beneficial to the country, through the income and foreign exchange earned, employment generated and support that local communities give to national tourism development and conservation policies. Also related to sustainable development is the concept of quality tourism.

This approach is being increasingly adopted for two fundamental reasons-it can achieve successful tourism from the marketing standpoint and it brings benefits to local residents and their environment. Quality tourism does not necessarily mean expensive tourism. Rather, it refers to tourist attractions, facilities and services that offer 'good value for money', protect tourism resources, and attract the kinds of tourists who will respect the local environment and society. Quality tourism development can compete more effectively in attracting discriminating tourists. It is also more environmentally and socially self-sustaining. Achieving quality tourism is the responsibility of both the public and private sectors. This concept should be built into the tourism planning, development and management process.

LONG-RANGE AND STRATEGIC PLANNING

Long-range comprehensive planning is concerned with specifying goals and objectives and determining preferred future development patterns. Tourism development policies and plans should be prepared for relatively long-term periods-usually for 10 to 15 and sometimes 20 years-depending on the predictability of future events in the country or region. These may seem to be long planning periods, but it commonly requires this length of time to implement basic policy and structure plans. Even development of specific projects, such as major resorts or national park-based tourism, can require a long time.

A planning approach which has received considerable attention in recent years, and is applicable to some tourism areas, is strategic planning. While the outcomes of strategic and long-range comprehensive planning may be very similar, strategic planning is somewhat different. It focuses more on identification and resolution of immediate issues. Strategic planning typically is more oriented to rapidly changing future situations and how to cope with changes organizationally. It is more action oriented and concerned with handling unexpected events.

Applied only by itself, strategic planning can be less comprehensive in its approach. By focusing on immediate issues, it may deviate from achieving such long-term objectives as sustainable development. But if used within the framework of integrated long-range policy and planning, the strategic planning approach can be very appropriate.

PUBLIC INVOLVEMENT IN PLANNING

Planning is for the benefit of people, and they should be involved in the planning and development of tourism in their areas. Through this involvement, tourism development will reflect a consensus of what the people want. Also, if residents are involved in planning and development decisions-

and if they understand the benefits the tourism can bring-they will more likely support it.

At the national and regional levels of preparing tourism plans, the common approach to obtaining public involvement is to appoint a steering committee. This committee offers guidance to the planning team and reviews its work, especially the draft reports and policy and planning recommendations that are made. A planning study steering committee is typically composed of representatives of the relevant government agencies involved in tourism, the private sector, and community, religious and other relevant organizations. Also, open public hearings can be held on the plan. These hearings provide the opportunity for anybody to learn about the plan and express their opinions. Another common approach, when the plan is completed, is to organize a national or regional tourism seminar.

This meeting informs participants and the general public about the importance of controlled tourism development and the recommendations of the plan. Such seminars often receive wide publicity in the communications media. In a large country or region, the usual procedure is for the tourism plan to be prepared by the central authority with public involvement. This can be termed the 'top-down' approach. Another procedure sometimes used is the 'bottom-up' approach. This involves holding meetings with local districts or communities to determine what type of development they would like to have. These local objectives and ideas are then fitted together into a national or regional plan. This approach achieves greater local public involvement in the planning process. But it is more time consuming and may lead to conflicting objectives, policies and development recommendations among the local areas. These conflicts need to be reconciled at the national and regional levels in order to form a consistent plan.

It is important that the development patterns of the local areas complement and reinforce one another, but also reflect the needs and desires of local communities. Often a combination of the 'top-down' and 'bottom-up' approaches achieves the best results.

THE TOURISM PLANNING PROCESS

The first step in the planning process is careful preparation of the study so that it provides the type of development guidance that is needed. Study preparation involves formulating the project terms of reference, selecting the technical team to carry out the study, appointing a steering committee, and organizing the study activities. The terms of reference (TOR) for the planning study should be carefully formulated so that the study achieves its desired results and outputs.

The TOR for a national or regional plan indicates the outputs and activities that are necessary to prepare the development policy and plan. The special considerations to be made in planning-such as economic, environmental or social issues and the critical institutional elements-should be specified in the

TOR. Identification of implementation techniques are also specified. The TOR format typically follows the planning process explained here, but it is tailored to the specific characteristics and needs of the planning area. Many places already have some limited tourism development, and these existing patterns must be considered in formulating the TOR. Other countries or regions will have considerable existing tourism development, but it may be declining or not be in a form that generates optimum benefits.

The TOR will therefore emphasize how to rejuvenate and improve existing development, along with how to provide guidance on the future expansion of tourism. It is common for a single study include various levels of tourism planning, such as national and regional plans along with detailed planning for priority development areas and projects. The planning for all these levels will need to be specified in the TOR.

BUDDHIST CIRCUIT

India is the birthplace of one of the most widely accepted religions in the world-Buddhism. The four holy places associated with Gautam Buddha in India are-Lumbini, his birthplace, which now lies in Nepal; Bodhgaya, where he attained enlightenment; Sarnath, near Varanasi, where he preached his first sermon; Kushinagar, near Gorakhpur, where he achieved Mahanirvana. The other important tourist places associated with Buddhism are: Sanchi, Vaishali, Nalanda, Amravati and Nagargunakonda.

All these places together are known as the famous Buddhist circuit in India. Bodhgaya is the most important Buddhist pilgrimage amongst all these places in India. Apart from being a significant archaeological site, it is renowned for the Mahabodhi Temple, which houses a 50 metre high pyramidal spire and an image of the Buddha. Sarnath near Varanasi is a vital centre of the Buddhist world where he delivered his first sermon and set in motion the wheel of law, the Dharmachakra. Buddhism germinated in Sarnath amidst the deer park. Nalanda is the famous education centre of Buddhism where the Chinese scholar and traveller Hiuen Tsang stayed in the 7th century to explore the roots of Buddhism.

Vaishali is significant to Buddhists as Lord Buddha announced his impending Nirvana here. One of the famous pillars erected by Ashoka to propagate Buddhism also stands here in Nalanda. Sanchi in Madhya Pradesh is known for its numerous stupas, monasteries, temples and pillars dating from the 3rd century B.C. to the 12th century A.D. Amaravati on the bank of river Krishna in the South India, is famous for its temple, dedicated to Lord Amarewara.

The temple is the dilapidated 2000-year-old Buddhist stupa that draws millions of archaeologists and pilgrims every year. Named after the great scholar of Buddhism, Nagarjunakonda, located on the banks of river Krishna retains its status as the greatest centre of Buddhist learning in the South of Vindhyas. Earlier known as Vijayapuri, Nagarjunakonda was the venue of the massive congregation of monks and scholars during the bygone era. The Buddhist circuit in India thus introduces you with the major townships in India that mark the evolution, development and propagation of Buddhism. After Gautam Buddha, it was Emperor Ashoka followed by his daughter and son Sanghmitra and Mahindra, who took the charge of propagating Buddhism in India as well as the South Asian countries like Burma, Nepal, China, Japan, Malaysia, Sri Lanka etc.

INFORMATION AND COMMUNICATION TECHNOLOGIES

"Atithi Devo Bhava"—Lets welcome tourists as guests and send them back as friends." The new advertisement by the Ministry of Tourism has been seen by all of us. Using Information Technology, this message, is being sent out for Tourists, Tour operators, Travel agents, public at large for the following two basic purposes.

- To create a sense of security amongst Tourists.
- To change the attitude towards Tourists in India.

ICT Information Communication Technologies have been transforming tourism globally. The ICT driven re-engineering has gradually generated a new paradigm-shift completely changing the Industry structure and developing a whole range of opportunities and threats. The new technologies enable the customers to customise, purchase and select the tourism products with pace and ease.

In fact the information technologies are undergoing a revolution world over. They are a key determinant for maximizing the gains. However the success of ICT deployment requires constant improvement and innovative management. The customer's decision risk has increased manifold because he has only information to rely on as he neither sees or inspects or tries out tourist services before deciding to use them. He can rely on the Internet, which is the latest product of Information Technology. It is possible once the customer has access to Internet site; he gets various opportunities out of which E-mail is one. The latest one to be used is video-conferencing, which is fast being identified as a powerful means of communication between the service providers of Tourism and the users of such services. In fact the communication technologies have completely revolutionized the Tourism Industry. Role of Communication Technologies is vital to any business and particularly to the tourism business. They are important for cost savings and improved communications that arise from an internal network. They help in reaching out and connecting with customers, suppliers and collaborators, which, in the case of Tourism Industry are:

- Airways, Railways and Roadways
- Hotels and all the other types of accommodation
- Tour operators and Travel agents
- Tourists and Travellers

To be precise, following benefits are offered by telecommunication to Tourism as well as other businesses:

- Enables sharing and dissemination of information of all tourism partners.
- Helps geographically separate persons to come together.
- Promotes new ways of tourism partnership.
- Restructure relationship with partners.

However the communication technologies are also prone to following limitations:

- High initial set-up cost
- Practical difficulties
- Security Risks

Inspite of the limitations, Information Communication Technologies are being used in a big way by the Tourism Industry. In fact, it will not be wrong to say that no successful Tour operator or Travel Agent can function without using information technologies. It is, therefore, extremely significant to the Tourism Industry. It will be appropriate here to extend the following quote. "A Journey of a thousand miles must begin with a single step" Lao Tzu. "No single step by a tourist can be taken without using Information Technologies".

OBJECTIVES

So far you have learnt about the concept of marketing and understood that Tourism marketing stands apart from marketing of other products and their advertising techniques and Public relations are also unique. After having this basic knowledge, with respect to tourism marketing, this session will deal with the basic concepts of information technologies in tourism marketing.

After having gone through this session, you should be able to:

- Define and explain different information technologies.
- Know various sectors of Tourism that require information technologies.
- Realise the benefits of information technologies for the user as well as Tour and Travel agents.
- Understand how the use of information technology has led to the growth of Tourism world over.
- Understand the role of Information Technologies in Information Centres.
- Understand Tourism with respect to changing communication technologies.

COMMUNICATION TECHNOLOGY: SIGNIFICANCE

The communication technology is significant in tourism industry in following ways:

- Allows organizations to use their resources more wisely and profitably.

- Creates a sense of security amongst tourists and also provides a friendly environment.
- Develops new avenues and new tourist spots.
- Enables central control and outsourcing of non-core functions.
- Helps in development of extensive growth between partner organizations and between employees, consumers and organizations.
- Helps in sustaining and promoting the existing ones.
- Information technology devices help in linking and sharing data and processes electronically, to build complementary services, expand, reach and enhance collaboration.
- Most devices result in information power storage and profitability.
- Possibility of handling complex details with increase in speed.
- Results in enhancement of processing capabilities.

Davis and Meyer state "Almost instantaneous communication and computation, for example, are shrinking time and focusing us on speed. Connectivity is putting everybody and everything on line in one way or the other and has led to the "the death of distance", a shrinking of space. Intangible value of all kinds, like services and information is growing explosively reducing the importance of tangible mass". The opinion clearly highlights the importance and impact of emerging communication technologies in this highly dynamic industry.

The concept of "Global Village" would be very appropriate in this scenario because it is growing communication technologies, which have opened doors for tourists and travellers and have made availability of information only with the press of a button, with the help of several new Information Technologies.

NEW INFORMATION TECHNOLOGIES

- Cable Television Technology
- Computer Technology
- Internet and Travel and Tourism
- Satellite Television
- Sky Track Technology
- Telecopy Technology
- Telefax Technology
- Teletex Technology
- Videotex Technology
- Websites

COMPUTER TECHNOLOGY

Computer is a tool, which is capable of processing a very large amount of data rapidly, or it is any device capable of processing information to produce a desired result. No matter how large or small they are, computers typically perform their work in three well-defined steps:

- Accepting input
- Processing the input just as to predefined rules
- Producing output

Computer is a multi-function electronic device that can execute instructions to perform a task. Therefore an electronic device that performs pre-defined or programmed computations at a high speed and with great accuracy; a machine that is used to store, transfer, and transform information is known as "Computer" to us.

It has made its entry in the field of tourism in a big way. In fact, computers are in use in some way or the other in various branches of tourism since the early sixties.

Be it travel agencies, hotels, Airlines or recently even in the Railways, Computers have played a key role in making the task of providers of travel services an easy affair. Not only this, through home terminals, computers are undertaking, among other jobs, the planning of vacations for an individual and his family.

Computer applications are used in:

- Airlines
- Cargo
- Hotels
- Terminals
- Travel Agency
- Railways

In the year 1983–Thompson Holidays first used computers using online programmes and introduced reservations via Prestel. Several other big tour operators, since then used similar to sell their various programmes.

SATELLITE TELEVISION

Satellite television is television operated by means of orbiting communication satellites located 37,000 km above the earth's surface. The first satellite television signal was relayed from Europe to the Telstar satellite over North America in 1962.

The first domestic North American satellite to carry television was Canada's Anik 1, which was launched in 1973. Satellite can also be described as a television system in which the signal is transmitted to an orbiting satellite that receives the signal and amplifies it and transmits it back to earth.

Therefore, it refers to courses that are broadcast, usually live, by an electronic signal sent to a satellite orbiting the earth and then retrieved by a satellite dish.

The satellite dish broadcasting the programme is called an "uplink", and the receiving dish is called a "downlink". For Tour operators, as well as Travel agents it serves as a linking device for making available the information of one corner of world to the other corner and Tourists are also, accordingly, benefitted by this linking device.

CABLE TELEVISION TECHNOLOGY

Cable television or Community Antenna Television is a system of providing television, FM radio programming and other services to consumers via radio waves transmitted directly to people's televisions through fixed coaxial cables as opposed to the over-the-air method used in traditional television broadcasting in which a television antenna is required. Cable system covering defined areas, such as the UK's franchise to install and operate a cable system granted by the Cable Authority and Department of Trade and Industry, offering TV channel output and, increasingly, local loop digital telephony services. The Cable Television Association is the CATV industry's representative organization.

Therefore it is a transmission system that distributes and broadcasts television signals and other services by means of a coaxial cable. Cable Television Technology has also greatly helped in information transfer and information sharing. Therefore, it has brought the tourists, the tour operators and the destinations close. It immensely helps in advertising and marketing of Tourism products.

VIDEOTEX TECHNOLOGY

Videotex is a system for sending of pages of text to a user in computer form, typically to be displayed on a television. It is computer technology of the 1980s that uses ordinary television sets, or similar low-cost monitors, to display computer information. Videotex systems, such as Canada's Telidon, were a complete commercial failure in North America, but achieved a modicum of success in Europe–*e.g.* France's Teletel and, to a much lesser degree, the UK's Prestel. Therefore, it is a form of electronic publishing consisting of computer-generated text distributed through telecommunications and received and viewed on home television.

It occupies a special position among the 'new media'. It plays a key role in the link between telecommunication and the computer sciences. Its advantage lies in the possibility it provides for linking computers and also in its interactive dialogue capabilities. Using Videotex, information and communication systems can be converted into interactive systems capable of communicating with one another. In fact, Videotex is a multipurpose instrument with multiplicity of uses.

It serves as:

- An instrument for data processing
- An information medium
- An organizational aid
- A communication system
- A marketing instrument

This relatively new service connects various forms of use of the facilities and at the same time offers some other possibilities. To operate this service, a television set with a decoder and telephone is necessary, without which the service cannot operate.

In Europe, nearly all the households have television sets and a telephone and with the help of Vedeotex, separate households can be reached in large areas. Members of German BTX service as well as Members of France Telecom services can now obtain all kinds of information from external computers or use data bank all through their television sets. In many other European countries and USA, similar systems are in use.

It is being used in a big way in Tourism, also in India because:

- It allows rapid message transmission
- Fast and inexpensive data collection
- Keeps up-to-date information, which is crucial for advertising

It has been found that Videotex is the most advantageous means of Communication, taking into account its low cost and wider range of applications. This technology enables the tour operators and travel agents or hoteliers to send complete pages of information text to the tourist to assist him in deciding and finalizing his tour plans. Satellite, Cable and Videotex technologies are very important because of their wider coverage and their technical methods of transmission, however, they have one shortcoming that none can be directed to one specific person. In addition, the person receiving information is only partially informed. The receiver of information cannot also start a dialogue or communicate. However, the following gives possibility of direct transmission of information to a single consumer:

TELETEX TECHNOLOGY

Teletex is a text and document communications service that could be provided over telephone lines. Teletex allows for the transmission and outing of Group 4 facsimile documents. It is neither like Telex nor like Teletex. Although it may not be as versatile a technology as some others that have been mentioned earlier in this session, but helps in transmitting information which is required by a tourist from a tour operator, Travel agent or a Hotel. Computer information and even copies of documents can be transferred to the tourist with efficiency. It is an improvement over telex and has in fact developed from it. The receiver for Teletex is an electronic 'typewriter', which can send electronically enriched 'letters' to owners of ordinary telex equipment. The transmission of message time is usually shorter in comparison with time taken with telex. Besides, it is also possible to transmit more office typewriters, symbols. A normal electronic typewriter can also be used as a receiver for telefax.

TELEFAX TECHNOLOGY

It is an electronic post office box system. Each member of the system has his or her 'post office box' in the computer, where other members can leave their message. The owner of each box can electronically contact the others.

All the means discussed permit the exchange of information electronically through a data 'network'. The exchange of information between the members with the assistance of electronic transmission is very fast. The data is also available in written form in printouts.

'Network' is a system of transmission linking facilities for automatic data processing. In this way, different computers are connected, permitting data exchange and processing over long distances. Telecommunication is possible only when there is such a network available. Telephone is the simplest and best communication network. In addition there is also separate clear data network for the exchange of data, which works digitally. In this way, a high transmission speed is achieved and there is a very low ratio of errors during transmission.

There are different types of networks, which can be used for telecommunication purposes either separately or combined. In Tourism, in addition to travel agents, tour operators, hoteliers, airlines, travel journalist's etc. use this technology.

TELECOPY

It provides the possibility of exchanging photocopies through a data network. Information, in the form of either written document or technical drawing, is remote copied. This means that two facilities for copying are connected. One at the sender's end and the other at the receiver's end. Transmission time is only a few minutes. Usually the details of packages, booking details or list of itineraries are sent to this tourist by the Tour operator, Travel agent or the Hotel.

INTERNET AND TRAVEL AND TOURISM

So far the information technology dealt with has been of the kind where intermediaries, travel agents, tour operators etc. are an indispensable part in the distribution and marketing of travel and tourism products, and as an important point of sale or product outlets.

This is an information technology where the producer and the consumer are directly communicating, by putting the indispensability of travel intermediaries in question.

As has been discussed earlier, the intangibility of the product where risk and uncertainty for the customer is higher, his need for reliable prepurchase information is stronger. Through Internet, which is the latest product of information technology, this need is fulfilled.

This interactive information-supplying medium is user friendly and gives enormous information of all kinds related to travel. Apart from supplying information about the world's leading and emerging tourist destination of all kinds, it is now possible to book and buy holidays through Internet using plastic money. It gives information on all Airlines, Hotels and Car hire companies, which are in its database. Microsoft is a travel agent. Its Internet site branded Expedia is one of the most important examples of the new generation of travel intermediaries.

Distribution of travel and tourism products using the Internet has a substantial cost reduction advantage for providers of tourism services. The cost incurred by suppliers in receiving a customer booking is the one, which is costly. So, Internet gives a practical aid both in supplying information and receiving bookings or selling tourism products on the principal's behalf. Marketing tourism products on the Internet is also possible. This is done through the page of the company's Internet site.

Once the company gets access to the Internet, it gets various opportunities. Of these, Electronicmail is one. As a tourism product supplier, especially with business travel as a selected target market, it can communicate with the person through his/her e-mail address wherever the client is. Unlike telephone communication, there is no need for the presence of the receiver of the message during message transmission.

It also gives a typed copy of the message. E-mail communication medium is very cheap yet efficient and effective. On the other hand, marketing on the Internet has an advantage of being used by all company's of all sizes as long as they can establish their Web Site on the Internet.

WEBSITES

A website is a collection of all pages under one domain. Sometimes, the subdirectories of large ISP(s) are also referred to as websites as they have been designed by different users and with different interests in mind.

Benefits of Websites

No matter how small or large a business is, one can profit enormously from a website in following ways.

- Reduces advertising costs.
- Information remains on line and always up-to-date.
- Pictures, product description, newly won awards, customer questions and instruction videos are possible on the web-site.
- Announcement of a package, deal, and sale can be promptly updated on the website.
- Customers find it simpler to surf the net and log-on to the websites for desired information.
- Websites almost eliminate waste of time in travelling for the desired information centre.

The tourist can make use of the websites, sitting back at home for making tour plans. Accordingly enormous websites are there by tour operators, travel agents, Hotels etc, some of which are given below.

- Luxury Resortsindia.com
- Destinations India.com
- Jaipur JodhpurUdaipur.com

- India Tours and Travels.com
- Asia Tours and Travel.com
- TravelinIndia.com

SKY TRACK

It is an automated airline reservation system, which enables travel agents to make bookings on hundreds of world's airlines using standard Prestel Television set and a keyboard. Possibility of direct transmission between tourists, tour operators and travel agents. This system invented by British Telecom is a way of providing computerized information terminal. The only requirement is a Telephone line and a standard colour Television set with an Adapter to link it to a decoder and keyboard. The information is transmitted quickly and accurately via ordinary telephone lines. The required information is rapidly transmitted through this technology and is very helpful in providing desired information to tourists.

INFORMATION TECHNOLOGY IN THE TRANSPORT SECTOR

Transport provides the essential link between tourism origin and destination areas and facilitates the movement of holidaymakers, business travellers, people visiting friends and relatives and those undertaking educational and health tourism. Before setting out on a journey of any kind, every traveller makes sure which Transport Company has a good safety record. To this effect, airplane coaches and even taxis are equipped with good communication equipment. An Airplane flies with the help of modern information technology equipment, which provides information ranging from weather, altitude and other information to the pilot, to communication made during emergency by the pilot with other airplanes and air traffic control stations.

In-flight entertainment is also a product of information technology, video games, video films are examples. In the case of buses/coaches and taxis, in many countries with developed tourism business, they are equipped with radio communication systems for various uses. For example, the driver or the tour guide updates the Tour Company headquarters about the progress of the tour throughout the touring period. This communication ensures the safety of tourists. Fast and easy information flow is of paramount importance to build confidence in the travelling public. In recent years, the confidence built due to the use of modern IT has been demonstrated by a tremendous increase in the number of travellers worldwide.

INFORMATION TECHNOLOGY IN THE ACCOMMODATION SECTOR

In the accommodation sector also the contribution of information technology is prominent. Any individual or group wishing to travel to any part of the world now has an easy access to the accommodation service providers. A visitor can access information about the kind of hotels at the destination, their ranges of product, the price and other relevant information without leaving his/her office or home. What one has to do is to ring up a travel agency and get the expert advice. This will help any visitor greatly as to where to stay during any kind of trip away from home.

Here the information can be obtained aided by still or moving pictures in order to give an exact feature of an accommodation, facilities and services of one's choice. At a destination also visitors are at ease during their stay in every respect, in getting information about their business, family or other information back home. They are also at ease to relaxing with the videos and television entertainment programmes, which nowadays are part and parcel of many accommodation units.

INFORMATION TECHNOLOGY IN THE ATTRACTION SECTOR

In the case of attractions, both man-made and natural the owners need to communicate or inform their customers and potential customers about their product. Information about the kind of attraction, where it is located and how to get there is of vital importance. The attraction owners, particularly the national tourist offices, discharge their duty of promoting their country's tourist attractions using the information technology products.

Information through promotional videos, Internet web Sites, television advertisements and travel documentaries are the main information dissemination tools. There is, in fact, competition amongst tour operation to create better and better sites for the user to enable the tourist to decide in their favour. More and more people around the Globe are getting computer literate or so to say computer savvy, due to which, they have increasingly become information seekers. Before deciding on the desired destination, they not only rely on the sites of tour operators or travel agents, they even take feedback from other travellers to find out about their experiences. In the Attraction Sector communication technologies are thus very significant.

INFORMATION CENTRES AND COMMUNICATION TECHNOLOGIES

Several information centres and tourist offices of Government of India are currently located at India and abroad. Overseas offices are located in Australia, Canada, France, Germany, Italy, Japan, Netherlands, Singapore, Spain, Sweden, UAE, U.K., U.S.A., New York, Israel, the Russian Federation and South Africa.

INFORMATION TECHNOLOGY AND GROWTH OF TOURISM WORLD OVER

It was in 1908 that the first move was made for promoting tourism by only three countries namely Spain, France and Portugal who founded the

France Hispano Portuguese. Federation of Tourist Association is considered the first international tourist organization. After first the World War, several other countries realised the need as well, but due to lack of communication technologies, the endeavour could not take off inspite of setting up the International Union of National Tourist Propaganda Organization in 1925.

After the Second World War, this endeavour was revived from the year 1963. With the revolution in the Information Communication Technologies the world Tourism, as a joint effort gained momentum. It was in the 1980s that the Tourist did not feel lost or insecure due to lack of information. Interestingly, during the same period, India was perceived as a country, which was backward and inhabited with wildlife and natives because India lagged far behind in growth of communication technologies.

It was only the late 1980s due to the advent of computer technology in a big way and satellite network that India could change that perception among foreigners. India also saw tourism increasing due to changed perceptions, advertising, marketing and attracting the tourists using information technologies.

Currently, tourist arrivals are predicted to grow by an average 4.3% a year over the next two decades, while receipts from international tourism will climb by 6.7% a year.

Tourism: Mega Trends for the 21st century:

- Globalization versus localization
- Electronic technology will become all-powerful in influencing destination choice and distribution
- Fast track travel–emphasis will be placed on facilitation and the speeding up of the travel process
- Customers 'call the shots' through technology such as CDROM atlases, internet, internet inspection of hotels and other facilities, brokers offering discounted rooms on websites, last minute e-mails, low fares etc.
- The tourist world shrinking by the day, due to technology, the tourist is nearly reaching 'space tourism'
- Growing impact of technologies, helping aggressive campaign is kindling the urge for travel consumption.

However, growth and related benefits of tourism cannot be taken for granted. The competition among countries, tour operators, destinations, etc. is becoming so fierce, that, in order to be a winner the following imperatives will have to be kept in mind by every country,

- Development focused on quality and responsibility
- Value for money
- Full utilization of information technology to identify and communicate effectively with market segments and niches.

TOURISM PROMOTION

Promotion means activities that communicate the merits of the product and persuade target customers to buy it. Ford spends about $2.3 billion each year on advertising to tell consumers about the company and its many products. The franchised dealers and salespeople assist potential buyers to buy a Ford car. Ford and its dealers offer promotions-sales, cash rebates and low financing rates as purchase incentives.

The promotion activities of marketing are concerned with communication with the customers that the product is available at the right price and at the right place. The promotional communication aims at informing and persuading the actual and potential customers into actual purchase of the product. An effective marketing programme moulds all the marketing mix elements–product, price, place and promotion to achieve the marketing objectives.

PROMOTIONAL OBJECTIVES

Effective promotion starts from an analysis and formulation of clear-cut objectives.

These include:

- Identification of the target audience to be reached;
- Identification of the purpose of the communication;
- Formulation of message to achieve the goal;
- Choice of media for delivering the message to the target audience;
- Allocation of the budget to achieve the desired purpose;
- Evaluation in terms of sales and feedback obtained from the customers.

The more carefully objectives are set the better promotion works.

Promotional planning can be done with a view:

- To create new ideas and attitudes: The purpose could be to create awareness of completely new tourism products such as Spa and Spirituality in Himalayas.
- To change the image: The purpose could be to change the unfavourable image of an existing tourism product in the minds of customers. For example New York, in late seventies changed the image of the city to promote tourism.
- To reinforce the image: Larger firms try to reinforce the attitude of customers to retain their existing market like visit to Disneyland and destinations like Goa, Uttaranchal and Singapore.

INTEGRATING COMMUNICATION PROCESS WITH PROMOTION PROGRAMMES

Every consumer goes through various stages of the decision-making process to arrive at a satisfactory decision.

The process of decision-making is a sequence of various steps:

- Need recognition
- Information search
- Evaluation of various alternatives
- Choice of product/services
- Post-purchase evaluation

The marketing communicator needs to effectively design the promotion programme in order to help the consumer in making a proper decision.

The good communication strategy should address target consumers needs and wants and help them to choose a particular tourism product. Steps in Developing Effective Market for Tourism Product The marketer needs to address various issues while designing the programme to effectively market the tourism product.

IDENTIFYING THE TARGET MARKET

A tourist organization needs to know their target market consisting of actual and potential customers. The target audience will determine the promotional campaign on what to say, how to say, when to say, where to say and who will say.

DETERMINING THE PROMOTIONAL OBJECTIVE

Once the target market has been identified, the marketer must decide about the purpose of promotional activity.

- *Awareness*: The target market may be totally unaware of the product. The communicator needs to make them aware and knowledgeable about the tourism product.
- *Preference*: If consumers know the product, they need to be made to feel favourably about the product and then moved to the stage of being convinced about preferring such a product to other products.
- *Purchase*: Some members of the target market might be convinced about the product, they need to be taken to the action stage of making an actual purchase of the product. Offering special promotional prices or rebates can persuade them.

DESIGNING A MESSAGE

It is an important step after deciding upon the promotional objective. The communicator needs to develop an effective message to decide what to say and how to say it. "Incredible India' campaign on television is aimed at capturing the attention of viewers about various tourist places all over the India.

CHOOSING THE MEDIA

The communicator must select between personal and non-personal channels of communication.

- Personal communication channels include face-to-face interaction, telephone or mail and are effective channels of influencing the customers of target market.
- Non-personal communication channels include media such as newspapers, magazines, radio, television, billboards, posters and websites. They are a major source to influence, create and reinforce the image of a product among consumers.

FEEDBACK

After deciding and sending the message, the marketing communicator needs to obtain feedback on its promotional efforts.

They need to know about target consumers' attitudes towards the product and company. Such feedback facilitates changes in the promotion programme or in the product itself. For example, most of the Airlines and 5-star hotels ask consumers about their experience after the flight or stay in the hotel.

THE PROMOTIONAL MIX

After knowing about the main objectives of promotion, let us understand the four main elements of the promotional mix. A company's total marketing communication mix-also called its promotion mix-consists of the specific blend of advertising, sales promotion, public relations, and personal selling that the company uses to pursue its advertising and marketing objectives.

The four major promotional tools of promotion are as follows:

- *Advertising*: Any paid form of nonpersonal presentation and promotion of ideas, goods, or services by an identified sponsor.
- *Sales Promotion*: Short term incentives to encourage the purchase or sale of a product or service.
- *Public Relations*: Building a good reputation of the company with the public by obtaining favourable publicity, good corporate image, and handling unfavourable events if any.
- *Personal Selling*: The sales force of the company makes personal presentations to make sales.

ADVERTISING

Advertising has been defined as any non-personal presentation by an identified sponsor for the promotion of ideas, goods, or services in exchange for value. While in designing the advertising programme, the target audience and message requirements should be analysed carefully. Advertising in tourism has many uses.

They include:

- Creating awareness;
- Advertising a special offer;
- Providing information on seasonal deals;
- Informing about special services;

- Direct selling;
- Soliciting consumer information;
- Overcoming negative attitudes;
- Reaching a new target audience;
- Providing a new use.

DEVELOPMENT OF ADVERTISING PROGRAMMES

Marketing management must make four important decisions when developing an advertising programme:

- Setting advertising objectives
- Setting the advertising budget
- Selecting advertising Media
- Evaluating Advertising Campaigns

SETTING THE ADVERTISING BUDGET

In general, marketing of products can be done with a variety of media options available but certain particular features exist with relation to advertising of travel and tourism in media:

- Tourism has a large and highly fragmented advertising market, consisting of few big enterprises with huge advertising budgets and a large number of small firms with less to spend on advertising.
- Print is the dominant medium in travel and tourism advertising. The higher cost of advertising on TV has made press a more economical medium to reach the target audience.
- Much of the expenditure on travel and tourism is done on brochures, destination guides, and point-of-sales displays. Tourist Boards, tour operators, and tourist information centres provide large amounts of information through printed material to prospective customers.

These specific factors should be kept in mind while setting the advertising budget for a tourism product.

SELECTING ADVERTISING MEDIA

The media planner has to essentially choose the most economical combination of media channels to reach desired target audience. There are various factors to be considered while appraising the media options.

Some of the main factors in media selection are:

- Readership or audience size;
- Geographical reach;
- Repetition and frequency of advertisement;
- Segment target market size;
- Unit cost and cost per thousand;
- Seasonal/period discounts available;
- Availability of medium;
- Reproduction quality.

SOME ADVERTISING TECHNIQUES IN TOURISM MARKETING

The advertiser creates the message in such a manner that will capture the target market's attention and interest. In tourism marketing some techniques of message presentation have been extensively used by advertisers over the years such as following:

SLICE OF LIFE

This technique shows some characters using or discussing the product's uses/benefits. For example, husband and wife recalling their experiences to a particular destination and decide to visit the place again.

LIFESTYLE

This style shows how a particular product fits in with a particular lifestyle. For example, Uttaranchal Tourism prints advertisement exhorting adventurous people to come for river rafting in Rishikesh.

TESTIMONY

The method of selling the product is through the testimony of satisfied customers. A single person, a number of people or a famous celebrity can do it.

MUSICAL

This method shows one or more people singing about the product. For example, Broadway actors sang the song 'I Love New York' to encourage tourists to visit New York. The tourist organizations often use a combination of the techniques while promoting tourist product.

SALES PROMOTION

Sales promotion can be defined as: Those marketing activities other than personal selling and advertising and publicity that stimulate purchases such as exhibitions, shows, and demonstrations. In a way they refer to short–term incentives offered to the consumer to induce a booking, reservation or sale.

OBJECTIVES OF SALES PROMOTION

The sales Promotion in tourism is done with the following objectives:

- *Creating awareness*: Sometimes companies devise special promotions like two or more companies join or tie up together to build awareness. For example, an Airline and hotel group tie-up to promote a particular destination.
- *Encouraging early bookings*: Tour operators often offer discounts at the start of the season to generate immediate bookings. For example, Deccan Airways providing airline tickets at auction to Pune, Bombay or Goa if booked in advance.

- *Increase trial*: The tourists are encouraged to try the product by giving incentives like free stays or trial coupons at much discounted prices.
- *Enhanced repeat buy*: Some promotions are done to encourage repeat stays or visits. For example, Indian Airline offers of multi-coupon discounts to frequent flyers.
- *Combating competition*: Tour operators or hotels may cut down their prices to combat any price cut by competitors or may be done to block competitors' moves in advance.
- *Promote use of tourist product during off-season*: When demand is low for hotel rooms, during low season, special season offers are used to attract customers. For example, Goa hotels offer special discounts during the rainy season; Jaipur and Agra hotels offer discounts during the summer season.
- *Motivating sales force*: The travel agencies give commission to travel agents for selling a certain number of tickets. The agents are also provided coupons, free offers, sales aids and training materials.

TECHNIQUES OF TOURISM SALES PROMOTION

Some of the sales promotion activities used in travel and tourism are as follows:

- *Rebates*: The tourist product is made available at special price less than original price for a limited period of time.
- *Discounts*: Certain percentage of price is deducted as discount from the original price to induce them to buy or buy more. For example, hotel stay for two children at discounted price for a particular package.
- *Refunds*: The seller offers to refund a part of the price paid by the customer on previous purchase of the product.
- *Contests*: These are another form of promotion. In these consumers are required to participate in some competitive event involving application of skills and winners are given some reward.
- *Quantity deals*: The tourist operator provides special package in which buyer is offered additional product at lower or no price. For example, a tourist operator coming out with the offer in family package 'two children for the price of one'.

Some other techniques of sales promotion are:

- Vouchers,
- Competitions,
- Prizes,
- Gifts and premium,
- Additional night stay,
- Slide shows,
- Point of purchase displays, and
- Posters.

4

Outdoor Adventure Tourism

INTRODUCTION

India offers plenty of scope for outdoor activities. Whether it's climbing or river-running, skiing or para- gliding, snorkelling or windsurfing, India has it all. The Himalayas, stretching in a majestic arc across the northern part of the country, are perfect for trekking and mountaineering; the rivers of the north, tumbling down from the mountains, are excellent for white water rafting. Auli and Narkanda, even if they aren't as well known as Switzerland, have ski slopes which are worth a run.

Further south, the Sahyadris and the Nilgiris are tailor-made for more relaxed trekking; set up base camp at the picture-pretty towns of Coonoor or Ooty, and strike out on your own- through tea gardens, coffee plantations and forests of fragrant sandalwood. Head for the coast- or for the islands of Andaman and Nicobar and the Lakshadweep, where windsurfing, scuba diving, snorkelling and swimming are just some of the ways of enjoying yourself. So put on your sneakers, haul on a backpack- and set out to conquer the great wilderness which lies beyond the teeming cities of India. You can be pretty sure to make some interesting discoveries every step along the way.

AERIAL SPORTS

Introduction

Centuries ago, when man first began to look up at the sky and wonder what lay above him, he's been captive to an inherent urge to fly to soar above and see what the earth looks like from way up there. Whether it's mythical Daedalus, or his unfortunate son, Icarus, whose wax wings melted in the heat of the sun; whether it's tales of angels and cherubs, flying gods and winged deities, world mythology has always reflected mankind's desire to take to the skies. Aeroplanes, zeppelins, hot air balloons and helicopters have all been a fulfilment of this desire.

But if you really want to go off on your own, and not as part of a crowd of people, aerial sports- hang gliding, paragliding and parasailing are what you should be doing. Soaring along on your own (and having chance encounters with curious birds!), getting a bird's eye view of a stunning landscape- that's what aerial sport is all about. Aerial sport, as a part of adventure travel, has only recently gained any level of popularity in India. A number of places, both in Himalayan and peninsular India, are suitable for gliding, but have little infrastructure or rescue facilities to speak of. For the time being, therefore, we're listing only the places where aerial sports facilities do exist, adequate enough to ensure that you're safe and have a good time.

Aerial sports can be divided into six types: hang gliding, paragliding, parasailing, skydiving, hot air ballooning and bungee jumping. Of these aerial sports, only hang gliding, paragliding and parasailing are popular enough in India to be offered as an adventure option by organisers. Bungee jumping, skydiving and ballooning are very limited in scope and are currently available only in large metros like Delhi and Mumbai; furthermore, the infrastructure for these hasn't been developed sufficiently.

When to Visit

When you go gliding or parasailing depends upon where you go. By and large, summer is when the Himalayan sites those in Himachal, for instance- are at their best; and winter is when the sites in peninsular India can be used for aerial sports. The Nilgiris tend to get chilly during the winter, and although it is possible to go gliding during this time, summer is generally much more suitable. The only time aerial sports come to a standstill is during the monsoon, when wind and rain can make it a dangerous activity.

What to Bring

Warm clothing and a windcheater are a must, as the higher you rise, the lower the temperature falls, and it can get quite cold. Make sure you're wearing sturdy ankle-support shoes, long trousers, and gloves. A pair of sunglasses and a liberal splash of suntan lotion are highly recommended too. Whatever you need in the way of bedding and other 'essentials'- mineral water, food, medicines, etc- will depend upon where you're going. Larger cities and towns like Ooty, Bangalore, Mumbai and Manali have virtually everything you'll need, but if you're headed further out, to Billing and smaller places, it makes sense to carry stuff you can't do without.

Training

More training is required for aerial sports than for a number of other sports like trekking or swimming. Both paragliding and hang gliding need a few days' training, in which trainees are taught the essentials of rigging up and dismantling a glider, aerodynamics, air safety, wind and land conditions, and so on. Theoretical training is followed by dry runs, then by short hops which do not rise high in the air and cover very short distances. Even when you've learnt gliding, it's best to go for short, easy glides in the beginning, and graduate to more difficult and higher ones later. Parasailing, in comparison, requires less training and can be enjoyed even by novices. Physical fitness is top priority for anybody who's keen on aerial sports. You've got be in good condition, and not overweight. Suffering from vertigo is obviously a no-no when it comes to aerial sports. A few institutions in India offer training in paragliding and hang gliding and other aerial sports. The length of courses varies, with private companies offering a short 4-day course which just about manages to get you flying. What's recommended, instead, is a good course from a reputed association which specialises in aerial sports training. Some of these organisations include:

ANGLING

Few anglers in the West realise that India, with its dozens of rivers and thousands of streams, offers vast opportunities for sportfishing and angling. Whether you're the type who likes to string a worm onto a makeshift line and catch your own dinner- or a thoroughbred professional angler with the latest in fishing tackle- India's waters, both fresh and salt, can be a pleasant surprise. The country has an estimated 50,000 km of waters- rivers, streams, and lakes included- and an additional 3,000 km of coastline, and although sportfishing is still the preserve of a very select elite, there's definitely a lot of scope for some satisfying angling.

Major rivers like the Ganga and its tributaries, the Yamuna, the Brahmaputra, the Mahanadi, the Krishna and the Kaveri are home to a wide spectrum of fish, includingmahseer, rohu, katli, and trout. The coastal waters lapping the shores of peninsular India harbour marine sportfish such as mackerel, marlin and sea bass.

What makes angling or sportfishing easy in India is that most major cities lie along rivers, as a result of which getting to a suitable fishing spot is generally not a problem. Furthermore, most states have well-organised Departments of Fisheries, where special hatcheries ensure that there's always a gene pool of local and exotic fish.

Fish sanctuaries and hatcheries in Jammu and Kashmir, Himachal Pradesh, Uttar Pradesh and other states through which major rivers flow, maintain a vast stock of fish which are specially bred for re-stocking rivers. It probably won't be long before veteran anglers will be able to attribute some of the 'biggest ones' to Indian rivers.

When to Visit

Angling or sportfishing is possible on Indian rivers almost throughout the year, although most state authorities forbid angling during the monsoon months, when fish are breeding. Regional variations in climate, can however, cause hindrances: most of the Himalayas, for instance, are too cold to allow any angling during the winter months. On the whole, October to November and mid-February to mid-May are the best times to go sportfishing in India.

Licenses and Permits

Fishing licenses are mandatory for all eager anglers, so go to the designated official before you throw your line into the water, or you just might find yourself being hauled off and penalised. In most cases, fishing licenses are not issued during the monsoon (when most fish species breed); in addition, most licenses are issued for only a specified stretch of water. Furthermore, there are stipulations that all fish caught must be released into the water, and anglers are restricted to a specified number of fish per day. Angling licenses can be obtained from the organisations and offices listed below, for fishing in the corresponding state or region:

- Kerala—High Range Angling Association, Munnar
- Coorg—Coorg Wildlife Association, Madikeri
- Karnataka—Wildlife Association of South India, Bangalore
- Tamilnadu—Palni Hills Game Association, Kodaikanal Assistant Director of Fisheries, Udhagamandalam
- West Bengal—Fisheries Department, Mirik
- Assam—Angling Association, Tejpur
- Maharashtra—Fish Association of Powai Lake, Mumbai Tata Hydroelectric Works, Lonavla
- Delhi—Assistant Warden of Fisheries, Delhi Administration,(at Okhla Barrage, Okhla)
- Uttaranchal—Fishing Association, Dehradun, Forest Department, Corbett National Park Municipal Corporation, Nainital (for fishing in Naini Tal)
- Jammu and Kashmir—JandK Department of Fish Preservation, Srinagar
- Himachal Pradesh—District Fisheries Officer, Dharamshala Himachal Fisheries Department (Katrain/Barot/Sangla/Rohru)

If you're a foreigner, and heading off to the Lakshadweep or Andaman and Nicobar Islands to do some sportfishing, you'll need a permit from the Ministry of Home Affairs in New Delhi- or an authorised official in the state. The same applies to certain areas of Himachal Pradesh, Jammu and Kashmir and other border states.

Things to Bring

Patience- and lots of it. Angling requires oodles of patience, and the ability to keep still and quiet for hours on end- and then the skill to battle it out with a heavyweight fish of up to 200 kg for the next hour or more. And now to the more mundane. The basic fishing equipment required includes rods, lines, hooks, reel, flies, spinners, spoons and bait- in the form of worms, paste or other lure. Light, waterproof clothing- brown or green in colour- is essential, as are waterproof shoes or light sandals which can easily be slipped off to drain out sand or water. Sunscreen, a light hat and dark glasses are necessary, and during the winter make sure you're well clad with sufficient woollens and a macintosh.High quality angling equipment for angling is not widely available for hire in India, although some outfits in popular areas like Garhwal and the Nilgiris do provide equipment on hire.

Accommodation and other Facilities

In most cases, finding suitable accommodation shouldn't be too much bother, as many of India's biggest cities and towns lie along rivers. Even if there's not much fishing within an urban area, fishing beats will usually be close enough for you to stay in a town and drive out in the morning to the beat you've chosen. In cases where beats lie far from urban areas, there are generally state-operated forest lodges or fishing lodges in close proximity. These won't be the height of luxury, but you can depend upon them for basic necessities. In rare cases you might need to take along a tent and pitch camp. In an attempt to encourage game fishing in India, the national and state tourism departments have started providing leaflets and brochures on areas where fishing is possible.

These leaflets usually contain fairly accurate and detailed information on where to go, what are the facilities available in the area, where angling equipment can be hired, and what licenses will be required. More information can invariably be obtained from the state tourism departments in India. Some travel agencies and tour operators in India cater to anglers and will provide everything from equipment and experienced guides to boarding, lodging and transportation. Major cities and those close to angling and sportfishing grounds often have such travel agents; further information and assistance can always be obtained from the local wildlife, forests or fisheries department.

Rivers and Beats

The main river stretches suitable for angling are in the lower Himalayas, the Satpuras, and the Aravalis, all of which have rivers teeming with a wide range of fish. India's rivers have approximately 31 species of freshwater fish which are of interest to anglers; these include trout (brown and rainbow trout, both introduced species); murrel, catfish and cyprinids. Unfortunately, some of northern India's best fishing beats, on the rivers of Jammu and Kashmir, are no longer recommended, because of the ongoing turmoil in the state.

In quieter times, rivers like the Lidder, Indus, Jhelum and smaller tributaries like the Bringhi, Aru and Sheshnag- all replete with fish, especially brown trout- were a haven for anglers. Until peace returns to the area, however, it's unsafe to venture out.

1. The Brahmaputra, 2. Peninsula Rivers, 3. The Ganga and Yamuna, 4. The Coastal Waters.

The Brahmaputra

Arising in the Himalayan mountains along India's easternmost frontier with China, the Brahmaputra works its way through the far eastern states of the country, foaming through gorges and gushing over rocky beds till it reaches the Sunderbans delta in Bangladesh.

The Brahmaputra, its tributaries and a number of smaller streams and rivers in eastern India- including the Rangeet, the Teesta and the Lohit (as the Brahmaputra's known in Arunachal Pradesh)- are home to two main sport fish, locally known as the katli (or bokar) and the jhungha. In places, brown trout and mahseer can also be found. The Teesta, in particular, is known for its excellent mahseer.

Arunachal Pradesh —Arunachal Pradesh, one of India's easternmost states, is also one of the best places to go angling in the east. The state is bisected by the Lohit river and a number of smaller streams, all of which offer ample opportunity for reeling in some of the biggest fish you're likely to catch. Try Tezu, on the Lohit, or Tipi and Bhalukpong (on the Bhoroli river), and Pashighat (on the Siang River). Itanagar, the capital of Arunachal Pradesh, is connected to the nearest airport (Lilabari) and the closest railhead (Harmuty) by road. Beyond Itanagar, accommodation and other facilities are rather sparse, so you'll probably end up staying in a camp, or, if you're lucky, in a guesthouse.

Assam—In Assam, mahseer fishing is possible on the Manas river, at the Manas Tiger Reserve. Manas is about 176 km from Guwahati, which is connected by air to most major airports in India. The nearest railhead is Barpeta Road, 41 km from Manas.

Peninsula Rivers

The Mahanadi, Kaveri, Krishna and Godavari —The four major rivers of peninsular India- the Mahanadi, the Kaveri, Krishna and Godavari- have the advantage of being open to angling and sportfishing almost throughout the year, barring a short spell in the monsoon when the fish are breeding. Prominent species in the peninsular rivers include the high-backed mahseer, the purree, the khudchee and the white carp.

Tamilnadu —The Nilgiris have a number of streams, rivers and pools where good trout fishing is possible. Among the best trout streams are the Peermund stream, Kalkundi stream, Portimund stream, Mekod river, and the Chembar stream. The Mukurthi Lake and the reservoirs created by the Avalanche and Emerald rivers also are well-stocked with trout.

Kerala-—Good angling is possible in the streams around Munnar, and Elephant Lake (in Munnar) is particularly renowned for its excellent trout. Munnar is accessible via road from Kochi- it's a four hour drive- and from other cities and towns in southern India. Karnataka—The Kaveri, in Karnataka, is the prime angling or sportfishing river. Mysore, one of the main cities in the state (and with road, rail and air links to the rest of India), is located conveniently close to the Kaveri, and anglers can stay either in the city or at the Kaveri Fishing Lodge, slightly outside Mysore. The waters around the lodge, which is on the banks of the river, are a good place to fish for mahseer.

The Ganga and Yamuna

The Ganga, the Yamuna and their tributaries —The rivers flowing southwards from the Himalayas harbour a vast number of fish, including the well-respected and much coveted mahseer, a cyprinid which is considered by veterans to be one of the most difficult fish to reel in- as good, some feel, as the famed Atlantic salmon. The mahseer's been dubbed the 'King of Indian sportfish', and with good reason too. The largest of the carp and minnow family, the mahseer includes a number of different sub-species such as the red-finned mahseer, the yellow-finned mahseer and the copper mahseer. The largest can weigh up to 220 kg, and they're capable of putting up a very stiff fight. The time taken to pull in a mahseer is supposedly in ratio to its weight- 5 minutes for every 5 pounds.

Other game fish found in the rivers of northern India include trout, rohu, katla, alwan, chhiruh, kalbose, murrel and catfish. Catfish are a particularly popular choice with Indian anglers, as they're easy to bait, are good fighters, and are prized for their tasty, boneless flesh.

Delhi—Although the polluted and muddy waters of the Yamuna at Delhi may not appear very promising to most anglers, they actually harbour about eight species, including catfish and a local humpbacked species known as the moh. The best beats in Delhi are along Okhla.

Himachal Pradesh—Ever since Jammu and Kashmir became off-limits for eager anglers, Himachal Pradesh has acquired the status of prime fishing locale. The Kullu Manali region, especially the Larji Valley, is crisscrossed by a number of streams which finally meet the Beas river. Most of these streams have good brown trout, besides other local species. Kullu, linked through domestic airlines to most major cities in India, is also accessible via road from almost anywhere in northern India.

Kullu has ample accommodation, and is a convenient base for angling tours around the valley. Further north, the Baspa river is replete with trout, and along the Sangla Valley are dozens of good beats where prime specimens can be caught. Kasol, Bathad and Banjar are more acclaimed for mahseer.

Uttar Pradesh and Uttaranchal—The Shivaliks, stretching across the mountainous state of Uttaranchal, offer good fishing- both in rivers and streams as well as in lakes. The Ramganga and Sharda rivers and the area's lakes- Nainital, Dodital in particular- are great for trout and mahseer fishing. On the Ganga, the stretches around Beasghat and Gangalehri are good for mahseer. Convenient bases for fishing beats include Rishikesh (linked by rail to Hardwar and by road to the rest of the country); the Corbett National Park and Nainital, both of which have road connections to cities and towns all over northern India.

The Coastal Waters

India's 3,000 km long coastline offers abundant opportunities for angling, and port towns like Mumbai, Kandla, Nhava Sheva, Marmagao, Kochi, Kolkatta/Haldia, Paradip, Vishakhapatnam, Chennai and Tuticorin have facilities for coastal fishing. Fishing is possible in coastal waters and in estuaries, and also at Chilka Lake in Orissa. The Andaman and Nicobar Islands and the Lakshadweep Islands too are rich in marine life, although conservation laws in these areas have put a large portion of the waters off-limits for anglers. The main saltwater fish found along India's coasts include snapper, perch, sea bass, shark, jacks, mackerel, marlin, tuna, tripletail, sailfish and snook.

CAMEL SAFARIS

Introduction

India's western desert, sprawling across the state of Rajasthan, has its share of dromedaries- ponderous, surly, smelly and generally unattractive. But spend a few days riding one, and you could just find yourself thinking they're not so very disgusting. Rajasthan, India's westernmost state, is the very essence of exotic India- barren desert and drifting sand dunes. Monotonous and dull- but only at first sight. Step in deeper, and you'll be overwhelmed by sounds and sights, colours and fragrances which will stay with you long after.

The vivid orange and green skirts of local women on the way to a distant well; the bright blue houses of an entire town; the beautifully folksy sound of a village musician playing on a four-stringed sarangi. The aroma of good, home-cooked food, redolent with pure ghee; the comforting warmth of a blazing bonfire on a chill desert nigh.

You can see Rajasthan on a jeep safari. Or, if you've a penchant for the high life, aboard the Palace on Wheels, Rajasthan's luxury train. But to really get a hands-on feel of the desert state, there's no beating a camel safari. Clamber up on one of these seemingly ungainly beasts, hang on for dear life, and let the good times roll- literally, for the Ship of the Desert walks in a way which would certainly remind any sailor of a rolling, pitching deck in turbulent waters!

When to Visit

Most camel safaris are organised in the winter, when the weather's good. Rajasthan's summers are almost unbearably hot and dry, so going on a camel safari during this time is virtually impossible. November to March, when days are cool (and nights cold!) is when most camel safaris are organised.

What to Bring

You'll almost certainly be doing your camel safari in the winter, when woollens are a necessary part of your packing. Desert nights, especially, can get very cold, so it's essential to take along plenty of warm sweaters and jackets when on a camel safari. Although mattresses are usually provided by whoever's organising the camel safari, you'll need to carry bedding- a warm sleeping bag is recommended, and an additional blanket or two can always be used.

During the daytime, the sun can be blistering, so make sure you've got along your sun hat, a pair of sun glasses, and suntan lotion. Carry a first aid kit along with you, as well as any other essentials you might need- out there in the desert, trying to find a shop which will sell you your favourite brand of soap can be a problem. It's a good idea to carry along extra blankets to cover the wooden saddle which you'll probably be sitting on. Blankets are excellent padding, and can protect you from a sore bottom after a hard day's riding.

Getting There

Most camel safaris start from Jaisalmer, which is connected by air, train and road to the rest of India. Rajasthan's capital, Jaipur, is also a convenient base for exploring the state, whether on camel or otherwise. Jaipur has a well-connected airport, as well as regular train and bus links to a number of cities across India. All camel-safari towns in Rajasthan, such as Bikaner and Mandawa, are connected by road to Jaipur. Buses run between all the major towns of the state, and private cars or taxis can be hired to do the trip.

Do's and Don'ts

It's important to check, when you're booking a place on a camel safari, what is included in the price you're paying. Find out what arrangements are being made for accommodation, food and drink and other essentials. In some camel safaris, mineral water is not a part of the package, in which case you'll have to bring your own. Find out for sure what you're getting before you book.

When you do start on the camel safari, keep a few things in mind. Remember that you're travelling through the desert- it's dry, and if you're not careful, you could get dehydrated. Drink plenty of water- at least 2 to 4 litres a day- and keep yourself well covered, to prevent sunburn. Wear a sunhat and sun glasses and slap on the suntan lotion if you don't want your skin to start peeling.

Rajasthan, although it's fast getting as commercialised as any other part of India, still is pretty unspoilt- especially as far as the desert is concerned. Keep it that way; please don't leave a trail of junk behind you or harm the ecology and culture of this beautiful region.

Popular Circuits

1. Jaisalmer, 2. Bikaner, 3.Mandawa

Jaisalmer

1. Jaisalmer-Badabagh- Baisakhai- Ramkunda- Roopsi- Ludharva- Chatrayil- Salkha- Beri of Kanoi- Masooradi- Jeseiri- Dedha- Deegasar- Kuldhara- Moolsagar- Amarsagar- Jaisalmer:

Jaisalmer, India's westernmost town, seems at first glance to be caught in a time warp. Dominated by one of India's most impressive forts- which is, incidentally, home to a quarter of the town's population- Jaisalmer is a city of cobbled streets, medieval architecture- and the desert. Golden sand dunes surround Jaisalmer, and this is where the camel reigns supreme- if you can call it that. From Jaisalmer, a camel sfari of a few hours takes you to Badabagh, where the tombs of the Bhatti Rajput kings (erstwhile rulers of Jaisalmer) are worth visiting. Close to Badabagh is the village of Baisakhai, with an interesting old Hindu temple. A brief halt at Baisakhai is followed up with a ride to Ramkunda, known both for its picturesque location and for its Hindu temples. Most camel safaris will halt for the night at Ramkunda, and carry on the next day to the village of Roopsi, with its wattle-and-daub houses, straight out of antiquity.

Further on from Roopsi, the camel safari wends its way to the village ofLudharva, which is dominated by a Jain temple. Chatrayil, a typical Muslim village, complete with a mosque, is the next halt, and is a nice place to spend the night before carrying on the following day to the Rajput village of Salkha, which is in close proximity to the sand dunes of Beri of Kanoi. When you get to this point, make sure you've got your camera handy. Beri of Kanoi has lots of traditional Rajasthani wells, and you'll invariably find village women, in colourful lehengas, fetching water.

Kanoi itself is a village of carpenters, and produces excellent handcarved wooden items- perfect for that 'souvenir from Rajasthan' for folks back home. From Kanoi, the camel safari proceeds to Masooradi village, and then on to the oasis of Jeseiri. After a wash-and-change at Jeseiri (that's what oases are for!), the camels move on to the Rajput village of Dedha and then to Deegasar, a lakeside hamlet which is picture-perfect.

After Deegasar, the next halt is the village of Kuldhara, where excavations have revealed ancient settlements dating back many centuries. From Kuldhara, the safari heads back to Jaisalmer, passing through the hamlets of Moolsagar and Amarsagar on the way. Amarsagar is home to a finely carved Jain temple, and is worth a halt. This route is really one of the longest camel safaris in the state; a number of shorter versions of it are available, if you don't have the time or the inclination to go the whole hog.

2. Jaisalmer- Moolsagar- Kuldhara- Masooradi- Padiyari- Moondardi- Jaisalmer:

An abridged version of the first camel safari, this one starts from Jaisalmer, and passes through Moolsagar, Kuldhara and Masooradi, before proceeding to Padiyari and then to the hamlet of Moondardi. From Moondardi, the safari heads back to Jaisalmer. A short trip, but enjoyable enough, especially for someone who doesn't have the time to spare for a longer expedition.

Bikaner

1.Bikaner- Naukh- Kanasar- Baru- Chayan- Sataya- Tadana- Mohangarh-Dungri-Jaisalmer:

333 km north-east of Jaisalmer lies the desert town of Bikaner, established towards the end of the 15th century and named after its founder, Bika. For many decades a busy market town which throbbed with activity, Bikaner still manages to preserve an aura of medieval bustle- although its economic structure has changed somewhat. Camel caravans from West Asia do not pass through Bikaner any more, but the town produces some of the best sweets, savoury snacks and rugs in India.

This route starts at Bikaner, where you can see the magnificent old Junagarh fort and the lovely Lalgarh Palace, before you get on to your camel and set off.The camel safari works its way southwards, passing through the hamlets of Naukh, Kansar, Baru, Chayan, Sataya and Tadana to Mohangarh. Mohangarh, although a small town, is dominated by an imposing sandstone fortress which deserves a visit. From the town, the trail continues to Dungri and then onto Jaisalmer, where it ends.

2. Bikaner- Charkhada- Teliyan ki Dhani- Kanasar- Baru Bhala- Bungri-Telansar- Chaku- Bharaiya- Jambo- Jaisalmer:

Another of the Bikaner-Jaisalmer camel safaris, but one which follows a different route. This one starts at Bikaner, and instead of heading directly south to Jaisalmer, makes a detour eastward into the neighbouring district of Jodhpur. Passing through the villages of Charkhada, Teliyan ki Dhani, Kanasar, Baru Bhala, Telansar, Chaku and Bharaiya along the way, the camel safari reaches the hamlet of Jambo, in Jodhpur district. From Jambo, it turns westward and goes to Jaisalmer, where it ends.

Mandawa

Mandawa-Dhakas-Khotia-Mandawa:

Mandawa, just a few hours' drive from Delhi, is known primarily for its wonderful old havelis, opulent mansions constructed by rich Marwari merchants who had amassed huge fortunes from trade. The havelis of Mandawa, decorated with colourful frescoes, are worth a visit before you set off on the camel safari.

From Mandawa, a camel safari of about six hours takes you to the hamlet of Dhakas, around 18 km from Mandawa. Dhakas lies amidst the dunes of the Thar, and its nearby villages, also in the middle of the desert, make for good exploring.

Most camel safaris halt for the night at Dhakas, then continue the next day to the hamlet of Khotia, a further six hours from Dhakas. A brief halt at Khotia is followed by a ride back to Mandawa. This camel safari is one of the shortest offered and though it's not full of exotica, it allows you a brief but enlightening glimpse of life in one of India's harshest but loveliest terrains.

These are just a few of the more popular routes; other camel safaris are organised throughout Rajasthan. Some, like the ones above, originate in Jaisalmer, Bikaner or Mandawa, while others 'do' the area around Jodhpur and Shekhavati, the latter rich with fresco-decorated havelis. Camel safaris like the ones in the vicinity of Jaisalmer and Shekhavati offer plenty of scope for touring medieval forts, visiting ancient temples and photographing some of Rajasthan's most imposing monuments.

The ones around Bikaner are, on the contrary, more suited for a glimpse of typical village life. You probably won't see too many famous forts or palaces on these circuits, but it's a grand opportunity to get a taste- often literally- of rural Rajasthan.

SKIING

Introduction

Talk of skiing, and most people will think of the powder-white slopes of Switzerland; India, tropical country that it is, will invariably not come to mind. Which is sad, because India too offers skiing- limited, but fulfilling. Gulmarg, in Jammu and Kashmir, was a skier's mecca for some decades before strife in the state effectively put a stop to nearly all tourism- but, in the meantime, other places have appeared on the ski map of India. Kufri and Narkanda (now getting a new lease of life, although they've been visited by in-the-know skiers for quite some time), Auli and Manali- both fast gaining a reputation for good slopes- all offer a very satisfying skiing holiday..

India's ski resorts are largely confined to the western half of the Himalayas- in Uttaranchal and Himachal Pradesh, high enough to get a good cover of snow during the winter months, yet low enough to be easily accessible.

Kufri and Narkanda in Himachal Pradesh have been frequented by skiers for decades now, while Auli is the new kid on the block- but what a kid. All across the Himalayas, January to March is the skiing season, when the resorts are at their snowy best. By late December, most slopes are already well covered, but places really start hotting up only once the new year starts.

Auli

India's premier ski zone, Auli lies high up in the mountains of Uttaranchal, above the town of Joshimath. About 2,500- 3,050 mt above sea level, it's surrounded by forests of oak and deodar, against a backdrop of towering snowcapped mountains- Nandadevi, Neelkanth and Kamet included. The view, as you'd expect, is spectacular, and a number of tourists come here just to feast their eyes on the beauty of the place. During the summer, the slopes of Auli are covered with grass and wildflowers, but once the snow starts falling, the entire scene changes.

The main snow slopes of Auli stretch for about 5 km, and include 500 mt long ski-lifts and 800 mt long chair-lifts. Snow beaters and snow-packing machines are continually used to keep the slopes dressed. Auli, in fact, is so good that French and Austrian experts have compared it favourably to slopes in Switzerland. The GMVN (Garhwal Mandal Vikas Nigam) handles all skiing activities at Auli, so you'll have to contact them for reservations. They'll be able to make arrangements for accommodation and transport, and will provide equipment too. Week-long and fortnight-long skiing courses are conducted by the GMVN at Auli as well.

Getting there —Joshimath, 13 km downhill from Auli, is the most convenient roadhead. Joshimath is connected by road to Haridwar (276 km), Rishikesh (253 km), Dehradun (295 km) and Delhi (about 500 km); from all these cities, and a host of other towns across northern India, daily buses arrive in Joshimath. Haridwar is the nearest railhead, with trains from Delhi, Varanasi, and Agra.

Jolly Grant, at Dehradun, is the closest airport, but is currently rather unreliable, with erratic flights and periodic shut-downs for repairs and extensions. Once you get to Joshimath, you can hire a car or taxi, or take the bus which climbs up to Auli.Much more exciting, however, is the cable car which runs between Joshimath and Auli. It covers a stretch of 4 km and rises from a height of 1,000 mt to 3,000 mt.

Where to stay —Basic accommodation facilities exist in the form of tourist bungalows at Joshimath and Auli. Rooms come with attached bathrooms, hot and cold running water, cable television and basic eateries- but that's about all. Be prepared to rough it out a bit, and don't expect any luxuries. Accommodation in Auli is rather limited, so reserve your rooms in advance.

Manali

Manali in Himachal Pradesh is known mainly for heli-skiing. The area around the town, including Deo Tibba, Hanuman Tibba, Rohtang Pass and Chanderkhani Pass, is where heli-skiing takes place. Skiers are taken aboard a helicopter up to a height of close to 14,000 ft, where they can then get off the copter and ski downhill. It's exhilarating- and expensive- and is fast becoming a popular alternative to just going to Manali for treks.Further out from Manali, good ski slopes exist at Solang; Solang Nallah, 10 km from Manali, also hosts an annual skiing tournament. The Directorate of Mountaineering and Allied Sports in Manali is one of the premier institutions for skiing in the Himalayas. The organisation offers ski courses throughout the winter, and can provide both assistance as well as advice on where and how to go skiing. The directorate also hires out equipment.

Getting there —The airport closest to Manali is at Bhuntar, near Kullu; domestic flights arrive here from most major airports in India, and connecting buses do the trip to Manali. The nearest railhead is Jogindernagar, 135 km from Manali. Manali itself has no train connections, although it's well linked to the rest of northern India by road. There's a large bus station on the Mall, with daily buses from Kullu, Chandigarh, Shimla and other major towns and cities in this part of the country.

Where to stay——Manali offers a reasonably wide range of accommodation. Some nice old hotels are situated on the outskirts of the town, while inexpensive lodges and privately owned guesthouses abound in the old town. Fortunately for skiers, Manali's most crowded during the summers, when hordes of families from all across India descend on the town, determined to enjoy their summer vacations. Winters are low season for everybody except skiers, and the chances of getting good accommodation at relatively low tariffs are bright.

Kufri

The ski resort which is perhaps the most easily accessible for anyone in northern India is Kufri. Just about 10 km from Shimla, Kufri's a quiet little town which becomes a busy winter wonderland once the snow starts falling. British officers in the Indian Army discovered this beautiful little place way back in the 1930s, and a serendipitous discovery it was- for Kufri, within a few years, became one of the hottest winter resorts in Himachal. The 1950s and 60s, especially, were boomtime for Kufri, although it's now been overshadowed by classier resorts like Auli. The snow still falls in Kufri, however, and a skiing trip here can be pretty satisfying. The Mahasu Ridge, just above Kufri, has some good slopes which are worth a try.

Getting there—Shimla, just about 10 km from Kufri, is well connected to the rest of India by air, rail and road. Shimla's Jubbarbhatti Airport has flights from Delhi, Chandigarh and Kullu, and a narrow-gauge train links Shimla to Kalka. Kalka has train connections to a number of cities and towns in India, including Delhi. Daily buses link Shimla to major towns in northern India. From Shimla, buses or hired taxis can be taken to get to Kufri.

Where to stay—Kufri's so close to Shimla that it's really not essential to stay in Kufri. You could, if you're willing to do the short trip to and from Kufri everyday, stay in one of Shimla's many hotels. Himachal's capital has a wide range of properties, all the way from economy to deluxe. If you'd rather stay in Kufri itself, there's a holiday resort, a winter sports club run by the Himachal Pradesh Tourism Development Corporation, a PWD Resthouse, and a few guesthouses.

Narkanda

64 km from Shimla is one of India's oldest ski resorts, Narkanda. Narkanda lies at an altitude of 8,100 ft, and is an important horticultural centre.

Fruit orchards on the surrounding hills produce some of Himachal's most luscious apples and cherries, making Narkanda one of Himachal's pleasantest settlements, no matter what time of the year. What's good about Narkanda is that it's still comparatively unspoilt and uncrowded, so you won't find yourself suffocated by hordes of fellow skiers. The slopes at Narkanda run the gamut from beginner's to advanced, from slalom to cross-country. Hattu Peak, 6 km from Narkanda, towers 2,000 ft above Narkanda and haspopular ski slopes.

Himachal Tourism manages all the skiing facilities at Narkanda. They hire out equipment, conduct training courses, and provide everything from accommodation to transport. The Directorate of Mountaineering and Allied Sports at Manali also plays a part in the skiing at Narkanda; they organise special skiing courses January onwards every year. Getting there

Fortunately for visitors, Narkanda is conveniently situated on the main highway from Shimla to Kinnaur. There are regular buses to and from Shimla (which, in turn, is connected to the rest of northern India by road and rail). The journey to Narkanda from Shimla is just about two hours, and both taxis as well as private vehicles can be hired in Shimla to do the trip.

Where to stay—Narkanda's list of tourist accommodation facilities is rather modest. The town has a pretty- but otherwise fairly unpretentious-resthouse, a small hotel operated by the Himachal State Tourism Development Corporation, and a handful of other properties. Most are clean and comfortable, but nowhere near luxurious.

Other Options

Besides Manali, Kufri and Narkanda, the other areas where skiing is being developed include Lahaul, Spiti, Kinnaur, Laka and Triund- the latter above Dharamshala. All of these have good ski slopes, and plenty of potential for pulling in crowds of eager-beaver skiers; all that's required is a lot of development in the way of infrastructure. Until access routes are developed, accommodation improved, and other facilities spruced up, they're unlikely to attract any but the most passionate of skiers. If you're one of the adventurous kinds who're willing to put up with a little hardship, you could contact the Himachal Pradesh Tourism Development Corporation- they'll be able to give you information on alternative destinations for skiing, and make the requisite arrangements.

TREKKING

Introduction

Trekking is the best way to see the world. If you really want to get a feel of the earth; if you really want to walk through the forests and feel the breeze on your face; trudge through unspoilt territory and explore for yourself- go trekking. And if you're an Indian- or have come visiting- then three cheers for that. Because this fabulous country offers some of the most awesome trekking opportunities anywhere.

All across, from north to south and from east to west, are a series of breathtaking trekking trails, ranging from even-kiddies-can-manage to the hardcore professional. Head for the Himalayas- for arid but gorgeously beautiful Ladakh and Zanskar, if you're looking for adventure; or make tracks through Himachal Pradesh- Lahaul, Kangra, Spiti, Kinnaur, and the Sangla Valley- for easier treks which take you through stunning landscapes and quaint villages where time stands still.

Go hiking through Garhwal and Kumaon, to the clearest of lakes and the holiest of Hindu shrines; or trek further south, where lie rolling hills, craggy peaks and cool valleys, just waiting to be explored. Try your hand (and foot) in the Satpuras near Pachmarhi, or go

to Tamilnadu, where the dreamy blue-misted hills of the Nilgiris make for great treks through coffee, spice and tea plantations, dense forests and tribal villages. Strike base at Ooty or Coonoor, and you can plan some great treks in the area. That isn't all, of course: there are plenty of other treks to try and to enjoy. The Sahyadris in Maharashtra; the hills around Shillong, Kalimpong, and Gangtok; the Valley of Flowers- and so much more.

Trekking: Ladakh

Hundreds of years ago, merchant caravans loaded with the treasures of the East- silk, musk, wool, livestock, borax, dry fruit, and semi-precious stones- would travel down the forbidding wastes of the Gobi desert, making their way through the Himalayas, along the Satluj river, and heading west. The Silk Road, as the route came to be known, invariably passed through a settlement which became, as time passed by, the most important market town along the border of India and Tibet: Leh. Starting off as a tiny settlement, the town grew over the years, into an important trading post. Merchants travelling from as far as Yarkand, Khotan and Kashgar would look forward eagerly to a halt at Leh, where they could have a brief respite from the gruelling conditions of the trail.

Leh is today regaining part of its former importance. The capital of Ladakh district, the town, a refreshing stretch of greenery along the bank of the Indus, lies amidst the stark, arid mountains of the far north. This region is one of heavy snows, biting cold winds, little vegetation and a beauty which is, in places, almost unbelievable. It's also an area of medieval Buddhist monasteries; of vivid red prayer wheels; of millions of prayer flags fluttering from every pole and every bridge. A land with a blend of mysticism, traditions, natural beauty- and yes, it must be admitted- swiftly growing commercialism- which is definitely worth a visit. Trekking through Ladakh isn't easy- its' harsh, rugged terrain and inhospitable climate is enough to tax the most seasoned of hikers- but once you've walked these trekking trails, you could easily get hooked for life.

When to visit —The passes which lead to Ladakh, whether Zoji La on the Srinagar-Leh road, or Rohtang on the Manali-Leh road, are choked by deep snow and ice for eight months in the year. Every year, when the snow melts, is when the roads are open- usually between late June and late October. This is, as you'll guess, about the only time you can get to Ladakh, other than by air. Although you can get to Ladakh in the winter by plane, it's really not recommended. Temperatures can drop to below -40ºC and frostbite, snow-blindness and hypothermia are very real risks. Time your trekking trip for summer; it's really the only time to visit Ladakh.

Access—Leh airport- the highest in the world- is connected by Indian Airlines (Alliance Air) and Jet Airways flights that come in from Delhi, Jammu, Srinagar and Chandigarh. Foreigners have to pay a US $10 entry fee. From the airport there are shuttle bus services and shared jeep-taxis to town. Weather conditions can be erratic in Leh and flights get cancelled at short notice. Check before travelling and book well in advance, since flights are usually full, particularly in summer.

Leh is connected by two major highway routes, one from Manali and the other coming up from Srinagar. Both traverse treacherous mountain routes and high passes, often getting blocked due to landslides. The Leh-Srinagar road runs close to the border with Pakistan and is often blocked by the army. The road connection to Leh is open only in the summer months from mid-June till end of September. You can do the route either by private car and jeep or by the tourist buses that run from Manali. Buses come in to the town bus stand, close to the main bazaar.

Precautions and Essentials —Special permits are required for visitors going to the Nubra Valley, Pangong Tso and Rupshu. The permits are available free of charge from the Collector's Office near the Polo grounds. You have to submit two photographs and photocopies of relevant pages of your passport. The permits are usually valid for seven days and are issued to groups of four or more travelling together. Several photocopies of the permits should be made as they need to be produced at the various checkpoints. Foreigners have to pay a fee of US$20 to enter the area.

Even in summer, although the days may be quite warm- even hot in places like Leh- evenings tend to get chilly. Pack sufficient protective clothing, including something to ward off the bone-chilling winds which whoosh down the mountains; they're deathly cold. Make sure to carry some Vitamin C and aspirin tablets for the high altitude. The scorching sun in the day can result in sunburn, so carry a protective lotion, hat and sun glasses. While trekking, take along your own food and plenty of fluid, preferably in the form of bottled water. The entire region of Ladakh- barring parts of the Nubra Valley- is very dry, and if you're not careful, there's a risk of dehydration.

Accommodation —Leh is full of hotels and guest houses, most of them clean, cheap and comfortable. Accommodation, therefore, is not a problem in Leh, but further out- in the wilds- you'll probably end up having to pitch tents or staying in the so-called 'guesthouses' in the larger villages. Settlements like Sumur, Diskit, Panamik, Hunder, Lamayuru and Dha-hanu have small guesthouses, most of them rooms let out by local villagers, but these are invariably few and far between. In most cases, a tent is what you'll have to sleep in.

Trekking Routes

1. Spituk-Rumbak-Yurutse-Ganda La-Skiu-Markha-Nimaling-Kongmaru La-Chogdo-Hemis-Leh: Starting at the tiny village of Spituk, only about 8 km from Leh, this trek goes right up to the lovely Markha Valley, and then to the renowned Hemis Gompa, the largest Buddhist monastery in Ladakh.
   Startby taking a tour of the Spituk Gompa, an 11th century Buddhist monastery which houses a fine collection of ancient thangka paintings, masks, idols and weaponry. From Spituk, travel along the Jingchen Valley to the Ganda La pass, going through Rumbak and stopping en route for the night at Yurutse. Ganda La, at an altitude of 4,900 mt, is one of the two mountain passes on this trek; once you've traversed it, you descend into the Markha Valley, stopping for the night at the village of Skiu. After Skiu, the track starts rising again, up to the alpine pastures of Nimaling, past the high reaches of the Kongmaru La pass, and on to the village of Chogdo. Camp for the night at Chogdo, then trek on to Hemis. The gompa, which lies in a mountain valley along the Indus, houses a number of valuable idols, scriptures and Buddhist paintings; at the height of summer, it's also the site of the heavily-attended Hemis Festival.
   A daily bus connects Hemis to Leh, so you can actually end your trek at Hemis and go to Leh by bus.
2. Lamayuru-Wanla-Hinju Valley-Konze La-Sumdo Choon-Stapski La-Alchi: One of the most popular treks in Ladakh, the Lamayuru-Alchi route connects two of Ladakh's most scenic villages, both with interesting old Buddhist monasteries. Lamayuru, 124 km from Leh along the road to Srinagar, is the start of the trek; once you've had a look at the fascinating Lamayuru Gompa – believed to have originally been a temple of the now extinct Bon Po religion- you can begin the trek. Start by ascending to the little-known Prinkiti La pass, then trekking down into the Shilakong Valley, where the village of Wanla is situated. Wanla, known primarily for its gompa, is a suitable place to pitch camp for the night.
   From Wanla, trek on to the Hinju Valley, which is a good base camp for a detour to Konze La. Konze La, at 4,950 mt, offers a wonderful view of the mountain ranges all around, and it's one of the few places in Ladakh where there's still a possibility of spotting the

elusive snow leopard or the highly endangered blue sheep.

From Konze La, you can return to base camp in the Hinju Valley, and continue, the next day, to the village of Sumdo Choon, where there's another gompa, profusely decorated with ancient paintings. After a night at Sumdo Choon, climb up to the Stapski La Pass, from where a day's descent brings you down into the valley to Alchi. Alchi, with its 11th century fresco-filled gompa, is worth a bit of sightseeing, before you go on to Leh.

3. Lamayuru-Prinkiti La-Wanla-Hinju-Konze-Sumdo Choon-Dung Dung La-Chilling: A variation on the Lamayuru-Alchi trekking route, the Lamayuru-Chilling route is basically identical to the trek to Alchi, at least till Sumdo Choon. From Sumdo Choon, instead of climbing up to Stapski La, ascend to the Dung Dung La pass. Dung Dung La, with its stunning views of the Zanskar Valley, leads down into a valley where the main village is Chilling. From Chilling, you can eithercross the Zanskar River- by a pulley bridge- and go on to the Markha Valley, or you can trek back to Lamayuru, and from there go on to Leh.
4. Trekking Routes in Zanskar: Bisected by the Zanskar river, the region of Zanskar is less visited than the rest of Ladakh, largely because it's harsher and has fewer facilities for accommodation, food, and the like. Trekking in Zanskar is possible, but should always be done with an experienced guide, and with sufficient supplies to see you through the trek.

   Among the more well-marked trekking trails are the Pensi La-Padum trail, the Padum-Darcha trail, the Padum-Leh trail and the Karsha-Lamayuru trail. The Padum-Leh and Karsha-Lamayuru trekking routes are particularly taxing, and should be undertaken only if you've had some experience of trekking in the mountains, and are physically in peak condition. If you're really adventurous- and a veteran at trekking-you could try trekking to Zanskar in winter, when the Zanskar river freezes over, and can be used as a trail. It's traditionally been used as a winter pathway by the local traders, but be warned: this requires a lot of fortitude and it's not going to be a cakewalk.

   Other popular trekking routes in Ladakh include the Stok-Khangiri round trek, the Lamayuru-Padum trail, and the Hemis-Markha-Padum trek. Trekking through the Nubra Valley and in the vicinity of the Pangong Tso lake is also possible, but less common, as in both cases, there are high passes to be crossed-Khardung La on the way to Nubra and Chang La on the way to Pangong Tso. Crossing these on foot can be arduous, and most tourists content themselves with admiring them from the comfort of a hired vehicle.

Trekking: Lahaul

Tucked away in the far northern corner of Himachal Pradesh, the valley of Lahaul lies in what would surely rate as some of the most beautiful alpine territory in the Indian sub-continent. Lahaul is a sub-division of the district of Lahaul-Spiti (of which Spiti is the other sub-division); the main town of Lahaul is Keylong, which is also the district headquarter of Lahaul-Spiti. The valley is bisected by the Chandra River, and lies along the border between the states of Himachal Pradesh and Jammu and Kashmir.

To the south are the apple orchards and green pastures of the Kullu Valley; to the north is the vast alpine desert of Ladakh. Sandwiched between these two extremes of terrain and vegetation lies the Lahaul Valley- with its glaciers, its barren mountains and the idyllic Chandratal Lake. A region of harsh terrain, friendly people and mountains which make for some memorable treks.

When to visit—Lahaul is connected to the rest of Himachal Pradesh by the Rohtang Pass, which is snowed under eight months of the year. When the snow melts somewhat during the height of summer, it's possible to pass through and get to Lahaul- usually between July and October, depending upon the condition of the road.

Entry—Lahaul was opened to foreign tourists less than a decade back- in 1992- and even now, any foreigners headed for the area require to get permits. Entry permits can be obtained from the District Magistrate at Simla or Keylong, or the Sub District Magistrate in Keylong or Udaipur. Foreigners travelling in a group of four or more can get a permit from the Additional Deputy Commissioner in Kaza. In all cases, foreigners will need to go through a recognised travel agency. A prepared itinerary, along with a passport, three photographs and the completed application form, will have to be submitted to the concerned official in order to pave the way for a permit.

Access—Lahaul's capital, Keylong, is connected by bus to Manali. It's a seven-hour ride, and during the summer months- July to October- there's a fair amount of transport on the road. A number of buses, both state-owned as well as those specially operated by the Himachal Pradesh Tourism Development Corporation, go from Manali to Keylong and back. Manali, in turn, is linked by bus to nearby Kullu, which has a small domestic airport at Bhuntar, 10 km from the city, and a busy bus station.

Alternatively, you can hire a vehicle and go all the way from Simla (158 km from Keylong), Delhi, Kullu, Chandigarh or one of the other main cities of northern India. Vehicles can be hired in all of these cities, although you won't be able to drive yourself. What you'll get is a vehicle driven by a chauffeur who knows the mountain roads like the back of his hand- hopefully.

Precautions and Essentials —Trekking through Lahaul require some preparation; a rucksack and a stout pair of shoes is not enough. Heavy equipment- such as tents and sleeping bags- will necessarily have to be carried, along with basic cooking equipment and food. Heavy woollens, waterproof jackets and spare clothing must be packed as well, because even during summer much of this area's bitterly cold, wet and windy. Other essentials include a good sunscreen and sun glasses- the air's so rarefied that the sun can really burn when it's bright and shining.

In all cases, hire a qualified guide to lead your trek; it's mandatory when foreigners go trekking, and highly advisable for Indians.

Accommodation—Lahaul is still pretty undeveloped, at least as far as tourism is concerned. Keylong has an HPTDC tourist bungalow, and a few hotels, but there's nothing in the way of luxury. Elsewhere, in Chhatru, Chota Dara and Batal, are PWD resthouses which offer very basic boarding and lodging facilities. The rest of the way you'll have to pitch a tent- out in the open, as there are almost no designated campsites as such.

Trekking Routes

The entire Manali-Lahaul area offers plenty of scope for trekking, whether you start off at Manali itself or strike base camp at Keylong and then go hiking through the surrounding area. Among the most popular trekking trails in the region are:

1. Manali-Chandratal-Keylong: A 120 km trek which takes you to the pristine blue lake of Chandratal, possibly the loveliest in all of Himachal Pradesh. Surrounded by mountains and glaciers, Chandratal- 'Moon Lake' is situated at a height of about 15,000 ft, and is aptly named; it's actually crescent shaped.

From Manali, take the road up to the Rohtang Pass, and from there onto Gramphu, where you can then walk beside the foaming waters of the Chandra River, travelling eastwards to Chandratal. The river takes you to Dorni (which can be the first halt; you'll have to pitch a tent here); then comes Chhatru. From Chhatru, continue to Chota Dara, the latter a major tourist centre as far as Lahaul is concerned- it has a PWD rest house, where you can actually get a hot meal and a room.

From Chota Dara, take the trail past the Bara Shigri glacier to Batal, at the base of the Kunzum Pass. Batal is the final halt- a windy and chilly campsite which has a PWD resthouse- before the final lap to Chandratal. Once you've ogled and taken all the photographs you want, head back- past Gramphu, to Keylong.

The trek from Manali to Chandratal and then on to Keylong should take about 10 days; it's high altitude and an arduous trek, so take it easy.

2. Manali-Bara Shigri Glacier-Keylong: A slightly shorter version of the Manali-Chandratal-Keylong trek, this one passes through Rohtang, Gramphu, Dorni, Chhatru, and Chota Dara, and up to the Bara Shigri glacier. The glacier's the longest in Himachal- all of 55 km long- and its mouth is 4 km from Batal. Bara Shigri's melting waters eventually feed the Chenab river.

3. Manali-Keylong-Suraj Tal-Baralacha La: 65 km from Keylong, the beautiful Suraj Tal lake is the source of the Bhaga river. It lies, hemmed in by soaring mountains, below the Baralacha La, the pass which connects Lahaul to Ladakh. Baralacha La, at a height of 16,400 ft, stretches for 8 km and lies on the road from Manali to Leh.

From Manali, take the road to Gramphu, then walk along the Chandra river till you get to Tandi. At Tandi, leave the Chandra and switch to its tributary, the Bhaga, which will take you onwards, 8 km to Keylong. Going along the Bhaga, travel north, pitching camp at either Jispa (which offers some accommodation) or Darcha, a campsite where there are a few tent restaurants. If you have the time to spare, do a short trek to the lovely Deepak Tal lake, 16 km from Darcha, before heading on north to Surajtal and Baralacha La. Once you reach the pass, you can either trek back or take one of the many buses which travel along this route between Leh (in Ladakh) and Manali.

Other possible trekking routes can be from Keylong to Udaipur and the Mrikula Devi Temple (a westward trek along the Chandra River and into the Pattan Valley); or from Manali to Koksar, the coldest place in Lahaul. Koksar, 21 km beyond the Rohtang Pass, is at an altitude of about 11,000 ft and is subject to sub-zero temperatures through much of the year; in summer it's a little bearable.

Trekking: The Nilgiris

Forming the junction of the Western Ghats and the Eastern Ghats, the Nilgiris- the 'Blue Mountains'- are amongst India's oldest mountain ranges. The hills, a part of the Nilgiri District of Tamilnadu, stretch across the borders of the state into the adjoining states of Kerala and Karnataka. Easier to traverse than the mighty Himalayas, the Nilgiris are often cited as being better suited for novice trekkers. The gentle slopes and temperate climate of the region mean that even those with little or no experience won't end up getting completely fatigued. The beauty of the Nilgiris, however, is such that even veteran hikers will enjoy themselves.

The three main towns of the Nilgiris- Udhagamandalam (better known as Ootacamund, or more familiarly, Ooty); Kotagiri and Coonoor- are perfect bases for interesting treks into the Nilgiris. Low, gentle slopes, where dense forests of shola trees alternate with tea estates, orange groves and coffee plantations; a land where tribes like the Todas, the Kurumbhas and the Irulas still live in a way which has changed little over the past centuries. The Nilgiris are interspersed with tiny villages, with tranquil blue lakes and elegant cottages where teatime is still the hour for hot buttered crumpets, scones and strawberry jam.

A trek through the Nilgiris is a great way to see the hills- to wander through forests of rhododendron in full bloom; to visit the wildlife-rich sanctuaries of Mudumalai and Mukurthi; to walk through rolling green downs and along rippling streams... It really doesn't get better than this. When to visit —The Nilgiris, unlike the Himalayas, are a year-round destination. Never do these hills get too hot or too cold for trekking; summer temperatures range between 12 and 25ºC, while winter temperatures never go below 3ºC. Summer, however, is when the area is pretty crowded, so winter- particularly between November and February- is a better time if you would rather give the crowds a miss.

Access —All three main towns of the Nilgiris- Ooty, Kotagiri and Coonoor- are conveniently located, with good connections via road and rail. Coimbatore, which is linked to the rest of India by air, rail and road, is just 112 km from Ooty and 80 km from both Coonoor and Kotagiri. Regular buses to the Nilgiris depart from Coimbatore; in addition, taxis and vehicles can be hired from Coimbatore or Chennai to do the trip.

A train also links Coimbatore- and other southern cities- to Mettupalayam, in the foothills of the Nilgiris. Mettupalayam is, in turn, connected by road to Ooty (54 km) and to Coonoor and Kotagiri (both 35 km). If you're in southern India, probably the most viable route would be by rail to Mettupalayam, and then by road into the Nilgiris. From another part of India, a flight to Coimbatore, followed by a bus ride to Coonoor, Ooty or Kotagiri is best.

Precautions and Essentials —As compared to the Himalayas, the Nilgiris are easier trekking, not just because they've gentler slopes and more equable climate, but also because there are fewer restrictions on moving around. No entry permits need to be collected from district officials, and it isn't essential to book a trekking guide, although you might like to hire one to help you out.

As far as clothing and other 'essentials' are concerned, remember that nights in the Nilgiris can get chilly, even during the summer, so take along light woollens for summer treks. During the winter, heavier woollens are necessary packing. On all treks, take along insect repellent, sun glasses, and a floppy hat. Bottled water and food is generally available all over the Nilgiris, so unless you're heading deep into tribal territory, you needn't stock up on either.

Accommodation —Ooty is, of all of the Nilgiris' hill stations, the mostcommercial. Overrun by successive generations of tourists wanting to escape the heat of the Indian summer, it has built up a fairly good tourist infrastructure, which translates into plenty of places to stay in and around town. These include guest houses, hotels and cottages, some of which are very elegant and old-fashioned.

Coonoor and Kotagiri too have their share of guest houses and small hotels, although most of these are not anywhere close to luxurious. Outside of the larger towns, accommodation options will invariably be limited to government-operated resthouses and forest bungalows; pitching tents will usually not be necessary, unless you're way off the beaten track.

Trekking Routes

Treks from Ooty—Ooty, once the summer capital of the British in India, as well as the place where snooker was invented by an officer called Neville Chamberlain-has a pretty, distinctly colonial charm which has managed to survive more than half a century of being totally Indian. The town itself is known for its exquisite Botanical Gardens- established in 1847- and is the base for a number of interesting treks, some long and some short, into the surrounding hills.

1. Ooty-Parson's peak-Porthimund-Mukurthi National Park-Pandiar Hills-Pykara Falls-Mudumalai National Park-Ooty: A long trek which headsnorth-west from Ooty, taking you through some of the prettiest and most unspoilt parts of the Nilgiris. Parson's peak, which towers over Parson's Valley, can be reached on foot or by bus- it's a three hour ride. Once you reach Parson's Valley, however, you should begin your trek: the area's so picturesque, it deserves every bit of time you can spend wandering through it. From Parson's Valley, trek on to Porthimund, a village lying deep in the hills. A tent can be pitched here for the night, before you go on to Mukurthi, a well-known wildlife preserve. Dominated by the Mukurthi Peak (36 km from Ooty and so named because it resembles a human nose), the Mukurthi National Park is a dense forest, inhabited by a fascinating cross-section of Indian fauna: leopards, elephants, tigers, the highly endangered Nilgiri tahr, and the more common deer, monkeys, birds, and reptiles.

   Mukurthi has a forest bungalow which, though not the height of luxury, is comfortable enough and makes an excellent base for exploring the sanctuary.

   From Mukurthi, head north, through the Pandiar Hills, pitching a tent along the way for the night. The next day, you can head for the lovely Pykara Falls, along the Pykara Lake, and then work your way north to the Mudumalai National Park. One of southern India's most important wildlife sanctuaries, Mudumalai is densely forested with bamboo, teak and sandalwood and has a large population of elephants. The park's also home to deer, monkeys, tigers, wild boars, sloth bears, gaur, and birds.

   From Mudumalai, you can trek back to Ooty, or you can take a bus- there are regular buses between the park and the city.

2. Ooty-Avalanche-Upper Bhavani-Kolaribetta-Emerald -Ooty: A shorter and more manageable trek, this one gives you a glimpse-tantalising in itself- of the Nilgiris. Although you'll see only the very fringe of the Mukurthi National Park along the way, there are plenty of pretty sights- a lovely lake, dense forests, and a quaintly named village- to make this a rewarding trek. Head south-west from Ooty,

past the Avalanche Dam, to the village of Avalanche, in the Avalanche Valley (nobody here was too imaginative when it came to choosing names!).

Named after an 'avalanche'- a landslide, really- in 1823, Avalanche is a riot of shola trees, rhododendrons, orchids, magnolias and a trout stream: absolutely lovely. You can stay for the night at the local forest department guest house, and trek south the next day to Upper Bhavani. A dam on one of the prettiest lakes in the Nilgiris, Upper Bhavani's good for a picnic, before you pass into Mukurthi National Park and head north towards Kolaribetta.At 2,625 mt, Kolaribetta is one of the highest peaks in the Nilgiris, and a trek to the summit, while not very tiring, will reward you with an unparalleled view of the surrounding countryside.

From Kolaribetta, go north-east, towards Ooty, stopping en route at the village of Emerald. Nobody seems to be very sure of why Emerald has such an unusual name- but nobody's complaining. It's a pretty place, and perfect for a picnic by the side of the lake. There are buses to Ooty from Emerald, so you have the option of completing the trip by bus.

Short one-day treks to Ooty's nearest tourist attractions are also possible; these include the thickly forested area of Glenmorgan, 17 km from town and rich in eucalyptus, wattle and rhododendron plantations; and Dodabetta, the second highest peak in the Western Ghats. Dodabetta, 2,638 mt tall, towers over the surrounding hills and lies about 10 km from Ooty. The hike to the top isn't much of a challenge, and will earn you a splendid view, as far as Coimbatore and even the Mysore plateau.

Treks from Kotagiri

1. Kotagiri-Kodanad ViewPoint-Catherine Falls-Elk Falls: Kotagiri- deep in the heart of the Nilgiris- is Kota territory, the home of one of the region's most important tribes. Kodanad View Point, about 20 km from Kotagiri, lies on the eastern edge of the Nilgiris and offers a fantastic view of the area for miles around. Picturesque tea estates and the Moyar River are among the attractions in the area. From Kodanad ViewPoint, on the way back to Kotagiri, you can stop at two of the best-known waterfalls in the region: Catherine Falls and Elk Falls. Both are within eight km of Kotagiri, and are popular with picnickers.

Treks from Coonoor

1. Coonoor-Lamb's Rock- Lady Canning's Seat-Dolphin's Nose-Law's Falls-The Droog-Coonoor: A trek which takes you through nearly all the tourist attractions which lie within reach of Coonoor. Start by trekking up to Lamb's Rock, nine km from Coonoor. The rock,

on a high precipice, overlooks the Coimbatore plains and offers excellent views of the tea and coffee estates in the area. Further along the road from Coonoor, past Lamb's Rock, lies Lady Canning's Seat, named for the wife of the viceroy. Like Lamb's Rock, Lady Canning's Seat offers a spectacular view of the Nilgiris.

Trek on from Lady Canning's Seat to the towering rock known as Dolphin's Nose. About 12 km from Coonoor, Dolphin's Nose is shaped much like the snout of a rising dolphin; it is, like Lamb's Rock and Lady Canning's Seat, great for taking photographs of the countryside- you can even see, nearby, the beautiful Catherine Falls. On the trek back towards Coonoor, do a detour to Law's Falls, about five km from Coonoor, along the road to Mettupalayam. The falls, near the junction of the Coonoor and Katteri rivers, are a popular tourist attraction. From Law's Falls, head for the Droog, about 13 km from Coonoor. Also known as Pakkasuran Kottai, The Droog, or Shankari Droog, is the site of a ruined 16th century fort which is believed to have been used by the legendary ruler of Mysore, Tipu Sultan, in his battles against the British. The fort, which is situated at a height of about 750 mt, has a number of medicinal springs in the vicinity, of which the most famous is the Maan Sunai ('Deer Spring'), which is never touched by the rays of the sun. When heading back to Coonoor, if you're feeling lazy, there's a bus which goes to the town; it, however, doesn't go to the summit of the peak, so you'll have to get to the foot of the hill- a trek of about 3 km- on your own two legs.

The Nilgiris Trekking Association, 31 D, Bank Road, Ooty, and the Nilgiri Wildlife and Environment Association (the NWLEA) at Mount Stewart Hills are among the best organisations from whom information on trekking in the Nilgiris can be obtained. Other options include the Tourist Information Office at Charing Cross, Ooty, and the Wildlife Warden at N Mahalingam and Co. Building, Coonoor Road, Ooty. Although no permits are actually required to trek through the Nilgiris, it's advisable to inform the District Forest Officer once your trek is planned- especially if you're going on a long trek through the forests. Keeping the DFOs informed of your route helps you get some much-needed help and co-operation at forest bungalows and from forest rangers.

Trekking: Sangla Valley

Tucked away in the south-eastern corner of Himachal Pradesh lies the Sangla Valley, part of the region of Kinnaur. The Valley, also known as the Baspa Valley, has been called the 'most beautiful valley in the Himalayas'. Although the indignant residents of countless other valleys across the mountains may disagree, there is definitely some justification for the claim. Stretching for 95 km, the Sangla Valley is watered by the Baspa river, which meets the Satluj at Karcham, and by several smaller streams and springs. The first 18 km of the valley are fairly narrow, with cedar, chilgoza pine and bhojpatra trees covering the slopes on either side. At Kupa, however, the valley opens up and widens into an unforgettably lovely vale, dotted with a pretty-as-a-picture villages, right up to Chitkul, beyond which habitation is almost nil.

The Sangla Valley stretches across what was once a glacier moraine but is today a gorgeous swathe of green, dwarfed by the surrounding mountains. The clear waters of the Baspa run between orchards of apple and apricot, through villages where the houses have exquisitely carved wooden doors and steeply sloped slate roofs; an area so amazingly lovely that the natives actually say that this is where the gods live. A week of trekking through the Sangla Valley and you just might end up agreeing.

When to visit—Winter, keeping in mind the Sangla Valley's northern location, is not a good time to go trekking here- it's bitterly cold from November to March. Summer, too, tends to be rather drippy, because of the monsoons. The best time to visit the valley, therefore, is late spring or early autumn- before or after the monsoons. Time your trekking visit for April to end of May, or September to mid-October.

Access —The Sangla Valley's largest and most important village is Sangla, which has regular bus connections to Simla and Rekong Peo. Alternatively, if you're coming from Rekong Peo (which has direct bus connections to Delhi, Chandigarh, Kalpa, Kaza and Simla), you can take a bus to Sangla. For most visitors, the most convenient route is by rail, plane or bus to Simla, and from there to Sangla by bus. The journey from Simla to Sangla is about ten hours; it's a distance of 230 km. Vehicles can also be hired at Simla, Delhi or Chandigarh to get to Sangla.

Precautions and Essentials —Even though the Sangla Valley lies fairly close to India's national border, no permits are required to visit the area. Don't venture beyond the valley without a permit, though, as treks to Spiti and northern Kinnaur require an Inner Line Permit.

As far as packing is concerned, you'll need to carry all the necessary equipment- tent, sleeping bag, cooking stove, fuel and the like. It's also prudent to take along supplies of food, just in case you set up camp at a place away from the larger villages of the valley. It's also recommended so that you don't put an unnecessary strain on the rural economy of the valley, a subsistence economy which depends almost entirely on the local annual crop. Adequate woollens must be packed, too: the Sangla Valley is far enough north to be fairly cold even during the summers. Between June and September, make sure you've got a good raincoat, waterproof boots and extra clothing to cope with the frequent monsoon showers.

Accommodation—Good camp sites exist in the Sangla Valley, most of them close to the junction of the Baspa and Satluj rivers. Further on, in the larger villages of the valley- such as Sangla, Kupa and Chitkul- local guesthouses and small hotels are available. Usually comfortable, they're a good option if you get sick of sleeping under the stars. In smaller villages, you might be lucky enough to find hospitable villagers who will let you have a room for the night, but be prepared to pitch a tent by the river or up on a slope.

Trekking Routes

If you want to restrict yourself only to the Sangla Valley, then the best trekking route to take is along the valley, following the course of the Baspa River from its junction with the Satluj up to the village of Chitkul. If you've got more time to spend in trekking, an alternative isto travel to the neighbouring areas of Kinnaur and Garhwal.

1. Along the Sangla Valley (Sangla-Kamru-Rakcham-Chitkul): The 'basic' Sangla Valley trek, this trekking route follows the course of the Baspa River, from Sangla to Chitkul, the last inhabited village in the valley. Start the trek at the Sangla village, the largest settlement in the valley. Close to the village are two of the valley's biggest attractions: the Kamru Fort and the saffron farm. Kamru village, about a forty-minute walk from Sangla, is an intriguing blend ofHindu and Buddhist religion: a Buddhist temple where a local mural combines the Buddhist Mahakala with the Hindu deity Hanuman is an interesting example of the native culture. Kamru is also home to an old fort, constructed from wood and stone and decorated with gabled roofs. On the outskirts of the village lies a saffron farm, considered better than the one in Pampore, Kashmir.
   From Kamru, walk on, 14 km along the bank of the Baspa river, to the village of Rakcham. Rakcham is home to apagoda-style temple decorated with fine wood carvings. The village has accommodation and dining facilities (although limited) and you can stay here for the night, before going on the next day to Chitkul.
   Chitkul, 25 km from Sangla village, is the last settlement along the Baspa; it has a campsite and a PWD resthouse. Chitkul is a base for the Kinner-Kailash pilgrimage; trekkers can either go further on the Kinner-Kailash trek, or walk another 4 km to Nagasthi, the last Indian outpost before the Tibetan border. Note that foreigners are not allowed to go beyond Chitkul without a special permit.
2. The Kinner-Kailash Circuit (Morang-Thangi-Rahtak-Charang La-Chitkul-Sangla-Kamru-Shang-Brua-Karcham): The mountain of Kinner-Kailash (not the Mt Kailash, which is actually on the bank of the Mansarovar lake in Tibet) rises to a height of 6,437 mt, towering over the Satluj river. The annual Kinner-Kailash yatra is an important pilgrimage for thousands of devout Hindus and Buddhists, but hundreds of avid trekkers also do the trip, for less religious reasons. The trek, which is best accomplished in July or August, takes about a week, and starts at Morang, on the left bank of the Satluj. Morang lies north-east of Chitkul and is connected by road to Rekong Peo and Tapri. You can spend part of the first day

exploring the old monasteries of Morang, before you proceed. The actual trek starts at Thangi, a short distance from Morang, along the gushing waters of the Turung Gad torrent.

From Thangi, walk 12 km up the valley to the village of Rahtak, where a tent can be pitched for the night. The next day is an arduous trek up to the 5,266 mt high Charang La Pass, after which the trail dips into the Sangla Valley. Follow the Baspa River to Chitkul, then make your way to Sangla village, stopping en route for a bit of sightseeing at Kamru. From Kamru, a trail leads, via Shang and Brua, through Karcham, up to Kinner-Kailash itself. The trek up the mountain takes a day in itself- or more, if you're not in peak condition.

The Kinner-Kailash trek is a difficult one, and it's essential to have an experienced guide along; don't try to attempt this on your own. Also, keep in mind the fact that this route passes through fairly uninhabited territory, so bring along adequate supplies and suitable equipment.

3. Chitkul-Doaria-Zupika Gad-Borsu Pass-Har ki Dun: This trek starts at the fag end of the Sangla Valley- at Chitkul- and heads eastward into neighbouring Garhwal, where it ends in Har ki Dun. Like the Kinner-Kailash trek, this one too is a fairly gruelling one and should be undertaken only with a good guide. The guide's necessary not only because you might otherwise get lost, but also to help you get the permits which are essential to pass through the area.

   The Sangla Valley-Har ki Dun trek starts at the village of Chitkul, at the end of the Baspa Valley, and continues across the river, up to the village of Doaria, from where the trail leads right, heading towards Garhwal. The trek then leads up to the Zupika Gad, and from there to the high Borsu Pass. Descending from Borsu, you'll come, in a few days' time, into the ethereally beautiful valley of Har ki Dun in Garhwal.

Trekking: Spiti

Spiti is a sub-division of the district of Lahaul-Spiti (Lahaul is the other sub-division); the main town of Spiti is Kaza. A high-altitude bare desert, Spiti is bisected by the Spiti River, which runs from the slopes of Kunzum La Pass to Sumdo. Spiti was, prior to India's independence, the domain of the Maharaja of Kashmir; it formed part of Ladakh, and is, in fact, much like Ladakh- treeless, harsh, bitterly cold and peopled by a race which is remarkably friendly, warm and hospitable. The little vegetation there is, stretches along the rivers and in places where, because of irrigation, the people have been able to plant crops and trees.

Spiti's still an undeveloped area- with few facilities outside the main town, Kaza- but its unspoilt beauty is such that not too many trekkers complain.

Walk along the Spiti river; trekking up to one of the thirty-odd Buddhist monasteries or labour up to one of the villages which cling to the mountainsides: Spiti is undeniably beautiful, whether you're looking for panoramic views, quiet old monasteries, or friendly villages.

When to visit —Like the Lahaul Valley, the Spiti Valley too is connected to the southern part of Himachal Pradesh through the Rohtang Pass, which is inaccessible through almost three-quarters of the year. Other than the Rohtang Pass, the Kunzum La Pass, between Spiti and Lahaul, also has to be traversed if you have to get to Spiti, which makes things even more difficult- because Kunzum La stays choked with snow even longer than Rohtang. As a consequence, the only months when you can actually visit Spiti are August, September and October.

Entry —Spiti was opened to foreign tourists less than a decade back- in 1992- and even now, any foreigners headed for the area require to get permits. Entry permits can be obtained from the District Magistrate at Simla or Kullu, or the Sub District Magistrate in Simla. Foreigners travelling in a group of four or more can get a permit from the Additional Deputy Commissioner in Kaza. In all cases, foreigners will need to go through a recognised travel agency.

A prepared itinerary, along with a passport, three photographs and the completed application form, will have to be submitted to the concerned official in order to pave the way for a permit. Kaza has a checkpoint where all permits need to be verified before you're allowed to proceed further.

Access—Kaza is connected by bus to Simla- which has its own airport- and Manali, whichis, in turn, linked by bus to nearby Kullu. Kullu has a small domestic airport at Bhuntar, 10 km from the city, and a busy bus station which is linked to a number of cities across northern India.

Alternatively, you can hire a vehicle and go all the way from Simla, Delhi, Kullu, Chandigarh or one of the other main cities in the region. Vehicles can be hired in all of these cities, although you won't be able to drive yourself. What you'll get is a vehicle driven by a chauffeur who knows the mountain roads like the back of his hand- hopefully.

Precautions and Essentials —Trekking through Spiti require some preparation; a rucksack and a stout pair of shoes is not enough. Heavy equipment- such as tents and sleeping bags- will necessarily have to be carried, along with basic cooking equipment and food.

Heavy woollens, waterproof jackets and spare clothing must be packed as well, because even during summer much of this area's bitterly cold, wet and windy. Other essentials include a good sunscreen and sun glasses- the air's so rarefied that the sun can really burn when it's bright and shining. In all cases, hire a qualified guide to lead your trek; it's mandatory for foreigners while trekking, and highly advisable for Indians.

Accommodation —Kaza, Losar and Tabo boast of PWD resthouses, and some of the larger- and more touristy- towns may have the odd privately-owned guesthouse or two, but don't count on it. Even in resthouses, accommodation will be very basic, and you'd better be prepared to rough it out. Anyway, once you've left Kaza, you'll probably end up sleeping in a tent pitched in a convenient valley.

Trekking Routes

1. Kaza-Langza-Hikim-Comic-Kaza: Start the trek from Kaza, the administrative centre of the Spiti Valley- and about the only place in the region which offers a selection, although limited, of accommodation and diningfacilities. From Kaza, head for Langza, at a distance of eight and a half km. The area's known for the wealth of fossils all around, but for the sake of Spiti's natural heritage, please don't pick up any- it's illegal, anyway.
   From Langza, follow the track up to the Buddhist monastery of Hikim. Hikim Gompa, built under the patronage of the Mongols, is modelled on a Chinese palace and is an unusual bit of architecture. From Hikim, walk on, to the rather amusingly named village of Comic, a further eight km from Hikim. The trek to Comic is a circuitous one, and you don't need to return to Kaza via Hikim or Langza- just follow the straight road back to Kaza, which is only about six km.
2. Kaza-Ki-Kibber-Gete-Kaza: One of the shorter, but immensely interesting, treks in the vicinity of Kaza. All three places on the trekking route- Ki, Gete and Kibber- lie to the north of Kaza, with Ki being a mere 11 km from Kaza. Ki is one of the largest, oldest and most important Buddhist monasteries in Spiti, and celebrated a thousand years of its existence in 2000, when the Dalai Lama performed a prestigious rite known as the kalachakra ceremony at the monastery. Home to about 300 monks, the Ki gompa has a noteworthy collection of traditional religious paintings (thangkas) and scriptures. At the monastery is a small guesthouse, and there are facilities for camping.
   Spend the night at Ki, then head for Kibber, 19 km from Kaza and one of the highest villages in the world. Kibber boasts of a small bank, a village and a post office, but the village of Gete, which claims to be the highest village in the world, is not quite so fortunate. Gete's at a height of close to 16,000 ft, and is approachable only on foot. From Gete, trek back to Kibber, where you can camp for the night before heading back to Kaza.
3. Kaza-Losar-Kunzum La: A westward trek from Kaza, the expedition to Kunzum La can be a very rewarding one, especially as it passes through some of Spiti's most scenic areas.

Heading west from Kaza, go towards Losar, the last village in Spiti- beyond it lies the Lahaul Valley. Losar, 55 km from Kaza, lies in an area which is starkly different from much of Spiti- instead of barren mountains and arid desert, you'll see apple orchards, poplar, willow and fields of vegetables. On the trekking trail to Losar, you can camp en route; there are a number of places along the way which are suitable for pitching a tent. When you reach Losar, you can stop for the night at the local PWD resthouse,before continuing, the next day, to Kunzum La, 18 km further to the west. Kunzum La-'The Meeting place for the Ibex'- doesn't harbour ibex any more, but it's still important. It's the pass which links Spiti to Lahaul, and, at a height of 16,000 ft, commands a magnificent view of the surrounding area.

From Kunzum La, you have the option of either heading back to Kaza, or, if you've got a permit to enter Lahaul, you can cross the pass and go to Batal, in Lahaul.

4. Kaza-Tabo-Sumdo-Nako: From Kaza, head east along the Spiti river to Tabo, 47 km from Kaza. Tabo is one of Spiti's largest settlements and the site of a prominent Buddhist monastery. The Tabo gompa, which is more than a thousand years old, has a fine collection of priceless old thangkas and religious manuscripts which are worth seeing. The town also has a small government-owned resthouse, and a few private guesthouses, where accommodation is available for the night. From Tabo, take the trekking trail onwards to Sumdo, on the border between Spiti and Kinnaur. Sumdo lies only about 20 km from the Chinese border, and recent efforts at afforestation have helped make the area a refreshingly verdant one.

Further on, in the district of Kinnaur, lies one of Himachal's highest and prettiest villages, Nako. Nako, besides being a beautiful place, is also reputed to be the final resting place of Padmasambhava, the first disciple of the Buddha to visit Tibet. Situated at the edge of a picturesque lake, Nako has little to offer in the way of accommodation, although you're welcome to pitch a tent on the outskirts of the settlement.

Sumdo lies within what is known as the 'inner line'- a border area which is adjacent to India's frontier with China. Special Inner Line permits are required to visit Sumdo, and may be obtained from the District Commissioner in Kaza or Simla. Permits are issued for a group of no less than four people, and that too only against an introductory letter from a registered travel agent.

Other trekking routes which are popular include the trek from Kaza to the Pin Valley National Park- the latter a well-preserved wilderness which is home to the highly endangered snow leopard- and the trek from Kaza to Dhankar. Dhankar, once the capital of Spiti, has an old and important Buddhist monastery which is known for its medieval murals. Dhankar lies 25 km from Tabo and can be a part of the Kaza-Nako trek.

WATER SPORT

Introduction

India's coastline, all of 7000 odd km, has some very pretty beaches,. A few are fairly famous- especially in 'beach bum' paradise, Goa- but there are also dozens of others in lesser known places, big and small, but perfect for water sports. Some are good for swimming; some offer a wider spectrum of facilities, including sailing, water skiing, snorkelling, wind surfing (or boardsailing, as it's known in many parts of the world) and scuba diving.

The fact that India's still not way up 'there' on the adventure tourism map means that water sports haven't been developed as major attractions in many destinations. Some states, however, like Goa and Kerala and certain specific resorts, such as Kadmat or Bangaram in the Lakshadweep Islands, have developed infrastructure; these are the places you'll find good equipment on hire, and institutions which conduct training courses. Good beaches in more obscure locations exist too, though they may not have too many facilities other than basic accommodation, eating places, and transport.

On the whole, the western coast is more suitable for water sports than the eastern coast, as the waters of the Arabian Sea tend to be calmer than those of the Bay of Bengal. So pack your swimwear, your snorkel and your suntan lotion- and head for the beach. For a watery adventure which will leave you wanting more.

When to visit—All of India's coastal areas- whether on the mainland or in the islands- lie in the tropical zone. Summers are hot and humid, and monsoons can be depressingly grey; the best time to visit, therefore, is in the winter. November to April is when the weather's at its best. It's warm enough to swim without having to invest in a wet suit, yet cool enough for comfort.

What to bring—Swimwear, suntan lotion, towels- obviously. Equipment such as scuba diving gear, snorkels, surfboards and other such stuff can be hired at major resorts such as Bangaram, Kadmat, the Andaman Water Sports Complex, and a number of beaches in Goa and elsewhere. Smaller and less touristy places will invariably not offer equipment for hire, so you'd be well advised to bring your own.

Precautions —Many of India's beaches, though with great potential for water sports, haven't been developed. They'll offer basic tourist infrastructure, but little else. These are the places you'll have to make sure- perhaps by asking local fishermen- that the seas are safe, and there aren't any sharks, sharp rocks, dirt and chemicals lurking below the surface. It's best, if you're even slightly unsure, to restrict your beach activities to sunbathing.

Even if the infrastructure's satisfactory, with life guards at hand, medical facilities and all the other essentials, it's wise to take some precautions. Although swimming by itself doesn't require too much skill, other sports will need specific training and a certain degree of physical fitness. Scuba diving, for instance, needs certified training, with rescue training and emergency care being an essential part of the course. And when you eventually get into the water, keep your eyes open for lurking dangers- octopus, sharks and the like.

Andaman and Nicobar Islands

The 3000-odd islands which form the archipelago of the Andaman and Nicobar group lie in the Bay of Bengal. A rather idyllic destination, with clear blue seas, colourful coral reefs, golden beaches, coconut palms and aboriginal people who are among the most isolated in India. While the Nicobar islands are off-limits to foreigners, the Andamans are not, and have some good facilities for water sports.

The capital of the Andaman and Nicobar Islands, Port Blair, is home to the Andaman Water Sports Complex, where there are facilities for a very wide range of activities, from those which require little skill to those for which you'll need to have prior experience. The water sports complex hires out rowboats, paddleboats, glass-bottomed boats, kayaks, bumper boats, surfboards and other equipment. There's also a swimming pool, should you want to paddle about a bit. Within the Andamans, other areas which are suitable for water sports include Havelock Island, Corbyn's Cove (for windsurfing and swimming) and Cinque Island, which is known for its stunning coral reefs-perfect for snorkelling. The Mahatma Gandhi Marine National Park is also especially recommended for keen snorkellers.

The Andaman Scuba Club in Port Blair conducts training courses in scuba diving and snorkelling.Port Blair has regular air and sea connections to Kolkata, Vishakhapatnam and Chennai. Port Blair, which offers a fairly comprehensive range of accommodation options, is linked to the other islands of the group by ferry.

Lakshadweep Islands

Formerly known as the Laccadives, the Lakshadweep Islands- 'Million islands'- may be somewhat inaccurately named, but are undeniably beautiful. In fact, the Lakshadweep islands, which lie in the Arabian Sea, are actually only 36 in number- a series of atolls and open reefs of which only 10 are inhabited.

Among the most popular sites for water sports in the Lakshadweep Islands are Bangaram (the only island accessible to foreigners) and Kadmat. Both have extensive facilities for windsurfing, parasailing, scuba diving, swimming, snorkelling and deep sea fishing. Bangaram, especially, has a wonderful coral reef, with an abundance of marine life- everything from stingrays, hawkbill turtles and green turtles to sturgeons, angelfish and clown fish. The southernmost isle of the Lakshadweep group, Minicoy has a large lagoon which is good for swimming; Kalpeni Island, further north, has seas suitable for swimming, kayaking and sailing.

Training courses in snorkelling and scuba diving are conducted by the deep-sea diving institute in Kadmat. Other sites which are being developed as tourist centres- and consequently are also acquiring the necessary infrastructure for sea sports- include Tinakara, Valiyakara, Cheriyam and

Suheli. Kochi, in Kerala, is the one place in mainland India which is linked to the Lakshadweep Islands by air and sea. Regular flights and ferries connect Kochi to Agatti, from where inter-island ferries go to the other islands of the group.

Maharashtra

The western state of Maharashtra stretches along the coast of the Arabian Sea, with the districts of Thane, Mumbai, Raigarh, Ratnagiri and Sindhudurg offering easy access to the sea. Further inland, amidst the low hills of the Sahyadris, lie a number of lakes which are excellent for sailing and windsurfing. The area around Pune, especially, is known for its lakes- Pawna, Panshet, Muslhi and Khadakvasla included. Of the four lakes, Khadakvasla has the best infrastructure; equipment can be hired at the Khadakvasla windsurfing centre and there are rescue facilities too by the lakeside.

Maharashtra's best opportunities for water sports, however, are in its coastal waters. The Royal Bombay Yacht Club and the Colaba Sailing Club are the two main organisations involved in the promotion of sailing and windsurfing in Mumbai's seas. Cuffe Parade, Chowpatty, Juhu and Marve are the four beaches from which surfboards can be launched, and the Ramada Inn Hotel also has a training school for the uninitiated.

Mumbai, the capital of Maharashtra, has excellent transport connections by air, sea, rail and road to the rest of India. It's also home to one of India's busiest international airports, with regular flights to a large number of destinations across the world. From Mumbai, trains and roads go further inland, to other towns and cities in the state.

Goa

Goa's miles of sunny golden beaches are every sunbather's dream come true, and they're also great for a number of water sports. Swimming, of course, is the most common, but there's plenty of scope for windsurfing, water skiing, deep sea diving and sailing too. Most resorts have their own beaches and will usually rent out the necessary equipment too. The most well known of Goa's beaches include Bogmalo, Candolim, Calangute, Anjuna, Baga, Colva, Sinquerim (Bardez), Vagator and Miramar. Goa can't boast of any stunning coral reefs, but its waters are a kaleidoscope of marine life. For a change from the ordinary, scuba divers could also head for one of the wrecks- dating back to British or Portuguese times- which lie along the shores. Be careful, though; there have been cases of accidents in the area.

Amateurs and those who're a bit nervous should plan on visiting Goa during the winter, when the waves are fairly easy to manage. Summers, and more specifically the days before the monsoons hit Goa, are when the waves are high and the winds are strong- plenty of challenges here for the expert. Monsoons are a tough time for everybody, when about the only option which remains is to go sailing on the Mandovi and Zuari estuaries, which are comparatively calm and navigable. Goa's Dabolim Airport has regular flights to and from Delhi, Mumbai, Ahmedabad, Bangalore, Cochin and Chennai. Besides that, there are ferries to Mumbai, trains from all across India, and convenient bus connections too.

Other Places

Other places where water sports facilities exist, though not always at such a high level as in Goa, Mumbai, the Lakshadweeps or the Andamans, include Gopalpur-on-Sea (Orissa), Kovalam (Kerala) and Kumarakom (Kerala). There are, obviously, lots of other pretty little beaches along the coasts with plenty of potential; a few years down the line, and you'll have many more options to choose from. For more information on water sports, you could contact the National Institute of Water Sports, at E-3, Dramila Apartments, Mangor Hill, Vasco da Gama, Goa. In addition, state tourism offices of the concerned states or union territories can provide information and assistance on the facilities available for water sports.

WHITE WATER RAFTING

Introduction

White water rafting in India is almost exclusively confined to the northern rivers which flow southwards from the Himalayas, gushing between densely forested mountains and through steep gorges. Rivers such as the Alaknanda, Bhagirathi, Indus, Zanskar and Teesta offer 'raft-worthy' rapids, and a trip down a river can be a great way to see the countryside. Whether the expedition's just a few hours of getting soaked and experiencing the thrills of a high-action Hollywood flick- or it stretches over a few days in which you spend time camping and trekking as well- this is an experience not to be forgotten.

White water rafting or river running, as an alternative way of spending your vacation, is being increasingly offered by a number of tour operators and travel agencies, including government tourist offices. Prices are generally reasonable, and will include food, equipment, lifejackets, helmets, an expert guide, and accommodation.

Check on what you're paying for, and whether any additional charges are likely to be levied. It also makes sense to scout around a bit before taking a decision on which agency you're going to book with. Most agencies allow anybody- as long as you're over 14 years of age- to book on river rafting trips. For basic trips, which pass through quieter waters, it isn't even necessary to know swimming, although those who can't swim may not be allowed on certain stretches of the river. Expectant mothers and people who suffer from epilepsy or other serious ailments, will usually not be allowed.

When to Visit —The Himalayan rivers, being the main river rafting routes, are virtually inaccessible during the winters. Some, like the Zanskar, are frozen over, and most of the others are too cold too allow rafting. Getting soaked could lead to a long and perhaps dangerous bout of hypothermia- or worse. The monsoon brings heavy rain to the lower reaches of the Himalayas, and melting snows in the mountains result in higher waters in all of the rivers. Summers, therefore, though a good time to go river rafting, can be a little unsafe, especially for novices who haven't travelled on a river in spate.

For novices, August and September- when waters are lower and more manageable- are the best months to go river running; veterans can opt for expeditions earlier in the summer. Spring or early summer is also usually suitable for river running. The Teesta is one of the few rivers where river rafting is confined to the winter months, between October and April.

What to bring—A love for adventure and a passion for the great outdoors is top priority. More practical things to pack include a good sunscreen, dark glasses, shorts, T-shirts (or other light, quick-dry clothing) and suitable shoes- sneakers or heavy duty rubber sandals may be a good idea. Also pack in a windproof jacket, a light sweater, towels, and a flashlight- and don't forget the first aid box and the camera!

Essentials —River rafting in some areas may require special permits from the government. Areas close to India's international borders, such as Nubra, Sikkim, Lahaul and Spiti may be off-limits to foreigners without a valid permit. Before venturing out with your oar and your life jacket, make sure you've got all the necessary permits which are needed.

Permits can usually be obtained fairly easily from District Commissioners, District Magistrates or other senior officials. Enquire at the Ministry of Home Affairs in New Delhi to figure out whether you need a permit, and who can give it to you.

Accommodation —Riverside tent camps exist along all the main routes, especially in Garhwal. These will generally consist of Swiss tents where accommodation is on a shared basis, with separate dry-waste toilet tents. All camps have their own arrangements for dining and entertainment- the latter invariably consisting of bonfires, beach volleyball and singing. Some of the longer runs may include stops en route at riverside villages or other settlements. In Ladakh, Lahaul, Sikkim and some of the less developed areas, pitching a tent will usually be the only course open for rafters.

Rafting Runs —There are two main sets of routes along the rivers, graded I to III (for amateurs) and IV to VI, for veterans. The Zanskar and the Indus, both in Ladakh, are graded I - III, while the more southern stretches of the Beas, Chenab, Sutlej and Teesta are graded IV – VI. Briefly,

Grade I : Small, easy waves; mainly flat water
Grade II : Mainly clear passages; some areas of difficulty
Grade III : Difficult passages; narrow in places and with high waves
Grade IV : Very difficult, narrow and requiring precise manoeuvring
Grade V : Extremely difficult. Very fast-flowing waters which can be manoeuvred only by experts

Grade VI : For all practical purposes, unmanageable- even suicidal

The Ganga and its tributaries; the Kali Ganga, the Indus, the Zanskar, the Teesta and the Rangeet are some of the rivers on which river running has been developed. Most of these have good riverside camps, and are well-frequented by organised rafting groups during peak season.

Other than these, there are other rivers, nearly all in northern India, where there are possibilities for river rafting. These include the Sutlej, the Chenab, the Chandrabhaga, the Beas and the Spiti rivers- all of which offer good river running, but have not been explored to a great extent, or (as is the case of the Sutlej and the Chenab) are practically off limits at present because of instability and unrest in the region of Jammu and Kashmir.

The Ganga

1. Kaudiyala - Shivpuri (Alaknanda): About 28 km upstream from the town of Rishikesh, on the Alaknanda, is one of India's best known- and most popular- stretches for white water rafting. The stretch between Kaudiyala and Shivpuri has several camps, each catering to river rafting outfits. Most of these operate between October to March, through the winter. The run starts at Kaudiyala and passes through thickly wooded hills; along the way are two of the river's best rapids- one known as the 'wall' and the other called the 'golf course'- which are succeeded by deep, tranquil pools. The river route makes it way past riverside temples, under the Laxman Jhoola. The run finally terminates at the dam beyond Rishikesh.

Rishikesh, which is about 257 km from Delhi,is well connected to most of northern India by road; the nearest railhead is at Hardwar, while the nearest airport is Jolly Grant, at Dehradun. There are regular buses to Rishikesh from Delhi, Hardwar and Dehradun. Once in Rishikesh, you can hire a vehicle to get to the river camp- in most cases, however, the tour operator will make arrangements for transport from Rishikesh to Kaudiyala. Besides the travel agencies who book Kaudiyala-Shivpuri trips, the Garhwal. Mandal Vikas Nigam (GMVN) and UP Tourism also offer river runs along the stretch.

2. Rudraprayag-Rishikesh (Alaknanda): Situated at the confluence of the Alaknanda and the Mandakini- two of the main tributaries of the Ganga, Rudraprayag is known to many wildlife buffs as the place where the famous Jim Corbett shot a man eating leopard in 1926. Although no longer as thickly wooded as it once was, Rudraprayag is still close enough to the jungles to make it a very charming place- and the starting point of an exhilarating, if strenuous, bit of river running.

Starting a little beyond the main town of Rudraprayag, the river makes its way through a series of rapids, narrow gorges and quieter stretches, passing through the towns of Srinagar and Devprayag (at the junction of the Alaknanda and the Bhagirathi). Further on, the river reaches Kaudiyala, from where the stretch to Shivpuri and on to Rishikesh is a fairly demanding one. The entire expedition takes about four or five days, depending upon the pace.

What is particularly appealing about the Rudraprayag-Rishikesh run is that other than the adventure of river rafting on one of India's best stretches, it also offers the chance to see the densely forested Himalayan foothills at close quarters. Furthermore, the river passes through the heart of 'sacred' India- with plenty of opportunity to visit old temples. Anyway, river rafting on the Alaknanda can mean loads of dips- intentional and otherwise- in the holy river!

There are regular buses to Rudraprayag from Rishikesh and Hardwar.

3. Tehri-Shivpuri (Bhagirathi/Alaknanda): The Tehri-Shivpuri run, on the Bhagirathi river, is considered to be one of India's best runs- scenic and heart-stoppingly exhilarating. Beginning at the town of Tehri, the district headquarters of Tehri Garhwal, this run goes down the Bhagirathi river, passing through foaming rapids- mostly grade III or IV- till it reaches Devprayag. At Devprayag, the Bhagirathi merges with the Alaknanda, beyond which the river becomes- in places- more manageable than in the upper reaches. Passing Kaudiyala, the run goes on to Shivpuri, and then to Rishikesh. Tehri is connected by bus to other major towns in northern India, including Rishikesh, Hardwar and Dehradun.

Other popular stretches for rafting on the Ganga and its tributaries are:

On the Alaknanda:	Kaliasaur to Srinagar (16 km, lower grades), Srinagar to Bagwan (20 km, lower grades)
On the Bhagirathi :	Matli-Dunda (12 km, a mixture of grades) Jangla-Jhala (20 km, a mixture of grades), Harsil-Uttarkashi,Dharasu-Chham(12 km, a mixture of grades)
On the Mandakini:	Chandrapuri-Rudraprayag (26 km, higher grades)

The Kali Ganga (Sharda)

Jauljibi-Tanakpur: The Kali Ganga's name is rather misleading- for it has nothing, actually, to do with the Ganga. The Kali Ganga, known in its lower reaches as the Sharda, flows into India from the neighbouring country of Nepal. Hurtling down from the foothills of the Kumaon region, the Kali Ganga meets the Gori river at Jauljibi, where this run starts. A taxing stretch of river running, this route- all of 117 km- passes through some of the fastest and most dangerous rapids along the river. Most of the river is Grade IV – or higher- and should be considered only after you've had some experience of river running.

The run down to Tanakpur takes about three days, and if you've still not had your fill, you can extend it to the lower reaches of the river, which are easier going. Jauljibi, which is the start of the run, is connected to major towns in Kumaon by road.

The Indus

Much easier and quieter than the Ganga and its tributaries, the Indus is suitable for Grade II and III trips. The river, which originates in Tibet, flows down through Ladakh, past Leh, and then passes into Pakistan.

1. Upshi-Khaltsi: The Upshi-Khaltsi run is somewhat long, but not too difficult. Most of the river along this stretch consists of grade I and II rapids, although there are some grade III rapids too. The run starts at Upshi, which lies upriver from Leh, along the road which leads south to Manali. From Upshi, the river makes its way westwards to Khaltsi, along the road to Kargil.
2. Spituk-Saspol: Spituk, just short of Leh and on the bank of the Indus, is the starting point for an easy and short trip downriver. The route goes up to the village of Saspol, near Alchi, and comprises a run of a few hours. A short and scenic run, the Spituk-Saspol route is relaxed enough to allow you to admire the beauty of the Indus Valley; beyond Saspol, however, the river starts getting a fraction wild, and is recommended only for experts.

Easier runs on the Indus include the run between Hemis and Choglamsar, a three-hour jaunt which goes through quiet, calm waters, and passes through the riverside villages of Stakna, Shey and Thikse,before ending at Choglamsar, just short of Leh city. Leh, the capital of Ladakh, is connected by air to Delhi, Srinagar, Jammu and Chandigarh. In the summer months, road traffic also links the town to Manali in Himachal Pradesh and to Srinagar, although the latter route is not recommended because of the unrest in the Kashmir Valley. Within Ladakh, buses ply between the main towns and villages, and vehicles can be hired in Leh to get to the more inaccessible areas.

The Zanskar

Born from the merging of the Stod and Tsarap rivers, the Zanskar arises near the border between Himachal Pradesh and Jammu and Kashmir, and makes its way northward, to meet the Indus at Nimmu. A beautiful stretch of water, the Zanskar isn't as wild and wicked as its southern sisters, the Alaknanda and Bhagirathi. It does have some grade III and IV rapids, but they're fewer and more far between. Among the most exciting runs on the Zanskar is the Padum-Nimmu run, a trip which takes several days and involves having to camp out in the wild. It's replete with exciting rapids, and is suggested only for those with a fair bit of experience in white water rafting.

Another good run is the Phey – Nimmu route, easier than the Padum-Nimmu one- it's mostly Grade II or III. The main attraction of the run is that it passes through astoundingly beautiful mountains, many of them with tiny villages and imposing old monasteries nestling among the valleys. The run starts at Phey and ends about 36 km from Leh, at Nimmu. Nimmu is situated at the confluence of Ladakh's two main rivers- the Indus and the Zanskar. Zanskar's administrative centre, Padum, is accessible from Kargil, to which it is connected by road during the summer months. Buses run between the two towns on alternate days between July and October, and vehicles may be hired in Kargil to do the trip. In both Ladakh as well as Zanskar, public transport and other facilities- including tourist accommodation- are very limited. In addition to this, parts of the area, especially those lying close to India's international borders, require special permits to be obtained. To overcome all these difficulties, it's essential to go through a specialised agency which organises river runs. They'll make all the necessary arrangements, including permits, transport, equipment and accommodation. Many such agencies have their offices in Leh, and some also have offices in other cities in India, such as New Delhi.

The Teesta

The main river in the north-eastern state of Sikkim, the Teesta originates at Cho Lhamu Lake and gushes down the mountains, creating foaming white rapids which are literally tailor-made for kayaking or rafting. Although this river isn't (as yet) as well- charted or developed as those in Garhwal or Kumaon, it's swiftly acquiring a reputation as a good stretch for white water rafting. Most of the Teesta is either grade III or IV, so it's advisable to have some experience of river running before you attempt it.

Probably the shortest run on the Teesta is the run between Makha and Rongpo, a trip of about two and a half hours. Among the longer and more gruelling runs on the river are the stretches between Dikchu and Teesta Bridge; Dikchu and Kali Johra (in West Bengal, a run of almost five days); and between Bordang and Melli. The tributaries of the Teesta, including the Lachung Chu and the Lachen, also make for good river running.

The Rangeet

The Rangeet demarcates the border between the states of West Bengal and Sikkim, and is known primarily for kayaking. Good river running, however, is also possible on the river, especially in the upper reaches of the Rangeet. The stretch between Likship and Teesta Bazaar (where the Rangeet meets the Teesta) is particularly popular, as is the stretch from Naya Bazaar to Teesta Bazaar. The runs between Jorethang and Bhaney Khola; Sikip to Jorethang; and Jorethang to Melli are short stretches where rafting can be done. More accomplished rafters can combine these runs and do a longer trip between Sikip and Melli. Sikkim's capital, Gangtok, is connected by road to the rest of India, and there are frequent buses to Gangtok from Darjeeling, Siliguri, Kalimpong and Bagdogra. Bagdogra, near Siliguri, is the nearest airport; it's about four and a half hours' drive from Gangtok.

Note that special permits are required by foreigners visiting Sikkim. 15 day permits are issued, both by Indian embassies overseas as well as by Regional Registration Offices, Sikkim Tourism Information centres, and Resident Commissioners of the Government of Sikkim within India.

5

Sightseeing in India

PARKS IN INDIA

Kanha National Park

The largest wildlife sanctuary in Asia, Kanha National Park was one of the first Project Tiger reserves in India. It is, in many ways, Project Tiger's biggest success story, with the tiger population having doubled since 1976. Over 1,945 sq km of bamboo thickets, extensive grasslands and dense sal forests make up Kanha- a series of plateaus which stretch across the eastern segment of the Satpura ranges in Madhya Pradesh. This is the land of the tiger, the leopard, and the wolves which inhabit the pages of Jungle Book.

Of this area, the core- about 940 sq km is the national park; around it is the buffer zone. Porcupines, jackals, sloth bear, jungle cat, macaque, dhole (wild dogs), bison and a stunning spectrum of birds inhabit Kanha, and make a trip to the sanctuary a must for any wildlife enthusiast. It is a truly thrilling experience, made more so by sightings of the tiger, 'gaur', or even the tiny mouse deer (muntjac) or the rare hardground barasingha, found only in Kanha. Go birdwatching on a misty winter morning, and you're likely to see beauties like the racquet tailed drongo, crimson breasted barbet, crested hawk eagle and golden oriole.

Entry Requirements

Visitors to Kanha National Park are required to obtain entry permits- a very nominal Rs 2

for Indians- at the entrance to the park. Additional charges are tagged on for vehicles (about Rs 15), for cameras, for guides and for elephant rides. Tourists are allowed to go on excursions in the park only at designated times, generally from sunrise to noon, and then from afternoon to sunset. Check with the park authorities about when you can go. Driving at night or moving around the park on foot is prohibited.

Access

The nearest airport is at Nagpur (266 km from Kanha), which has connections to a number of major cities in India, including Mumbai. The nearest railhead is Jabalpur, at a distance of 169 km; Jabalpur has trains coming in from all across the country, and from here there are convenient buses to Kanha. The MPSRTC operates two buses daily, the earlier of which leaves Jabalpur at about 7 in the morning, to reach Kanha by noon.

Other cities and towns which are connected to Kanha by road include Raipur (219 km) and Mukki (25 km). From all these towns, there are regular buses to Kisli, and to the two park entrances, at Khatia and Mukki.

Once you're in the park, you can hire a jeep from the MPSTDC office at the park. Jeeps can be booked through the manager of the MPSTDC log huts at Kisli, though elephant-back is a far better and quieter vantage point, to explore the park. You can go on mapped circuits accompanied by guides from the forest department who help you to identify the animals and birds. If you are a birdwatcher, Kanha will give you hours and hours of fun – the early morning being the best time to spot the birds. Also within the park is the Kanha Museum, which focuses not just on the flora and fauna of the area, but also on the local tribal population.

Best Time to Visit

Kanha Tiger Reserve is closed to visitors during the monsoon months, from July to November. Winter, between November and January, is a comfortable time to visit the park, when the weather's pleasant. April to June is when the summer sets in; it can get pretty hot at this time, but if you're a die-hard wildlife fan, this is when a visit can reward you with satisfactory wildlife-watching at the park's waterholes.

KAZIRANGA NATIONAL PARK

Welcome to the land of Rhinoceros Unicornis. The great Indian one-horned rhino, more than two tons of frightening muscle and tank-like belligerence. With its armour-plating hide and its 24" long horn- which really isn't a horn, but compressed hair- the Indian rhino once ruled the roost in the wetlands of north-east India. Hunted mercilessly, it was on the brink of extinction when conservationists awoke to its plight.

The result, and a successful one at that, is Kaziranga National Park, in Assam. Stretching over an area of 430sq km on the south bank of the Brahmaputra river, Kaziranga is one of the last refuges of the Indian rhino. A vast stretch of coarse, tall elephant grass, marshland and dense tropical forests, it has managed to survive the onslaught of poachers, urbanization and burgeoning human populations. Plans are already afoot to extend the park's boundaries to include the Brahmaputra river to the north and a part of the Mikir hill ranges to the south.

Fairly early on- in 1908, in fact- Kaziranga was declared a reserve forest and was officially closed for shooting; at the time it could boast of only a few dozen rhinos. By 1950 the area was a wildlife sanctuary, and in 1974 it was designated a national park. Bounded by the misty blue hills of Barail and Karbi Anglong to the south, the national park was declared a UNESCO World Heritage Site in 1985.

Today it's one of the few places in India where it's possible to see the rhino out in the open- an awesome sight indeed. And, what's better still, the rhino population of Kaziranga now numbers more than a thousand of the creatures. Endangered, no doubt, but protected too.

Kaziranga is home also to elephants, sloth bears, tigers, leopard cats, jungle cats, hog badgers, capped langurs, hoolock gibbons, pigs, jackals, porcupines, pythons, wild buffaloes, Indian bison, swamp deer, sambhars and hog deer. Besides these, the park has a respectable avian population, which increases considerably in the winter, when migrating birds visit the park.

Entry Requirements

Visitors to the Kaziranga National Park are required to register at the Tourist Centre in the Bonani Tourist Lodge while entering the park. The entry fee for foreigners is about Rs 200; for Indians it's Rs 10. Charges for cameras and vehicles are additional (even if you bring your own vehicle, you'll pay a fee for it). Rented vehicles and elephant rides cost between Rs 750 to 800 for a ride of about an hour and a half. The fees for Indian visitors are appreciably less- generally between Rs 50 for an elephant ride and Rs 150 for a hired jeep.

Access

The two most convenient bases for getting to Kaziranga are Jorhat and Guwahati. Jorhat, 96 km from the sanctuary, is the nearest airport, but Guwahati's Borjhar Airport, 239 km from Kaziranga, is connected by more flights. Cars are available on rent at both airports. There are also direct train services to Guwahati from Calcutta, New Delhi, Mumbai, Chennai, Bangalore, Cochin and Trivandrum. In addition, both Jorhat and Guwahati are accessible by road from all the neighbouring states- West Bengal, Meghalaya, Manipur, Mizoram, Nagaland and Arunachal Pradesh. From Jorhat and Guwahati, taxis and buses are available to get to Kaziranga.

Once within the park, wildlife-watching trips can be taken at dawn on elephants that wade through the tall elephant-grass and give you a vantage view of animals waking up to the day. Elephant trips cover Baguri, Hole Path, Mihimukh, Kohora-Central Path and Arimarah. On an elephant ride, do wear trousers that fully cover your legs to avoid abrasions from the coarse elephant-grass.

Best Time to Visit

The best season to visit Kaziranga is the winter- approximately November to April. The weather's hot and humid through much of the rest of the year. During the monsoons (June to September), when there's heavy rainfall and the park is closed.

CORBETT NATIONAL PARK

In the foothills of the Kumaon Himalayas, close to Ramnagar, lies the Corbett National Park. The first Reserve forest of its kind, the park was established in 1936- when it was known as the Hailey National Park- mainly through the efforts of Jim Corbett, the conservationist. Corbett lived throughout his childhood in the area of Kaladhungi between Nainital and Ramnagar.

He had a deep insight into the ecology of the area, and in later years he was called upon by the locals to shoot down man-eating leopards and tigers that stalked the villages. Locally referred to as "Carpet Sahib", he turned to photography and writing, authoring books on wildlife, like "My India", "Jungle Lore" and "Man-eaters of Kumaon".

Corbett National Park was the first to be designated a Project Tiger Reserve in 1973. Situated at a distance of 260 kms from Delhi and 128 kms from Nainital, the Corbett National Park is best known for its big cats, especially the tiger. Despite the efforts of conservationists, the tiger population of India is dwindling rapidly, and Corbett National Park is one of the few parks where the tiger can still be seen. There are around 50 tigers in Corbett, besides other wildlife like leopards, several lesser cats, the wild dog, porcupines, jackals, civets, sloth bear, black bear, wild boar and a few hundred elephants.

Stretching over 520 sq km with a core area of 330 sq km, the Corbett National Park consists of mixed deciduous and sal forests and stretches of savannah grasslands where antelope, chital, hog deer and sambar graze. The Rhesus monkey and common langur are ubiquitous, while the long-snouted gharial, marsh crocodile, cobras and pythons can be seen on the mud banks of the Ramganga. The Ramganga reservoir, in the main Dhikala camp area of the park, has over 600 species of birds, including the pied kingfisher, crested serpent eagle, fishing eagle and Himalayan grey headed fishing eagle. The river is also home to the famous river carp mahseer, a favourite catch for anglers.

Entry Requirements

Entry to Corbett is strictly regulated and permits are needed from the park administration in Ramnagar. For foreigners, the fees are Rs 350 for the first three days at Dhikala and Rs. 75 for every additional day. Charges for boarding and lodging are additional.

Access

The nearest railhead is at Ramnagar, 50 kms. from the main park campsite at Dhikala. Convenient trains connect to Delhi, Lucknow and Moradabad. It is also possible to rent a car and take the road from Delhi, passing through Moradabad; the bus journey from Delhi takes about 7 hours. There are daily buses from Ramnagar to Moradabad and Ranikhet. From Ramnagar, buses run to Dhikala (within the park); jeeps too are available for hire, at a tariff of about Rs 800 per day.

Elephant rides and jeep rides can be arranged once in Corbett National Park; private vehicles and jeeps are also allowed. Elephant rides are the recommended way to see the animals, the charges are Rs. 100 per person or Rs. 400 per elephant for two hours.

Note that movement within the camp is restricted and moving out on foot is forbidden.

Best Time to Visit

The Corbett National Park is out of bounds during the monsoons- usually from about June 16th till November 14th. Once the park reopens after the rains, the best time to visit is between January and mid-June. In the winter months from December till February the Ramganga reservoir is full of migratory birds. Summer is the best season to view wildlife, especially the tiger, that come out of the deep forests for water.

GREAT HIMALAYAN NATIONAL PARK

Hemmed in on three sides by the towering peaks of the Himalayas, Himachal Pradesh's Great Himalayan National Park is undoubtedly the place to go for a rendezvous with the wildlife of these mountains. Here, amidst dense forests of blue pine and cedar, in high alpine meadows and mountain slopes which remain covered with snow throughout the year, lives one of the densest and most impressive populations of Himalayan wildlife. Created in 1984, the Great Himalayan National Park (officially known as the Jawaharlal Nehru Great Himalayan National Park) includes, in a wide swathe of land covering 765 sq km, the previously-established Tirthan Sanctuary.

Adjacent to the park are two more important protected areas- the Pin Valley National Park and the Rupi Bhabha Sanctuary- a vast expanse of land sheltering many of the species, both animal and plant, endemic to the Himalayas. The Great Himalayan National Park lies in Seraj Forest Division (in Kullu District), in the upper catchment areas of the Jiwa, Sainj and Tirthan rivers. A park where the altitude varies from 1,500 mt to about 6,000 mt, encompassing within it snowcapped mountains, river valleys, and steep cliffs.

The diversity of terrain and altitude is reflected in a corresponding diversity of vegetation. Deciduous broadleaved forests of oak and bamboo alternate with pine and deodar woods, while grasses and colourful wildflowers crowd alpine meadows in the upper reaches.

Inhabiting this stretch of land is a dazzling array of animals and birds. Among the most prominent mammals are leopards, Himalayan black bears, brown bears, langurs, rhesus macaques, and wild sheep such as the Himalayan thar, bharal and the ibex. Rarer animals like the highly endangered musk deer are also found in the park, and there have been reports of snow leopard sightings. The Great Himalayan National Park is unsurpassed in its bird life, with almost 68 resident species and close to 50 migrant species being sighted here. Pheasants, such as the gloriously beautiful monal, the kaleej and the Western tragopan, are among its many attractions.

Entry Requirements

Special permits are required by visitors to the Great Himalayan National Park. These permits can be collected, for a nominal fee of Rs 2 (for Indians) or Rs 4 (for foreigners) from the office of the Park Director at Shamsi, or the range officers at Larji, Sairopa and Sainj. Charges for guides (who are provided by the park authorities, and are mandatory for anybody visiting the park) are extra, as are fees for cameras. Visits to the Great Himalayan National Park are allowed only between sunrise and sunset.

Access

The town closest to the Great Himalayan National Park is Kullu, which is about 60 km from the park. Kullu, as one of the most popular tourist destinations of Himachal Pradesh, is very well-connected to the rest of the country. Kullu's airport, at Bhuntar, receives flights from across India, while the local bus station has links to most major cities in northern India, such as Shimla, Chandigarh, Delhi and Ambala. The nearest major railhead is at Chandigarh, although there's a smaller rail station at Jogindernagar. From Kullu, National Highway # 21 (to Manali) leads to Aut, from where a motorable road leads part-way to the park. A vehicle can be hired at Kullu to do the trip to Gushaini or Neuli, the end of the road. From here onwards, visitors need to go on foot, as no motor transport or horses are allowed.

Within the Great Himalayan National Park, the only form of transport is your own two legs- so make sure you're physically fit and wearing a sturdy pair of boots. A qualified guide is mandatory for everybody visiting the park; you'll be able to hire one at the park's office. A trek through the park is definitely the best way to see the beauty of this area, and with some luck you should be rewarded with some great sightings of birds, bharal, langurs, and even a leopard or bear.

Best Time to Visit

The Great Himalayan National Park is best visited in early summer or autumn- April to June and September to November are the times when the weather's at its best. Beyond November, and right up to April, heavy snowfall can block roads and trails, besides making it a little too cold for comfort! Rainfall hits the park between July and September, sometimes resulting in landslides and muddy trails.

KEOLADEO GHANA, BHARATPUR

Amongst India's premier wildlife sanctuaries is the Bharatpur Bird

Sanctuary, on the border between the states of Rajasthan and Uttar Pradesh. Formally known as the Keoladeo Ghana National Park, it's a marshy area, stretching over 29 sq km of kadam forests, grasslands and shallow lakes. Created by the Maharaja of Bharatpur in the 19th century by diverting water from an irrigation canal, Keoladeo was founded as a shooting preserve, but given the status of a bird sanctuary in 1956. Upgraded to a national park in 1982, the area today ranks as one of the best waterbird preserves in the world- and it's a World Heritage Site.

Keoladeo Ghana, Bharatpur harbours some of India's richest birdlife, including the gorgeous shocking-pink tinted painted stork, several species of cormorants, egrets, pelicans, ibises, cranes, ducks and geese. One can see over 350 species of birds, both native as well as migratory. Among the latter, the highly endangered Siberian Cranes, which come to nest in winter, are the rarest.

Bharatpur is the Siberian Crane's only known wintering ground in India; at last count, only 2 cranes nested at the park, definitely a cause for worry. In addition to the birds, Keoladeo is home to a wide range of mammal and reptile species, including deer, jackals, blackbuck, fishing cats, otters and blue bulls.

Entry Requirements

All visitors to Keoladeo Ghana, Bharatpur need to obtain an entry permit from the Warden or Ranger at the entrance to the park. Foreigners need to pay an entry fee of Rs 200; Indians pay Rs 25. Extra charges are levied for cameras and photographic equipment.

Access

Keoladeo Ghana is situated just two km from the town of Bharatpur, which is connected by train and road to Delhi (176 km away) and Agra (50 km away). There are regular buses plying to Bharatpur from Delhi, Agra, and other cities, and taxis can also be hired to do the trip. Within the park, walking or cycling is easily the best way of seeing Keoladeo's fabulous range of avian life. Taxis or private vehicles, however, are allowed into the park and can be used.

The forest department also operates mini buses and boats within the park. If you decide to pedal through the sanctuary, cycles can be hired at the entrance to Keoladeo; a map of the park's walking trails can be obtained from the reception counter at the entrance.

Best Time to Visit

Keoladeo Ghana Bharatpur is open throughout the year for visitors, although winter is definitely the best time to visit. Summers are too hot and monsoons too wet for comfort, but the months between October and February are very suitable for a trip. Besides the fact that the weather's good at this time, the park's migratory birds arrive during the winter.

SARISKA TIGER RESERVE

A hot favourite on many tourist itineraries, Rajasthan is an exotic and heady combination of desert, history and culture. Come winter, and the state's flooded with tourists eager to go on camel safaris, to shop, to visit medieval palaces- and, in an increasingly large number of cases, to go wildlife-watching. Of Rajasthan's more than a dozen Protected Areas, Sariska is easily one of the best. Sariska Tiger Reserve lies amidst the Aravali Hills- 800 sq km of grassland, dry deciduous forests, sheer cliffs and rocky landscape interspersed with the ruins of medieval buildings.

Nearly 90 per cent of the area is covered with thickets of scrubby dhok trees, within which lives an impressive array of wildlife - including the elusive and majestic tiger. Apart from the tiger, a variety of other wildlife like the leopard, sambhar, chital, nilgai, four-horned antelope, wild boar, rhesus macaque, langur, hyena and jungle cats are found in the park.

Also a highly visible section of Sariska's inhabitants are its many birds- the park is home to India's largest population of peafowl, and harbours quail, sandgrouse, golden- backed woodpeckers and crested serpent eagles, among other species. The Siliserh Lake, on the edge of the park, has a large number of crocodiles.

Like many of India's other wildlife reserves, Sariska too has its own set of issues relating to poaching, pollution and conservation. Despite these problems, however, Sariska has endured. Local forest protection societies have been set up in neighbouring villages, and efforts by regional NGOs have helped generate a certain level of interest among the decision- makers as well as the local villagers.

Entry Requirements

All visitors to Sariska Tiger Reserve need entry permits to get into the park. These permits, available at the office of the Field Director, or at the gate to Sariska, cost Rs 25 per person. Extra charges are levied for cameras (about Rs 10) and vehicles (Rs 100 for a minibus, Rs 75 for jeeps and cars).

Access

The town closest to Sariska is Alwar, and the park itself lies off the Delhi-Alwar-Jaipur highway, just over 100 km from Jaipur, and about 200 km from Delhi. Alwar, a mere 21 km from Sariska, is the nearest railhead, and has frequent trains from Deeg, Bharatpur, Jaipur and other towns. In addition, the high-speed Shatabdi Express comes daily from Delhi, except on Sundays. The train stops only for two minutes at Alwar, so you'll have to be quick on your feet, getting on or off.

The nearest airport is Jaipur, which, by virtue of its being the state capital, and an important tourist destination, is well connected to the rest of the country. Regular buses connect Alwar to Delhi and to other towns and cities within Rajasthan as well. From Alwar, there are buses to Sariska, and rented vehicles or taxis can be taken to get to the park. Within Sariska, jeeps can be hired from the Forest Reception Office to tour the park. The other option for avid wildlife-watchers is to hire a machan or 'hide' near one of the waterholes.

Best Time to Visit

Sariska is open to visitors throughout the year, although certain jungle tracks are closed during the monsoon and the breeding season. The best time to visit the park is late in the winter around January or February. If you don't mind the heat, April to June is a great time to see animals at the waterholes.

RANTHAMBHORE NATIONAL PARK

The Ranthambhore National Park stretches across an area of 1,334 sq km on the eastern edge of the Thar Desert. Once the hunting grounds of the erstwhile ruling family of Jaipur, today it is one of the last sanctuaries of the big cat, the Royal Bengal Tiger. Ranthambhore actually consist of not one, but three, wildlife preserves: the Ranthambhore National Park itself, the Sawai Mansingh Sanctuary and the Keladevi Sanctuary. Ranthambhore is an oasis of dense dry deciduous forests amidst a vast tract of semi arid scrub and thorny desert vegetation surrounded by the hills of the Vindhyas and the Aravalis.

An ancient fort lies within the park boundaries of Ranthambore, adding to its charm. Ravines, nallahs, water bodies and waterfalls add to its beauty and offer many natural hideouts for tigers and the other wildlife endemic to this park.

Part of Project Tiger (one of Asia's most important conservation efforts), Ranthambhore is the favourite haunt of wildlife buffs and professional wildlife photographers from around the world who come to see tigers, panthers, wild cats, hyena, jackal, marsh crocodile, wild boar, bears, many species of deer and a rich birdlife of over 300 species, including the great Indian horned owl. Ranthambhore encompasses three lakes: Raj Bagh, Malik Talab and Padam Talab, where aquatic birds can be seen. Although latest reports show that the tiger population of Ranthambhore is on the decline, it's still one of India's bestplaces to see the great cat in all its glory.

Entry Requirements

Entry to the Ranthambore National Park is limited; all visitors must obtain a permit at the entrance to Ranthambhore before they're allowed to enter. Foreigners pay an entrance fee of Rs 200; for Indians, the fee is Rs 25, while Indian students pay Rs 5. Additional charges are levied for cameras.

Access

The Ranthambore National Park is 145 km from Jaipur though the nearest railhead is at Sawai Madhopur, 12 km away. Sawai Madhopur, which lies on the main Delhi-Mumbai railway route, is connected by train to a number of cities and towns across India, including Delhi, Mumbai and Jaipur. The nearest airports are at Kota and Jaipur, from where a bus or train can be taken to Sawai Madhopur, where a taxi may be hired to get to Ranthambhore; alternatively, you can take the bus which goes to the park. Within the park, hired vehicles- especially jeeps- can be hired at the entrance to Ranthambhore. The RTDC (Rajasthan Tourism Development Corporation) organizes jeep and truck safaris for tourists, besides which you may bring your own vehicle into the park.

Best Time to Visit

Ranthambhore is open for visitors between October and June. Summers are very hot in this part of the country, and temperatures rise so high that you'll probably end up being utterly uncomfortable. However, the summer heat attracts animals to the waterholes, so there's greater chance of seeing wildlife in May or June. The best time for a trip remains between December and April, when the weather's great and there's plenty of opportunity for doing some hardcore wildlife-watching. March and April, especially, are months when tiger-spotting is more common.

RAJAJI NATIONAL PARK

Lying in a 820 sq km swathe across the Shivaliks, at the foot of the Himalayas, the Rajaji National Park spreads across three districts of Uttaranchal- Haridwar, Dehradun and Pauri Garhwal. In 1983, the three wildlife sanctuaries of Rajaji, Motichur and Chilla were amalgamated into a single contiguous park consisting of several distinct vegetation zones. These include broadleaved deciduous forests, riverine vegetation, grasslands, and pine forests in the upper reaches.

Inhabiting these dense green jungles are an impressive array of creatures- furred and feathered, docile and dangerous. 23 species of mammals- including tigers, leopards, elephants, deer, jungle cat, wild boar and sloth bear- and 315 species of birds are found in Rajaji.

The most prominent avian species include pea fowl, woodpeckers, pheasants, kingfishers and barbets, supplemented by a number of migratory species during the winter months. Besides that, the rivers which flow through the park harbour fish such as trout and mahseer. Rajaji's history of conservation has been rather rocky in the recent past. The park's been besieged by a host of problems, ranging from soil erosion to poaching. Despite all these issues, Rajaji continues to be one of northern India's major wildlife reserves- and one of the best places to see the fauna and flora of the terai.

Entry Requirements

All visitors to Rajaji National Park need entry permits in order to be allowed into the park. Permits are available at each of the gates to the park, and cost Rs 30 for Indians and Rs 350 for foreigners.

These permits are valid for three days; if you wish to stay longer, you'll have to pay Rs 20 a day (if you're Indian), Rs 175 per day if you're not. Additional charges are levied for cameras and vehicles. Still cameras are free for Indians and Rs 50 for foreigners; vehicles are Rs 500 for both Indians and foreigners.

Access

One of the reasons for Rajaji's popularity is that it's conveniently situated for anybody coming from Delhi. The national capital is only 231 km from the park, and there are convenient overnight trains from Delhi to Haridwar and Dehradun, from where there are connecting buses to Rajaji. Similarly, the capital of Uttar Pradesh, Lucknow, is linked by bus to Haridwar and Dehradun. From Rajaji, the nearest airport is Jolly Grant, at Dehradun, while the most convenient railheads are Haridwar and Dehradun. Both have railway connections to the rest of the country.

Rajaji is accessible through different gates; the Ramgarh Gate and Mohand Gate are within 25 km of Dehradun, while the Motichur, Ranipur and Chilla Gates are just about 9 km from Haridwar. Kunao Gate is 6 km from Rishikesh, and Laldhang gate is 25 km from Kotdwar. Within the park, the only way of getting around, if you haven't got your own vehicle, is by elephant. Elephant rides of about 2½ hours each are organized by the park authorities and cost between Rs 50 and 100 per person.

Best Time to Visit

Rajaji National Park is open to visitors between November and June. The months from December to March are usually the best time to visit, as the weather's at its best. Beyond April, things start hotting up, though it never gets unbearably hot.

SUNDERBANS TIGER RESERVE

Sunderbans, the world's largest delta and mangrove swamp, is formed by the merging of three rivers- the Ganga, the Brahmaputra and the Meghna- and has a 2,585 sq km wildlife sanctuary that extends into Bangladesh. The Wildlife Sanctuary, which is the world's largest estuarine sanctuary, has some of India's most interesting wildlife, and is worth a visit. Spreading over a series of densely forested islands and saline water channels, Sunderbans is home to spotted deer, wild pigs, monkeys, herons, kingfishers, white bellied eagles and almost 270 Royal Bengal tigers.

The tigers of Sunderbans are known to be mostly man eaters- mainly because of the lack of other suitable prey in the area- and the entire estuary has become, over the past decades, a place where you have to be on the alert all the time. Hunters, honey-collectors and fishermen from the neighbouring areas wander through the sanctuary throughout the year, and there are an average of 40 maulings a year.

This is an improvement on past figures, however, as the forest department has introduced a number of measures- including masks and electric dummies to scare off maneaters. According to local folk culture, it is still believed that Bonbibi, the goddess of the forest, protects the villagers on their hazardous missions.

A possé of armed policemen accompanies all visitors who venture into these 'beautiful forests'. Sunderbans' other creatures include estuarine terrapins, Olive Ridley turtles, estuarine crocodiles, Ganges dolphins, water monitors and a wide variety of birds, fish and crustaceans. Also part of Sunderbans is the Sajnekhali Bird Sanctuary. Besides a heronry, theSajnekhali Visitors' Centre has a crocodile enclosure, a shark pond, a turtle hatchery and a Mangrove Interpretation Centre.

Entry Requirements

A boat trip through Sunderbans outside the sanctuary requires no prior permission. Permits are however necessary to visit the estuarine delta area, and can be obtained from the office of the Field Director, Sunderbans Tiger Reserve, Port Canning, 24 Parganas. These permits allow you to visit the Sajnekhali Bird Sanctuary and the Project Tiger reserve areas within Sunderbans. Permits to visit other parts of Sunderbans can be obtained from the Divisional Forest Officer, 24 Parganas, 35 Gopalnagar Road, Kolkata. For foreigners, permits are available at the Forest Department in the Writer's Building, Kolkata. Note that the core area- the National Park- is off-limits for tourists; you'll only be able to visit the wildlife sanctuary.

Access

The capital of West Bengal, Kolkata, is just 131 km from Sunderbans, and is well connected to the rest of India (and to a number of destinations abroad, too), so you shouldn't have much trouble getting to the estuary. The railhead and roadhead closest to Sunderbans Tiger Reserve is Port Canning, which is connected to Kolkataby train. From Port Canning, regular buses go to Sonakhali, Raidighi, Najat and Namkhana, from all of which launches can be hired to tour the waterways of the reserve.

The WBTDC organizes guided tours- mostly of a duration of two or three days, starting and ending at Kolkata. They're a good way of visiting Sunderbans without some of the adventure which accompanies making your own arrangements, and cost between Rs 1,000 and 3,000. Within Sunderbans, the only way to get around is by boat; you can take a boat ride, along with an official from the Project Tiger office.

There are, in addition, watchtowers at a few places- such as Netidhopan, Sajnekhali, Sudhanyakhali and Haldi- from where you can keep a look out for passing wildlife.

Best Time to Visit

Sunderbans is open to visitors from October to March. Winter is anyway the time when the area isn't as hot and humid as the rest of the year, so it's best to time your visit for between December and February.

CHILKA LAKE NATIONAL PARK

The Chilka Lake in Orissa is Asia's largest inland salt-water lagoon. Studded with small islands- including the picturesquely-named Honeymoon Island and Breakfast Island- the lake is separated from the Bay of Bengal by a sandy ridge. The pear-shaped lake spreads across 1,100 sq km, and has a unique ecosystem with a range of aquatic flora and fauna found in and around its brackish waters. An impressive array of bird life, both native and migrant, makes Chilka one of the best places in India for a bit of satisfying bird-watching.

White bellied sea eagles, greylag geese, purple moorhen, jacana, herons and flamingos are among the many species which make the lake a bird watcher's delight: Chilka, in fact, is home to one of the world's largest breeding colonies of flamingos.

Other than the birds, Chilka's shores are home to blackbuck, spotted deer, golden jackals and hyenas, and the lake is rich in aquatic life- its waters harbour around 160 species of fish, crustaceans and other marine creatures, including the famous Chilka dolphin.

Prawn, crab and mackerel fishing are an important source of livelihood for the local people, and hundreds of small fishing boats set sail each morning to bring in the day's catch from the lake.

He Nilgiri Biosphere Reserve harbours India's second largest pachyderm population, and the chances of seeing elephant herds is pretty high, especially during the dry season.

Access

Chilka is approximately 120 km from Bhubaneshwar, the nearest airport; state transport, OTDC tour buses and private operators ply the roads between Chilka, Puri, Behrampore, Bhubaneshwar and Cuttack. The nearest railway stations are at Rambha and Balugaon, both of which have train connections to cities as distant as Kolkata, Puri, Hyderabad and Chennai. From both Balugaon and Rambha buses are available to the lake.

Local transport is basically limited to three wheel rickshaws and auto rickshaws, bicycles and cars are sole modes of private transport. The services of local boatmen and the OTDC's motorboats are available for access to the islands though outboard motors are not allowed near the bird sanctuary. OTDC boats can be hired at Barkul, and cost between Rs 410 (for a 7-seater boat) to Rs 790 (for a 34-seater boat) per hour. A special tour is operated by the OTDC between Barkul and Kalijai, and costs Rs 40 per head.

Best Time to Visit

The weather remains moderately warm the whole year round, so come any time of the year except during the rainy season from June to September. The best time, however, is from October to March, when the lake is crowded with migrating birds, usually at least 50-70 species. Pilgrims flock here in January during Makar Mela (at the time of Makar Sankranti) to pay obeisance to the Goddess Kalijai, whose temple is situated on Kalijai island in Chilka Lake.

FORTS AND PALACES IN INDIA

Red Fort, Delhi

India's first Independence Day on August 15, 1947 was celebrated with the unfurling of the Indian tricolour on the ramparts of Delhi's Red Fort: a fitting tribute indeed to a building which has few parallels when it comes to sheer grandeur. The largest of Delhi's many medieval monuments, the Red Fort is (and this is not a cliché!) one of those places where history was made-it remained the epicentre of Indian governance for close to 200 years, and its pavilions and gardens, till today, retain a magnificence highly reminiscent of its past glory.

Constructed between 1638 and 1648 by the greatest of the Mughal emperors (in terms of architectural ability, that is), Shahjahan, the Red Fort was then known also as the Qila Mubarak ('The Auspicious Fort'). And auspicious it was- and grand, rich, magnificent- as befitted the castle which was to be the capital of one of the medieval world's wealthiest empires. Surrounded by solid walls of red sandstone, the Red Fort's main entrance is through the Lahore Gate- so named because it faces Lahore, in Pakistan. Beyond the gate lies the Chhatta Chowk or Meena Bazaar, a covered market which in its heyday harboured wares as varied as gemstones and midgets, Persian carpets and eunuchs- but is today home to sellers of touristy souvenirs.

The main fort begins beyond the Naubat Khana, which is the reception counter for the fort. Beyond it spreads a vast complex of gardens and pavilions, once threaded by a canal known as the Nahar-e-Bihisht, the Stream of Paradise. Here, in a state which is a mere shadow of its medieval splendour, are the many palaces of the Red Fort, including the white-marble Diwan-e-Khas which housed the legendary Peacock Throne, and the somewhat less ornate Diwan-e-Am, built of red sandstone and once decorated with heavily gilded stucco work.

Also part of the Red Fort are the ostentatious Moti Masjid, a small but extremely ornate mosque of white marble, constructed by the emperor Aurangzeb; the Rang Mahal, that at one time used to be a gloriously ornate creation adorned with gold, silver, mirrors and paint; and the Hammams, the royal baths.

Best Time to Visit

The best time to visit Delhi is between October and March, when the weather is very pleasant. During the peak of winter in January, however, pollution causes a thick fog to envelop the city. Summers are searing hot and dry, so avoid the city at this time- or come prepared. The Red Fort is open daily from Tuesdays to Sundays from sunrise to sunset, approximately 9.30 am to 4.30 pm. Entry tickets to the fort cost Rs 10 per person (for Indians) and Rs 150 per person (for foreigners). Entry to the fort is free on Fridays.

Getting there and Around

The gateway to India, Delhi is served by two airports to the southwest of the centre. The Indira Gandhi International Airport -Terminal II receives all the international flights, while the domestic airport, Indira Gandhi Terminal I, has flights arriving from destinations within India. Delhi's three railway stations- New Delhi Station, Old Delhi Station and the quieter Hazrat Nizamuddin Railway Station have a host of trains connecting the capital to almost anywhere in India. Buses from across northern India arrive at Delhi's three ISBTs (Interstate Bus Terminals), near Kashmiri Gate, at Anand Vihar and at Sarai Kale Khan. Once you're in Delhi, taxis, hired cars, buses and autorickshaws are among the options for getting around.

JAIGARH FORT, JAIPUR

Of Jaipur's three forts, Jaigarh is perhaps the most interesting. Not if all you want to see are pretty palaces (for that Amer's perfect); but if you want a peek at a hard-core fortress, this is it. Jaigarh (literally, 'Victory Fort') was built between the 15th and the 18th century, and stands 15 km from Jaipur, amidst rock-strewn, thorn-scrub covered hills, its forbidding stone ramparts visible from Jaipur itself.

A steep road goes up to the main gate, the Dungar Darwaza, from where the view is stupendous. Jaigarh, once responsible for the security of both Jaipur and Amer, is a huge moated fort and contains all the accoutrements of a full-fledged citadel. 1 ½ or 2 hours are usually enough to explore it don't bother taking a guide; there isn't much use for one, and sections like the armoury and the museum have adequate signs.

Begin with Jaigarh's biggest draw the Jaivana, the world's largest cannon on wheels. Jaivana was constructed in Jaigarh's foundry in 1720, and its barrel alone weighs close to 50 tons. According to popular belief, Jaivana's been fired only once (the ball falling 35 km away in a very unfortunate village!). Actual inspection of the cannon has revealed, however, that the number of times it's been fired has been considerably higher. Wander around a bit you can walk the ramparts and peer down the loopholes for guns and boiling oil, or check out the wide water channels. These were part of a very efficient system for rainwater harvesting, bringing in water from across the hills and into Jaigarh's 3 underground tanks. The largest of the tanks stored 60,00,000 gallons of water, and was, till not long back, supposed to house a treasure (that myth was shattered by the Indian government, which searched it).

Also part of the fort are the armoury and museum: both have a good collection of items pertaining to Jaigarh. The Armoury's treasures include a 50-kg cannonball, various swords, shields, muskets, war bugles, armour and guns (bullock-cart, wheel, and camel-mounted!). It also has photographs of two of Jaipur's maharajas, Sawai Bhawani Singh and Major General Man Singh II, both once senior military officers in the Indian Army.

The Museum has more of the same, though not all military. Here too there are photos- some delightful ones of old Jaipur, its maharajas (especially Madho Singh, Man Singh II and Bhawani Singh), palace guards, royal processions and the Jaipur State Cavalry.

There's an interesting photograph of India's many rulers at the Conference of Ruling Princes and Chiefs (Delhi, 1917), along with other knick-knacks- maps of Jaigarh, spittoons, leather and metal oil containers, and 18th century circular playing cards. Among Jaigarh's other structures are a series of open halls, of which the Shubhat Niwas (the Meeting Hall of Warriors) has a few weather-beaten odds and ends lying about mostly ramshackle sedan chairs and drums.

Best Time to Visit

The best time to visit Jaipur is between October and March. During this period, the heat of the desert sun is less intense, the weather is cool and it is the best season for going sightseeing. The Elephant Festival and the Gangaur Festival are held in Jaipur at the tail end of March; another good reason to plan a trip as winter is on the wane and summer is yet to set in.

Getting there and Around

One of India's hottest tourist destinations, Jaipur is well connected to the rest of the country: the domestic airport has regular flights to and from all across India, and trains- including superfast Shatabdis- link the city to Delhi, Mumbai, Kolkata, and a host of other cities in Rajasthan, Gujarat and other nearby states. Besides that, buses (regular as well as deluxe and air-conditioned) are operated from neighbouring states, and within Rajasthan, by the Rajasthan State Roadways. The Rajasthan Tourism Development Corporation (the RTDC), also run special daytrips to Jaipur from Delhi, Agra and elsewhere.

Getting around Jaipur is best done by autorickshaw, tourist taxis or cycle rickshaws, as public buses are usually crowded and uncomfortable. Alternately, you could try hiring a car: chauffeur-driven jeeps, buses, cars, minivans and MUVs are readily available for hire within the city and to the attractions round about.

AMER FORT, JAIPUR

Exotic, fascinating, historic, amazing, colourful— all are soubriquets applied with (more often than not) gay abandon to the many Indian cities that form part of the average traveller's itinerary. But one city, at least, where these appellations are singularly appropriate is the 'Pink City' of Jaipur. A strikingly beautiful city, historic and interesting, dominated by the imposing 16th century Amer Fort, a brooding bastion of pavilions and palaces, looking down over Jaipur. Amer (or Amber) was once the capital of the Kachhwaha rulers of the state of Dundhar, all of seven hundred years before the city of Jaipur came into existence.

The Amer Fort itself owes its construction to three rulers: Raja Man Singh, Mirza Raja Jai Singh and Sawai Jai Singh- and took a full two centuries to build, much of it having been made in the 1500s. Looking at the splendour of the fortress, one can well imagine why it took so long to complete: it is, to put it simply, exquisite. The citadel rises above the waters of the Maotha Lake, and although a motorable road leads to the main gate of Amer, the touristier alternative is to ride an elephant up to the gate. Once inside, you'll get the chance to see one of India's best-preserved medieval citadels, a stunning complex of gardens, temples, pavilions and courtyards. The Amer Fort is, in roughly equal proportions, a pleasure-palace, a former centre of administration and a military stronghold- all worth seeing.

The fort's first courtyard is a wide expanse, dominated by two buildings the pillared red sandstone Diwan-e-Aam (the Hall of Public Audience) and the intricately painted double-storeyed Ganesh Pol gate. Beyond these lies a series of pillared corridors, centring around a typical Mughal 'charbagh' garden, bounded on one side by Sukh Niwas and on the other by Jas Mandir, a lovely piece of architecture which combines Rajput and Mughal features: delicate mirror work, stucco, paint and carving (look out, especially, for the exquisitely carved jaalis or screens). The Amer Fort's pièce de resistance, though, is the exquisite Sheesh Mahal- the Mirror Palace- which is, as you'd imagine, liberally mirrored. Patterned mosaics, coloured glass and mirror decorate the Sheesh Mahal from floor to ceiling, creating a palace of almost unbelievable beauty.

Fountains and waterways, gardens and courtyards spread out across the rest of the fort, the ramparts of which actually weave their way into the mountains for miles around.

Best Time to Visit

The best time to visit Jaipur is between October and March. During this period, the heat of the desert sun is less intense, the weather is cool and it is the best season for going sightseeing. The Elephant Festival and the Gangaur Festival are held in Jaipur at the tail end of March; another good reason to plan a trip as winter is on the wane and summer is yet to set in.

Getting there and Around

One of India's hottest tourist destinations, Jaipur's well-connected to the rest of the country: the domestic airport has regular flights to and from all across India, and trains link the city to Delhi, Mumbai, Kolkata, and a host of other cities in Rajasthan, Gujarat and other nearby states. Besides that, buses (regular as well as deluxe and air-conditioned) are operated from neighbouring states, and within Rajasthan, by the Rajasthan State Roadways. The Rajasthan Tourism Development Corporation (the RTDC), also run special daytrips to Jaipur from Delhi, Agra and elsewhere.

Getting around Jaipur is best done by autorickshaw, tourist taxis or cycle rickshaws, as public buses are usually crowded and uncomfortable. Alternately, you could try hiring a car: chauffeur -driven jeeps, buses, cars, minivans and MUVs are readily available for hire within the city and to the attractions round about.

GWALIOR FORT

The Mughal emperor Babar referred to the Gwalior Fort as "the pearl amongst fortresses in India" and although you may beg to differ, you will probably agree that this, the dominating feature of Gwalior's skyline, is definitely a citadel worth seeing. With a turbulent and pretty eventful past, the Gwalior Fort spreads out over an area of 3 square km, bounded by solid walls of sandstone, which enclose three temples, six palaces and a number of water tanks. Regarded as North and Central India's most impregnable fortress, the Gwalior Fort was built by Raja Man Singh Tomar in the 15th century.

In the five hundred years since then, the fort has changed hands many times it has been held by the Tomars, Mughals, Marathas and British, who finally handed it over to the Scindias. Today it's a must to see sight on any Gwalior itinerary, and just the ride up to the fort gives you a taste of what's coming: the southern path is bounded by rock faces with intricate carvings of the Jain tirthankars. As you enter the fort, you'll see lots more to impress and interest you: palaces and temples, impressive gates and historic water tanks. Of the temples in the Gwalior Fort, the most famous are the Teli-ka-Mandir- a 9th century Dravidian-style shrine which is notable for its profusely sculpted exterior; the Saas-Bahu Temples— two pillared temples which stand next to each other, one larger than the other; and the Chaturbhuj Mandir, a Vaishnavite shrine dating back to the 9th century.

Among the fort's most prominent palaces is the amazingly ornate Man Singh Palace, built by Man Singh in the 15th century. Embellished with a vivid pattern in tile and paint, the palace spreads over four levels, and despite its picture-pretty appearance, has a somewhat gory history: Mughal emperor Aurangzeb imprisoned and later murdered his brother Murad here. Equally grisly is the Jauhar Kund, which marks the spot where the women of the harem burnt themselves to death after the defeat of the king of Gwalior in 1232. Other palaces within the Gwalior Fort which are worth seeing include the Karan

Palace, the Jahangir Mahal, the Shahjahan Mahal and the Gujri Mahal (the latter built by Man Singh for his favourite queen, Mrignayani).

Best Time to Visit

The best time to visit Gwalior is the winter, from the end of October to early March. The last weeks of December and early January are the coldest time of the year here, and can be a good time to visit Gwalior. Summers should be avoided, if possible, as it gets extremely hot. For those who are musically inclined, the annual Tansen Festival- a celebration of Indian classical music- is held in Gwalior every November, and is worth attending.

Getting there and Around

If you're short on time, Gwalior is best reached by plane, the domestic airport has connections to Delhi, Mumbai, Bhopal and Indore. A wider range of options are offered by the railways, with regular trains to and from many of India's larger cities. A number of trains on the main rail routes between Delhi-Mumbai and Delhi-Chennai halt at Gwalior, and for people arriving from Delhi, there are daily superfast services on the Taj Express and the Shatabdi Express: both enable convenient day-trips from Delhi to Gwalior. There are, in addition, frequent connections to other cities in Madhya Pradesh, Uttar Pradesh and Rajasthan, including Bhopal, Indore, Agra, Mathura, Jaipur and Bikaner.

A good network of roads link Gwalior to the rest of the country, and a bus service operates between Gwalior and other major cities, such as Delhi, Bhopal and Agra. Within Gwalior, the options for public transport are many, from metered taxis, private cabs, auto rickshaws, cycle rickshaws, tongas (horse drawn carts) and city buses to rattletrap three wheeled tempos. For those who'd prefer more comfortable means of transport, hired chauffeur-driven cars are available.

AGRA FORT, AGRA

The original 'Red Fort' (although that title has since been usurped by the more well-known fort in Delhi), the fort at Agra stands next to what is perhaps India's best known monument, the Taj Mahal. More often than not, the Agra Fort is overshadowed by the pristine beauty of the Taj, but for those looking for something beyond romance; the Agra Fort is worth seeing. Akbar, the greatest empire-builder of the Mughals, commissioned the Agra Fort in 1565, and his grandson Shah Jahan, pulled down many of the original buildings and replaced them with marble ones, while Aurangzeb added the ramparts. The fort was for some time occupied by the British; today, much of it is with the Indian Army and is out of bounds for tourists

The main point of entry for tourists to the Agra Fort is the Amar Singh Gate; the main entrance, the Delhi Gate, is now closed. Once past the gate, some of the fort's most splendid architectural structures are on view: keep your camera ready. The first of these is the Diwan-e-Aam (the Hall of Public Audience), a pillared hall centred round a throne alcove of marble with a delicate pietra dura inlay of floral motifs. The throne alcove was initially made to house the Peacock Throne (which was later taken to Delhi by Shah Jahan, looted by Nadir Shah and then carried away to Persia).

Like the Diwan-e-Aam, the Diwan-e-Khas, where the emperor held audience with visiting dignitaries, is also splendid. Built in 1635, it had two thrones on the terrace, one in white marble and one in black slate. Emperor Shah Jahan is believed to have used the marble throne for repose, and the slate throne to watch elephant fights in the courtyard.

Other than these, the fort's main structures include the Khas Mahal, where the emperor slept (the Khas Mahal has cavities in its flat roof to insulate it from the hot winds of summer) and the Macchi Bhawan, or fish chamber, with its fountains, tanks and water channels stocked with fish. The emperor and his courtiers amused themselves by angling here.

Also within the fort is the marble Nagina Masjid, built by Shah Jahan to house the women of the zenana or harem. Below it is the Zenana Meena Bazaar, where the ladies could examine and buy trinkets, finery and the like- all without actually emerging from their purdah (veil). The Sheesh Mahal (the Palace of Mirrors) has mirrored walls, which reflected and enhanced the lamplight, and was used by the women for bathing. Last but not least is the two-storied octagonal tower known as the Musamman Burj, said to be the place from where Shah Jahan last saw his beloved Taj Mahal before dying.

Best Time to Go

The best time to visit Agra is in winter- between November and March, when the weather's at its best and the city plays host to some interesting festivals. Of these, arts and crafts fair known as the Taj Mahotsav (February 18-27) is perhaps the best-known, although the Sharadotsav (Octoebr), a cultural festival featuring famous performers from across India, is also worth attending. The Agra Fort is open to visitors from sunrise to sunset.

Getting there and Around

Definitely among India's top tourist destinations, Agra is well connected to the rest of the country by air, rail and road. Domestic flights link it to Delhi, Khajuraho and Varanasi, while trains from a number of cities arrive at Agra's six railway stations (of which Agra Cantonment is the largest, receiving trains from Southern India, Delhi, Gwalior and Jhansi, among others). For those coming from Delhi, the Shatabdi Express is very convenient. By road, Agra is linked to Mathura, Delhi, Gwalior, Jaipur and several other major cities. UPSRTC and private buses ply to and from Agra and other cities, using the Idgah Bus Stand as the main terminus. Within Agra, the wisest option for getting around is to hire a chauffeur-driven car to taek you around the sights. Local buses are available, but are crowded and unreliable. For a spot of local colour, try a cycle rickshaw or an auto rickshaw; but bargain or you may be taken literally for a ride!

GOLCONDA FORT, HYDERABAD

Considered one of India's most outstanding citadels, the 13th century Golconda Fort was built by the Kakatiya kings and later switched hands and came into the possession of the Bahmani dynasty. Still later, the Qutb Shahi dynasty took over, and it is to them and more specifically Mohammad Quli Qutb Shah that the Golconda Fort owes much of its present grandeur. During the late 17th century, the fort was besieged by the Mughal Emperor Aurangzeb, who finally gained control of it. The Golconda Fort is impressive all the way: it stands, magnificent and majestic, atop a 120 mt high granite hill.

The path up to the fort was once a bustling market that sold everything from carpets to precious stones- especially diamonds and pearls. The path's deserted these days- except for tour groups- but the fort's as imposing as ever. Make your way up the road and you'll come to a colossal gate, its outside studded with long iron spikes, to deter invading armies from battering it down. Once you get past the gate, you'll come to the remarkable portico known as the Balahisar Gate. The Gate is spectacular not for its decoration or proportions, but for its amazing acoustics a feature you can check for yourself by clapping your hands; supposedly even this can be heard at the Durbar Hall which stands at the summit of the hill.

Also worth having a look at are the royal Nagina Gardens, the Bodyguards' Barracks, and the three water tanks, all of 12 mt deep, which once formed part of an intricate water system in the fort. The crowning glory (quite literally) of the Fort is, however, the Durbar Hall, which stands atop a hill overlooking the twin cities of Hyderabad and Secunderabad. It's approached by a thousand-step stairway, and if you can summon up the energy to accomplish the climb, you will be rewarded with a great view of the cities below- including (on a clear day) the famous Charminar itself. Outside the fort, about a kilometer to the north, are the tombs of the Qutb Shahi kings, distinctive buildings topped with bulbous white domes.

Also near the fort are the Taramathi Gana Mandir and the Premamathi Nritya Mandir, the two palaces where the sisters Taramathi and Premamathi, the king's favourites, lived. In close proximity to the palaces is the Kala Mandir, where the two women danced daily for the king's pleasure.

Best Time to Visit

The most pleasant months in Hyderabad are October to February, when the maximum temperature hovers around 28 º– 29ºC. The nights are cool, with an average minimum temperature of 16ºC. Hyderabad is best avoided in summer, when day temperatures can touch 40°C or more and drop by about 10ºC with nightfall. The monsoons hit the city during June to December.

Getting there and Around

Hyderabad ranks as one of India's largest and busiest cities, and getting here should not be a problem. Hyderabad's local airport receives flights from all across India, with regular connections to Delhi, Mumbai, Chennai, Kolkata and other major destinations; in addition, there are flights to and from the Middle East.

Hyderabad's three railway stations at Kacheguda, Hyderabad (Nampally) and Secunderabad are major junctions on the South and West Zone sectors of Indian Railways' network, and receive a large number of trains from all parts of India. The city is, in addition to its rail and air connections, linked to the rest of the country by good highways going as far as Kolkata and Mumbai. State roadways and private bus operators run buses to and from a number of other towns and cities in Andhra Pradesh, and even go as far as Mumbai and Nagpur in Maharashtra. Within Hyderabad, the options for getting around include a good local bus service, which surprisingly enough, is fast, efficient and relatively uncrowded.

Other than that, there are autorickshaws, taxis, cycle rickshaws and cars for hire.

HAWA MAHAL JAIPUR

The Hawa Mahal, or the Palace of Winds, is arguably Jaipur's best-known monument. For one, it is unlike any other Rajput monument – fort, palace or temple. Secondly, it's a bit too whimsical and delicate, almost like a magical structure from the Arabian Nights. Despite its towering height and length, the Hawa Mahal looks like a light, airy structure which might blow away with the slightest wind. Placed right in the middle of the bustling Johari Bazaar, near the Badi Chaupad (the big square), this reddish-pink building made of red sandstone is a constant reminder of Jaipur's colourful history which refuses to just curl up and die. Adjacent to the City Palace (where the family of the last Maharaja of Jaipur still lives) is the Hawa Mahal Jaipur, built by Sawai Pratap Singh and designed by Lalchand Usta in 1799.

If anyone views it from a distance, it looks like a palace with the promise of big, spacious rooms inside. But once you cross the road for a closer inspection, you realise that it is little more than a finely chiselled facade. Out of its five floors, the top three are just a room deep while the lower floors are connected to rooms and courtyards. Hawa Mahal, Jaipur, is an enormous tapering structure with numerous arches, spires and a mind-boggling 953 latticed casements and small windows. If you observe it closely, you'll realise that it is actually a portion of the zenana palace (women's quarters) and what you can view from the road is merely the back of the building.

Constructed for the Royal Ladies of the Court

The building is a bit of an enigma as nobody knows precisely why it was built. A couplet ascribed to Sawai Pratap Singh, a poet and a devotee of the Hindu deities Radha and Krishna, suggests that the monument was dedicated to them. However, the most widely accepted conjecture is that it was a viewing gallery for the ladies of the royal household. Sitting in the cool, airy interior of the Hawa Mahal, they could watch the goings-on below while remaining hidden themselves. The carved screen balconies meant that the windows caught even the slightest whiff of breeze, making the ladies comfortable as they watched the royal parades and processions.

FORT PALACES IN ORCHHA

Introduction

Raja Rudra Pratap founded Orchha in the early 16th century, but most of the early construction work in the town was carried out by his successor, Raja Bharti Chand. He built the city walls, and the citadel that, unfortunately, is in ruins now. Work on the Raja Mahal was started by Raja Rudra Pratap, but he died in 1531, leaving the construction incomplete. His son, Bharti Chand, completed the front and the main portion of the palace, but could not complete the building during his lifetime. The final touches to the Raja Mahal were added by one of the most prominent rulers of Orchha, Madhukar Shah built several other monuments in the town as well. The Raja Mahal is a fine example of Mughal architecture with typical stone jali (lattice) work and multifaced arches at the entrance.

The palace is in the shape of a perfect square that is further divided into two courtyards. The main courtyard is flanked by the palace which has a four-storeyed building at one end of it. The other three sides have five-storeyed apartments. The Raja Mahal's facade is simplicity personified with hardly any ornamental detailing, but the interiors house some splendid paintings. The outer courtyard has some beautiful arches arranged in floral patterns and carved out in lime mortar.

Main Attractions inside the Palace

Inside the Mahal, the two places worth a look are the Durbar-e-Khas and the Diwan-i-Am. The Durbar-e-Khas, or the Durbar Hall, is situated on the first floor of the palace and is surrounded by high battlement walls. It is well fortified, and right above it are a number of musket holes through which the enemy was shot at. The Diwan-i-Am is an assembly hall where the king often held meetings with his council of ministers.

The hall has three platforms, and from the highest one, the king held forth on affairs of the state. The Diwan-i-Am has massive columns and the ceiling has been decorated with paintings belonging to the Mughal and the Bundela schools of art. The exterior of the palace is decorated with elephant and lotus-shaped brackets. The entire architecture of the Raja Mahal is exquisite and speaks loftily of the stone carvers who sculpted it.

Jahangir Mahal

The intricately carved Jahangir Mahal has an aura of grandeur and opulence. Built on the lines of Emperor Akbar's Hamam Saras in Agra, it is nevertheless representative of the Bundela school of architecture. The palace is five-storeyed and houses as many as eight pavilions. The third floor has a court where the rulers of Orchha met with their subjects.

The court is raised over superimposed arcades with a wide gallery overlooking it. A long line of elephant brackets flanks the entrance to the monument, and a reddish-brown cornice runs along the periphery of the court. The façade of the Jahangir Mahal is decorated with a plethora of geometric patterns, and paintings of peacocks and flowers.

As the very name of the monument suggests, it was built in honour of the Mughal Emperor Jahangir, by the Orchha ruler, Vir Singh. The friendship between the two went back a long way, much before either of them became monarchs.

Before he became Maharaja, Vir Singh owned the fief of Badoni, situated midway between Orchha and Gwalior. Meanwhile, in the Mughal Court, the relationship between Emperor Akbar and his eldest son, Salim (later to be known as Jahangir), was always a tempestuous one. Prince Salim was a bit too susceptible to affairs of the heart, and his dalliance with Anarkali had riled the emperor no end.

Abul Fazl, one of the Navratnas, or Nine Jewels, in Akbar's court thrived on the rift and persuaded Akbar to forfeit Salim's heirship to the Mughal throne. Inevitably, Salim revolted against this, and Akbar deputed none other than the Machiavellian Abul Fazl to quell the rebellion. Fazl began a march to Agra to meet Salim's army in battle, but first he had to travel through Badoni, which was en route. At this crucial juncture, Vir Singh decided to help his friend Salim in his hour of trial by attacking Fazl's army and vanquishing it. Not content with that, he chopped off Fazl's head and presented it to Salim. This was in 1602, and three years later when Akbar died and Jahangir replaced him as the emperor, it was time for him to repay the favour to his old friend.

Accordingly, he bestowed the whole of Bundelkhand to Vir Singh and even attended his coronation in 1606. It was on this occasion that Vir had the Jahangir Mahal built to receive Emperor Jahangir when he visited Orchha. The palace today stands as a memorial to the great friendship between the two erstwhile rulers.

Rai Praveen Mahal

Built in circa 1618 by Maharaja Indrajit Singh, the three-storeyed palace is also variously known as the Anand Mandal Bagh and the Rai Praveen Manika Bhavan.

A lush garden, with shrubs and flowerbeds pruned in very many artistic shapes, surrounds the palace. Quite obviously, the art of topiary has been in existence in Orchha for centuries. The Mahal was built in honour of the 'Nightingale of Orchha', Rai Praveen, and the second floor is resplendent with scenes of Nritya Mudra, the poses and postures of Indian dance.

The Glorious Beauty of Rai Praveen

Rai Praveen was as well known for her enchanting beauty as for her poetry and music. The paramour of Indrajit Singh, in whose court she performed, her fame inevitably spread far and wide and finally reached the Imperial Court of Akbar. The Mughal emperor was smitten by her, and he arrogantly summoned her to his durbar. Indrajit Singh, Rai Parveen's paramour, was too weak-kneed a ruler to defy the Imperial summons.

Emperor Akbar Moved by Charms of Poetess

So, Rai Praveen went to Akbar's court, where, accompanied by her tutor, Keshava Dasa, she regaled the court with her singing and dancing skills. A bewitched Akbar asked her to jilt the contemptible Indrajit (who had abandoned her to her fate in any case) and take up residence with him in his harem.

He enticed her with the fabulous riches of the Mughal court, which, he told her, were more suitable for a lady of her accomplishments. However, Rai Parveen refused.

Akbar, finding all his inducements falling on deaf ears and touched by her loyalty, decided to restore her to Orchha. Rai Praveen returned to Orchha with both her dignity and that of her kingdom intact. The palace is a fitting memorial to this lady.

The fort also houses a Tope Khana (canon foundry) which kept a vigil round the clock, guarding against any external threat from the enemies of Orchha.

AHHICHATRAGARH FORT (NAGAUR FORT)

Hadi Rani Mahal

Although the fort is in a fairly dilapidated state it does house some beautiful palaces. One of the most beautifully decorated palaces is the Hadi Rani Mahal which has intricately carved designs all over its walls and ceilings. It is further embellished by exquisite mural paintings mostly displaying Maharani Hadi Rani (one of the most well known maharanis of Nagaur) along with her retinue. It also has a particularly fascinating frescoed ceiling which is worth travelling miles to see.

Deepak Mahal

The other palace to look out for is the Deepak Mahal which is decorated with beautiful floral designs from wall to wall. In rain parched Nagaur the temple is like a breath of fresh air, and it is natural that the desert fiefdom, deprived of any greenery, painted pictures of beautiful flowers and shrubs. Deepak Mahal represents a fantasy for the people of Nagaur.

Bhakt Singh Palace

Also worth looking out for is the Bhakt Singh Palace although the history behind it is particularly gory. Bhakt Singh was the ruler of Nagaur in the first half of the 18th century. His brother Abhay Singh was the heir apparent to the throne of Jodhpur and was persuaded by the Mughals to become the ruler by murdering his own father.

Abhay Singh assigned this task to his brother Bhakt, promising him Nagaur if he commited the foul deed. Bhakt willingly commited the patricide and became the ruler of Nagaur and built a splendid palace for himself inside the ancient fort.

Amar Singh Mahal (Palace)

The fort also houses the Amar Singh Mahal, which is decorated from floor to ceiling with intricately carved designs. Amar Singh was the ruler of Nagaur during the Mughal emperor Shah Jahan's reign to avenge the death of a Mughal courtier called Salabat Khan. The palace is a fitting tribute to his memory. Although he was cremated on the banks of the Yamuna, his wives commited sati (self-immolation) in Nagaur itself, and their palm impressions can be found nearby.

Akbari Mahal

Nearby lies the Akbari Mahal, which was built to commemorate the recapture of Nagaur by the Mughals from the governor of Ajmer in 1556. The art and architecture of the palace clearly indicates a confluence of both Rajput and Mughal art. In fact, the Mughal style and influence can be seen in most of the airy palaces and pavilions.

Rani Mahal

Also to be found in the fort is the Rani Mahal and the Zenana Deori. The Rani Mahal was obviously the dwelling place of the wives of the rulers of Nagaur as was the Zenana Deori. The Zenana Deori has paintings on its ceilings rather similar to the Sistine Chapel in Rome.

They must have had a local Michaelangelo in their midst in medieval Nagaur. Also in the women's quarters is the Baradari, which is another residence where the royal ladies lived. It also contains a small swimming pool. In one of the palaces is also housed an ornate hammam or bath.

Magnificent Fort Gateways

As seen, the gateways to a fort in Rajasthan are no diminutive ones - as they were massive stone structures with reinforced doors to ward off elephants and even cannon shots. Mostly, there are notched parapets at the top of the gates from where archers could shoot at their tormentors.

The Nagaur Fort had Three Main Gates

Sireh Pol

The outermost gate has heavy wooden doors fitted with iron spikes to prevent elephant charge.

Beech Ka Pol

This is the second gate of the impressive fort.

Kacheri Pol

The last gate is known so because it housed the judiciary of Nagaur in ancient times.

Fort Temples

Ahhichatragarh also houses two temples, the Krishna Mandir and the Ganesh Mandir dedicated to the two gods respectively. The interior of the Krishna temple is laced with pictures – from very primitive sketches of cows and buffaloes (Krishna was a cowherd), to beautiful murals of Lord Krishna in the company of divine gopis (milkmaids). The Ganesh Mandir has a brick-red façade, which is in reasonably good shape, and the inner sanctum houses a marble statue of the elephant god.

Krishan Mandir

The Ahhichatragarh fort houses the Krishan Mandir, dedicated to Lord Krishna. The interiors of the Krishna temple are decorated with pictures - from very primitive sketches of cows and buffaloes to beautiful murals of Lord Krishna in the company of Gopis (milkmaids).

Mosques

The fortress houses the Shah Jahani Mosque, which was built by the Mughal emperor Shah Jahan during the time when Nagaur was under Mughal control. In a decrepit state; the mosque is no Taj Mahal but an important historical monument nonetheless. It represents the time when the Mughals enjoyed uninterrupted power in Nagaur from the time Akbar conquered it in 1556 to when his grandson Shah Jahan voluntarily bestowed it to Amar Singh in 1638. A few kilometers away from the fort is the Akbari Masjid constructed by the Mughal emperor himself in the 16th century. The monument has stood the test of time with the interiors still quite well preserved although the façade is in a shabby condition. The inner part is lined with blue tiles and all the inscriptions inside are intact. The mosque serves a dual purpose as it is used as a madarsa (school) in the morning where local children assemble for their lessons. However, the main mosque in Nagaur as in virtually every town and city in India is the Jama Masjid. Located a short distance away from Ahhichatragarh fort the Masjid is an impressive monument, and has four huge minarets which are almost as high as a skyscraper. The monument has become a little worse for wear over the years. Jama is a corruption of Jumma, which means Friday and is the Muslim holy day. Therefore, Friday prayers are held in the main mosque across the country.

Shah Jahani Masjid

This masjid within the fortress was built by the Mughal Emperor Shah Jahan during the time when Nagaur was under the Mughal control.

In a frail state ; the mosque is no Taj Mahal but was definately an important historical monument. In a way, it represents the time when the Mughals enjoyed uninterruped power in Nagaur from the time Akbar conquered it in 1556 to when his grandson Shah Jahan voluntarily bestowed it to Amar Singh in 1638.

PURANA QILA (OLD FORT) IN DELHI

Humayun: The Mughal Emperor Costructed The Fort

When the second Mughal emperor Humayun decided to make a city of his own he decided on the site of the ancient city of Indraprastha. Humayun was quite a scholar with a fine grasp on such matters and so it is certain that the site was chosen deliberately. When his Sher Shah Suri overthrew him, he destroyed most of Dinpanah (refuge of the faithful) as the city of Humayun was called to make way for his own Dilli Sher Shahi or Shergarh. Incidentally, Humayun was probably the only emperor in history who built a city in Delhi and did not give it his own name – this was typical of Humayun's rather sophisticated and dreamy character. The Layout of The Massive Colossal

In plan the Old fort, now simply called Purana Qila by Delhites, is irregularly orbital. The walls of the immense Qila tower down on the road that takes one to Pragati Maidan from the height of 18m, and run on for about 2km. It has three main gates – the Humayun darwaza, Talaqi darwaza and Bara darwaza (which one uses to enter the fort today). The double-storeyed gates are quite huge and are built with red sandstone. of all the gates entry was forbidden from Talaqi (forbidden) darwaza, the northern gate. It is not clear why this was so. Other Attractions of The Fort

Sher Shah Suri and his successor could not complete the city, and when Humayun defeated Sher Shah's son to take back his city, he did not deal with Dilli Sher shahi as the latter had done with Dinpanah. In fact the Mughal emperor very handsomely completed the city and even used several of the buildings like the Sher Mandal, a rather pretty two-storeyed octagonal building. Humayun used this as his library and, then tripped to his death from its steps.

Excavation of Grey Ware Pottery

Several excavations have taken place in the Purana Qila in an attempt to prove, or disprove as the case may be, whether it is indeed the site of Indraprastha or not. Diggings have yielded Painted Grey Ware pottery which has been dated to 1000BC. Similar stuff has been noticed in other sites associated with the epic Mahabharata as well, which seem to conclusively prove that this indeed was the place where Indraprastha once flourished. These excavation have also thrown up material, like coins, associated with the Gupta (about 4-5th century AD) and post-Gupta ages (700-800AD) of Indian history as well.

Qila-i-kuhna Masjid

One of the most fascinating buildings, and also one of the few that still survive, in the Purana Qila is the Qila-i-kuhna masjid. Sher Shah Suri built it in 1541 (also see History) and he was obviously out to make a definite style statement.

The mosque is quite a place; its prayer hall measures 51.20m by 14.90m and has five doorways with the 'true' horseshoe-shaped arches. Apparently the idea was the build the whole mosque in marble, but the supply ran out and red sandstone had to be used instead. But the builder used the material at hand very skillfully and the result is quite spectacular – the red sandstone and the marble contrast beautifully with each other to give the mosque a very distinctive air.

The mihrabs (prayer niches) inside the mosque are richly decorated with concentric arches. From the prayer hall, staircases lead you to the second storey where a narrow passage runs along the rectangular hall. The central alcove is topped by a beautifully worked dome. In the courtyard at one time there was a shallow tank, which had a fountain.

The mosque has an inscription which says 'As long as there are people on this earth, may this edifice be frequented, and people be happy in it.' A noble thought – amen to it.

TUGHLAQABAD FORT IN DELHI

Fort Stands in Isolation

'Ya base gujjar, ya rahe ujjar.' (May [this city] be the abode of nomads or remain in wilderness.) These words, with which the great Sufi saint Hazrat Nizamuddin Auliya cursed Ghiyas-ud-din's city, seem to still echo all over the ghostly ruins of Tughlaqabad. The citadel frowns down ominously like some Gothic palace all over the Qutub-Badarpur road and seems to prefer its splendid isolation. Which is of course not exactly what Ghiyas-ud-din Tughlaq had in mind when he started out building it. It would have broken the old sultan's heart if he had seen just how swiftly the saint's curse went into action; soon after his death in fact.

Ghiyas-ud-din Tughlaq Raised the City

It seems that even when he was far from being a king Ghiyas-ud-din Tughlaq had dreamed of raising his city, Tughlaqabad. Earlier, Ghiyas-ud-din had been a general (he rose to being the governor of an important province like Punjab, but that's another story) in Ala-ud-din Khalji's army. Once while on the road with Ala-ud-din, Ghiyas-ud-din, on spotting this area, mentioned to the sultan what an ideal setting it seemed to provide for a new city. Upon this the king indulgently (and, knowing Ala-ud-din, also perhaps patronizingly) replied, 'When you become king, build it.' Knowing full well, as every boss, that while he was around there was not a shadow of a chance of anyone else taking his place. After the death of Ala-ud-din various events conspired to put the general on the throne at last. Then he fulfilled his long-cherished dream.

A Stratigical Layout of the Fort

Romanticism apart, Tughlaqabad also made perfect strategic sense. Those were the times the Mongols were a real menace to society and generally a pain in the neck for all the sultans of the Delhi Sultanate. Almost everything that the sultans built was aimed baffling the Mongols with sheer structural magnificence (read somewhere to duck in and hope for the best).

Tughlaqabad fort, situated as it was on high rocky ground, was ideally located to withstand sieges. Ghiyas-ud-din Tughlaq helped matters along by putting up formidable walls which, though short on aesthetic value, are excellent examples of solid unimaginative masonry and not the type that any invading army could hope to scale in a hurry. Tughlaq put ramparts towering at heights of anywhere between 9m (30ft) to 15.2m (50ft), and rising up to 29.8m (98ft) around the citadel, between himself and the Mongols.

The fort is half-hexagonal in shape and Ghiyas-ud-din seems to have built defenses around and in it till he was blue in the face. The outer walls are built around the silhouette of the surrounding land and, what with their height and width, add formidably to the natural barriers. They were also well defended. On the north, east and west sides it is protected by trenches that go far down, and in the south a lake acts sentinel.

To Reach the Inner Complex of the Fort

The parapets have small loopholes all over them from where Ghiyas-ud-din's soldiers to spot invaders quickly and start saying it with arrows. The fort has or at least had thirteen portals and the inner citadel has three more. If you could reach them that is, because it was defended in depth by three layers of battlements.

For all the defense, the city of Tughlaqabad hardly saw any warfare. Perhaps that is why it bears such an air of dejection – it could never fulfill the task it was built for. You enter the fortress by a highway, which was set one

27 arches, almost all of them have vanished now. Water being prized commodity (and allegedly one of the reasons why Tughlaqabad was finally abandoned) there was a huge reservoir to store rainwater in the fortress; you can still see it. When one enters the fort, the first impression is of emptiness; the ruins begin registering later. It is difficult to imagine that if one was somehow transported a few centuries back, these very walls would come alive, with people brushing past you and if things got really lively one could even find oneself in the midst of a full-scale Mongol invasion.

As you enter, to the left, used to be the palaces and to the right still stand the ruins of the a tower (Bijai Mandal, not to be confused with the one in Jahanpanah; also see *Bijai Mandal*), several halls and a subterraneous passage that led to the Bijai Mandal in Jahanpanah. Just beyond was the city, with its streets (all laid out in a grid), houses, mosques, peoples and bazaars.

An Excellent View

A walk up the walls is well worth the while and, well, one of the main reasons why people come here at all. The vista is glorious; the ruins inside the fort, Ghiyas-ud-din's tomb next door and remains of the Adilabad fort (built by Ghiyas-ud-din's son Muhammad) lay scattered in front of you like petty detail.

Walking along the southern side of the fortress next to the outer wall is a way out of the impregnable fortress which one supposes was reserved for dire emergencies in case of prolonged sieges. This was a standard practise all over India; a secret escape route was part of the building plan in any fortress. Don't feel tempted to try it, if you value your neck. Further towards the west there is an abysmal tank which you don't want to go falling into – it is called the road to hell (Jahannum ka raasta) and for obvious reasons.

For a place of its size, Tughlaqabad was built with surprising speed, just four years. and of course abandoned with equal speed in 1327. Muhammad-bin-Tughlaq, probably being one of those modern free thinking guys who didn't want to be known by his father's laurels, chose to make a city of his own called Jahanpanah. One of his first achievement being to do away with Ghiyasuddin by arranging one of those accidents that were so frequent in medieval ages; a pavillion built to welcome Ghiyas-ud-din fell on him, of all things. Anyway, with the sultan's death, the city's short-lived glory to an abrupt end.

JAISALMER HAVELIS

Salim Singh ki Haveli

Salim Singh ki Haveli: The haveli or mansion was initially occupied by the influential Mehta family of Jaisalmer. It was built around 1815, possibly on the remains of an earlier building of the late 17th century. The building was commissioned by the then Prime Minister of Jaisalmer, Salim Singh, a man with a reputation for Machiavellian cunning. His father Diwan Swaroop Singh, also Prime Minister of Jaisalmer in his time, was murdered as a result of a palace intrigue when the young Salim was a mere dozen years old. Salim took it upon himself to avenge his father's death. As soon as he came of age, Salim eliminated all of Jaisalmer's courtiers, princes and hangers-on with such dexterity that he was appointed premier by Maharawal Mool Raj.

Salim built his eight storeyed pleasure palace and lived in it with his seven wives and two concubines. It is a magnificent monument with every structure carved with elaborate detailing. He demanded the best and got it; anything that did not please him was summarily rejected. The mansion boasts of 38 balconies, each with a different design. As you enter you are confronted by an imposing stone elephant, while the upper storeys of the building jut out proudly like a ship's prow, which is why the haveli is also called the Jahazmahal or Ship's Palace. The monument as a whole has the appearance of a great ocean liner, with a narrow base which widens at the top. It has a beautifully arched roof, topped with blue cupolas, and brackets in the form of peacocks.

As Salim Singh's power grew so did his ambition, and he reckoned it was time he usurped the power of the maharwals themselves. He came up with a scheme to knock off the top two floors of the haveli and build a gateway from his house right upto the maharawal's palace, but this proposal was nipped in the bud by the monarch himself. This incident marked an about-turn in his political fortunes for soon he was killed in one of the numerous court conspiracies he himself had encouraged for long. The Salim Singh saga was a classic illustration of the old maxim that ultimately 'the schemer always falls into the pit which he digs for another'.

Nathmal's Haveli

The haveli (mansion) was built circa 1885 for Diwan Mohata Nathmal, then Prime Minister of Jaisalmer. Designed by two Muslim brothers Hathi and Lulu, the haveli was ordered for Nathmal by the then maharawal Beri Sal. The sibling-architects worked in an unusual manner; each carved out one-half of the building developed according to the same plan. However, when the building was completed, the two sides turned out to be very dissimilar to each other though the haveli remains unsurpassed in Jaisalmer in terms of the quality of the work. Like the Salim Singh's haveli (mentioned above), the entrance to Nathmal's haveli is zealously guarded by stone elephants; and the entire façade is embellished with a slew of detailing – horses, elephants, soldiers, flowers and birds. There are also carvings of trains and bicycles, gadgets of the then new age which the artisans themselves had never seen but carved out of hearsay

The Imposing Interiors of Haveli

Another extraordinary part about its construction is that the main chamber is carved out of rock and the entire frontage of the first floor is carved out of one solitary boulder. The interiors of the havelis are decorated by beautiful miniatures. The workmanship of Jaisalmer's havelis is an amalgam of both Rajput architecture as well as Islamic art that was imported via the traders' caravan through the desert

Patwon-ki-Haveli

The five Patwa havelis were the first ones to crop up in Jaisalmer and are known locally as the Patwon-ki-haveli. The first was constructed circa 1805 by a merchant called Guman Chand Patwa and is the biggest and the most ostentatious. Patwa was a man of considerable means, and for his five sons he built the elaborate five-storeyed complex which reportedly took 50 years to finish. All five houses were constructed in the first 60 years of the 19th century. The havelis are also known as the 'mansion of brocade merchants' as the family ostensibly dealt in threads of gold and silver used in embroidering dresses. However, they reportedly made their fortune elsewhere; through opium trade and by moneylending.

The Decor of Patwa Haveli

The unsung heroes as far as the Patwa mansions are concerned are the unnamed stone carvers who wielded the chisel with as much skill as a surgeon handles a scalpel. Every square inch of space has been carved exquisitely, with jali (latticed) friezes providing ventilation to the interiors as well as offering privacy to the women to look out without exposing themselves to Peeping Toms. The havelis are built in yellow sandstone with a different design on every window and arch. As you enter the haveli through its magnificent arched gateway, you come across its delicately carved yellow-brown frontage with as many as 60 balconies overlooking it. Another prominent haveli of Jaisalmer is the Nokhatmal haveli, which unlike the other mansions is a fairly recent addition to the city having been constructed only a few years ago.

UMAID BHAVAN PALACE

Construction of the Palace

The palace built by Maharaja Umaid Singh who ruled from 1911-47 was the last expression of princely architectural extravaganza during the British Raj. It was in 1925 that Umaid Singh went to London in search of an architect and commissioned the firm of Lancaster and Lodge to build the palace. The foundation stone was laid in 1929 at Chittar Hill- a sight dictated by astrological considerations. "Striking indeed is the impression of romance and dignity which this occasion conveys" said Col. Windham at the time of its inaugaration, adding while addressing the king "It conjures up both a retrospect of the past and a prospect of the future Your Highness."

Chittar-ka-Bangla

It took some 3000 people working round the clock some 15 years to complete and ranks as one of the world's largest residences. The massive structure is also referred to as Chittar-ka-Bangla or Chittar Bungalow. The 347-room building was designed by Henry Lanchester, an understudy of Edwin Lutyens (who designed most of New Delhi) it contains two huge wings separated by a double dome 185 feet tall.

Rajmahal

The primary entrance to the palace is called the Rajmahal, which contains the traditional Rathore coat-of-arms, bearing the sacred kite, an incarnation of the family goddess. Its symbol is omnipresent in the palace and as a mark of reverence, kite hunting is not allowed in Jodhpur. It houses several banquet halls and ball rooms where the monarch used to entertain his guests (usually European), a billiard hall and an imposing Durbar Hall.

And that's not all. It has libraries panelled with teak, circular reception halls, magnificent double staircases, marble flooring, a swimming pool embellished with tiles depicting the zodiac. The wings include courtyards, staff offices and zenanas (women's quarters), a cinema house and opulent royal suites. Suffice to say a visit to the palace will simply knock your breath away. The unique feature of the palace is that it is not mortared at all, but like the Jaisalmer fort it was built out of solid interlocking blocks of stone. The chunks of rock were cut from the Sursagar quarry located 13km away.

Palace Served as a Military Base During Second World War

During the Second World War even while the structure was unfinished, the palace became a military base for the allied troops. Christmas dinners for the entire military community were organised annually at the palace, with the Jodhpur royals playing a key role in keeping up the morale of the soldiers during the war. When Umaid Singh died in 1947, his son Hanwant Singh became maharaja but he too was killed in a plane crash five years later. While his heir Gaj Singh, who was only four at the time was being educated in England the palace remained unoccupied. One year after Gaj Singh returned to India, the then Prime Minster derecognised the princes and ended their privileges. Initially at a loss as to what to do with the palace, after much dilly-dallying Gaj Singh did what many other princes did as well-coverted his residence into a luxury hotel in 1977. Part of the palace, which was once the audience hall has now been converted into a museum.

MOUNTAINS AND HILLS IN INDIA

DHARAMSHALA

Introduction

The Himachal hill town of Dharamshala sits on a narrow ridgeline along the Dhauladhar range. Dharamshala is roughly divided into two sections - the lower town with its traditional settlement and market areas and the upper town of McLeodganj, famous for its celebrity resident, His Holiness The Dalai Lama. The heights of the two sections vary from 1,250 metres to about 1,770 metres with a steep winding 10 km road linking the two sections. Around a 150 kms from Mandi, Dharamshala lies in the Kangra Valley of northern Himachal Pradesh and is the most important town of the district. Surrounded by pine forests, the grand Dhauladhar ranges tower like sheets of rock over Dharamshala.

Once a British hill resort, this sleepy little hill town revived with the influx of Tibetan refugees after Chinese occupation in 1959. The Dalai Lama set up his temporary residence at McLeodganj. Many western visitors have come to Dharamshala in search of spiritual guidance and an audience with the Dalai Lama. In McLeodganj, the Tibetans run most of the hotels and restaurants as well as handicrafts shops. The lower town of Dharamshala is crowded with shops, local houses and government offices and the Museum of Kangra Art. McLeodganj has a distinctly different character, with its brightly painted buildings, Buddhist temples, prayer flags fluttering in the air and saffron monks and nuns hurrying along the streets. The main Buddhist temple or Tsuglagkhang is a five-minute walk from the bazaar.

The residence of His Holiness the Dalai Lama is surrounded by high walls and sits on the edge of a cliff overlooking the valley. The Dip Thekchen Choeling Monastery nearby stands out with its golden roof amidst tall pine forests. The Library, open from Monday till Friday, has an exhaustive collection of books, manuscripts, and archival photographs on Tibet. Besides the overpowering Tibetan presence, a few remaining Raj edifices like the Church of St. John in the Wilderness are worth visiting. And if you want to make excursions out of Dharamshala, visit the pretty Kangra towns of Palampur, Naddi and Andretta.

Getting there and Around

The nearest rail station for Dharamshala is at Pathankot, 150 km. From Dharamshala and McLeodganj there are regular bus services to Dalhousie, Chamba, Manali, Shimla and further down to Delhi. You could drive in by rented car from any of these towns as well.

Best Time to Visit

The winters are cold and Dharamshala is quiet and empty, perfect for that peaceful vacation away from the hustle and bustle of city life. The best time to visit Dharamshala is between October and December or from March to June. Carry heavy woollens, rain protection and walking shoes.

KULLU

Deep in the heart of Himachal Pradesh, at an altitude of 1,219 mt on the banks of the Beas River, lies one of northern India's most popular hill stations Kullu. Kullu lends its name to the idyllic valley which surrounds it an area dwarfed by snowcapped peaks which soar high into the sky, an area of apple orchards and beautiful ancient timber temples. This has been the favoured destination of thousands of travellers for generations altogether, and although many just use Kullu as a stepping stone to the nearby hill station of Manali, Kullu too has its own charm. Its reputation as the heart of the 'Valley of the Gods' (as the Kullu Valley is known) means that Kullu's greatest sights are its temples.

Check out the Raghunathji Temple, dedicated to the guardian deity of Kullu, a manifestation of Lord Rama.

Legend has it that a ruler of Kullu, Raja Jagat Singh, brought the idol within the temple all the way from Ayodhya, the birthplace of Lord Rama. Another important shrine, 10 km from Kullu across the Beas, is the Bijli Mahadev Mandir, where the main lingam is topped with a trident, which is believed to attract lightning. Also worth visiting is the Basheshwar Mahadev Mandir, 15 km from Kullu and famed for its fine scrollwork. For the adventurous, Kullu has more surprises up its pretty sleeve: there's plenty of opportunity round about for angling (in the Beas), trekking, nature walks, and more. The town is the transit point for treks such as the one over the Chanderkhani Pass to Malana; the Jalori Pass and Bashleo Pass to Shimla; and the Pin Parvati Pass to Sarahan. The town also lies in close proximity to some of Himachal's best-kept secrets: the temple-town of Naggar; the quiet retreats at Katrain and Kaisdhar, and the ancient town of Mandi.

Getting there and Around

Bhuntar Airport has regular flights both on Indian Airlines and private carriers connecting the town to Delhi and Shimla. The most convenient railhead is Chandigarhay, and with good connections to the rest of the country. Buses and taxis ply between the two cities regularly. Alternatively, one can drive to Kullu— good roads link the town to Delhi, Shimla, Chandigarh and other nearby places, and there are regular bus connections to and from Delhi, Shimla, Pathankot, Palampur and Ambala.

Best Time to Visit

The best seasons to visit Kullu are from Mid-March to Mid-April and again mid-September till mid-November. Summers are more crowded, though that is the main season for treks. The festival of Dussehra in October is an extravaganza in Kullu, and reason enough in itself to visit the town at this time.

DARJEELING

At 2,134m, Darjeeling is quite the picture-perfect hill station with its fantastic mountain views, trekking trails, Buddhist monasteries and balmy climate. Darjeeling has that rarefied mountain air and a lofty beauty, amplified by the world's highest mountains looming in the distance.Staggering above the clouds, the majestic Kanchenjunga and her entourage of lesser peaks are clearly visible from Tiger Hill, the highest vantage point in Darjeeling. Even the elusive Everest puts in an appearance when the skies are clear. On cloudy days, the mist-shrouded peaks make an awe-inspiring backdrop to Darjeeling's own beauty. The Senchal Lake at a height of 2,448m is a charming picnic spot nearby.

Darjeeling became a favourite haunt of Kolkata-wallahs during the days of the Raj. Being a border town, the influence of its neighbours, Bhutan, Tibet and Nepal is palpable — it is here that you can feast on momos and kebabs, have a typical English tea with cake and crumpets, shop for ethnic bric-a-brac or simply hang around the main market at Chowrasta.

Hindu and Buddhist cultures rub shoulders all over town. The Dhirdham Temple is the most prominent Hindu temple here, but Darjeeling's Buddhist monasteries stand out with their prayer wheels and colourful pennants fluttering in the breeze. The Bhutia Busty Gompa, stands out with the majestic Kanchenjunga as a backdrop. Its library holds the original copy of the Tibetan Book of the Dead. Shrouded under a cloud of mist is the Yogachoeling Gompa popularly called Ghoom, which enshrines an image of the Maitreya Buddha. This is one of the best-known monasteries in Darjeeling, 8 kms out of town. The other monasteries in Darjeeling are the Samdenchoeling, Sakyachoeling, Phin Sotholing, Aloobari, Thupten Sangachoeling and Sonada Gompas.

Another place worth visiting in Darjeeling is the Bengal Natural History Museum with its amazing collection of Himalayan flora and fauna, and the Padmaja Naidu Himalayan Zoological Park that houses rare species like the snow leopard, Siberian tigers, red pandas and the Tibetan wolf. For mountaineering enthusiasts a visit to the famous Himalayan Mountaineering Institute (HMI) is a must, if only to view the mementos from all the Everest expeditions of the past. Tea has for long been Darjeeling's major claim to fame. The steep slopes are intricately patterned with a maze of tea plantations. The fragrance of tea blossoms wafts through the town and the markets are flooded with uniquely packaged pouches of tea - pleasing gifts to take back home. While you are in Darjeeling, visit a tea plantation and savour some of the local brew at any of the wayside cafés.

Getting there and Around

Darjeeling is 651 km from Kolkata and 51 km from Kalimpong by road. Bagdogra, 96 km away, is the nearest airport, connected to Kolkata, Delhi, and Guwahati. From here a bus or private taxi can get you to Darjeeling in 3 hours. New Jalpaiguri is the nearest railhead with connections to major cities in the country. The Toy Train to Darjeeling takes a picturesque 7-hour route via New Jalpaiguri. Within Darjeeling, jeeps and Land Rovers are available on hire.

Best Time to Visit

The best time to visit is from April to June and September to December. Average summer temperatures hover between 14°C and 8°C and the winter temperatures fall to between 6°C and 1°C. You will need light woollens for summer and heavy woollens for winter.

SHILLONG

Get a birds' eye view of Shillong from the sky, a lively city that paints a pretty picture. A vision of snug wooden cottages and red tiled roofs rubbing shoulders with each other, nudging at terraced hills. Shillong, the capital of the eastern state of Meghalaya lies on a 1520 m high plateau. The Diengiei Hills and the Assam Valley peaks loom up in the distance, hemming in the Umiam gorge and the Umiam River. The view from Shillong Peak is amazing; this is the highest point in the city, from where you can glimpse the entire city veiled in clouds. Shillong by night will take your breath away, with its millions of lights glimmering like a galaxy.

Within Shillong city is the flower bedecked Ward's Lake encircled by whispering pine groves. This is a pleasant place to go boating or to feed the colourful fish while standing on the bridge across the lake.You'll love the walks in this city although it does get a little crowded with cars in the afternoon. Lady Hydari Park doubles up as a miniature zoo and is a short distance away from Ward's Lake. A visit to the St Mary's Christian Cathedral at Dhankheti is a must - it has beautiful stained glass windows and the grotto is carved out of a single rock. The bells of the cathedral resonate across the city at dawn, in the afternoon and at dusk.

Shillong is a city of waterfalls - feel the spray from the Crinoline Falls, from the two Gunner's Falls, Spread Eagle, Elephant Gait and Elephant Falls, Beadon and the Sweet Falls. Quite the most spectacular falls, however, are at Cherrapunjee, 56 km away, a town that was once billed as the wettest place on earth. Shillong is a throbbing city, full of vibrant energy and one that enjoys keeping abreast of development. Yet it has a serenity and beauty that add to its unassuming simplicity. This, combined with the comfortable climate, makes Shillong a great holiday getaway from the Kolkata fast lane.

Getting there and Around

Shillong is 1181 km from Kolkata. The quickest route to get here from Kolkata is via Guwahati in Assam, 128 km away. Guwahati has the nearest airport, Borjhar and the closest rail junction. From here, buses and taxis take about 4 hours to get to Shillong.

Best Time to Visit

Shillong is a year round destination that is particularly beautiful in the monsoons (June to September), if you are willing to put up with the heavy showers. The temperatures range from 10ºC to 30ºC. Carry light woollens and an umbrella, no matter what season it is.

GANGTOK

Mesmerising, picturesque, colourfulGangtok is the exuberant capital of Sikkim that lures for an unforgettable vacation. Cool breezes blow over the lush mountainside and the air is fragrant with the profusion of wild orchids and rhododendrons. Gangtok's bazaars bustle with the animation of trendy youngsters, elderly matrons in their traditional bakus and lamas in colourful maroon and mustard robes. Prayer flags flutter in front of pretty Buddhist shrines and pagoda-style houses that cling to the hillside. At about 1,770 mt, Gangtok offers panoramic views of the Himalayas, especially from Tashi Viewpoint.

Though you will be charmed by Gangtok's serenity, for energetic moments make a trip to the famous Pemayangtse Monastery to see its priceless antiques and idols, and to the nearby ruins of Rabdantse, the 17th century capital of Sikkim. The Institute of Tibetology, the Enchey Monastery, and the Rumtek Monastery are other interesting places in Gangtok. The Do-Drul Chorten is a splendid temple capped by a golden tower, with 108 prayer wheels. The sacred Changu Lake at 3,780 mt, 40 km east of Gangtok remains frozen through the year and comes alive during summer when rhododendrons, irises, primulas and poppies burst into bloom on its banks and on the adjoining hill slopes.

Getting there and Around

Gangtok is 721 km from Kolkata, 589 km from Guwahati and 584 km from Patna. The airport closest to Gangtok is at Bagdogra, 124 km and the nearest railhead is New Jalpaiguri (125 km), with connections to all the major cities of India. You can drive to Gangtok from either of these West Bengal cities in 5 hours or from Siliguri 114 km away or Darjeeling, 139 km from Gangtok. The drive to Gangtok is facilitated by numerous taxis, shared jeeps and hired cars with chauffeurs.

Best Time to Visit

The best time to visit Gangtok is between October and mid-December when clear views of the Himalayan peaks are guaranteed or again between March and May when the flowers are in bloom. January and February means snow in the higher altitudes and visits many of the tourist spots are not possible. June to September brings heavy rains causing landslides that often disrupt communication. Carry light woollens for summer and heavy woollens for winter. Rainwear is a must in any season.

MAHABALESHWAR

Mahabaleshwar, within easy distance of Mumbai, is a peppy hill station that was once a colonial retreat during the British Raj. Mahabaleshwar is liberally perked up with a dash of interesting ingredients for that delicious holiday you've always been meaning to take. Perched in the Sahyadri Mountains at a height of 4500 ft, Mahabaleshwar has a magnificent view of the evergreen valleys of the Deccan and the Konkan coast. In the midst of thick forests is that beautiful plateau where many a box office hit film has been picturized; a woody haven that tempts you to break forth into a song and dance routine! There is much to see and do in Mahabaleshwar. Start by drinking in the breath-taking vistas and varying perspectives of the valley from over 30 different vantage points.

Mahabaleshwar sights: See spectacular sunrises and sunsets from Wilson Point; let your eyes sweep across the valleys of the Rivers Koyna and Savitri from Connaught Peak and Elphinstone Point; and admire panoramic views of the Sahyadri Ranges from Marjorie Point. Arthur's Seat overlooks awesome canyons and cliffs; from this vantage point you can see the geological differences between the rocks of the Deccan Plateaus and the Konkan coast. A short climb down the steps near Arthur's Seat leads to the source of the River Savitri at Tiger's Spring.

You must see the cascading waterfalls like the Chinaman, Lingmala and Dhobi Falls. The imposing fortress of Pratapgadh, an hour's drive outside Mahabaleshwar, and a number of old temples, are also part of the local attractions. The Panchganga Temple is considered the source of five important rivers of the region.

While away the hours at wayside coffee shops in the markets in Mahabaleshwar or sip coffee or fresh fruit juices at the roadside cafes. Admire the seasonal flowers in the park, amble off on gentle mountain ponies, and go for a boat ride on Venna Lake.

Shop for locally made shoes, varieties of honey, fruits and an enormous range of soft fruit like strawberry, raspberry and mulberry from the surrounding Brahma Aranya forests. As you drive up to Mahabaleshwar, the road passes by farms that put up stalls selling fresh fruits, ice creams, jams, jellies and crushes... take some home with you so that the taste of Mahabaleshwar lingers on.

Getting there and Around

Mahabaleshwar is 290 km from Mumbai via Pune, and 266 km via Mahad. It is 120 km from Pune, the nearest airport and most convenient railhead. The best way to get here is by road - bus, taxi and car - on a good, motorable road.

Best Time to Visit

Mahabaleshwar is a year round destination. The summer is cool enough and the winter warm enough for a pleasant vacation. The monsoons are torrential and best avoided. Carry light woollens in winter and a wrap for summer evenings.

MOUNT ABU

Set amidst green, wooded hills, Mount Abu is Rajasthan's only hillstation, and the perfect destination for those who like sleepy, relaxed holidays. Small, quiet and deliciously cool, Mt Abu usually inundated by weekend crowds, Gujarati honeymooners and pilgrims- but finding a little bit of solitude amidst the crowd is never a problem. Fortunately for those who can't imagine a holiday without a bit of sightseeing thrown in, Mount Abu offers a few attractions to choose from few, but adequate. Go boating on the pretty Nakki Lake, or go strolling along the many paths that wend their way through the hills, offering some of the most spectacular views around.

The attraction in Mount Abu is the architectural wonder known as the Dilwara Temples. One of the most splendid temple complexes anywhere in India, the Jain Dilwara temples are carved entirely from white marble two of the temples, the Vimal Vasahi (built in 1031, the oldest in the complex) and the Tejpal Temple (built in 1231), are especially exquisite and will leave you spell bound. The carving here is so intricate and delicate that they appear to be made out of ivory rather than marble. Drink in loads of clean, cool air. Feast your eyes on greenery; trail a hand in the refreshingly cool water of the lake.

Getting there and Around

Abu Road is the nearest railhead, an hour's drive from Mt Abu and connected to Delhi and Ahmedabad by good superfast and express trains. The closest airports are at Udaipur and Ahmedabad from Mountt Abu. The easiest access is by road from any city in Rajasthan or Ahmedabad in Gujarat via the city of Udaipur.

Best Time to Visit

Mt Abu has fairly temperate climate even though summer temperatures range between 23 °C and 34°C. Winters are balmy at a cool 28°C with minimum temperatures of 11°C. It rains fairly heavily in the monsoon (65-177 cm) so the very best times to visit are between February and June or any time after the rains between September and December. Lightweight clothes will do very well for the summers but winters (November-January) will require a warm jacket or sweater.

PANCHMARHI

Time stands still at Pachmarhi, an evergreen plateau in the Mahadeo Hills of Madhya Pradesh. Pachmarhi's pristine beauty lies in its innocence and its unspoilt splendour. The area is a visual treat - red sandstone cliffs and deep gorges cleave the valleys; verdant forests and flower-filled vales are drenched by numerous streams and brooks. The hills that surround Pachmarhi are washed in green. Waterfalls cascade down every conceivable rock face and create pools.Groves of jamun and bamboo are scattered about the countryside, while the forests are thick with sal trees.

Many a trail leads you to blissfully secluded forest glens. The Satpura National Park is home to exotic bird and animal species - the gaur, sambar, leopard, barking deer, langur and the occasional tiger; spotted pigeons, gold-throated chloropsis, great pied hornbills and kingfishers, to name a few.

Beauty apart, the Mahadeo Hills are a pilgrimage centre, with ancient shrines to Shiva concealed in deep ravines and cliffs. The sacred site of Mahadeo in Chauragarh is the spot where the God tricked the demon Bhasmasur, and Jata Shankar, as the name suggests, resembles Shiva's untamed locks. A dark cave in Jata Shankar has two naturally formed Shivlingas on which water drips constantly from a pool. The mythological Pandava kings are said to have spent part of their exile in the Pandava Caves or Panch Mathi, which lent their name to Pachmarhi.

There is a colonial side to Pachmarhi, too. Red-roofed bungalows with pretty gardens, jacarandas and laburnums overhanging pebbled paths, churches with stained glass windows, and a typical cantonment area complete the picture.

This sublime landscape is offset by a historical heritage of Stone Age cave paintings, the oldest of which is 10,000 years. Pachmarhi is a place that has escaped the onslaught of reckless development - a fate suffered by so many other hill stations in the country - and the area has been declared a biosphere reserve. Pachmarhi extends an open invitation: to wildlife enthusiasts, bird watchers, trekkers, hikers, bikers, history-buffs, pilgrims and lotus-eaters.

Getting there and Around

Pachmarhi is 864 km from Mumbai and 211 km from Bhopal, the nearest airport with connections to all major cities of India. The quickest way to get here is to fly to Bhopal and then take an onward bus or taxi to Pachmarhi. The closest railhead is Piparia, 47 km, on the Mumbai-Howrah mainline, from where buses and taxis are available for Pachmarhi. Within the city you can walk, hire a bike or a jeep to see the sights.

Best Time to Visit

This is a year-round destination with a pleasant climate. Summer temperatures rarely exceed 37ºC and winter temperatures never fall below 7ºC. Carry light woollens for summer evenings and heavier woollens for winter.

KEMMANAGUNDI

Come to Karnataka's Kemmanagundi, a picturesque hill station near Chikmagalur. Kemmanagundi is a great place to get away to at any time of the year— summer, winter and even the monsoons, a season that can be quite spectacular, with waterfalls gushing over and the trees on the hills wearing a sparkly rain-washed look. Driving up to Kemmanagundi, you are greeted by pleasing mountain scenery. The landscape is lush with forests and waterfalls that tumble down the rock face. Many a shady walking trail through the woods leads you to untrodden paths and quiet glens, where you can picnic, ramble and commune with nature.

Kemmanagundi lies in the Baba Budan Hills and was once the summer retreat of the Maharaja of Mysore, the Wodeyar King Krishnaraje Wodeyar IV, after whom the hill station is also, named the K.R. Hills. The Royal Horticultural Society of Karnataka has its base at Kemmanagundi, with beautifully landscaped gardens and a riot of flowers. About 8 km walk from Kemmanagundi are the Hebbe Falls. This 168 m high waterfall is broken half-way by a rock ledge before it crashes down hill. Hebbe Falls is a lovely picnic spot, with the spray turning the surroundings dewy. The Kalahatti Falls that cascade down 122 metres is another major attraction, about 10 km from Kemmanagundi. Kemmanagundi has that delightful ability to carry your thoughts away from the routine. So the next time you are looking for a quiet holiday destination where you can spend a few peaceful days in tranquillity, head for the hills and discover the joys of refreshing Kemmanagundi.

Getting there and Around

Kemmanagundi is 260 km from Bangalore, 225 km from Mangalore (the closest airport), and 55 km from Chikmagalur. Trains halt at Tarakere, the nearest railhead. State Transport buses come to Kemmanagundi from Bangalore, but the most convenient way to get here is to drive.

Best Time to Visit

Kemmanagundi is pleasant throughout the year - the temperature never rises above 28ºC. Summer is peak tourist season, while the crowds thin during the monsoons, making it a great time to be here.

CHAMBA

When you seek an unusual break from the hackneyed hill station theme, turn your searchlight towards Chamba, a scenic Himalayan town just 50 kms from Dalhousie. Chamba blossomed as the ancient capital of the Pahari Rajas; it was named after King Sahil Varman's daughter Champavati. Today it is the quintessential valley township, famous for its myriad temples, forests and charming hill folk. At 915m, Chamba rises above the river Ravi as it rages by, leaving verdant valleys and dense deodar forests in its wake. The forests surrounding Chamba are rich in wildlife, marmot and snow leopard haunt the upper reaches above the snowline, and musk deer, brown bear, leopards and wild boar inhabit the lower elevations.

Mountain birds such as the partridge and pheasant flit across the vale. Pretty waterfalls and streams tumble down the mountainside and at every turn, the valley's beauty seems to grow. Chamba is strewn with intricately carved temples topped by spires in the Shikhara style. The shrines are dedicated to Shiva and Vishnu. The 10th and 11th century temples of Laxmi Narayan and Hari Rai are particularly ornate and popular with pilgrims and sightseers alike. The Chowgan, a huge grassy field, is the centre of town life in Chamba - the gathering point for all things religious, political and social. The Gandhi Gate on the Chowgan's south-west face was built to commemorate Lord Curzon's visit to the town in 1900. Other interesting places are the Akhand Chandi Palace, now a museum and the Bhuri Singh Museum that houses a collection of ancient Chamba artefacts and manuscripts.

Many a trek into the Himalayas is launched from Chamba - through Bhaderwah to Kashmir, through the Sach Pass into Pangi Valley and to other peaks in the Dhauladhars, Peerpanjal and Laskar mountains. Bharmaur (65 km), the ancient capital of Chamba, is a popular village that can be accessed by road. The Gaddi tribes lead their goat and sheep to pasture at Bharmaur in summer. While in the area, visit the sacred Manimahesh Lake where thousands have a holy dip around Janamashtami. Chamba is bound to bowl you over with its scenic beauty, temples and its sense of tranquillity.

Getting there and Around

Chamba is 580 km from Delhi and120 km from Pathankot, the closest railhead. The nearest major airports are at Jammu and Amritsar, both 245 km away, from where buses, taxis and tourist vehicles are available. Dalhousie is just 50 kms away from Chamba. Within Chamba, you can move around in taxis, jeeps, buses and minibuses.

Best Time to Visit

Summer - April to October - is quite the best time to be in Chamba; the weather is pleasant barring the monsoon months of July and August. Summer temperatures range from 8°C at night to 39°C during the day, while winter temperatures drop to freezing - between 10°C and 1°C. Cotton clothes and light woollens are fine for summer, but heavy woollens and snow clothes are required in winter.

BEACHES AND SEASIDES IN INDIA

Goa

Goa- the name conjures up images of sun-baked sands and palm fronds waving in a cool sea breeze. All that may sound a wee bit clichéd, but Goa definitely isn't. One of India's hottest destinations for well over two decades now, Goa was and still is where everybody goes to party.

A sunkissed land dotted with coconut trees and rice fields, old Portuguese churches and the prettiest of beaches- where February means Carnival and every day is an occasion for celebration. Goa's beaches are where much of the action is; some of the best beaches in India, these are the major reason why Goa attracts so many thousands of tourists- Indian and foreign- every year. The state's beaches stretch all along the coastline, from the northern border with Maharashtra right down to the south, where peaceful stretches like Palolem are a godsend for anybody looking for an escape from the crowds.

The three main areas where Goa's best beaches are concentrated include Mapusa, Panaji and Margao. Along most of the major beaches are resorts, hotels, cottages, restaurants and souvenir shops by the dozen, and usually an interesting flea market as well. All of which means that you can get a fairly complete vacation- with accommodation, dining, entertainment and shopping- all on one beach. What more could one ask for?

Best Time to Visit

Goa is a year-round destination, but the best time to go is in winter, between late October and early April. The winter weather is balmy, the days are sunny and the nights cool, especially on the beach.

The summers are very hot and humid and it rains heavily from June to August, making it unsafe to swim. The carnival period in the month of February through to early March is another peak time, attracting a lot of tourists to Goa. It is a great season with parades, pageants and merrymaking late into the night.

Access

Goa is well connected to Mumbai and other major cities by air, rail, road and a limited catamaran service, the latter only from Mumbai. Dabolim Airport, 30 km from Panaji, is the only airport in the state, but it's got plenty of flights coming from the rest of the country. Goa is also well connected by train, with Margao being the main station for the Konkan Railway plying between Maharashtra and Karnataka. Trains come in from Mumbai, Delhi, Bangalore, Trivandrum and other major cities of the country.

National Highways link Goa with other cities and there are regular overnight coaches and buses. Driving down from Mumbai is also a good idea, since its usefulness to have a vehicle in Goa. The best way to get around Goa is to hire a vehicle, as public transport systems can be a bit unreliable: there are no metered taxis and the bus service is erratic. Riding pillion on motorcycle taxis is extremely popular and inexpensive. You can also rent cars or two-wheelers for the day.

GOPALPUR-ON-SEA

Gopalpur-on-Sea is a lovely laidback seaport village, far removed in spirit from the nearby temple towns of Orissa. Starting life as an obscure little fishing village, Gopalpur-on-Sea became a prominent trading port during the days of the British East India Company. Today, neither the British nor the wealthy Bengalis who once made Gopalpur a vibrant, happening place are here any more. Gopalpur has gone back to being a quiet, relaxed place, but with one major difference- it's today growing into one of India's prettiest beach resorts.

Nowhere as commercial and trendy as Goa, but with a charm all its own.

This languorous beach with coconut groves, casuarina coppices and gentle sand dunes is deserted for miles. Picture blue waters and high waves, sleepy lagoons and tiny creeks, a place where you can loll on the sand, stroll down the beach and gorge on seafood.

Or tackle the high waves on a yacht moored at the crumbling ancient jetty... and then climb up the ancient lighthouse for a spectacular view of the bay. The best thing about Gopalpur, besides the golden beach, is he seafood. This is a seafood lover's paradise, but, like everything else in this resort, don't expect meals in a hurry. The restaurants, shacks and even the locals are quite willing to cook a special meal for you – just remember to give them plenty of notice.

Best Time to Visit

Gopalpur is a year-round destination, but the best time to go is from October to April. The temperatures range from a summer high of 35°C to a winter low of 16°C. The monsoon season (June to September) sees some hot and some very wet days.

Access

The nearest airport is at Bhubaneshwar, 180 km from Gopalpur. Bhubaneshwar is a one-hour flight from Kolkata, to which it is also connected by rail and road. From Gopalpur-on-Sea, the nearest railhead is Berhampur (16 km) on the Kolkata-Chennai line. You can drive in to Gopalpur on National Highway 5 from Berhampur, Bhubaneshwar and Barkul (75 km). Buses, minibuses, tourist taxis and even auto-rickshaws can be hired from Berhampur. Auto rickshaws are available for moving around within the town.

GOKARNA

The term 'Gokarna' actually means cow's ear but it is a mundane way of describing a place as pretty as this. Named for the ear-shaped confluence of two rivers which marks Gokarna, the place is a small town, known more as a pilgrimage centre than as a beach. This is a pity, really- because Gokarna, with its coconut palms, its blue seas and clean sands, is perfect for an idyllic vacation by the sea. Situated along the Karwar coast, in northern Karnataka, Gokarna is beach-utopia if you're looking for minimal luxury but maximum privacy, with only the sun, the surf and the seagulls for company. A somnolent one-street town consisting almost entirely of wooden houses, Gokarna is in close proximity to four beaches. Of these, Kudle, a kilometre-long stretch of white sand fringed by palm trees, is the nearest; just about 20 minutes' walk from Gokarna. Half an hour further from Kudle is Om beach, so named because it's shaped like the auspicious 'om' symbol. Gokarna's two other beaches- Paradise and Half-Moon- are smaller and lesser known, but equally great for a bit of sunbathing and swimming.

All of Gokarna's beaches remain pretty empty, except for the odd 'in-the-know' traveller, the hippy who's tired of Goa, or the many pilgrims who come to Gokarna for 'darshan' at the Shiv Temple. Gokarna, like nearby Udipi, is a sacred place for Hindus, who believe it to be the place where Shiva emerged from the earth after a long penance in the netherworld. The town's main shrine is the Mahabaleshwar Temple, home to a very holy lingam that was reputedly rescued by Shiva's elephant- headed son, Ganesh.

Best Time to Visit

Gokarna is pretty much a round-the-year destination, although you'd be well advised to avoid it during the monsoon, when heavy rain can make it muddy and messy. In February-March, festivities mark Maha Shivratri, and along with other celebrations, there's a colourful procession in Gokarna. January and February, when the weather's good, are anyway a great time to visit the town.

Access

Gokarna is 60 km south of Karwar and 7 hours from the city of Mangalore. One of the best ways of getting to this town is aboard the Konkan Railway, which traverses the prettiest parts of India's western coast. Konkan Railway trains pass through Gokarna Road (10 km from the town), Ankola (25 km), or Karwar (23 km). From either of these railheads, a bus can be taken to Gokarna.

Gokarna has good bus connections to a number of towns within Karnataka and along the west coast; Goa, for instance, is only about 5 hours away.

KOVALAM

Kovalam is a famous hippie paradise. No longer an undiscovered rural idyll, Kovalam has made rapid strides towards 'resort-isation' and is now one of the biggest draws to 'God's own Country'-Kerala. Highly commercialised and very crowded through most of the year, Kovalam manages, against all odds, to retain much of the charm which made it a popular beach in the first place. It still has a lovely shoreline and beautiful beaches lined with coconut trees, and local fishermen from the villages still go out at night for the daily catch. A towering promontory of rock dominates Kovalam, looking out over a bay of clear blue water. Golden sand slopes down into the sea for as far as 100 mt, and dotted along the coast are a few interesting coral reefs, which make for good snorkelling. Surfing and swimming are among the other water sports possible off Kovalam beach. Beachwear, light cottons, sandals and sun protection are, obviously, essential luggage to this beach town, although surfboards are available on loan for water buffs. And that's not all.

Kovalam has also acquired a reputation as being one of the best places in Kerala-or India, for that matter- for an invigorating ayurvedic course of treatment or rejuvenation. Ayurvedic massage parlours, spas and yoga centres are a dime a dozen in Kovalam, and there's really nothing that can buck you up as much as a course of therapy- with herbal oils and soothing massages- at one of these!

Best Time to Visit

Being near the sea makes Kovalam really a year-round destination weather-wise. The actual season is from September to March. The prices shoot up during the Christmas-New Year week as do the number of tourists, so it might be wise to avoid this period.

Access

Kovalam's just 16 km south from Kerala's capital, Thiruvananthapuram, so the nearest airport is obviously the international one there (10 km). Thiruvananthapuram's railway station is well connected to the rest of south India, with a number of trains coming in from other parts of the country too. The capital also has extensive road connections to other cities and towns in Kerala and its neighbouring states. Inexpensive buses run every half-hour from Thiruvananthapuram to Kovalam. There are also direct services from Kollam, Kanyakumari (Tamil Nadu), Ernakulam and Thekkady. Taxis and auto-rickshaws will also make the trip but at comparatively greater expense. Kovalam is small enough to cover on foot without much effort. There are local buses for trips out and one can hire two wheelers by paying a security deposit and producing a valid driver's license.

MAMMALAPURAM

The coastal town of Mahabalipuram or Mammalapuram is only 58 km from Chennai. Lying along the pretty Coromandel Coast, Mammalapuram is known primarily for its ancient rock-cut temples. The eight Rath Temples date back to the 8th century and have been carved out of monoliths. Each one is associated with one of the Pandava brothers, heroes of the epic Mahabharata. Close to these are the two-spired Shore Temple, the Krishna Mandapam—the world's largest bas-relief with detailed carvings of gods, animals, insects, and birds- and eight rock-cut caves decorated with depictions of scenes from various legends. The temples are all very well; a good way to while away the time between hours when you're sunbathing, swimming, or simply lolling on the beach. But what really matters to beach buffs is the sand and the sea, and both are good here.

It is suitable for day lazing on the beach and for a leisurely swim, followed by a satisfying lunch of freshly caught fish. You can't go far wrong here. About 20 km north of Mammalapuram is the beach of Covelong, a fishing village which is not as touristy as Mammalapuram, but is great if you want to get away from the crowds. Covelong Beach is good, and there are facilities for water sports such as windsurfing. At about the same distance from

Mammalapuram is Muttukadu, a water sports complex which offers a range of sports, including boating, kayaking and windsurfing.

Best Time to Visit

The best time to visit this pleasant seaside temple town is in the winter, between November and February. And within this period too, mid-January and mid-February are when Mammalapuram's at its best. The weather's great, the sand's nice and warm, the sea's deliciously cool, and there's plenty of opportunity to enjoy yourself. This is also the time when the annual Mammalapuram Dance Festival is held; exponents of Bharatnatyam, Kuchipudi, Odissi and Kathakali perform on weekends through the month.

Access

Mammalapuram is fairly well connected to the rest of the state of Tamil Nadu. The closest airport is at Chennai, which is 58km from Mahabalipuram. The road is good and you can rent a car and be driven along the coast – it's a pleasant and pretty drive. The nearest railway station is at Chengalpattu. Mahabalipuram is well connected with the rest of the state. Buses from Chennai, Pondicherry and Chengalpattu and Kanchipuram are frequent.

BEACHES OF MUMBAI

Mumbai, the capital of Maharashtra is a beautiful city filled with many enchanting beaches, having shimmering sand, sun and surf. These beaches are like the soul of this city of dreams, where people enjoy their evenings. Some of these wonderful beaches of Mumbai are given below:

Juhu Beach

One of the largest and frequently visited beaches of India, Juhu Beach is located 18 km north of the city center. This beach is one of the most exotic beaches on the shores of Arabian Sea. Areas near Juhu beach are one of the posh localities of Mumbai where bungalows of the famous film personalities are located. It is also the venue of many film shootings.

Juhu beach is a famous hangout zone of Mumbai. The southern end of the Juhu beach is surrounded many Luxury hotels and apartments.

Juhu beach has many stalls selling the famous snack of Mumbai, Bhelpuri, which people enjoy eating while visiting the beach. A popular weekend spot, Juhu, also offers horse and donkey rides. Here you can enjoy yourself by watching dancing monkeys, acrobats, cricket matches, toy sellers and other type of Indian beach entertainment. Versova Beach is towards north of Juhu, which is a home to Mumbai's largest Koli fishing community.

Marine Drive in Mumbai. Marine Drive, the Jewel of Mumbai, is located in the central Mumbai. It was built in the 1920s and 1930s on land rescued from the sea. It is Mumbai's most famous pathway, where people walk and sit in the evenings. It is also known as "Queen's Necklace" because of the dramatic line of street lamps lit up at night that surround the beach. Recently it's name has been changed to "Netaji Subhashchandra Bose Road". Marine Drive is a fun place to be, here you can enjoy yourself by watching children playing with sand and vendors selling toys and food. Marine Drive is really a colourful and beach.

Chowpatty Beach

Chowpatty beach is situated at the top end of Marine Drive. It is the only beach in the central part of Mumbai. This beach is the venue where many Hindu religious ceremonies can be witnessed like the annual thread-tying ceremony initiating young boys into the Brahmin caste. Another festival 'Nariel Purnima' is celebrated towards the end of the monsoons.

Here the idols of Ganesha are immersed on the last day of 'Ganesh Chaturthi'. At the beach there are statues of Lokmanya Tilak and Vithalbhai Patel. The beach is also famous for a huge line of stalls, selling 'Bhelpuri', 'Kulfi' and 'Paan'. Other attractions at the beach are shooting galleries, snake charmers, monkey trainers, balloon sellers and masseurs. Recently, a "Nana-Nani Park" has been added to the beach, specially for elderly people.

Marve and Manori Beach

The Marve and Manori beaches are located approximately 19 miles from Mumbai. These attractive beaches are pleasant for bathing. At Marve there is a 5-star resort hotel to spend a refreshing weekend. On the way to these lovely beaches lies the Madh Beach, another favorite picnic spot.

KANYAKUMARI BEACH

The legendary end of India's land Kanyakumari or Cape Comorin is surrounded by three seas, Bay of Bengal, Indian Ocean, and Arabian Sea. Therefore the meeting point is called 'Thriveni Sangamam". This place is famous for outstanding views of the sunshine and sunset. The beach of Kanyakumari is an unique beach having multi colored sand. At the Kanyakumari beach the sea is quite rough. It is a wonderful sight to see when the huge waves of the sea hit itself against the rocks and then weaken, before it gathers itself up for another hit. There is a variety of shells found on this beach and you can even buy some of them.

ATTRACTIONS AT KANYAKUMARI BEACH

The Sangam

The Sangam at Kanyakumari beach is the point that arks the merging of the three major bodies of water, the Bay of Bengal, the Arabian Sea and the Indian Ocean. There's also a major bathing ghat here having steps that lead into the water and a kind of lagoon formed between land by a series of rocks.

People visiting this place bathe and enjoy themselves, getting lightly washed by the the remains of waves, which strike over the rocks.

Vivekananda's Rock

One of the major attractions at Kanyakumari is the Vivekananda's rock, a huge stone emerging out of the sea. It is said that Swami Vivekananda meditated on this rock. Now there's a statue of Vivekananda here, as his memorial. Thus, many followers of Swami Vivekananda visit this place, specially Bengalis. Other famous attractions of this mesmerizing beach is Gandhi Mandapam. This Mandapam marks the place where the vase containing the ashes of Mahatama Gandhi was kept before being immersed in the sea. Kanyakumari Amman temple on the shore is another attraction. According to the Hindu mythology Goddess Sakthi remains a virgin to save mankind.

HERITAGE MONUMENTS

India is blessed with number of world heritage monuments showcasing the breathtaking architecture and intricate work. Taj Mahal, a unique masterpiece is the wonder in itself, an absolute epitome of Indian culture, heritage and civilization.

Behind each monument is an underlying sense of mystery, intrigue and romance. Five thousand years of Indian History has given us the treasure of thousands of monuments across the country, monuments belonging to Hindus, Buddhists, Muslims and Christians.

Visit the monuments of India, they are not only fairy tales carved out of stones, bricks, and mortar narrating the tales of valor and courage of Indian rulers. Monuments in India form a great heritage of India and they are evidence of India's historical past. These monuments reflect the culture and the heritage of yore days.

Visit India in order to spectacle the miraculous beauty of Indian monuments. Be it Taj Mahal or Khajuraho temple, Indian monuments forms an attractive tourist spots for travellers from all over the world. Plan your monument tour to India and come across the diversity of culture and heritage.

Mohenjodaro and Harappa Civilization Related Monuments

The famous monumental heritage of India—the forts, palaces, temples, mosques, churches etc. is an evidence proving that architecture in India had been a form expression.

The era of architecture in India began with the settlement of the cities of Mohenjodaro and Harappa. The Great Bath, the Assembly Hall and the Drainage System are a few examples of the earlier architectural forms. Architecture in India evolved over a period of time, incorporating definitive influences from its various rulers, be it Hindus, Muslims or British.

Religious and Spiritual Monuments

Hindu architecture concentrates immensely on the religious and spiritual. The construction of Temple was what architecture was all about. The famous Khajuraho Temples, Jain shrines at Dilwara, Jagannath Temple at Puri, Konark Sun Temple and Kailashnath Temple at Ellora are some of the finest medieval specimens of famous Hindu Architecture.

The Muslim invasions brought about a tremendous change in the forms of architecture, with the features like arches, tombs, mosques, minarets etc. Qutub Minar, Taj Mahal, Jama Masjid (Delhi) remain unexcelled even today.

British Style of Architecture

Leaving more than a lasting impact on India's architecture, the British followed various architectural styles - Gothic, Imperial, Christian, English Renaissance and Victorian being the essentials. The Rajabai Tower at Mumbai (Bombay), Victoria Memorial at Calcutta, Law Courts at Chennai (Madras) and the layout of the cities of New Delhi and Chandigarh are few of the examples symbolizing the British colonial architecture in India.

TAJ MAHAL OF AGRA

A Symbol of Love

Take a constitutional down Shahjahan Park in the chilly mauve light of dawn, and the pale white dome of the Taj Mahal, India looms in the distance. Set against the azure skyline, it looks like a mirage in a desert. Inch closer and the supreme majesty of the greatest monument to love comes into focus – with its dew-coated lawns and its pearl-white mausoleum.

Travel to Taj Mahal Agra to baptize into the true glory of this passion of love. As the sun rises to cast a reverential beam on the sepulchre, the 'dream in marble' turns from lavender to yellow, while nightfall sees the monument bathed in moonlight – looking like a woman wreathed in smiles while waiting for her lover.

There are many theories as at which time the Taj Mahal, India looks the best, but there is no substitute to viewing it at all hours of the day and the night if you want to understand its myriad facets. Taj Mahal, India is a microcosm of the universe – it contains within it both the yin and the yang, taking on a new personality to suit the occasion. It can be harsh, dry and strong like alabaster, delicately chaste and fragile like porcelain, noisily populous or quiet and secretive.

The Monumental Heritage

A copious amount has been written about the Taj – Agra's window to the world. Nobel laureate Tagore called it 'a tear on the face of eternity', while the painter William Hodges wrote in 1876 that 'it was like a most perfect pearl on an azure ground'. From Princess Diana to President Clinton to Yanni – the Taj draws every éminence grise from across the 'seven seas' to it like a magnet. As Clinton said during his presidential visit to India, "the world is divided into those who have seen the Taj and those who have not." The American President joined the list of 'haves' this year, but for anyone bitten by the travel bug, a visit to the luminescent monument is an essential part of their resume.

To say the 'miracle in human design' is the Mughal Empire's magnum opus is to state the obvious. Like Picasso's 'Guernica', Omar Khayyam's 'Rubaiyat' or Beethoven's 'Eroica', the Taj instills in you a sublime passion. It uplifts you – one feels more significant as a human being within its confines than outside it.

The History Manifest

Taj Mahal in India was made in commemoration of Arjumand Bano Begum. The queen was married at the age of 21 to emperor Jahangir's son Khurram. During all the phases of Khurram life, Arjumand Bano Begum supported him through out. She was like a supporting pillar in his life. In AD 1628, Khurram became king after a bloody battle of succession. He changed his name from Khurram to Shahjahan or the King of the World. Arjumand Bano also changed her name from Mumtaz Mahal.

Mumtaz Mahal was not destined to be a queen for a long period of time. She died at the age of 39 while delivering a child at Burhanpur. That auspicious day turned into a mournful event. When Arjumand Banu Begum (better known as Mumtaz Mahal) died in childbirth in 1629, her husband, Emperor Shah Jehan immortalised their love by building the 'dream in marble' – the finest illustration of Mughal architecture. The dream took over 22 years to fructify and over 20,000 craftsmen were employed to build it.

Taj Designing

Who designed the Taj Mahal India is shrouded in mystery – some historians credit the Venetian architect Veroneo with its construction, while others believe it was the work of a Persian called Ustad Isa.

But we do know of the lesser luminaries connected to it with certainty – the central dome was built by Ismail Effendi from Turkey, the calligrapher was Amanat Khan from Shiraz, the mosaicist, Chiranji Lal hailed from Delhi while the goldsmith, Qazim Khan was summoned from Lahore. A story which is probably apocryphal but has been doing the rounds for generations, says that Shah Jahan had the chief mason's right hand amputated to preclude him from replicating the 'marvel in marble' anywhere else in the world.

Taj on the Banks of the Yamuna River

Located at the southern end of the city on the banks of the Yamuna River, the site where the Taj stands belonged to a Hindu nobleman, Raja Man Singh.

Abdul Rehman Lahori, the court historian recorded that five million rupees were spent on the building – a king's ransom in those days.

Once complete, the upkeep of the mausoleum and its 42-acre garden was funded with the revenue obtained from 30 neighbouring villages. There are three lofty gateways to the Tajmahel complex. The central portal is richly decorated with floral arabesques and is inscribed with passages from the Koran. A huge forecourt leads onto a lush garden, which is divided by an aqueduct.

The main monument is a two-storeyed octagonal building with a huge rotunda as its crowning glory. Four sky-scraper tall minarets position themselves as sentries on each side of the monument – all built out of brick and encased in marble. The graves of the celebrated duo, Shah Jahan and Mumtaz Mahal are housed in the catacomb below. The Taj is remarkable for its perfect proportions and rich pietra dura, and every minutiae in the monument has been etched with consummate skill. In a nutshell, the Taj is the 'Embodiment of the Islamic Concept of Paradise'

Paradise on Earth

It is unmistakable that Shahjehan conceptualised the Taj Mahal as 'heaven on earth'. As you enter the gates of the Taj, it is like an ingression into heaven. The watercourses divide the garden into quadrants. It was Babur who had introduced the char-bagh (four-garden) concept into India. The imagery is threefold: it is a symbol of paradise to reward the faithful; an oasis from the dry desert heat; and a summation of the secular tradition of the royal pleasure garden and the watercourse, which divides the garden into four, epitomises both, the life source and the meeting of man and God.

In this context, the spacious lawns surrounding the Taj Mahal become as important as the mausoleum itself.Your travel trip to Taj definitely leaves you mesmerize, a 'Paradise on Earth' really summarises its ethereal appeal – the monument rivals any of the other wonders of the world.

Taj Mahotsav

The best time to visit this 17 th century monument is during Taj Mahotsav. Taj Mahotsav is 10 day saga held annually at Shilpgram, near Taj Mahal. Bedecked elephants and camels, drum beaters, folk artists and master craftsmen together recreate the glorious past of the Mughals.

During this fest, Taj Mahal comes alive with culture and traditions. Taj Mahostav provides an opportunity to its artisans to perform their art and craft. You can actually purchase crafts which include wood carvings from Saharanpur, handmade carpets of Badohi, the pottery of Khurja, chickan-work of Lucknow, the silk of Banares and much more. Through Taj Mahotsav, performers get a platform to showcase profusion of folk music and dances of Dundelkhand, 'Nautanki' (Drama), 'Sapera' dance of Rajasthan, Lavani of

Maharashtra. Just at the entrance, there are number of shops. These shops sells exquisite crafts and arts at affordable price. You can purchase leather work, footwear and embroidery. Infact, you small Taj Mahal miniature made of white marble are quite popular amongst the tourists.

QUTUB MINAR IN DELHI

As A Holy Minar

The world famous towering Qutub Minar, started in 1192 by Qutub-ud-din Aibak (1192-98), breathes down the neck of the Quwwat-ul-Islam mosque. There is a slight difference of opinion as to its purpose: it probably was a tower of victory, but then again it could have been built to be a minar (tower), attached to the Quwwat-ul-Islam mosque, for the muezzin (priest) to climb up top for a prayer. Among Delhites there are lots of other theories about the origin of the tower. Some say it was the observatory of the great scientist Aryabhatta of ancient India, other claim that it was built by Prithvi Chauhan for his daughter to see the Yamuna.

In fact everything short of an extraterrestrial origin has been attributed to it. The presence of the ancient non-rusting Iron Pillar within the complex further appears to add credence to the first theory. However the tower, its entire design and architecture are undisputedly Islamic and all the other theories are just matters of wild surmise. Considering how shortchanged he was for time, it is doubtful that Qutub-ud-din got much further than a couple of levels of the minar, in fact many suggest that lived to see only the first storey complete. Altamash, his successor, completed the remaining tower.

Taking Caring the Minar

It is clear that the tower was very close to the sultanate's heart, since repeated efforts were made to keep it in perfect shape. In its long career, the tower got hit by lightening twice – something that, of course, with its height it was literally asking for. Once during the reign of Muhammad-bin-Tughlaq, who very decently repaired the ensuing damage. The next time was in the indefatigable builder Feroze Shah Tughlaq's time, when the topmost storey got damaged. Feroze Shah, who of course couldn't well leave things alone, not only repaired the floor, but also sneaked in another level. The result of this combined effort is an interesting mix in styles that is clearly discernable all over the tower. Each of the original three storeys has different designs.

The base storey has alternate angular and circular flutings while those of the second one are round and the third one has only angular flutings. Their alignment is mercifully similar, so giving the tower a rhythmic harmony. The pretty projecting balconies have a very interesting pattern, with icicle-shaped pendentive (an intricate design in which triangular pieces of vaulting spring from the corners of a rectangular area and support a rounded or polygonal dome) type of brackets. The attractiveness of the balconies is heightened by the bands of sonorous inscriptions. The diameter (at base) of the Qutub Minar is 14.32m and about 2.75m at the top. The tower had a crowning cupola on the top at one time, however this was struck down sometime in the early 19th century, an earthquake felled it. This was replced by a well meaning English engineer Major Smith. However it must have looked quite an eyesore for when Lord Hardinge was Governor-general of British India, he had it removed.

JANTAR MANTAR, JAIPUR

A Colossal Observatory

Jantar Mantar, built between 1728 and 1734, literally means the 'instruments for measuring the harmony of the heavens'. Jai Singh, the brain behind the grand project, chose stone with marble facing. This was the biggest of all his observatories and the only one built of stone. He used it daily, often with his astronomy gurus Pandit Jagannath and Kewal Ram. In all there are 17 instruments in the Jantar Mantar complex. The function of each instrument is rather complex but serves a particular function where time plays the main theme.

The instruments and their functions are given below in the order of their anti-clockwise position in the complex. The large Kranti Yantra was employed for the measurement of the longitude and latitude of the celestial bodies. The Diganta Yantra was deviced to measure the azimuth (arc of the celestial great circle from Zenith to horizon) of planetary bodies. Similarly, the Small Ram Yantra and the Large Ram Yantra are used to find the altitude and the azimuth. The Chakra Yantra gives the angular measurement of an object from the equator. The Jai Prakash Yantra determines the precise coordinates of celestial bodies and the small iron plate strung between the crosswires gives the sun's longitude and latitude and the zodiacal sign that it is passing through. Its main function is to keep an eye on all the other instruments.

Adequacy of Specific Yantras

The Rashivalayas Yantra operates in the same manner as that of the Samrat Yantra and has one sundial for each of the zodiac signs. Five of them (Gemini, Taurus, Cancer, Virgo and Leo) are at the back from north to south. Aries and Libra face them followed by Aquarius, Pisces, Capricorn, Scorpio and Sagittarius from north to south. It helps in taking readings the moment each zodiacal sign crosses the meridian. The Large Samrat Yantra is based on the same principle as that of the small one but in size it is 10 times larger and more accurate by 2 secs. The sundial is 27.4m high and is still used on the Guru Purnima (full moon day in the month of Jul/Aug) to forecast the onset of monsoon.

The Dakshina Yantra is a wall is aligned along the north-south meridian. It is mainly used to observe the position and movement of the celestial bodies when they pass over the meridian.

The Disha Yantra has only one function and that is to point towards the north. The Unnathamsa Yantra is used to find the altitudes of the astral bodies. Observations can be made round the clock and the sunken steps help in taking readings from any portion of the dial. The Raj Yantra or the King of Instruments is used only once a year to calculate the Hindu calendar, the details of which are based on the Jaipur Standard. To do so a telescope is fixed over the central hole. A bar for sighting is then attached at the back of the instrument. The plain disk is used to record the sightings.The Observer's Seat belonged to Maharaja Jai Singh and was used for observing the wonders of the sky and universe. The Narivalya Yantra is a sundial with two dials; one facing north when the sun is in the Northern Hemisphere (21 Mar-21 Sep) and the other facing south for the rest of the year.

The Dhruva Yantra helps in finding the position of the Pole Star at night and also those of the 12 zodiac signs. It is based on an entirely different system to what is used today for the same purpose. Traditionally, human breath, approximately of 6 secs was used as the standard unit of measurement. The Small Samrat Yantra is a triangular structure and has a large sundial with quadrants at the borders given in hours and minutes. The arc on the left displays the time from sunrise to midday and the one on the right from midday to sunset. The sundials have been constructed on Latitude 27°N and the reading can be adjusted to the Indian Standard Time (84°N) but that must be done according to the month and the solar position.

FATEHPUR SIKRI MONUMENTS

The Historical City

Sikri was a decrepit little village till the Mughal Emperor Akbar came visiting in 1568. Despite marrying the Amber princess Jodhabai in 1562, and having over 300 concubines at his beck and call, the monarch was childless. Desperate for an heir, Akbar visited the saint, Shaikh Salim who was encamping here and who predicted that Akbar would have a son within 3 years. As fate had willed it, Jodhabai bore him a son the next year. The emperor named him after the mystic. Not only that, he decided to move lock stock and barrel to the place and named it Fatehpur, or the 'City of Victory'. His military conquest of Gujarat might also have persuaded him to shift base as must have the local abundance of red sandstone. In fact, apart from the marble-white mausoleum of Salim, nestling in one corner of the Jami Masjid – the city is entirely built out of red sandstone.

Many Attractions of the city

Diwani-i-Am —The Diwani-i-Am (Hall of Public Audience) is where the monarch sat and lent a patient ear to all the petitions he received. A paved courtyard called the Pachisi was where the monarch played chaubar, a game that closely resembles chess– using slave girls as pieces.

Diwani-i-Khas —TheDiwani-i-Khas nearby housed theIbadat Khana or the 'House of Worship' where the emperor debated various systems with noted theologians.

Although semi-literate, Akbar was the most liberal of the Mughal emperors, and in 1579, he was declared the highest authority in matters of religion by the famous 'infallibility decree'. Three years later, the emperor founded Din-a-Ilahi or the 'Religion of God' which was an amalgam of all the major religions of the world. Decried by religious zealots from his own community as an apostate, Din-a-Ilahi disappeared as a faith after Akbar's death in 1605.

Ankh Michauli —As you enter the Ankh Michauli (Closed Eyes) pavilion, you realise that Akbar could be as flippant as he was profound. Here the Mughal played 'blind man's buff' and indulged in frivolous pranks in the company of his harem.

Jodhabai's Palace —Jodhabai's Palace is befittingly the grandest of all palaces in Fatehpur Sikri – as she was his most favoured wife and the mother of the crown prince. Other notable palaces at Fatehpur Sikri are the five-storeyed Panch Mahal and the Hawa Mahal.

Friday Mosque—Begun in 1571 and completed four years later, the Friday Mosque was the largest of its kind in India at the time, measuring 168 metres by 144, with a huge inner courtyard.

Buland Darwaza—The Buland Darwaza or 'Sublime Gateway' was added later to commemorate Akbar's military conquest of Gujarat. The gateway, which rises to a height of 45 metres, presents an awesome spectacle of isolation, and has exquisite Persian calligraphy inscribed on it.

Salim Chisti's Mausoleum—A trip to Fatehpur Sikri would be incomplete without visiting Salim Chisti's Mausoleum – the sage who played an important role in Akbar's life. Issueless parents visit his shrine in droves to pray for sons as Akbar did over four centuries ago. They tie little cords and paper wishes to the screens and any other object they can find.

The Everlasting Glory of Fatehpur Sikri —By 1585, Akbar wearied of the dry, hot climate of the city and moved to the cooler climes of Lahore. Within a few years, the pomp and pageantry of the city vanished – but the sandstone monuments endure to this day. Such were the construction methods employed, that there is not a single derelict monument in the city. The Mughal Empire has long since vanished from the firmament but the greatest of the Mughal emperors, Akbar etched his name forever in the sands of time by building the Fatehpur Sikri.

INDIA GATE

A War Memorial

India Gate is constructed as a memorial and was built in the memory of 90,00 soldiers who laid down their lives during world war I. Located at

Rajpath, India Gate is 42 m high and is popular relaxation area during the summer evenings. India Gate also act as popular pinic spot during winter. Also known as the All India War Memorial, India Gate was designed and constructed by Lutyens. He was the who is considered the chief proclaimer in designing the New Delhi plans. A tour of Lutyens' Delhi just has to kick off with the stately India Gate at the east end of the broad Janpath (earlier Kingsway) that leads to the Rashtrapati Bhawan. Another additional 13,516 names engraved on the arch and foundations form a separate memorial to the British and Indian soldiers killed on the North-West Frontier in the Afghan War of 1919.

The foundation stone was laid by HRH the Duke of Connaught in 1921 and the monument was dedicated to the nation 10 years later by the then Viceroy, Lord Irwin. Another memorial, Amar Jawan Jyoti was added much later after India had said goodbye to its imperial rulers. It is in the form of a flame that burns day and night under the arch to remind the nation of soldiers who perished in the Indo-Pakistan War of December 1971. The entire arch stands on a low base of red Bharatpur stone and rises in stages to a huge cornice, beneath which are inscribed Imperial suns. Above on both sides is inscribed INDIA, flanked by MCM and to the right, XIX. The shallow domed bowl at the top was intended to be filled with burning oil on anniversaries but this is rarely done.

Spectacular View of India Gate

Nowadays, if you drive down the smooth wide expanse of Rajpath on a midsummer night, you might be excused for assuming that a huge glittering carnival is in progress at India Gate. The entire boulevard up to the monument is lined with cars, scooters, motorcycles and what-have-you. In fact all of Delhi seems to have converged to the emerald lawns of India Gate. The air is thick with chatter, laughter and the cries of assorted vendors peddling their wares. You can snack on anything from fruit chaat (fruit salad with hot, spicy dressing), through bhelpuri (a snack of puffed rice, spices and hot, sweet and sour chutney), chana jor garam (spicy chickpeas), dal ka pakodas (fried lentil-flour dumplings), potato chips to ice cream, candy floss and aerated drinks.

RASHTRAPATI BHAWAN

The Viceroy Palace remains Lutyens most significant achievement. It is befittingly the crowning glory of the British Empire and architecture in India. Today, it is perhaps India's best known monument after the Taj Mahal and the Qutub Minar. Bigger than the Palace of Versailles, it cost a whopping £12,53,000 and now houses the President of India. It is unquestionably a masterpiece of symmetry, discipline, silhouette, colour and harmony. of course, it has come in for much criticism too but that has mostly been limited to the imperial intent behind it rather than its architecture. Better known now as the Rashtrapati Bhawan, the sprawling palace straddles the crown of Raisina Hill and is the focal point of New Delhi. The majestic Rajpath (earlier Kings Way) leads up to the palace on Raisina Hill and here comes into view the one fatal flaw in design. Lutyens and Baker had a major showdown about the height of the slope approaching the palace which was at that time caricatured as the 'War of the Gradient'. Lutyens wanted the palace to come into view as one climbed Raisina Hill. Unfortunately, Baker miscalculated. The palace disappears from sight till only the copper dome is visible. Furious with Baker, Lutyens said he had 'met his Bakerloo'. The palace is flanked by the two Secretariats and the three together, open into a huge square called the Viceroy's Court where the Jaipur Column stands tall. The Viceroys Court, which frames the main entrance to the house, has lateral entrances on the axis of the Jaipur Column. Here the levels were reduced artificially and cascades of steps are flanked by huge sandstone elephants and ranks of imperial lions modelled by the sculptor C.S. Jagger.

The Attractions of the Palace

The main entrance is approached by a broad flight of steps which lead to a 12-column portico. Do notice the enormous projecting cornice or chajja, a Mughal device, which blends so effortlessly with the classical style of the monument. Lutyens' ability to smoothly incorporate light oriental touches is all the more remarkable given his active and profound dislike for Indian architecture. The most outstanding feature of the House – you can spot it while you are still a kilometre away – is the huge neo-Buddhist copper dome that rises over a vast colonnaded frontage. Beneath the dome is the circular Durbar Hall 22.8m in diameter.

The coloured marbles used in the hall come from all parts of India. The Viceroy's throne, ceremonially placed in this chamber, faced the main entrance and commanded a view along the great axial vista of Kingsway (now Rajpath). At present the hall is the venue of all official ceremonies such as the swearing in of the Prime Minister, the Cabinet and the Members of Parliament. It is in this very chamber that the President annually confers the Arjuna Awards for Excellence. The columns at the front entrance have bells carved into their capitals. Lutyens reasoned that 'the ringing of bells sound the end of an empire and stone bells never sound'. Despite this, the empire came to an end a brief 16 years later.

The Great Interiors of the Palace

The principal floor comprises a magnificent series of state apartments. The State Drawing Room is barrel-vaulted and plainly treated with domestic fireplaces. The State Ballroom is enriched with Old English mirror glass. The State Library is based on the form of Wren's St Stephen's, Walbrook. The State Dining Room is lined with teak panelling enriched with the star of India. The concept of Imperial order and hierarchy permeates the entire house. Marble staircases flanking the Durbar Hall provide access to the private apartments above. There are 54 bedrooms together with additional accommodation for guests. Lord Irwin, its first occupant, 'kept losing his way' but insisted that "in spite of its size, it was essentially a liveable-in-house."

Mughal Garden

To the west the palace overlooks an enormous Mughal Garden designed by Lutyens. Here the principles of hierarchy, order, symmetry and unity are extended from the house into the landscape. A series of ornamental fountains, walls, gazebos and screens combine with scores of trees, flowers and shrubs to create a paradise so delightful that Indians called the garden 'God's own Heaven'. The Irwins supervised the planting of the garden which grew in tropical profusion softening the formal pattern of lawns and waterways. Popularly known as the Mughal Garden, it is open to public every spring but be prepared for the tight security check.

The Glory of the Palace

After India became independent, the sheer size of the building overwhelmed its new keepers. Mahatma Gandhi suggested it be turned into a hospital. Thankfully, nobody took him seriously. The Durbar Hall served as a museum for several years till the building which now houses the National Museum was completed. Here's what Mark-Bence Jones remarked about life at the Viceroy's House in his book Palaces of the Raj. Do note the then-and-now comparison he makes on a later visit to the palace, long after the British had gone. "Then there were the banquets held during sessions of the Chamber of Princes, when every other guest at the long table was the ruler of a State. The gold plate glittered in its crimson-lined niche, the lustres glinted, the scarlet and gold khitmagars moved deftly against the teak-panelled walls, and from an adjoining room came the music of the Viceroy's band."

"In India that replaced the Raj, Lutyens' Palace has managed to keep some of its glory. As the home of a modern democratic President, it is certainly on the large side, but the Indians have been wise enough to maintain a Presidential establishment worthy of the setting. Scarlet-clad guards still sit on their chargers beneath the stone sentry boxes, khitmagars in white, red and gold line the corridors."

GAITOR MONUMENTS

Just opposite the Man Sagar Lake, Gaitor lies in a narrow valleywith its marble and sandstone chhattris (cenotaphs) of the rulers of Jaipur.This was the site where the Kachhwaha royalty ended their stay on earth. It has been the royal cremation ground of the kings and princes of the ruling clan of Jaipur from Sawai Jai Singh II onwards. It has cenotaphs of all the Jaipur rulers except Sawai Ishwari Singh who was cremated outside the Jai Niwas garden. The marble memorials mark the places where the Kachhwaha kings were cremated and the smaller ones standing with them are those of the princes who died young. After the capital was shifted to Jaipur Sawai Jai Singh chose Gaitor as the cremation ground for the royal family. Then from 1733 onwards the final rites of every Kachhwaha king were conducted here. These chhatris are open domed pavilions set on a raised platform. Slender pillars hold up the roof and the platform has smaller chhatris at its corners.

The Architectural Brilliance of Cenotaphs

Each chhatri or cenotaph has a different design and is styled according to the majesty and power of the king during his lifetime. The most beautiful one is that of Jai Singh II himself with intricatecarvings and a graceful shape in marble, built by his son Ishwari Singh. It is a white marble dome built on 20 carved pillars that rise from a square platform lavishly engraved with scenes from Hindu mythology. The Chhatri of Madho Singh I, second son of Jai Singh II, is a pillared two storeyed structure with a smaller pavilion on the roof. The Chhatri of Pratap Singh is also of marble alongwith a dome and square pillars to give company. The Chhatri of Madho SinghII is in white and pink stone. A lamp is lit everyday at the cenotaph of Sawai Man Singhsince his death. Another familiar spot here is that of the miniature shrine of the two sons of Madho Singh II from his mistresses. The whole scene set between the gardens presents a picture perfect shot.

6

Policies for Tourism in India: Sport Tourism Perspectives

AN INITIATIVES

The Government of India announced the first Tourism Policy in November 1982. It took ten long years for the Government to feel the need to come up with a possible improvement over this. Thus the National Action Plan for Tourism was announced in May 1992. Between these two policy statements, various legislative and executive measures were brought about. In particular, the report of the National Committee on Tourism, submitted in 1988 needs special mention. In addition, two five-year plans - the Seventh and the Eighth - provided the basic perspective framework for operational initiatives. The Seventh Plan advocated a two-pronged thrust in the area of development of tourism, viz., to vigorously promote domestic tourism and to diversify overseas tourism in India.

While laying stress on creation of beach resorts, conducting of conventions, conferences, winter sports and trekking, the overall intention was to diversify options available for foreign tourists. The Tourism Policy, 1982 was more an aggressive statement in marketing than a perspective plan for development. Its main thrust was aimed at presenting India to the foreigners as the ultimate holiday resort. With a view to reach this destination, the following measures were suggested by the Policy:

1. To take full advantage of the national heritage in arriving at a popular campaign for attracting tourists;
2. To promote tourist resorts and make India a destination of holiday resorts;
3. To grant the status of an export industry to tourism;
4. To adopt a selective approach to develop few tourist circuits; and,
5. To invite private sector participation into the sector.

TOURISM AS AN INDUSTRY

The Planning Commission recognised tourism as an industry by June

1982. However, it took ten years to make most of the States to fall in line and accord the same status within their legislative framework. At the beginning of the Eighth Plan (1992-97), 15 States and 3 Union Territories had declared tourism as an industry. Four States had declared hotels as an industry.

The National Committee on Tourism was set up in July 1986 by the Planning Commission to prepare a perspective plan for the sector. Within the broad framework of the Seventh Plan, the Committee had to evolve a perspective plan for the coming years.

The Committee, headed by Mr. Mohammed Yunus, submitted its recommendations in November 1987. The list of Members was as impressive Mr. S.K. Mishra (Secretary, Department of Tourism), Mrs. Kapila Vatsayan, Mr. K.L. Thapar, Mr. Rajan Jaitley, Mr. A.B. Kerker, Mr. R.K. Puri and Mr Pran Seth.

The Committee in its Report recommended that the existing Department of Tourism be replaced by a National Tourism Board. It suggested that there be a separate cadre of Indian Tourism Service to look after the functioning of the Board. It also submitted proposals for partial privatisation of the two airlines owned by the Union Government.

By September, 1987, the Central Government declared more concessions for the sector: these included tax exemption on foreign exchange earnings from tourism (a 50 per cent reduction on rupee earnings and a 100% reduction on earnings in dollars), a drastic reduction in tariff on import of capital goods, and concessional finance at the rate of 1 to 5% per annum. The Tourism Development Finance Corporation was set up in 1987 with a corpus fund of Rs. 100 crores. Until then, the sector was financed on commercial lines by the Industrial Development Bank of India, Industrial Credit and Investment Corporation of India and other commercial banks.

NATIONAL ACTION PLAN

The National Action Plan for Tourism, published in May 1992, and tabled in the Lok Sabha on 5 May 1992, charts 7 objectives as central concerns of the Ministry: 1. socio-economic development of areas; 2. increasing employment opportunities; 3. developing domestic tourism for the budget category; 4. preserving national heritage and environment; 5. development of international tourism;6. diversification of the tourism product, and7. increase in India's share in world tourism (from the present 0.4 per cent to 1 per cent during next 5 years)

As per the Action Plan, foreign exchange earnings are estimated to increase from Rs.10,000 crores in 1992 to Rs.24,000 crores by 2000 AD. Simultaneously, the Plan aims at increasing employment in tourism to 28 million from the present 14 million. Hotel accommodation is to be increased from 44,400 rooms to 1,20,000 by 3 years. Other provisions in the Action Plan include a discontinuance of subsidies to star hotels, encouraging foreign investment in tourism and the setting up of a convention city for developing convention tourism. The Action Plan envisages the development of Special Tourism Areas on lines of export processing zones. Special Central assistance is to be provided for the States to improve the infrastructural facilities at pilgrimage places. It proposes to set up a National Culinary Institute, and projects a liberalised framework for recognition of travel agents and tour operators.

EIGHTH PLAN

The Eighth Plan document makes a special mention that the future expansion of tourism should be achieved mainly by private sector participation. The thrust areas as enumerated in the Plan include development of selected tourist places, diversification from cultural related tourism to holiday and leisure tourism, development of trekking, winter sports, wildlife and beach resort tourism, exploring new source markets, restoration of national heritage projects, launching of national image building, providing inexpensive accommodation in different tourist centres, improving service efficiency in public sector corporations and streamlining of facilitation procedures at airports. The Eighth Plan aims at luring the high spending tourists from Europe and USA. It also envisages a 'master plan' to integrate area plans with development of tourism. This is envisaged to ensure employment opportunities for the local population.

In April 1993, the Government announced further measures aimed at export promotion. The existing Export Promotion of Capital Goods Scheme (EPCG) was extended to tourism and related services. Against the existing 35 per cent, the tourism sector would now pay an excise duty of 15 per cent only on capital goods import, subject to an export obligation of 4 times the cargo, insurance and freight (CIF) value of imports. With an obligation period of five years, this came as a boon to the hotel industry. The cost of construction had also come down by 20 per cent.

In addition to the above policy pronouncements by the Union Government, our planners had envisaged the possibilities of developing specific regions on a zonal plank. Special area programmes like the Hill Area Development Programme and the Western Ghats Development Programme form part of the overall national plan.

The Eighth Plan document stipulates that the strategy in such designated special areas is to devise suitable location-specific solutions, so as to reverse the process of degradation of natural resources and ensure sustainable development.

This approach perhaps needs to be integrated into the project of special tourism areas, now being made popular by the Government. Administrative Control and Developmental Compromises The federal principles enshrined in the Indian Constitution require that the tourism sector be treated as a State subject. As such, the Department of Tourism (under the Ministry of Civil Aviation and Tourism at the Centre) undertakes certain promotional and developmental activities with a view to enhance the sectoral potential. The Department has certain regulatory functions to perform involving the hotel industry, travel agencies and tourist operators. Over the years, there has been considerable erosion of powers so far as State Governments are concerned.

GOVERNMENT ACTION FOR STATES

The sustained campaign for privatisation in all the policy documents has left limited space of operation for the States. The public sector is increasingly being perceived as an agent of inertia than of change and hence the pressure for a hands-off policy. On the other hand, the Union Government has been usurping the powers of the State with some pretext or the other. Promotion schemes, designed at the Centre, are transferred for implementation at the State level.

The special Central Assistance, for example, granted for the development of infrastructure at the pilgrim centres, carries with it a pre-defined scheme and mode of execution. Furthermore, there are occasions when the Centre forces the State Governments to extend certain subsidies and concessions to the sector. The terms of such concessions would have been fixed by the Centre and the States would have no choice but to fall in line. For example, during the State tourism minister's conference in December 1991, the States were urged to freeze water and electricity rates for 10 years. They were also asked to exempt certain hotels from local and state taxes for 10 years.

Seventeen circuits and destinations were identified under the National Action Plan for development through Central assistance and investment by the States and the private sector. The centres were identified by the Centre and the States were asked to do the needful. There were also times when the federal division of power resulted in operational contradictions. For instance, by 1989, many foreign hotel chains like Hilton, Hyatt, Penta and Kempinski had applied for licenses for investing in India. However, the revenue departments of the respective States failed to locate and allocate land for the construction of hotels.

The scheme, thus, fell flat. Curiously, the Union Government was not hesitant to make use of Constitutional provisions when it suited its interests. As has been stated earlier, the Yunus Committee had suggested the creation of the Tourism Board on lines of the existing Railway Board. (Perhaps, it was the brainchild of Mr. K.L. Thapar, then adviser to the Planning Commission, in charge of Transport and Tourism Sector. Being from the Railway Service, it is not surprising that Thapar thought about a 'Tourism Board'). To begin with, the empowered committee of secretaries challenged the idea of creation of a Board.

PRIVATISATION PROCESS

It was said that the Railway Board as an independent entity was created for historical reasons. It would be difficult for tourism to be looked after by a

Board, because legally the sector would come under the Industrial (Development) Act. It was also found that such a Board would not be viable financially. In 1991, the think-tank on tourism created by Minister Madhavarao Scindia rejected the idea of a Board in toto. It was emphasised that the Board cannot be in charge of a sector that is basically under the jurisdiction of the States. Scope for Federal Interventions The previous section highlights the dubious ways by which the Centre attempts to hijack initiatives at the State-level. This is achieved essentially by threatening to curtail Central assistance or by cajoling through promises of more financial aid.

It is common knowledge that the resource-base of the States is very narrow, making them vulnerable at the negotiating table. However, States have the freedom to resist the Centre's strong- arm tactics, provided State assemblies stand-by the interests of the States. For instance, State legislatures may refuse to freeze water and electricity rates on grounds of revenue generation. In that event, the concerned Chief Minister or the Minister of Tourism may convey the intensity of resistance that he is confronted with, and thus refuse to comply with the Centre's diktats. It is heartening to realise that the States have often exercised their power of self-determination and consequently refused to toe the line drawn by the Centre. This offers enough scope for possible interventions at the federal strata of our political system in matters of policy formulation. Privatisation and its Implications

According to the Approach Paper to the Seventh Plan, " there is a vast potential for development of tourism in the country. Tourism should be accorded the status of an industry. Private sector investment will have to be encouraged in developing tourism and public sector investments should be focused only on development of support infrastructure". Thus the seeds of private initiatives were sown during the Seventh Plan. The Government took the matter of privatising the tourism sector seriously by 1988. It was during the tenure of Mr. S.K. Mishra as Tourism Secretary that the talk of inviting private investment into the sector began. The Government permitted foreign equity participation up to 5 1 %in tourism projects. Foreign charters were allowed to operate in the country for the first time. Foreign companies were allowed to repatriate their profits to the extent of 3%. The structural adjustment programme, initiated in June, 1992, paved the way for privatisation in almost all sectors of the economy. The Annual Plan (1992-93) document emphatically enunciated the Government's position vis-a-vis tourism.

DEMERITSOF PRIVATISATION

The future growth of tourism will have to be achieved mainly through private initiative. The State will contribute to tourism by planning broad strategy of development, provision of monetary and fiscal incentives to catalyse private sector investment." The process of privatisation brought in its wake big investments and private involvement at various levels. As an offshoot, environmental considerations were thrown to the winds and there were instances of large scale human rights violation. The self- correcting nature of policy made provisions for stricter controls in this regard. More seriously, privatisation meant alienation of the majority of our population and their deprivation. Employment generated in tourism is generally seasonal and ill paid. The private sector- induced pockets of tourism had the potential of turning into centres of pollution, drug trafficking and prostitution. Industry Status Granted to Tourism The Seventh Plan proposed that tourism be declared an industry. However, it took time for the States to implement this, even though they agreed in principle. The smokeless industry had the advantage of generating maximum value-added, because of low-cost inputs.

The Tourism Policy Statement carried certain provisions in favour of the hotel industry. It stated that there should be provision for depreciation in the balance sheets of hotels. Being an export industry, hotels were to be given excise concessions. The provisions of the Monopolies and Restrictive Trade Practices (MRTP) Act were relaxed for hotels, because any hotel with 300 or more rooms would have incurred an investment of Rs. 25 crores. The document also hinted at lower tariffs for power and water and regulations for easy import of equipment. As a follow-up, hotel and shipping were added to the list of 27 industries exempted from Section 22 A of the MRTP Act. The consequences of declaring tourism as an industry need to be studied in detail. It is not possible to capture its implications in an exploratory work like this.

However, it is obvious that the private sector has primarily benefited to a great extent by this measure. Importing Modifications to Policies We have earlier stated that the arena of policy formulation should be self-evaluating and self-correcting. In the case of Tourism Policy, this has proved to be the plus point. As an illustration, the Policy statement of 1982 made no mention of infrastructure development. The successive governments at the Centre failed to create proper tourism infrastructure, thus resulting in loss of traffic. This lacuna was corrected in the National Action Plan. However, much of this change was due to intensive lobbying by such agencies like the Indian Association of Tour Operators (IATO), the Travel agents Association of India (TAAI) and the Indian Hotels and Restaurants Association (IHRA). It is for the voluntary agencies and pro-people forces to exploit the avenue of lobbying at various levels.

ENVIRONMENTAL ISSUES

The environmental implications of tourism development did not form part of the 1982 Policy. The consequences are too obvious to be written about. However, the NAP, 1992 did carry specific provisions for environmental protection and harnessing. From Policy to Cartooning Policy statements may also lead to justifiable flights of fantasy. Two examples would illustrate how policies were used to justify stands taken by the politicians: a. Shri Devi Lal, the then Deputy Prime Minister wanted a 50 per cent discount for farmers at Five Star Hotels run by India Tourism Development Corporation. The scheme had teething problems since it was not easy to distinguish a farmer from amongst the clients who visit such hotels. However, on his insistence, the so-called CHAUPALs recreated a village ambience to the amazement of foreign tourists, who took a liking for them. b. Pursuing the objective of the Seventh Plan to diversify overseas tourism to its logical conclusion was what prompted Aand. Jagdish Tytler to float the idea of casinos. It was an attempt to provide some entertainment for foreigners during the evenings.

It was said that Indian classical music would not provide much needed entertainment for foreign guests because the artistes spend a lot of time tuning their instruments. Folk dances get over in an hour. So much for our much touted cultural diversity. It is embarrassing to believe that the consultative committee attached to the Ministry of Civil Aviation and Tourism had endorsed the idea. Conclusion broadly, our successive policy pronouncements in the realm of tourism fall within the "liberalising" framework of the macro-economic policy environment. The Finance Bill, 1988, had assured 50 per cent tax exemption on foreign exchange earnings in the sector, and a further 50 per cent exemption if re-invested. In effect, it amounts to 100 per cent tax concession. Luxury hotels enjoy exemptions of all kinds with a view to encourage tourism earnings.

These tax exemptions coupled with provision of soft loans to the sector led to a boom in the tourism related private investment. The Economic Survey 1991-92 aptly summarises the ultimate aim of such incentives for private sector participation: " The Government has tried to expand the economic space in which the people can exercise their initiative and ingenuity. It hopes to do more to expand their opportunities, to enhance their potential. But what shape the economy takes ultimately depends on what the people make of it.

In that sense, the future is in their hands." We should not forget that tourism is an industry which emerges in the context of unresolved socio-economic structural issues, such as land distribution patterns or the take over of traditional occupations by modem mechanised capital. Tourism happens to be a source of livelihood for millions in India and aggressive privatisation does not ensure social and economic safety nets. In the face of the unhindered entry of international capital and successive alienation, perhaps, it is difficult to agree that "the future is in our hands"

ECOTOURISM

The Draft Tourism Policy 1997 states that "in the context of economic liberalisation and globalisation being pursued by the country, the development policies of no sector can remain static." The policy further states that "the emergence of tourism as an important instrument for sustainable human development including poverty alleviation, employment generation, environmental regeneration and advancement of women and other disadvantaged groups in the country" requires support to realise these goals. India's tourism resources have always been considered immense, in a tourism audit.

The geographical features are diverse, colourful and varied. The coastline offers opportunities for developing the best beaches in the world. There are a wealth of eco-systems including bio-sphere reserves, mangroves, coral reefs, deserts, mountains and forests as well as an equally wide range of flora and fauna.

The Policy further states that "international tourists visiting interiors of the country for reasons of purity of the environment and nature contributes to the development of these areas particularly backward regions". Thus Tourism "should also become a reason for better preservation and protection of our natural resources, environment and ecology".

The policy recognises that sustained growth of tourism can give rise to conflicts. To ensure that the growth of tourism takes place along desired lines, certain guidelines have been framed: 1.to remove the constraint of the information gap. 2. to create a tourist product that is desirable and supported by an integrated infrastructure. 3. to involve all agencies, public, private and government, in tourism development.4. to create synergy between departments and agencies that have to deliver the composite tourist product.5. to use both the circuit and scheme approach so that peoples participation through panchayats, local bodies, NGO's, and youth organisations will create a greater awareness of tourism.

The Central Government can thus concentrate on larger investment oriented projects. 6. to create direct access for destinations off the beaten track.7. to diversify the product with new options like beach tourism, forests, wild life, landscapes and adventure tourism, farm and health tourism.8. to ensure that the development does not exceed sustainable levels.9. to develop the seven north-eastern states, the Himalayan region and Islands for tourism.10. to maintain a balance between the negative and positive impacts of tourism through planning restrictions and through education of the people for conservation and development.

Development Plan

The strategy for development should take into consideration the carrying capacity, local aspirations and benefits likely to accrue to the community. In particular specific policies and guidelines for ecotourism development and adventure tourism are to be formulated, primarily through a regulatory framework. The Draft Guidelines have been approved at a State Ministers Conference and have been circulated to various trade and industry bodies.

The guidelines draw a distinction between mass or resort tourism and nature or ecotourism, as the kind of tourism that has a lower impact on the environment and requires less infrastructural development. The Ministry hopes that the environment conscious international tourist will be made aware that India is taking steps to protect its ecology and environment.

Apart from the do's and don'ts, the guidelines are governed by a tourism management plan, the key elements of which are the protection of natural resources and a positive involvement of local communities, along with an optimum number of environmentally conscious visitors.

The principles of management are scientific planning, effective control and continuous monitoring, development of physical infrastructure, zoning and a Management plan for public use of natural sites. The management plan should establish standards for resort development, style and location of structures, waste disposal, treatment of sewage, control of litter, use of public spaces and fragile areas.

The operational guidelines rely on sensitisation of all the role players and this programme is based on a self-regulated environmental code. Area specific rather than universal development plans keeping in mind the unique character of the location and its economic and social environment are important. This would help the State Government to coordinate with the industry in managing visitors and their activities.

NGO's working on socio-economic programmes in forest and remote areas could have a closer coordination with tourism service operators to transfer economic benefits, particularly the handicraft production and marketing sector. The guidelines are only a beginning, and it is hoped that with increasing awareness of the visitor the industry will regulate its practices.

Tourism Advisory Committee

There is an emphasis on the needs and perceptions of the international tourist running through the discussion on the guide lines although the data from the National Parks makes it evident that the domestic tourists outnumber international visitors, although they do not pay the same amount as the foreign visitor either in entry fees or for board and lodging and transport facilities. They do however demand a much higher per capita use of resources like water, fuel for heating and cooking and transport. They also make the same intensive use of time and try to maximize their stay by the number of animals and birds they can view in the 24-hour period.

It is interesting to note that no democratic participation has been called for in the policy formulation process, and all the amendments to the policy have come from trade associations and government think tanks. The tourism Advisory Committee also consists of eminent persons and community representation has been ignored. The elite nature of the policy makers is well represented in the quotations given above from the policy document.

The policy clearly recognises the debate on the tourism issue which has surfaced wherever tourism development, particularly in the case of tourism projects relating to the "gifts of nature" like beaches, rivers, mountains and forests, have already been developed. However, mere recognition of the hostility of people to tourism development is not enough to change the nature of tourism development or the resistance to tourism or what many have termed a poor tourism culture.

Perhaps to understand this in a better perspective, we should look at the issue of sustainable development in a critical way. Perhaps we can question the impact of sustainable development on the environment and sift through the jargon of development planners, international agencies, and environmental activists to see how sustainable development can be achieved without all the contradictions that are apparent as in the case of the tourism sector.

Sustainable Development in Tourism

The concept of sustainability originated in the context of renewable resources like forests and fisheries and was subsequently adopted by the environmental movement. In most cases it is understood to mean "the existence of the ecological conditions necessary to support human life at a specific level of well being through future generations." However, in addition to ecological conditions there are social conditions that influence ecological sustainability in a nature-people interaction. The social connotations have been described by Barbier (1987) who has defined social sustainability as "the ability to maintain desired social values, traditions, institutions, cultures or other social characteristics."

The term sustainability came into usage in 1980 when the IUCN presented the World Conservation Strategy where sustainable development was linked to conservation of living resources. However, the fundamental goals have often been lost sight of because of operational goals (e.g. food, water, shelter, health are fundamental goals to be realised through self reliance, cost effectiveness, appropriate technology, people centred-ness etc.) Consequently, the WCED made its definition brief: Social Development is development that meets the needs of the present without compromising the ability of future generations to meet their own needs. They did not make any assumptions on the direction in which changes in demand would take place. (e.g. equity, social justice, self-determination, or cultural diversity).

India's tourism policy follows the mainstream SD (Sustainable Development) thinking by adopting all the critical objectives: revive growth change the quality of growth meet essential needs for jobs, food, energy, water and sanitation ensure sustainable levels of population conserve and enhance the resource base reorient technology and management risk merge environment and economics in decision making reorient international economic relations make development more participatory. These objectives are responsible for building a very broad consensus on the issue of sustainable development, yet the debate at the operational level continues. Most participants in the debate now accept that many human activities are reducing the long-term ability of the natural environment to provide goods and services, which will eventually affect human health and well being.

Causes of Enviromental Degradation

Many also accept that poverty is devastating the lives of millions in the Third World since there is no consensus between what is environmentally necessary and what is economically and developmentally feasible. The level of inter-dependence between the two insights is yet to be incorporated in the concept of Social Development. Some problem areas are: Environmental degradation, already affecting millions in the Third World, is likely to reduce human well being across the globe. Who is responsible for this rapid degeneration? Is it the poor or the rich?

The poor have no option but to exploit resources for short-term survival. If we take the example of forests and their resources, which have been traditionally outside the market system and in the sphere of tribal or indigenous peoples rights, they are today seen as exploiters of the forests as against tourists, with all their demand for infrastructure and superstructure, who are seen to be conservationists. The inter-linked nature of the problem of sustainability is such that the impact of degradation will be quicker on the poor than on the rich.

Can Sustainable Development be the metafix it claims to be in reconciling increasing industrial, agricultural and resource use productivity with environmental needs. The weakness of the Social Development argument lies in the techno-economic approach to solutions with regard to common property resource management, through know how transfers, resource pricing, subsidy policies and building management capabilities. (World Bank, 1987) Deeper processes such as land reforms, industrial demands on raw materials, over consumption, changing legal and political structures are either ignored or looked at in a cursory manner.

For instance how can we claim a consensus between those who are concerned for the survival of future generations with those who are concerned with the survival of wild life, or human health and subsistence? Unless we can identify the trade-offs necessary for each specific objective of sustainability, we will not have clarity in the discussion. We will also fail to understand why, even when there is a broad consensus, projects on the ground result in conflicts.

Suggested refinements could be:— 1. a distinction between ecological and social sustainability and in the process an identification of the inter-linkages a distinction between renewable and non-renewable resources, between environmental processes crucial to human life and crucial to other forms of life dependent on the resources. a distinction between the techno-economic aspects of social sustainability (infrastructure, services, government) with political and cultural sustainability.2. a distinction between equitable development and local participation, and decentralisation, what many have called NGOisation of sustainable development. This is because no rigorous testing of local participation leading to social equity or to sustainable resource use have been reported.

Environmental Impact

Case studies reflect personal, organisational or political preferences. Tourism is one of the activities which have caused concern because of the effects of increasing human traffic on fragile environments. Countries which are looking towards Tourism as a means of economic growth, like India, have limited resources and cultural restraints and they have the greatest need to pay heed to the possible negative impacts of tourism. The environmental impact of tourism is a basic issue, whether we are looking at a developed or an underdeveloped area, region or country. The costs of tourism for a country like India include extensive investment in fixed assets with a low rate of return for infrastructure, transportation, accommodation, cultural institutions, exhibition centres, and park facilities.

To this maybe added the social and cultural costs like additional demands on infrastructure like land, water, health services; the creation of new jobs for displaced people; the cost of positive community relationships; the disparity between the lifestyle of visitors and those who serve them; the possible friction between local residents and new users of valued local resources; the perception of local residents of the spending of scarce capital resources on what they consider low priority areas like tourism; cultural cost of alterations in local ceremonial or traditional values; loss of privacy for local communities as tourists come to gape at their living conditions and rituals.

Tourism also causes increasing congestion and pollution as thousands of visitors flock to parks and sanctuaries in motorised vehicles; there are changes in accessibility, landscape and the ecological balance between man and nature; there is the cost, both monetary and human, of creating conservation zones (core/buffer) with unforeseen or undesirable side effects; which have been observed in the ecotourism movement.

The benefit of revenue from tourism does not always redress these problems but goes towards the cost of administering the project. The tourism industry is generally self-centred and not given to educational, cultural or exchange programmes on a philanthropic basis. The natural environment, with the best will in the world, cannot escape damage with the volume of visitors. As more and more tourists, both domestic and international seek the exotic and remote destinations around the world, the likelihood of the environment suffering as a result become greater.

Forests can suffer from trampling, fires, tree felling for facilities and waste. Wildlife, despite the protection in national parks, has suffered a loss of habitat, hunting and poaching, viewing and photographing, leading to an interruption of feeding and breeding patterns or hunting for food undisturbed. These are the prized moments for the viewer. The trade in wild life trophies or tourist souvenirs is the more deliberately destructive aspect of such tourism.

Wild Life Sanctuaries Management

The building of tourist lodges in materials that are not integrated with the environment and the pressure they put on the land and water bodies is also wilfully destructive. Management techniques that include being less user friendly or control of numbers by closing access or by multiplying the number of attractions and areas or charging higher admission fees are generally not popular with the tourist or the tour operator and are also difficult to implement because of high administrative costs. Conclusion: EQUATIONS, through its involvement in the field have had a variety of experiences relating to the debate on ecotourism and sustainable development. The major issues that have emerged after the policy of notification of wild life sanctuaries and their management by the Forest Departments are quite disturbing. Wherever notification has led to displacement of people the experience of rehabilitation has not been successful and the conservation aims have not been met. Several sanctuaries have witnessed militant action by displaced communities against the developers of tourism. In many cases the tourism aims have also not been met in making the sanctuary accessible to viewers, naturalists, wild life photographers. Tourism has not been able to counteract poaching and the most extensive and the oldest conservation project, Project Tiger has not been able to save the tiger population.

The commercialisation of the experience, like the privileging of one species, for example the tiger, has led to congestion and noise pollution and this has put a pressure on the management of the sanctuary to organise tiger shows which are putting a pressure on the feeding and mating habits of the tiger. These are very invasive techniques of experiencing the wild. On the plus side, the concept of beneficiary led development has helped indigenous people to organise against their displacement and exploitation as well as to fight for the retention of their traditional rights and life styles. Environmentalists have not only been involved in such organisations and movements but have done valuable documentation. This has influenced many urban visitors to be more sensitive to the wild and to follow the rules when participating in ecotourism. This has also led to the development of a code of conduct for the tourist, the industry and the administrator. These attempts are in a very nascent stage. The kind of co-ordination that is required between the environmentalist and economist is just beginning to emerge and have still to counter the myths of neo-classical economists in the field of tourism. But a beginning has been made.

COASTAL ISSUES

The Coastal Regulation Zone (CRZ) came into existence on February 19,

1991, with the gazetting of the notification by the Union Ministry of Environment and Forests (MoEF) under Sec. 3(1) and Sec. 3(2)(v) of the Environment Protection Act, 1986, and Rule 5(3)(d) of the Environment Protection Rules, 1986.

Through the Notification the Central Government declared the coastal stretches of seas, bays, estuaries, creeks, rivers and backwaters, which are influenced by tidal action (in the land ward side), up to 500m. from the high tide line (HTL) and the land between the low tide line (LTL) and HTL as CRZ. In the case of rivers, creeks and backwaters, the Notification stated that the CRZ could be modified on a case by case basis, on the basis of reasons to be recorded during the preparation of the coastal zone management plan (CZMP). However, the width of the CRZ from each bank could not be less than 100 m., or the width of the water body, whichever was less.

Activities Prohibited in the CRZ

1. Setting up of new industries and expansion of existing ones, except those directly related to waterfront or requiring foreshore facilities.
2. Manufacture, handling, storage or disposal of hazardous substances.
3. Setting up and expansion of fish processing units including warehousing (excluding hatchery and natural fish drying in permitted areas).
4. Discharge of untreated wastes and effluents from industries, cities, towns or other human settlements. The existing practices would have to be phased out by the concerned authorities within three years.
5. Dumping of ash or any waste from thermal power plants.
6. Land reclamation, bunding or disturbing the natural course of sea water with similar obstructions. Exceptions are made for activities required for the control of coastal erosion, the maintenance of water ways to ports; clearing sand bars; and for the construction of regulators, storm water drains and structures for the prevention of salinity ingress.
7. Mining of sand, rocks and other substrata materials, except those raw minerals not available outside the CRZ areas.
8. Drawing or harvesting of groundwater and construction of mechanism within 200 m. of the HTL. Between 200 and 500 m. it will be permissible only if done manually through ordinary wells for drinking, horticulture, agriculture and fisheries.
9. Construction activity in ecologically sensitive areas.
10. Any construction activity between LTL and HTL except facilities for carrying treated effluents and waste water discharge into the sea, facilities for carrying sea water for cooling purposes, oil, gas and similar pipelines and facilities essential for facilities permitted under the notification.

11. Dressing or altering of sand dunes, hill, natural features including landscape changes for beautification, recreation and other such purposes, except as permitted under the notification.

Regulated activities (requiring environmental clearance from MoEF): 1. Construction activities related to defense requirements for which foreshore facilities are essential. Residential office, hospital, workshops will not normally be permitted in the CRZ, except in very special cases.2. Operational construction for ports and harbors and light house.3. Foreshore facilities of thermal power plants for transport of raw materials, in-take of cooling water and out fall for discharge of treated wastewater or cooling water. 4. All other activities with investment exceeding. 5 crores.

Coastal Zone Management Plan (CZMP): All the coastal states have to prepare, within one year, CZMPs identifying and classifying CRZ areas as per the Notification guidelines. These plans have to be approved by MoEF All further development activities should be within the framework of these plans. In the interim period, before the approval of the plans, development activities should not violate the provisions of the Notification. Violations are punishable under the provisions of the Environment Protection Act of 1986. For regulating developmental activities, the coastal stretches within 500m of the HTL are classified into CRZ-1, CRZ-11 and CRZ-III.

CRZ-I — Areas that are ecologically sensitive and important (national parks, coral reefs, mangroves, areas close to the breeding and spawning grounds of fishes, areas of high natural beauty, historical heritage, high genetic diversity, and those likely to be inundated by global warming, 'etc.); and areas within the LTL and HTL.

Regulations in CRZ-I — 1. No new construction shall be permitted within 500 m of the HTL.2. No construction activity except for facility for carrying treated effluents and waste water into the sea or carrying sea water for cooling, oil, gas or similar pipelines will be permitted between the LTL and the HTL.

CRZ-II —Areas that have already been developed up to or close to the shore-line. 'Developed areas' that come within municipal limits or other legally designated urban areas which have been substantially built up and which have been provided with infrastructural facilities like drainage, approach road, water supply and sewage mains.

Regulations in CRZ-III— 1. Buildings will not be permitted in the seaward side of existing roads (or those proposed in the CZMP) nor on the seaward side of the existing authorised structures.2. Reconstruction of authorised buildings to be permitted subject to the existing floor space and without change in existing use CRZ III Areas that are relatively undisturbed and do not belong to either CRZ-I or CRZ-II.

This will include coastal zones in the rural areas and also areas within municipal limits or urban areas that are not substantially built up. Regulations in CRZ-III. 3. Areas up to 200 m. from the HTL earmarked as no development zone (NDZ). No construction will be permitted within this zone except for repairs of existing authorised structures not exceeding the existing plinth area and covered apace. Raising of horticultural crops, gardens, pastures, parks, play fields, forestry and salt manufacture from sea water permitted in this zone.4. Development of vacant plots between 200 m. 500 m. from the HTL, in designated areas with prior approvàl of MoEF, permitted for hotels and beach resorts.5. Construction or reconstruction of dwellind units between the 200m and 500m of the HTL permitted so long as it is within the ambit of traditional rights and customary uses such as existing fishing villages and gouthans.

Building conditions would be based on the conditions that the total number of dwelling units does not increase more than double of the existing units; the total covered area is not more than 33 per cent of the plot area; the overall height is not more than two floors and 9 m. Guidelines for development of beach resorts in the designated areas of CRZ-III · No construction within 200 m. from the HTL and in the area between LTL and HTL.6. The total plot size should not be less than 0.4 hectare and the covered area should not be more than 33 per cent.

The total height of the construction should not be more than 9 m. and the building should not be more than two floors. Groundwater cannot be tapped within 200m of the HTL. Between 200 and 500 m. it can be tapped with the concurrence of the State or Central Groundwater Board. 7. Extraction of sand, leveling or digging of sandy stretches, except for the structural foundation will not be permitted within 500 M. of the HTL.8. The quality of treated effluents, solid wastes, emissions and noise levels etc. must be within the standards laid down by the central or state pollution control boards.

Untreated effluents and solid wastes should not be discharged into the water or beach .9. To allow public access there should be a gap of 20m. width between two hotels. Two consecutive gaps should not be more than 500 m. apart.

THE WORLD SCENARIO AND INDIAS POSITION

In recent years tourism has emerged as a major economic activity that is employment oriented and earns foreign exchange. Its share in the worlds GDP in 1994-95 was 10 per cent which is more than the world military budgets put together. In global terms, the investment in tourism industry and travel trade accounts for 7 per cent of the total capital investment. Today 21.2 crore people around the globe are employed in travel trade and tourism. In future, this industry is likely to see unprecedented growth.

According to the World Tourism Council at Brussels, the revenues from travel and tourism in Asia Pacific region will grow at the rate of 7.8 per cent annually over the next decade. Amongst the economic sectors, the tourism sector is highly labor intensive. A survey by the Government of India notes that the rate of employment generation (direct and indirect) in tourism is 52 persons employed per Rs.10 lakh investment (based on 1992-93 Consumer

Price Index). This is much higher than the rates of employment generation in most other economic sectors.

Indian tourism industry has also recorded phenomenal growth. The rate of international arrivals in India in recent years has been to the tune of about 19 lakh arrivals per year. The unprecedented growth in tourism in India has made it the third largest foreign exchange earner after gem and jewellery and ready-made garments.

This is not surprising since India possesses a whole range of attractive normally sought by tourists and which includes natural attractions like Iandscapes, scenic beauty, mountains, wildlife, beaches, major rivers and manmade attractions such as monuments, forts, palaces and havelis. However, in global terms, in spite of such attractions, tourist arrivals in India are a mere 0.30% of the world arrivals. Receipts are similarly low, just a 0.50 per cent of the world receipts. We are still quite far from the target of 50 lakh tourist arrivals per year.

Tourism in the State

In 1973, a separate Tourism Department was established to identify and develop the tourism potential in the State. This was followed by the creation of Tourism Corporation of Gujarat Limited in 1978 which was entrusted with the task of undertaking and developing tourism-related commercial activities. The Corporation is presently engaged in a variety of activities such as creation of lodging and boarding facilities for the tourists and other aspects of tourist facilitation such as transportation, packaged tours, wayside catering along the National and State Highways, arranging cultural festivals, organizing exhibitions and producing and distributing maps, posters, brochures and pamphlets. The Corporation has set up accommodation facilities at Chorwad, Ahmedpur Mandvi, Porbandar, Veraval, Hajira, Ubharat and Tithal.

Similar facilities at pilgrimage centres like Palitana, Somnath, Dwarkja, Pavagadh and Dakor have also been set up by the Corporation. One of the recent tourist attractions introduced by the Corporation in collaboration with the Indian Railways is a special tourist train. The Royal Orient Train which connects up various tourist destinations straddling the Gujarat and Rajasthan State. However, the Corporation has suffered losses due to a number of organizational constraints. In order to minimize these losses and also to provide better services to the tourists, the Government has undertaken privatisation of some of the commercial property units of the Corporation.

In spite of possessing a variety of tourist attractions such as wildlife, scenic beauty, pilgrimage centres, exotic traditional crafts and festivals, beaches, hospitality of the region and a varied healthy and tasteful cuisine, the State has not been able to accelerate the pace of tourism in comparison to other states. In 1991, the State did declare a tourism policy but it did not elicit adequate response from the private sector since the policy contained only a handful of benefits while the implementation was tardy due to legal and administrative constraints.

This was at a time when the Government of India had already declared tourism as an industry and a large number of states had followed suit. This enabled the tourism industry to avail of incentives, reliefs, benefits available to the industry in those states. While other state Governments made successful efforts in developing tourism within their states, the relative inability of the Gujarat State to harness and develop its full tourist potential may be attributed to a combination of factors such as lack of effective policies, inadequate infrastructure, ineffective marketing and lack of decent facilities for the tourists.

The main rationale for formulating a comprehensive tourism policy is rooted, on one hand,in the convergence of socio-economic spread benefits, environment - friendliness and employment potential of tourism industry and on the other, in the growing demand for tourism products in the State, brought by a rapid industrial growth in the State during the recent years that has led to tremendous increase in number of business travellers.

Objectives

The main objective of the States Tourism Policy will be to undertake intensive development of tourism in the State and thereby increase employment opportunities. The following related objectives are dovetailed with main objectives:

1. Identify and develop tourist destinations and related activities.
2. Diversifications of tourism products in order to attract more tourists through a varied consumer choice.
3. Comprehensive development of pilgrimage centres as tourist destinations.
4. Create adequate facilities for budget tourists.
5. Strengthen the existing infrastructure and develop new ones where necessary.
6. Creation of tourism infrastructure so as to preserve handicrafts, folk arts and culture of the state and thereby attract more tourists.

Approach and Strategy

In addition to the facilitation role assigned to itself by the Government in the development of tourism, the Government will adopt the following strategy towards the private sector with the objective of securing its active involvement in leading the development of tourism in the State.

1. The tourism will be given the status of industry in order that the facilities and benefits available to the industry are also made available to tourism projects.

2. A special incentives package will be made available for encouraging new tourism projects as well as expansion of existing tourism units.
3. Infrastructural facilities will be strengthened and developed within the State, particularly in Special Tourism Areas which will be notified latter and which will be developed by adopting an integrated-area.
4. Effective mechanisms will be set up to build meaningful co-ordination with the Central Government and the State Governments agencies, the local self-government bodies and the NGOs.
5. Government will encourage building effective linkages with the relevant economic agents and agencies such as the national and international tour operators and travel agents of repute, hotel chains and global institutions connected with tourism such as WTO.

POLICY PROPOSALS

Tourism as Industry

Like other industrial projects, tourism projects too involve professional management, capital investment, special skills and training. The Government of India and a number of other states have declared tourism as an industry. Gujarat State which is at the forefront of the industrial development will also declare tourism as an industry. This will enable the tourism projects to be reliable to get benefits contained in the paras 5.1.2 and 5.1.3 below.

Availability of land is a primary requirement of any project. The process of grant of land will be facilitated in urban areas for the projects concerning setting up of hotels, restaurants and apartment hotels etc. Existing arrangements for grant of government waste land to industrial units will be made applicable to various tourism projects.

Arrangements will be made to acquire private land under Land Acquisition Act for various tourism projects by companies registered under the Companies Act. The existing commercial rates of NA assessment applicable to land involving tourism projects would be reviewed and rates of NA assessment for industrial purposes will be made applicable to them.

As one of the sets of infrastructural institutions, the State Financial Institutions have made an important contribution in creating conductive environment for industrial entrepreneurs. They will be called upon to do the same for tourism entrepreneurs in terms of making available adequate finance.

So far, the lending from the State Financial Institutions has been largely confined to hotels only. In reality, the range of activities for tourism projects is far larger than just hotels as can be seen from the following illustrative list:

Accommodation Projects

1. Hotels
2. Resorts
3. Motels

4. Apartment Hotels
5. Heritage Hotels

Food Oriented Projects

1. Restaurants
2. Wayside Facilities on the State Highways.

Other Tourism—Related Projects

1. Amusement Parks and Water Sports
2. Handicraft Village Complexes
3. Fairs and Festivals.
4. Camps and Facilities Encouraging Adventure
5. Train Travel Projects
6. Sea/RiverCruise Projects
7. Sound and Light Shows
8. Museums
9. Natural Parks/Zoos
10. Safari Projects
11. Ropeways
12. Sports/Health Facilities Complexes
13. Training Schools for the managerial expertise for Hospitality Industry.
14. Golf Courses.

Service Oriented Projects

1. Travel Agency
2. Tour operation
3. Transport Operation
4. Linkage with the International Hotel Chains (Franchise)
5. Human Resources Development (HRD) for Tourism Industry and necessary training facilities.

Most of the projects on this illustrative list are not eligible for loans from the banks or the State Financial Agencies. It will be necessary to make suitable changes in the lending criteria for viable projects in the listed activities in order than their financial requirements are met. The modification of the lending criteria of the State Financial Agencies will be made with regard to the financial ceiling, debt equity ratio, recovery period, moratorium etc. Necessary arrangements will be made to ensure that the State Financial Agencies and the banks attach adequate priority to the financing requirements of tourism projects.

As referred to in Para 4(b), a new incentive pac kage will be made available to replace the existing incentive policy instituted in 1991. A tax holiday of 5-10 years in respect of following taxes will be made available upto 100 per cent of capital investment to various tourism projects located in Special

Tourism Areas whether declared by the Central Government or the State Government, located in designated areas and located on National and State Highways. The scope and the extent of the benefits of tax holiday will vary according to certain considerations such as the admissible expenditure, the size of the capital investment etc. The benefit of tax holiday will also be made available for the purpose of expansion of the existing tourism projects in these areas:

1. SalesTax
2. Purchase Tax
3. Electricity Duty
4. Luxury Tax
5. Entertainment Tax

Necessary administrative arrangements will be made at the State and District Level to operationalize the incentive schemes. Suitable schemes will be designed to market tourism products, and particularly wide publicity will be secured in respect of various facilities being offered by the travel agents, tour operators etc. Special paying guest scheme will be formulated for providing adequate and inexpensive lodging and boarding facilities too take care of seasonal flows of tourists to the pilgrimage centres during festivals. Financial assistance will be provided for the preparation of feasibility reports by consultants in respect of tourism projects. Structure of the taxes and tariffs, e.g. luxury tax, entertainment tax, sales tax, etc., will be reviewed with reference to developmental needs of tourism sector and necessary amendments will be made.

Redefining the Roles of the State and the Market

Since the approach of the Tourism Policy focuses on market-led developments, the role of the State would be as follows :

The Government proposes to make commercial services available entirely through private sector or in association with it. The States role will primarily focus on strengthening and upgrading existing infrastructure and development of new infrastructure. Reputed consultants will be hired to prepare area development master plans/feasibility studies in respect of important tourist destinations and areas of tourism potential, e.g. Sardar Sarovar Project Area, Kutch, Beach sites and area covering Porbandar,Gir Forest, Veraval, Somnath, Ahmedpur-Mandvi, Saputara, Modhera etc.

Efforts will be made to get funding for development of infrastructure for these destinations/areas from national and international agencies. To ensure timely provision of necessary funding, the Government will earmark funds in the annual budgets of the departments concerned for securing the purpose mentioned in 5.2.1.

In conformity with States promotional role in the development of tourism sector, all competitive and commercial activities of Tourism Corporation of Gujarat Limited will be privatised except where no entrepreneur is coming forward to meet the existing need. This privatisation would help strengthen the financial position of the corporation and also help provide qualitative services to the tourists. Tourism Corporation of Gujarat Limited will assume a catalytic role focused on acting as clearing house of information, production and distribution of promotional literature, policy advice etc. The Tourism Corporation will assist entrepreneurs and agencies in tourism sector and will try to help alleviate their difficulties particularly vis a vis the Government and its agencies. A Computerized Information Centre will be set up at the State level to make available necessary information to the agencies/entrepreneurs who wish to set up tourism projects.

In addition to its existing offices in Bombay, Delhi and Madras, the Tourism Corporation will also open its offices in other major cities of India to give wide publicity and disseminate information on Gujarat Tourism and market tourism products through these offices and through reputed travel agents in other big cities. Thus, the information about Gujarats tourist destinations and related information would be made available to tourists from outside the State in their own cities. There is already a scheme of 50 per cent matching grant from the State Government to the local self-governing bodies for the development of local tourist destinations. This scheme will be made more effective and attractive and necessary provisions in the budget will be made. This will help centralize the process of developing tourist destinations.

The process of decentralization will be further strengthened by delegation of administrative and executive powers of approval of incentives to small tourism projects to District Level Bodies headed by the Collector. These bodies, in addition, will also secure co-ordination from other departments / agencies of the Government in development and promotion of tourism. Representation will be given on this body to the experts, individual agencies and individuals connected with the tourism.

A Single window clearance system will be instituted for speedy clearance of various permissions, approvals required under different laws and rules. Necessary modification/amendment will be made to various administrative arrangements and laws which are not consistent with the approach of this Policy. Care will be taken to ensure that prospective investors do not have to suffer protracted and complex administrative process.

Intensive efforts will be undertaken to attract investors from outside the State as well as from other countries including non-resident Indians to invest in tourism sector on large scale. Tourism Corporation of Gujarat Limited and Directorate of Tourism will play active role to ensure that investors get various permissions easily and are provided with all the necessary facilities.A High Powered Committee under the Chairmanship of Chief Secretary with Director of Tourism as the Member Secretary will be constituted with the objective of securing effective co-ordination among various Government departments and agencies as also to speed up decision making proceeds concerning tourism. The committee will meet regularly and enjoy full powers of Government, provided the approval of the Chief Minister and the Council of Ministers will be obtained wherever required.

In order to create a participate forum for deliberation and discussion concerning tourism industry, a Tourism Advisory Council headed by the Chief Minister will be set up.

The Ministers and Secretaries of administrative departments concerned will be the members. The representatives of tourism industry, experts and related organisations will be nominated as members. The Additional Chief Secretary (Tourism) will be the Member Secretary of this Council. The Council will meet periodically to deliberate upon policy as well as individual issues and offer suitable advice to the Government.

Perspective Planning

Perspective plan for tourism development will be prepared in consultation with experts. An overview of possible tourism products is offered below :

Religious (pilgrimage) and Archaeological Tourism

Gujarat has a preponderance of pilgrimage centers as in some other states. Somnath and Dwarka - some of the well known and revered sites of ancient Hindu temples are situated in the State. The temple architecture has reached heights of excellence in Jain temples at Shetrunji, Girnar and Taranga. The temple of Ambaji situated in Aravalli range in North Gujarat is an important religious centre for devotees in the country. Dakor, Pavagadh, Bahucharaji, Shamlaji, Narayan Sarovar, Sudamas Porbandar, Kabirvad Shuklatirth, Kayavarohan, Bhadrakali Temple Ahmedabad and Tankara - Maharshi Dayanand Saraswatis birth place are also important pilgrimage destinations which have kept alive the religious sentiments of the people. Lakhs of pilgrims visit these places every year.

These places are visited not only by the devotees from all over the country but also by non-resident Indians and travellers especially from the eastern part of the world. Necessary accommodation facilities and related services will be created on these sites. For ensuring orderly and planned development of pilgrimage centres, the State Government has constituted Pavitra Dham Vikas Board chaired by the Chief Minister.

The Board will prepare and implement plans to provide necessary facilities to the devotees and also ensure conservation of cultural atmosphere consistent with sentiments of visiting devotees. Shamlaji is an ancient site for Buddhists. The excavated relies of Buddhist period at the site are now kept in a museum at Baroda.

There are a number of places of archaeological importance is such as the temple-town of Palitana, Modhera with its Sun temple, historical Ranki Vav at Patan with relics of an ancient capital, the Girnar Hills with Hindu and Jain temples, Junagadh with a historical fort, Dabhoi, Champaner, Pavagadh, Shaking Minarets, Gandhi Ashram, Siddi Sayed Jali etc. These can be developed by providing necessary infrastructural facilities and marketed as tourist destinations to attract tourists.

Heritage Tourism

A large number of old palaces, havelis, darbargadhs exist in the State. These historical buildings can be converted into hotels, restaurants or museums by providing suitable incentives to owners. Wildlife and Pilgrimage Tourism circuits can be linked to heritage properties exploiting the geographical congruity. Development of this sub-sector will not only attract foreign tourists but also provide encouragement and support to local art and craft. Government will take necessary steps to promote Heritage tourism in the State.

Wildlife Tourism

There is substantial scope for development of tourism based on wildlife in the State. Gir Forest of Gujarat is the last stronghold of Asiatic Lions. The Bear Sanctuary at Ratan Mahal (Dist.Panchmahal, Black Buch Sanctuary at Velavadar (Dist.Bhavnagar), Bird Sanctuary at Nalsarovar (Dist.Ahmedabad), Wild Ass Sanctuary at Kutch etc. can be effectively developed into tourist destinations by providing infrastructural facilities. In order to facilitate visitors to these areas, coordination among various agencies will be established.

Coastal and Beach Tourism

The Gujarat State has the longest coastline among Maritime States of the country. Identified stretches of coastline can be developed into beaches from tourism point of view. It will be the endeavour of the State to develop beach potential by providing such facilities as may attract foreign tourists. Various tourist destinations easily accessible from the coast will be linked through coastal shipping circuits.

Tourism Based on Traditional Art and Craft and Cultural Activities

Banni in Kutch, Khambhat, Junagadh etc. are known for their craftsmanship. Similarly, there are hundreds of fairs that are celebrated through out the year with enthusiasm. Tarnetar Fair in Surendranagar District, Chitra Vichitra Fair at Poshina (Sabarkantha District), Kanwat Fair at Chhota Udepur (Panchmahals District), Dang Darbar in Dang. Bhavnath Fair of Junagadh, Vautha Fair of Ahmedabad etc. have immense tourism value. By developing accommodation, transport and other facilities, these fairs and festivals will be promoted nationally and internationally. The places of importance from art and craft point of view will be included in the tourist circuits and necessary facilities provided to tourists.

Corporate Tourism

Private sector will be encouraged to build the state of the art convention centres, seminar halls etc. so as to attract corporate events like seminar, workshops and annual general meetings. Participants in such events generally have high purchasing power and provide a boost to local economy.

Adventure Tourism

This is also a territory with possibility of development as a sub-sector which will be examined and new activities like Camel Safari in Kutch, Horse-riding in Aravalli hill ranges, Parachuting in Saputara, Trekking in Dang, Pavagadh, Palitana etc. will be promoted. Such activities will create large scale employment opportunities for guides, coolies, traders for hire of tents and equipments etc. and will also encourage paying guest accommodation in such areas. Private entrepreneurs and institutions will be encouraged to develop such facilities.

Highway Tourism

There is a good network of State and National highways which criss-cross the State and a large number of travellers prefer road journey. Because of large geographical expanse of the State, these journeys tend to be quite long and boridng. There is a need for creating necessary facilities like hotels, restaurants, picnic spots, water parks etc. along the highways at suitable intervals for the highway travellers to relax. In fact, travellers can be induced to follow certain traffic routes if such facilities are better developed. Highway facilities and wayside amenities are so well developed in some states that this has become the mainstay of tourism. State shall encourage private investors to create such facilities on highways.

Various sub-sectors of tourism activities listed above will be encouraged by marking new tourism units eligible for incentives under Tax Holiday incentive scheme in designated areas.

As mentioned earlier, the State Government intends to designate certain areas having significant tourist potential as Special Tourism Areas. To this end, reputed consultants and institutions will be engaged to prepare area development plans in respect of various areas such as Kutch District, areas around Sardar Sarovar project area, South Saurashtra areas covering Gir, Porbandar, Veraval, Somnath, beaches and areas of pilgrimage/heritage towns.

These areas will be developed by following integrated area development approach. The State Government will make efforts to tap all the source of national and international funding for development of these areas and provide special encouragement to tourism projects being established therein. For ensuring faster development of these areas, area development committees will be constituted.

Human Resources Development

Human Resources Development is an important aspect of service industries. Tourists depend upon travel agents, guides and hence trained manpower is a sine qua non of tourism industry. On the basis of available statistics, training facilities can be safely said to be totally inadequate. If trained manpower is not available locally, the objective of local employment will not be achieved. Keeping in view the approach of market-led development, the State Government will encourage and support creation of training facilities in the private sector by private agencies/individuals.

Hotel Management course, courses meant for guides, caterer and other supervisory and non-supervisory staff of hotel will be introduced in Industrial Training Institutes (I.T.Is). Approved hotel associations and private entrepreneurs will be encouraged to create new training facilities by making available land to them for this purpose and by giving other appropriate incentives.

The Government will consider setting up a Hotel Management Training Institute at the State level preferably in private sector.

Residents of Gujarat, especially local youths, would be encouraged and facilitated to take part in such training courses.The Institute of Hotel Management, Catering and Nutrition which is working under the administrative control of the Central Government will be utilized to start new training courses so that the residents of Gujarat can get admission and manpower requirement of this sector is met. The residents of Gujarat undergoing such training will be reimbursed a part of the tuition fees through scholarships.

FEEDBACK AND MONITORING

To make the New Tourism Policy result oriented, implementation will be monitored by a High Powered Committee under the Chairmanship of Chief Secretary. A Management Information System will be set up to assist the Committee to make available information on various aspects of implementation on a continuous basis. The Committee will also review the policy from time to time.

New Tourism Policy

In line with the new directions and priorities envisaged for India tourism, the Government of India has formulated a new Tourism Policy to guide development of the tourism sector. The key elements of the National Tourism Policy, 2002 are :

1. Position tourism as a major engine of economic growth
2. Harness the direct and multiplier effects of tourism for employment generation, economic development and providing inpetus to rural tourism.

3. Focus on both international and domestic tourism
4. Position India as a global brand to take advantage of the burgeoning global travel and trade and the vast untapped potential of India as a destination.
5. Acknowledges the critical role of the private sector with overnment acting as a proactive facilitator and catalyst.
6. Create and develop integrated tourism circuits based on India's unique heritage in partnership with States, private sector and other agencies.
7. Ensure that the tourist to India gets physically invigorated, mentally rejuvinated, culturally enriched and spiritually elevated.

Index